RUSSIA AS A 'DEVELOPING SOCIETY'

By the same author

PEASANTS AND PEASANT SOCIETIES

THE AWKWARD CLASS

THE RULES OF THE GAME: Models in Scholarly Thought

INTRODUCTION TO THE SOCIOLOGY OF THE
'DEVELOPING SOCIETIES' (*with H. Alavi*)

LATE MARX AND THE RUSSIAN ROAD:
Marx and the Peripheries of Capitalism

RUSSIA, 1905–07: REVOLUTION AS A MOMENT OF TRUTH
The Roots of Otherness: Russia's Turn of Century, Volume 2

RUSSIA AS A 'DEVELOPING SOCIETY'

The Roots of Otherness: Russia's Turn of Century

Volume 1

Teodor Shanin

YALE UNIVERSITY PRESS
NEW HAVEN AND LONDON

First published in the United Kingdom by The Macmillan Press Ltd.

Published in the United States by Yale University Press 1986

Printed in Great Britain

Library of Congress Catalogue Card No. 85–40905
International Standard Book Number: 0–300–03659–0 (cloth)
0–300–03660–4 (paper)

To the memory of Paul Baran, a human bridge between three worlds, stranger in a strange land, a landsman

'The Western precedence would prove here nothing at all . . .'

Karl Marx

Contents

List of Tables, Figures and Maps

Acknowledgements

My intellectual debts are too extensive to be fully acknowledged. I shall name only those who are particularly significant. I would like to thank for encouragement, advice and comment Hamza Alavi, Perry Anderson, Philip Corrigan, Boguslav Galeski, Iris Gillespie, Leopold Haimson, Jan Owens and Israel Shahak. I owe gratitude to a number of Soviet scholars–friends whom I shall not name individually. My work could not have progressed without effective library 'back-up', for which I owe particular thanks to Jenny Brine of CREES, Birmingham, and Agnesa Valentinovna Mushkan of TsGIA, Leningrad. I would like also to thank Sandy Simpson, Pauline Brooks and Jarmila Hickman for constant and effective technical help.

As to the institutional help, I owe particular thanks to the British Academy and especially to Peter Brown and Jenny Lynden of its staff. I would like also to thank the Russian Institute, Columbia University, New York, the ESRC and my own University of Manchester for support and indulgence. The same goes for the other type of institutional back up – the Shula and Aelita general support team.

Preface: 'The Roots of Otherness'

Chronicles are written only by those to whom the present matters.
Goethe

The first Russian attempt at self-understanding in terms of contemporary social theory took the form of a debate between the Slavophiles and the Westerners. Russia was seen as *either* totally unique *or* as a backward section of Europe, a rung behind on a single evolutionary ladder. It was neither. Russia was not unique, nor was it on the threshold of becoming another England. It was not 'feudal' nor was it consequently and simply 'capitalist', or a transitionary mixture of both. At the turn of the nineteenth century Russia became the first country in which a specific social syndrome of what we call today a 'developing society' had materialised; it combined this type of social structure and international setting with a long imperial history, an entrenched state apparatus and a highly sophisticated and politically committed intellectual elite.

The fundamental distinction between human reality and nature at large is the way consciousness, comprehensions and miscomprehensions are woven into it, structuring human action. During the last decades of the nineteenth century the alternatives and strategies of the tsardom's rulers and administrators were laid out in terms of 'catching up with Europe' (or else, deteriorating into 'another China'). Vigorous state intervention along 'German' lines, with Friedrich List as its theoretical forerunner and Bismarck as the symbol of success, produced by the beginning of the twentieth century not another Germany, but a shattering economic and social crisis, a military defeat and, by 1905, a revolution. Consequently this was the time and the place where the relevance of the West European experience for the rest of mankind was first fundamentally challenged. Russia was to produce in actual political deed two major programmes and tests of radical transformation of the type of societies referred to today as 'developing'. Those polarly opposing yet theoretically complementary strategies were symbolised by the names of Stolypin and Lenin, but represented on both sides a spectrum of goals, views, analytical achievements and personalities. Little was added during the three generations to follow to the store of conceptual alternatives then created.

The level of theoretical understanding lagged behind the political strategies. Marx had once remarked on the historical tendency to act out new political drama in costumes borrowed from past generations. The French revolutionaries of 1791 saw themselves in the mould of leaders from the ancient Roman republic. The fact that Russia's political leaders consistently understated the newness of their experience and solutions and bent fact and ideology to present them in West European garb makes it the more instructive. While the government has measured itself by the German imperial successes, the leaders of the Russian dissent related their present and future to the English parliamentarism or to the French revolutions.

The 1905–7 revolution was to Russia a moment of truth. By proceeding in a way unexpected to both supporters and adversaries, this revolution has dramatised a new pattern of social characteristics and promoted unorthodox solutions, political as well as theoretical. A new Russia begins there, with monarchists who learned that only revolutionary social transformation can save their tsardom; and with Marxists who, under the impact of a revolution that failed, looked anew at Russia and at their Marxism. In historically quick succession, both were to gain power for the political exercise of their new understandings. Those who refused to learn have as speedily found themselves 'on the rubbish heap of history', to use a terrible but realistic description of biographies-cum-historiographies.

The growing acceptance of the specificity of the reality, problems and theories of 'developing societies' that has come to the fore since the 1960s, permits the placement of the Russian experience in a new and more realistic, comparative context. This can add to our understanding of Russia/the USSR. It can throw new light on a conceptual transformation – the most significant result of the 1905–7 revolution, decoding Lenin's comment about this 'dress rehearsal' without which 'the victory of the October Revolution in 1917 would have been impossible'. It may also make Russia's history and its contemporary theorising serve the fuller understanding of the 'developing societies' of today. The argument is presented in two separate books.

Russia as a 'Developing Society' looks at Russian society at the turn of the nineteenth century. It attempts to untangle the different yet related themes of the history of Russia on its way towards the revolutionary periods of 1905–7 and 1917–21. Mark Bloch once warned that 'the knowledge of fragments, studied by turns, each for its own sake, will never produce the knowledge of the whole; it will not even produce that of the fragments themselves'. He continued: 'But the work of re-integration can come only after analysis. Better still, it is only the continuation of analysis, its ultimate justification.' This book has chosen as its fundamental 'fragments' the Russian state, peasantry and capitalism, that is, the main power structure, the way of living of the mass of the population, the most challenging economic dynamism in view and their interdependence – a fundamental triangle of social determination. Its initial chapters are set out accordingly. The book then proceeds to consider the peasant economy and the general picture of Russia in flux during the period discussed.

The companion volume, Russia 1905–07: *Revolution as a Moment of Truth*, is devoted to the Russian revolution of 1905–7. It begins with the revolution's build-up and its two major strands: the struggle in the cities for political freedom and/or socialism and the struggle of the villages for land and for liberty understood from the peasant's perspective. It is followed by an analysis of the interdependence of these struggles and of its main social actors. The concluding chapters are devoted to the conceptual revolutions and persistences, relating the revolutionary experience of 1905–7 and its interpretations to the future history of Russia. A Postscript considers some issues of method and of goals concerning contemporary history and historical sociology.

* * *

The beginnings of the research that went into both books of the two-volume series 'The Roots of Otherness' go back to a study which was eventually published in 1972 as *The Awkward Class*. Further research, debate and experience made me refuse its publishers' kind offer simply to have it reprinted when the stock of its copies ran low. By that time I came to believe that while the essence of the book stood the test of criticism, its form of presentation carried two major weaknesses. It centred on the Russian peasantry and the analytical problems of its differentiation. Looked at from the distance of time it seems clear that one must broaden the focus, that is, to link peasantry more explicitly to general society and to relate the issue of socio-economic differentiation to other fundamental dimensions of analysis. Second, such an analysis must be related more explicitly to historical periodicity. A sequence of books identified by major periods of the history of Russia is therefore to replace the 1972 version of *The Awkward Class*, which will suffer partial dismembering and major readjustment. The research and elements of the text that appeared in the first two chapters of the initial version of *The Awkward Class* have entered parts of *Russia as a 'Developing Society'*, especially in the first and second sections of Chapter 2, and the second sections of Chapters 3 and 5. Even in those places, the reader will find considerable changes resulting from further research. The historical juncture to which this book and its companion volume, *Russia, 1905–07: Revolution as a Moment of Truth* directly relate was followed by distinctive periods representing the two major political conclusions from the 1905–7 experience, when these have dominated strategies of Russia's effective rulers, and a new revolutionary epoch. The first is the period of 'Stolypin's reforms', 1906–11, that is when the tsar's government had the field to itself after defeating the revolutionary challenge. Its conclusions from the 1905–7 experience were expressed in a concentrated effort immortalised by Stolypin's words about 'putting the wager on the strong'. Next came the revolutions of 1917, a civil war and as a major part of it, the peasant war of 1917–21 expressing the particular livelihood and struggle of the great majority of Russians in the most decisive period of Russia's contempory history. In the historical sequence, this was followed by the period of Lenin's Russia of NEP, a period to be covered by a new largely revised and partly refocused version of *The Awkward Class*. In addition to the original discussion of the socio-economic differentiation and mobility, the new version of *The Awkward Class* will incorporate a more extensive consideration of Lenin's rural Russia, 1921–8. New introductory chapters replacing the discussion transferred elsewhere will relate this book more directly to the conceptual revolution discussed in *Russia 1905–07: Revolution as a Moment of Truth*, and update it, considering the changing views concerning the Russian peasantry also as against the civil war of 1917–21 and its aftermath. It will look particularly at Lenin's diverse 'agrarian programmes', formulated as he progressed through the stages of the political experience biographical to him, historical to Russia.

Introduction: *Russia as a 'Developing Society'*

The book's title is self-explanatory of its content and the case it makes. It looks at the morphology of Russia's 'backwardness' and the rhythms of the Russian history at the turn of the nineteenth century, a period that led to the crucial 1910–40 era of revolutions 'from below' and transformations 'from above'. It relates it to what we have learned since about the so-called 'developing societies'.

The word 'introduction' describes particularly well Chapters 1, 2 and 3 of this volume. They are introductory in the sense of offering basic information and relevant analytical categories to readers who have heard of, but never studied, the Russia of the period. The first section of Chapter 1 is in this sense an introduction to the introduction, presenting the early historical origins of the contemporary Russian state, ethnicity and society. The issue of historical processes as well as of actuality are then pursued in three chapters devoted to Russia's 'fundamental triangle of social determination': state, peasantry and capitalism at the turn of the nineteenth century.

Readers' attitudes to statistical materials are notoriously ambivalent. To some, this is the quickest route to illumination, to others it is something one 'skips over' to get to the 'real text'. With that in mind, Addenda 1 and 2 single out issues that can be handled only via statistical data: the diversification of the Russian population revealed by its 1897 census and the divisions within its rural society, especially its socio-economic differentiation.

Chapters 4 and 5 are an 'introduction' in a different sense. They introduce the major points of debate, that is, the issues that have divided those who analysed Russia and will doubtlessly do so in the times to come. It brings further substance to the book's motto – Marx's heretical statement devoted to rural Russia of the 1880s that foretold a debate a century later.[1] The questions of Chapter 4 are those of the nature of the Russian peasant economy. Chapter 5 considers Russia's political economy and socio-political structure *in toto* and looks at the major

forces that subverted them, that is, a type of capitalism and an
ideological and political dissent at the turn of the nineteenth century and
their historical roots.

As with every introduction, a reader sufficiently informed can omit
some of the material. The text permits such reading, while the preface
and the list of contents will help in the selection. On the other hand, to
live and to teach in Western Europe, is to learn daily how outstandingly
sparse is the knowledge of Russia despite its global significance. Yet,
strong views are held and constantly debated about its characteristics,
with a spoonful of fact mixed in an ocean of rhetorical zeal. That is why,
in this field particularly, facts matter and substantial introductions must
precede analytical text, discourse and debate.

1 The Russian Tsardom: Past and Present

> To the Emperor of All the Russia, belongs the unlimited autocratic power.
> Submission to his supreme will, not only out of fear but also for conscience'
> sake, is ordained by God himself.
>
> *Code of Laws of the Russian Empire*, ch. 1, section 1

A. THE MAKING OF RUSSIA

The Russian empire grew out of Moscow, initially a small outpost of the
duchy of Rostov, later a duchy and a direct vassal to the Mongol khans
of the Golden Horde. In an almost ever-ascending curve spanning five
centuries, a dependency of less than 600 square miles has risen to become
the world's largest territorial state. This spectacular, one may say
incredible, rise, offered extensive scope for disputes, conjecture and
speculation, romance, fairy tale and outright lies. For our purposes it is
important to untangle from the outset some of the major threads of the
'past within the present' in the Russian tsardom at the turn of the
nineteenth century, looking selectively at issues that are important for a
better understanding of its political and social character. It is important
to look also at the tales, beliefs and claims attached to early Russian
history, not only because 'the traditions of all the dead generations
weigh like a nightmare on the brain of the living'[1] but also because 'a
fraud is in its own way a piece of evidence'.[2] In every generation anew
the representation of the past can teach us about the contemporary
realities of power, about collective patterns of self-understanding and
about the ways those are exercised and transformed.

The Russian tsardom and the Russian nation derive from two
ancestries and three different social 'models', all represented by
powerful political entities locked in a violent confrontation of arms,
economies and ideologies. As to the ancestries, one was ever proudly
displayed by the mainstream latter-day Russian leaders and analysts,

1

the second often rejected as devilish slander or else treated as the explanation of all of Russia's ills. Kiev, Christianity and Europe was the first; the second was Mongols, Steppe and Asia. The three societal alternatives were the Great Novgorod, the grand duchy of Lithuania, and the grand duchy of Moscow. Of those, the ideological 'reading of history backwards' has usually stressed the last, relegating the others to footnotes. There were historians, however, who believed that the Russian autocratic tendencies resulted from a particular piece of ill-luck, by which it was Novgorod that was defeated in the struggle for the supremacy over the Russian lands.

The whole period referred to as the 'late Middle Ages' was to the states and the ethnic entities of Europe a period of contradictory processes, of frequent rapid rise and equally rapid decline, which usually left some ethnic and political remnants to feed into future processes. To exemplify, the Great Moravia state of the Slavic tribes, for a while a major power in Central Europe, followed just such a short trajectory of rise, decline and disappearance in the ninth century. On the other hand, the ninth to tenth centuries have seen also the composite processes of state formation, ethnic crystallisation and Catholic conversion of Hungary, Poland and Bohemia, into moulds that are essentially still with us, despite centuries of territorial division, foreign rule and assimilatory policies by alien conquerors.

The grand duchy of Kiev was formed in the ninth/tenth-century wave of East European 'statisation' and destroyed by the Mongol attack in the thirteenth century.[3] It came into being along the Volkhov and Dnieper, the major river route of merchants and pirates from the Baltic to Constantinople. Through the same territories ran the major east to west track of nomads and trading caravans. The Viking traders–pirates and soldiers–mercenaries (*Varyag* to the Slavs) came into the area during the age of the Norse conquest throughout Europe. They called the country *Gardariki* – the 'land of the cities', indicating a sequence of autonomous, small and fortified market towns along major waterways, involved in exchange as much as in forest production and farming, and run by local oligarchies and/or by popular assemblies – the *Veche*. The ethnonym *Russ* came first to describe Scandinavians, which under the chieftanship and later the dynasty of Rurik, established themselves as the rulers of Novgorod and eventually of most of the waterway of the Dnieper, including Smolensk and Chernigov and with a capital and main operational base in Kiev (Map 1).

The new state of the Varyag, who traded and raided in summer and collected tribute from the subject populations in winter, rapidly grew

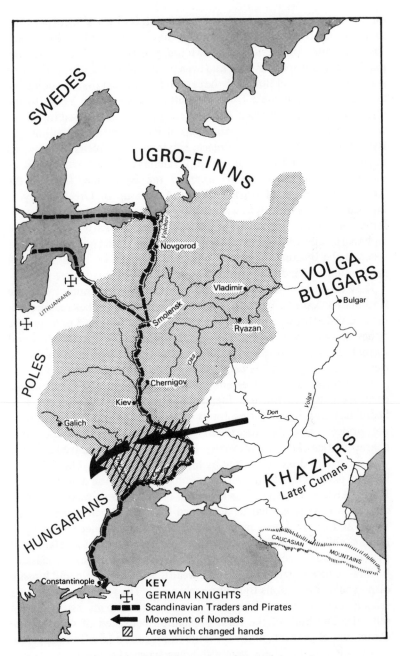

MAP 1 *Kiev in the tenth to thirteenth centuries*

into a major military and political power subjecting and incorporating extensive territory and populations of Slav, Finnic and Turkic tribes. They inhabited the territories known today as Belorussia, the Ukraine, much of the European Russia and even parts of Poland. Kiev fought the states of Khazar and Bulgar to the east and south-east that straddled the alternative trading route from the Baltic Sea down the Volga to the Caucasus and Persian coast. Close relations were maintained for a time with Scandinavia, but the central axis of Kiev's external relations was Byzantium, the main trading place, employer of mercenaries, coveted prize of piracy and cultural centre of reference. In the year 988 Kiev under the rule of Vladimir accepted the Byzantine, that is, the 'Orthodox' version of Christianity, and a group of Greek clergy to introduce it. They brought with them also a script developed earlier to serve the Slavic languages of Moravia and Bulgaria (the Cyrillic alphabet). The alliance was clinched by the marriage between the sister of the Byzantine emperor and the Grand Duke Vladimir, a full recognition of Vladimir's status as a royal ally of the empire.

Kiev was now open to Christendom (the inherited conflict with the Catholics accepted). Its trade, diplomacy and dynastic ties reached out far and wide through Europe. International relations and prestige, the riches amassed by successful wars and trade, the growth of literature and formal law left a powerful memory of a golden age of Kiev in the eleventh century, and the early part of the twelfth century.

The Kievian state was essentially a decentralised affair, not unlike early feudalism in Europe. Elements of it can be traced directly to Scandinavian political forms, for example, the role and organisation of the princes' retainers (*druzhina*). The grand duchy of Kiev had characteristics of its own, however. Each province was centred on a city with a resident duke supported by his court of retainers. The dukedom was the patrimony of the ever-increasing lineage of the descendants of Rurik. Always assuming Rurik's blood to be in his veins, a provincial duke was usually elected or acclaimed by the freemen assembly, the *Veche* and/or the 'great men', but his rule was ever-dependent upon military ability to hold on to his throne.[4] As time went by the retainers of the prince have merged into local oligarchies to establish a class of boyars – a new aristocracy of arms, wealth, landownership and kinship or personal connections to the princely court. The townsmen formed a second social stratum of freemen, usually with its own institutions of self-rule. The bulk of the rural population consisted of *smerdy* – the communes of peasants under a tributary obligation (*dan'*) to the prince and/or his boyars. There were also some slaves (*kholopy*).[5]

The princely authority meant military leadership, the right to tribute, the administration of justice, and some legislative powers that were limited by custom, by the boyars' *duma*, and/or by the popular *Veche*. A grand duke, his seat initially in Kiev, was considered the supreme sovereign of all the duchies of Russia, but in fact his rule became increasingly one of a multiplicity of princely patrimonies engaged in never-ending wars of succession. The pressure of nomads, which grew particularly with the destruction of the buffer of the Khazar state to the south-east, was met with increasing difficulty. As a result, there was a gradual retreat from lands south of Kiev and a shift of population to the forested north-east with the subsequent growth in significance of the frontiersman dukes of Rostov-Suzdal' on the upper Volga. By the second half of the twelfth century they took over the title of the grand dukes of the Kievian Rus', while keeping their capital in Vladimir. Since the thirteenth century the Kievian lands also came under pressure from the German, Lithuanian and Swedish military advance from the north-west.

The major territories of Kiev and its neighbours had been shared for centuries by sedentary agriculturalists and pastoral nomads in complex patterns of symbiosis, exchange and confrontation. *Nomads* – a Greek word for cattle drivers – represented a specific type of economy and social organisation based upon the use of natural pasture for animal produce, a system parallel and often superior to farming, especially in less fertile regions.[6] Contrary to the views often shared by the sedentary populations, the usual life pattern of the nomads has been not one of 'free wanderers', but based on strict cyclicity of movement, in which different parts of a specific area are used subsequently and seasonally. This involved periodic returns to the same areas and settlements and some measure of subsistence farming and gathering that supplemented the animal production. Nomadic life of Euro-Asia has centred in the Steppe – the broad stretch of grasslands interspaced by mountains – and other areas less suitable for grazing between Manchuria in the east and the Hungarian Pushta, at which nomadic tribes and confederations have circled for thousands of years. Under conditions of ecological, political or military crisis, this cyclicity time and time again turned linear; the nomads united in large masses and the Steppe became a corridor of massive 'migration of nations' through which mounted armies of exceeding striking force rode to loot, conquer and resettle.

The nomad political and socio-economic system combined loose control of land by the tribal confederations, free access to it for every tribesman, family ownership of cattle, low division of labour and animal husbandry. This carried considerable military potential. Horsemanship and hunting, the need to defend one's cattle and camp from robbers, the harsh experience of pastoral life, turned every man into a resourceful and tough warrior. Tribes and lineages divided the nomads' world, but also offered ready-made patterns for military organisation. The glitter of wealth accumulated in settled communities and cities offered constant provocation to reach out for those riches and strip them from the sedentarists, usually despised as unmanly and slavish by the Steppe code of honour. Raiding, war and 'mercenary' service were, to many nomad groups, a constant source of income on par with the animal production and trade. Once inter-tribal unity was established or imposed, the military strength of the pastoralists increased dramatically. Armies of mounted archers, the nomads' main striking force, spawned a variety of dynasties and states.[7]

Throughout history and as late as the twentieth century (for Saudi Arabia), nomad-created kingdoms came into existence, usually to decline rapidly after fierce blossoming: the Scythians, the Huns, the Avars, the Madiars and the Cumans to name but few. In the sixth century A. D. a world empire of nomad Turki stretched from China to Europe.[8] The first-known historiography of state formation, that of Ibn Khaldun in the fifteenth century, was actually based on the consideration and generalisation of the nomad conquests and their aftermaths.[9]

The nomads of the Kievian lands and frontier, mostly Turki of the Khazar, Bulgar, Patzinak and Cuman tribes, have been true enough to the general picture presented. Their relation with the Slavs and Ugro-Finns with whom they shared much of the physical space were fairly close and often peaceful, based on mutual trade, political alliances or even on shared statehood. Turki nomads (part-nomads in fact), for example, the Barendai's and Kavui's of Chernigov, formed a part of the Kievian/Russian army and nation on equal footing with its Scandinavian and Slav ethnic components. The prince identified most with the 'golden age' of Kiev; and the father-in-law of Henry I of France, Yaroslav 'the Wise' (1019–54), came to power with the help of Cuman allies and kept that alliance in his main campaigns. The records of election to the princely throne of the grand duchy of Kiev state that Mstislav was 'called to it' in 1125 'by the people of Kiev and the Karakalpak', that is, by the 'Russian' nobles and urbanites together with the major nomad group and cavalry force of the Kiev realm. Russ princes frequently married daughters of the nomad chiefs – a way to secure an alliance in the dynastic struggles and war.[10] It took a massive ideological operation by the Orthodox church in the latter days to suppress these memories, separating the sedentary, controllable and Christian sheep from the nomad goats. Nomads enter the later Russian lore mainly as a synonym of evil and 'otherness': strange, predatory and hostile. Russian language reflected it clearly. The word Christian became the synonym of a peasant (*krest'yanin*), while the various descriptions of the nomads became an insult, an abomination assigned to the realm of pagan (later Islamic) enemies outside the pale of civilisation: the *yazychnik*, the *Koshchei*, the *Polovets*.[11]

* * *

At the beginning of the thirteenth century, the Steppe had overboiled once more, and arguably, for the most spectacular occasion. A Mongol tribal federation was put together by Temuchin, who took the title of Chingiz Khan. He called into being the most effective military organisation of his world, establishing by the right of conquest an empire that was to stretch from south China to Poland, Hungary and Syria.[12] The new onslaught began by massive destruction, slaughter, enslavement and looting of the lands conquered. It proceeded to establish a world-wide *Pax Mongolica* – an international system with considerable political unity, excellent postal communications (*Yam*), roads open to trade, a unitary system of law (*Yasa*) and of taxation. Contrary to the contemporary tales, the supremacy of the 'locust-like' Mongolian army, the Gog and Magog of the European monks-chroniclers, lay not in its numbers but in its organisation. The Mongol military structure, discipline and chain of command became the core of the political organisation, within what can rightly be called an army-state. All the conquered lands (indeed, the world at large) were treated as the property of the 'golden family' of the descendants of Chingiz Khan and of the Mongols at large. The Mongol global realm was divided into regions (*Ulus*), under the sons of Chingiz Khan and their descendants, one of whom was to assume the supreme authority of *Kogan*. Subject to total obedience in political matters, the payment of tribute and the supplying of soldiers, conquered people were left to themselves, their ways, chiefs and religions.

As before, the empire of the nomads proved fairly short lived. By 1294, with the death of Kublai Khan – the fifth supreme ruler of the dynasty – the Mongol empire split into independent regional components, which proceeded to subdivide further as the Mongol conquerors assimilated into the local people and the Chingiz dynasty gradually lost control over the conquered lands. The momentum of the Mongol drive, though, was not quite at its end even then. In 1370–1405 Timur was to establish a new late-Mongol empire based on conquest, while his descendant Babur moved to establish the Moghul empire in India as late as 1526.

The end of Kievian state was brought about by the Mongol march into Europe. A Mongol force first defeated a combined Russian–Cuman army in 1223 and came back to conquer under Batu Khan (a grandson of Chingiz Khan) in a short and violent campaign of 1237–40. In that war the Mongols overran the Kievian Steppe as well as parts of its woodlands and obliterated most of the Russian cities, including Kiev and Vladimir. They also defeated, exterminated or enslaved many of its people as well as their ethnic neighbours, sedentary and nomad alike, and established on the lower Volga the new *Ulus Kipchak* (i.e. the Cuman region of the Mongol global empire), better known as the 'Golden Horde'.

The population at the core of the new state consisted of Turki nomads of the Steppe, incorporated and assimilated into military, political and legal patterns of Mongol statecraft and arms-craft with a sprinkling of 'real' Mongols at its top. They used the ethnonym Tatar rather than Mongol, spoke a Turki dialect and under the Uzbeg Khan (1313–41), became Muslim in religion. The Golden Horde exercised sovereignty also over the northern and north-western forest regions where different processes of ethnic crystallisation and political transformation were now set afoot. The Slav and Ugro-Finn sedentary populations with admixtures of some settled Turki and Scandinavians were being shaped and delimited by the Orthodox religion and the political and legal context of the vassal relation to the Golden Horde.[13] Their dukes claimed descent from Rurik or at times from Gedymin of Lithuania, but ruled under the revocable patent (*Yarlyk*) of the khan of the Golden Horde and subject to the Mongolian law and provision of tribute and recruits. They were usually watched by the resident representatives of the Khan – the *baksaks*. Following the Mongol law, the *Yasa*, all clergy was granted extensive autonomy and immunity from taxation. In the conditions of the decline of the institutions of the Kievian state, and orthodox Christian church came to play an increasing political and ideological role and to define who was considered 'Russian' among the subjects of the Golden Horde.[14] This entity, the 'Russians', for a time more a potential than a definable group, has extensively differed in its ethnic, economic and political characteristics from the Kievian realm but never abandoned some of its links and claims to these origins.

The Khans of the Golden Horde (referred to as 'Tsars' by their Slav subjects) made good use of the 'divide and rule' and 'indirect rule' principles. The forest-and-Christian provinces were eventually divided into four 'grand duchies' and a number of duchies. One of those was Moscow. In 1328, for services rendered in the collection of tribute and the suppression of an anti-Tatar rebellion in Rostov and Tver, after some crafty dynastic manipulations, the Duke of Moscow, Ivan – nicknamed Kalita ('the moneybag') – was promoted by the Khan to the grand-dukedom of Vladimir. A prudent and suitably nasty politician, he had considerably increased his territories by buying and conquering more land and had the 'metropolitan of all the Russias' (the head of the Orthodox Church within the Golden Horde) transfer his seat to Moscow. Ivan subsequently began to style himself the grand duke of 'all the Russias' (*vseya rusi*) – a claim clearly too ridiculous to provoke his Tatar masters to put a stop to it. In 1380, his grandson Dmitrii led the first major attempt by a coalition of Russian princes to use the dynastic squabbles within the Golden Horde to break 'the yoke' of Tatar sovereignty. In the event, a single victorious battle was followed by a lost war. Dmitrii and his allies were forced to swear allegiance to a new Tatar overlord. Despite that, the struggle further enhanced Moscow's standing between the Russian duchies of the Golden Horde.

When at the end of the fourteenth century the armies of Tamerlan smashed the core regions of the Golden Horde but did not proceed against its Russian provinces, the Tatar/Russian balance shifted irreversibly. The Golden Horde was rapidly disintegrating into competing princedoms and Hordes. From the mêlée of the wars of succession in which the Tatar, Russian and Lithuanian armies fought it out in ever-changing coalitions, the Muscovite state emerged as the most successful. As a sign of the new times, in the fifteenth century some of the Tatar princes chose Moscow's 'protection', that is, declared themselves its vassals. In 1480, the Grand Duke Ivan III ('the Great') renounced Moscow's dependency to the remainders of the Golden Horde. It was also under his protracted rule that Muscovy finally settled its rivalry with the grand duchy of Tver and the city-republic of Novgorod by conquering and submerging them both, establishing a realm with territories thirty times those of the duchy of Moscow at its inception. In a gesture of high ideological significance, pregnant with new images and claims, Ivan III married in 1472 the niece of the last emperor of Byzantium, recently conquered by the Turkish army. The code of law (*Sudebnik*) promulgated by Ivan referred back to the Kievian legislation. Symbolically, it was as if the era of Kiev was returning, but the claim to succession laid by the rulers of Muscovy was by now amplified even further. In the language of the monk Filofei of those days: 'two

Romes [i.e. Rome and Byzantium] have fallen, the third [Moscow] stands fast and a fourth will never be'[15] – a manifest claim to an empire, temporal and spiritual. A new age of Moscow's pre-eminence had dawned and was declared.

*   *   *

Braudel has forcefully presented the new social trends that reshaped the 'Mediterranean world' in the fifteenth and sixteenth centuries.[16] A period of massive changes was recorded throughout Europe. Lingering vestiges of major states of the past were being wiped out, never to rise again: Byzantium came to its end with the conquest of Constantinople in 1453; the Moorish Spain disappeared with the fall of Grenada in 1492. The significance of the Italian republics and tyrannies declined. At the core of those developments within the 'Mediterranean world' was, in Braudel's view, the general crisis of the city-states, which for a long time provided the focus of economic and political life of southern Europe. Modern technologies of war, exceedingly expensive in goods and manpower, have favoured the centralised and large territorial state able to mobilise extensive agricultural surplus and numerous recruits or mercenaries. What followed was the 'irresistible advance' of Aragon under John II, of France under Louis XI, of Turkey of Mahmood II and of the Hapsburgs. The sixteenth century had consequently become an age of growing empires and at its very centre the simultaneous rise of the Hapsburgs and the Ottomans as the new 'superpowers', political as well as ideological. Charles V's imperial crown was matched by Selim's claim to the Califat of Islam.

At the Russian plain the Mediterranean age of imperial ascent was closely matched by the rise of Moscow and its claim to the mantle of tsardom of 'all the Russias'. Broudel's logic of resources also holds in this different context. In the long term, sedentary agriculture proved to have a higher capacity than pastoralism to extend production, or at least for a higher share of produce to be appropriated by the rulers – a 'material base' for a standing army and use of firearms. The Russian rulers also proved better than their Tatar overlords at immobilising and demobilising direct producers as well as in resolving dynastic problems of succession. The Golden Horde disappeared. Novgorod, Tver, Vyatka and Pskov, as well as the Kazan' and the Astrakhan remainders of the Golden Horde, were conquered and incorporated, their separate political identity lost for ever. History never repeats itself entirely and it is the specificity of the Russian case that may be well expressed as the tale of confrontation of three 'models' of political organisation; and, one may say somewhat anachronistically, of three ideologies, represented by

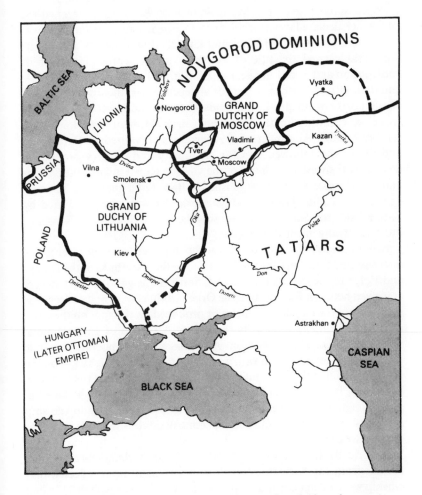

Map 2 *Muscovy and its neighbours in fourteenth and fifteenth centuries*

the three states: the Great Novgorod, the Grand Duchy of Lithuania and the Muscovite 'tsardom of all Russias'.

The Lordship of Novgorod the Great (*Gospodin Velikii Novgorod*, to give it its full title) was the most significant Russian equivalent of a European city-state.[17] The Mongols of Batu Khan never reached the city, which declared its vassal allegiance to them, paid its tribute and was left at that. In a world of kings and kinglets it was the city and not its duke that carried the title of lordship – a fair representation of its constitution and its self-image. Lordship stood for sovereignty, self-rule and the control of extensive territorial dependencies incorporating most of the northern fur-producing lands as far as the Urals. The Mongol 'yoke' sat relatively lightly on the city's neck. Mongol super-lords were far away. Duke Alexander of Novgorod was favoured by Batu Khan and those who followed him for his loyalty and military prowess in defending the western frontier of the Golden Horde against the Swedes and the German knights established at the Baltic shore – in Estonia, Latvia and Kaliningrad of today. Alexander was even appointed by Batu Khan's son Sardak to be the singular grand duke of the Russians, but that arrangement did not last.

Economically, the city of Novgorod has been a major centre of international trade relating the Baltic Sea to the waterlinks of the Dniepr and Volga to the east and south-east. Some of the goods exported were conveyed between Europe and 'the Orient'; others were first collected as tribute from the city dependencies or produced on the spot on the city's own lands (*Putina*) and by its craftsmen. A system of guilds, unique within Russia, was in operation. Any image of a democratic republic should be, of course, taken with a pinch of salt. An oligarchy has on the whole controlled the city's main offices and dominated its political life. Moreover, boyars rather than merchants were the city political elite, even though many of the boyars also engaged in trade. Landownership as well as external trade and colonial control established their grip over the city wealth.

Historically, it was Novgorod that could rightly claim real and direct descent from the Kievian state. Its political institutions reflected that kinship with a democratic accent of their own. A city revolt in 1136 had made the *Veche* assembly and the oligarchy much more powerful and weakened its Duke. The Duke's prerogative was narrowly defined by a contract (*ryad*) turning him into a city's official – the commander of its armies and a co-judge.[18] The Duke and his retinue were not permitted to own land within the city's territories. Major decisions concerning war, taxes and laws were made by the city assembly, its officers and notables.

A major aspect of city life and cohesion was its relation with the outside world in which trade intermingled with conquest, diplomacy and war. From the north, the west and the south-west came the pressure of the Scandinavians, Lithuanians and of the German crusading orders against whom spectacular battles were fought and won. To the east and the south-east were the complex relations with the Tatar overlords and the ever-repeated attempts of the Russian princes, specially of Tver and Moscow, to extend their control to the richest city of Russia's land. The decline of the Golden Horde, the rise of Moscow and a growing internal crisis created new conditions in the second half of the fifteenth century. In the major confrontation that followed, the results proved uncannily similar to those described by Braudel. The city-state was no longer a match for the large territorial powers. The boyars of Novgorod subsequently opted for the acceptance of Lithuanian sovereignty, but the majority of commoners and the low clergy seemed to have preferred the Orthodox Moscow tsar. The armies of Ivan III brought this debate to an end, defeating Novgorod and making it into a vassal of Muscovy in 1478. Shortly afterwards, at the first stirrings of opposition to the new sovereign, the Moscovite army marched into the city and abolished its autonomy, symbolically removing to Moscow the bell used to call its *Veche* meetings. The city notables were executed or deported and their lands seized. The city's elected institution disappeared altogether. In 1570 any remainders of rebellious spirit and wealth were beaten out of the city by an army of Ivan IV, which laid it waste, and by further waves of deportations.

The main remaining challenge to the claims of the Moscow's tsars to inherit Kiev and more as the rightful rulers of 'all the Russias' was that of the largely Russian state created by the Lithuanian conquest.[19] In contrast to the struggle over Novgorod, the confrontation of the Moscovite and the Lithuanian states was that of territorial powers which were initially much more alike in population and size. The difference was mostly that of social organisation. During the thirteenth century, the pagan Lithuanian tribes of the forest area bordering the Baltic Sea had united to fight off the German orders of crusading knights from the west and north and to raid and conquer new lands to the south and east. They were successful in both. The German advance was essentially contained. By the middle of the fourteenth century the Lithuanian grand dukes Gedymin and his son Olgerd came to rule the city of Kiev and most of its original lands, controlling the area from the Baltic to the Black Sea. Gedymin set his capital in Vilno/Vilnius. Unlike the Tatars, the Lithuanian conquerors rapidly assimilated into the Slav population, adopting Russian language, laws and the Orthodox religion. They reaffirmed many of the 'old' laws and 'Kievian' privileges of the Russian cities, boyars and clergy. Their main Code of Laws was written in Russian.

In 1385 Olgerd's son Iagailo/Jagello converted to Catholicism to become the King of Poland, a step followed by other Catholic conversions and the advance of Polish cultural influence in Lithuania, of which he remained the supreme sovereign. At the beginning of the fifteenth century, the German crusaders were defeated by this Lithuanian–Polish dynastic alliance. In the east, Vitov, the next grand duke of Lithuania (Jagello's cousin and vassal but increasingly independent in his actions), was challenging in a succesion of campaigns Tatar sovereignty over their Russian provinces. Olgerd and Vitov were quick to lay claims of their substantively Russian grand duchy to the full inheritance of Kiev, confronting Moscow in war, diplomacy and the struggle for the allegiance of boyars and retainers.[20]

This struggle of West and East Russia was more than a simple dynastic confrontation, for the two countries represented political and ideological structures of considerable difference. To quote a major historian, it was 'a centralised autocracy of the Tsars, gradually building up' in Moscow as against 'not a centralised state but a political federation . . . [in which] an aristocratic regime essentially came into being' in so far as the Lithuanian state was concerned.[21] Also, Lithuania remained pagan until the fourteenth century. The impact of Orthodox Christianity was new and partial, limited mostly to the nobles and now increasingly subverted by Catholicism. In the ex-Kievian provinces of Lithuania the commoners stayed mostly loyal to the 'Orthodox' religion for which Muscovy was increasingly acting as the political champion. All of these differences grew as time went by.

The loose dynastic tie to Poland was in the sixteenth century substituted by the incorporation of the Grand Duchy of Lithuania into a unified Polish/Lithuanian/Russian state, with the Polish composite as its senior partner. Within this state, the power of the lesser nobility has proceeded to increase, establishing eventually what was in fact a multiethnic republic of nobility – the *Rzeczpospolita*, with a powerful nobility Parliament and an elected king, bound on his election to sign a constitution of privileges of his nobles.[22] Self-government (the Magdeburg laws) was also extended to most of the cities. The autonomy of different churches was accepted, and considerable religious tolerance turned the country into a major place of exile for those persecuted elsewhere. All the same, the Catholic church has never accepted anything less than its own supremacy and/or dominance, at least in the long term. Neither had the ethnically Polish section of the nobles.

The rise of the power of the nobility and its self-government was parallel to the increasing enserfment of the peasant majority of the population. The peasant response in the 'core' areas of old Poland and Lithuania was limited but there was growing confrontation between the Polish or polonised and mostly Catholic nobility, its church and its *Rzeczpospolita* and the peasants and Cossacks of the mainly Orthodox south-eastern regions who spoke, neither Polish nor Lithuanian. New ethnic entities had been forming there, the Beloruss on the Lithuanian lands and the much more sharply delineated Ukrainians in the area of the direct Polish rule. Cossack brotherhoods of armed frontiersmen were established there. The ethnic–class Cossack–peasant uprisings in the Ukraine were to play a major role in the further advance of the Muscovite state. While the links of the upper classes of the *Rzeczpospolita* shifted towards the West, the field to the East was increasingly left to Moscow: ideologically and eventually politically and militarily.

In its foreign relations the *Rzeczpospolita* inherited from the Lithuanian state its 'eastern problem' of the military struggle against Moscow and the Tatars (later also against the Turks and the Cossack/peasant rebels). It did reasonably well to begin with, and even for a time attempted to subjugate Moscow. Then a series of military disasters, and, an internal political crisis struck at the very core of the *Rzeczpospolita*; it failed to quell a Cossack rebellion, lost a war and in 1667 surrendered to the Muscovite state a major slice of its territories inclusive of Smolensk and of Kiev. It was to lose more of them in 1772 and 1793 and to disappear in 1795 from the map of Europe by the final partition of its lands between the tsardom and its allies – Prussia and Austria. Much before that the short episode of an independent Cossack state in the Ukraine was brought to an end by the Muscovite army and political pressure. The 'competition' of the political 'models' in Eastern Europe was over. The tsardom of all the Russias reigned supreme, stretching from the Pacific Ocean to the River Bug and later to Vistula, and from the White to the Black Sea. Muscovy was Russia.

*   *   *

Muscovy was neither the richest of 'Russias', nor was it economically the 'most progressive'. Always assuming that an increasing division of labour and the indices of manufacturing or of trade per capita count as 'progress', the Novgorodians have excelled in all of those over the Muscovites. Nor was Muscovy the most populous of 'Russias'; Lithuania and later the Russian part of the *Rzeczpospolita* were larger.

The initial geographical placement of Moscow was fortunate, central to most of the Russian duchies and neither too far nor too close to the Tatar masters-enemies. Such was, however, also the placement of Tver, while Novgorod stood close to the place where the later Russian capital of Petersburg was to be built as Russia's 'window into Europe'. Moscow's claim to the Kievian heritage was dubious at best, the actual city of Kiev (with a masive Orthodox population and clergy) has blossomed for centuries as part of Lithuania and later of the *Rzeczpospolita* while Kiev's main political institutions of old were reflected, if at all, in the city state of Novgorod. Even in sheer military strength Muscovy did not win easily or at once. Its capital was overrun and sacked by the Crimean Tatars as late as 1571. In the wars with its western neighbours it fared poorly. Against all those odds, and within a few centuries, Muscovy defeated and swallowed all of its main competitors–neighbours.

The temptation to uncover the reasons for this formidable rise of Muscovy and/or to fit it into a more general scheme of analysis was ever powerful. Historical origins, religion, military organisation and extra-ordinary personal capacities of the Muscovite princes were claimed in explanation, but no simple comparison or solution has ever seemed to work. Muscovy repeated neither the decentralisation of Kiev nor the instability of the Tatar state, and it was indeed the extent of its centralisation and consistency that formed its major characteristic. The Orthodox religion was no panacea for political success either. Nor were all of the Russian rulers particularily wise. Russia was a state of conquest engaged in continual wars – a 'state in arms' – but in that experience Muscovy was not unlike its less fortunate neighbours. Plekhanov suggested the model of 'Oriental Despotism' in explanation of the specific characteristics of the pre-Petrine era, that is, before the seventeenth-century assault of the Westernising reforms. Without the 'hydraulic agriculture', that view offers little more than a tautology where Russia is concerned. Class analysis of the Russian state has often been undertaken in search for the answers to its strength. Such a task is made difficult by a context in which, as suggested by the dean of the Russian historians at the turn of the nineteenth-century, Klyuchevskii, it was the Russian state that seemed to generate class structures (contrary to the social experience of the countries that produced the class theory itself). While pertinent to many analytical problems, the class analysis used unspecifically or singly has been less than illuminating when the nature of tsardom was considered. To exemplify, Klyuchevskii's contemporary Rozhkov, an eminent Marxist historian of his day, has suggested that the rise of Moscow absolutism was simply part and parcel of the world-wide late-feudal pattern of ascent of the lesser nobility.[23] Yet, an 'ascent' that meant the nearly total power to the nobles in Poland and their seamless servitude to the tsars in Russia does not offer much insight into these matters.

For our immediate purpose it will be sufficient to say here that at the centre of the issue clearly stands the institutional history of the Russian state and its effectiveness as a system of controlling population, mobilising surpluses and waging war, as well as its structural capability of readjustment and regeneration. Directly related to its characteristics – a structure linking coercion to consensus, was the ethnogenesis of the Russians and the nature of the Orthodox church. That is not 'all' but that is salient, made the more important by a powerful bias that colours our social sciences. The nineteenth century escape from history locked into the 'books of kings' towards the analysis of social processes has enhanced the discipline as well as our understanding of society. Yet, that accentuation of social structure and/or of political economy has only too often led to the treatment of the state and of related patterns of collective cognition as epiphenomenal, that is, as a simple reflection of the essential laws and processes located elsewhere. To understand Russian history one must overcome such reductions. Or, to express the same view positively, one must admit the realism and recover for analytical use, if critically, the major conceptual duality of *state* and the *civil society* that formed the eighteenth-nineteenth-century point of departure of the political theory in Rousseau, Hegel and Marx or, more implicitly, in Adam Smith, de Tocqueville and later in Weber and Michels. It means to focus specifically on the nature, contradictions and the discrete history of each of those analytical poles and not only at their interdependence, manifest and central as it is.[24]

B. THE STATE: FORMATION OF AN EMPIRE

From its inception the Moscow State claimed unlimited powers for its rulers. Its duke ruled solely by the patent of the Tatar khans (the *yarlyk*), and once those had lost control, 'by God's will' and his own whim. The organisation of the army, the framework of state administration and the definition of the princely power, owed much to the Tatar statecraft and to Byzantine canonic law. A dukedom, which to many Europeans represented 'the back of beyond', approximating to nineteenth-century Britishers' Timbuktu, was thereby injected with a potent combination of the two most advanced and centralistic modes of political administration of the day. The Kievian political structures of popular, aristocratic and/or local power, were weaker or non-existent in the north-east There was no record of a *Veche* or of an election of a duke being established in Moscow. Its boyars rapidly became courtiers, officials and advisers of an absolute monarch. Its commoners' tribute developed into bondage. A complex system of law and bureaucratic administration was rapidly built up.

A new vocabulary of autocracy documented the rise of Moscow, and the actual assertions by its dukes of their claims to absolute power. This was noted by contemporaries: 'for it was never before that a grand duke was called *gosudar* [sovereign], for he was called *gospodin* [lord]'.[1] The significance of that fifteenth-century comment becomes clear when related to the fact that the earlier Russian documents have used the term *gosudar'* for a ruler of serfs and slaves, while the word 'lord' was used for the rulers of free men. The Russian term 'state' (*gosudarstvo*) derives directly from the word *gosudar'*. By the sixteenth century, the title 'grand duke' was increasingly replaced by that of 'the Tsar by God's will'. From the beginning of the seventeeth century the word 'autocrat' (following the Byzantine *autokrator*, i.e. unlimited ruler) was added to the title. Those ideological and legal images were directly linked to the twentieth-century laws of the Russian empire. Until the last days of the tsardom, the Section 1, Part 1 of the Code of Laws of the Russian empire proclaimed: 'To the Emperor of all the Russias, belongs unlimited autocratic power. Submission to his supreme will, not only out of fear but also for conscience sake, is ordained by God himself.'[2] For four centuries of Russian history it meant just that.

The 'autocratic' rule of one man over an extending realm meant an ever-extending apparatus of central administration. At its top was the royal court: a closely knit, often overlapping and ever intriguing group of royal aides, kinsman, lovers, those boyars who had the sovereign's ear, army commanders, managers of tsar estates and properties, supervisers of tax collection, body-servants, guards, clergymen and diplomats. A *Duma* of boyars and chief bureaucrats acted as the official advisory body to the tsar, while the day-to-day administration was carried out by *'Prikazy'*, led by *Diaks*, a rough equivalent of ministries of the realm intermixed with offices administering the tsar's personal welfare.[3] Significantly, the posts of the bureaucratic tier were filled neither by clergy (to be 'secularised' later, as in Western Europe) nor by hereditary landed aristocracy, but by a stratum of lay commoners, increasingly specialised since the seventeenth century.

The rise of the autocracy was reflected in the nature of class division that was established in law, to run parallel and at times in contradiction to the actual diversities of wealth.[4] The state rulers and top administrators were restructuring the entire system of duties and privileges. From the fifteenth century, men and lands became increasingly subject to a unitary royal and bureaucratic will. The traditional division of land between the grand duke's sons into apanages had disappeared during the sixteenth century. The rights of an hereditary noble to transfer allegiance between different dukes, one of the Kievian political customs that did apply in Moscow, was disappearing also. Such action came eventually to be treated as high treason and punished as such.

The weakening of the hereditary nobles went hand in hand with the rise of those who served the tsar directly, mainly in his army, and were granted land and serfs in lieu of payment. Service tenure was established already in the era of Mongol domination. The destruction of Great Novgorod facilitated and dramatised that process. Most of the land and peasant dependants of its executed or exiled boyars were divided into small parcels and granted in lieu of military service to the Moscow tsars. The lands and peasant 'souls' given in fiefs were being further extended by new conquests and new confiscations aimed at boyars charged with treason, plus some properties of the church. The growing grip of the state over free peasant communities and their enserfment led to similar results.

A new socio-legal estate of 'servitors' was thereby established, directly relating state service to land holding and privileges within the hierarchy of social and political power. One face of this stratum was a cavalry army of about 25 000 (which could be increased by contingents of the Cossack frontiersmen, allied nomads, etc. to about 100 000).[5] It was ever ready for service and seasonally called up, mostly against the Tatar forces in the south with whom it shared much in equipment and tactics, but with important 'technical inventions' or adaptations of its own – the *gulai gorod* of anty-cavalry moving walls-on-wheels, and since the sixteenth century the use of firearms.[6] The other facet of it was that of fief-holders with tributary peasants attached. Specific administration (the *razryadnoi prikaz*) was established to supervise the fief-holders (the *dvoryane*) and to secure that military service was actually rendered by them, or else that land and the rent-paying peasants were taken back and reassigned. The fiefs varied considerably in size, ranging from large estates to units as small as that of a dozen serf families and their land, granted to a man of lowly rank. As time went by the fief-holders increasingly merged with the hereditary nobility. Their common denominator and the official legitimation of the rights of the tsar to take over and redivide the lands of his nobles and of the church, were made explicit by the law of 1572, which stated as its aim: 'to secure that *the service* does not suffer, and that landownership is used for this purpose'.[7]

The accentuation of the duty of service to the tsar (*sluzhba gosudar'eva*), mostly military, went hand in hand with the disappearance of other duties by those who 'served'. To pay a tribute or a tax (*tyaglo*) had consequently become a badge of the under-dog, the sign of exclusion from the serving-and-ranking hierarchy. An overwhelming share of not less than 95 per cent of the population had entered that category. The description of people of lower status as the 'tax-paying classes' was retained in the Russian law until the twentieth century.[8] Other privileges, or lack of them, went together with that major division; for example, in contrast to the servitors, the 'tax-paying classes' were open to corporal punishment, could not freely take up residence of their choice, etc.

The 'tax-paying classes' of Muscovy divided into two major sub-categories: the townsmen and the ruralites. The townsmen (*posadskie*) were organised into merchant and 'black' (i.e. lower) 'hundreds'. On the margin between the servitors and the merchants stood the *gosti*, rich private traders operating as the direct suppliers to the tsar and granted special privileges related to that service. (These could include freedom from taxation, and the very important right not to stand trial before the local governor and judges, but have cases referred to the *kazennyi prikaz* in Moscow.) The status of the majority of the urbanites was close to that of the rural 'tax-payers' in their duties and by being bound increasingly to the locality in which they resided. There were no 'municipal freedoms' within Muscovite Russia.

The tax-paying ruralites were organised into communities (*volost'*) which carried the collective responsibilities for the tax and labour duties due to the state and to the servitors, if any, to whom they were 'granted' or to landowners on whose land they settled. Internally they seemed to have operated as small peasant land communes of neighbours. (There is considerable argument about those matters to which we shall return in the next chapter.[9]) The villages/hamlets were small. Diversities have been reported in them between the poor and the rich, the holders of taxable land-units (*vit'*) and those who were not. There were also extensive differences between the villages, not only ecological but man-made, that is, between those tributary to monasteries, to the servitors or else to the state only (the 'black' *volost's*). Some of their labour was used by their lords but the mass of the agricultural production took place within peasant family farms.[10] The control by the state, the servitors, the hereditary landowners and the clergy was exercised over peasant produce rather than over production.

The tightening state regimentation of the population led to the growing exclusivity of its different legal categories. The right to possess land and serfs was eventually limited to those in service and to the monasteries, the right to keep shops in towns to the officially recognised urbanites (which for a time included the foot soldiers of the musketeer regiments – *strel'tsy*). In line with that, the transfer between different categories of the population was forbidden.[11]

The Moscow State was increasingly establishing yet another hierarchy, in addition to that of 'service', riches and tax. The conquest and colonisation were making the country multi-ethnic. With the Orthodox church acting as the main agency of that assimilation process, many of the new subjects were rapidly and fully assimilated into the Russian majority, for example, the Ugro-Finn inhabitants of Vyatka, many of the Tatar nobles, etc. Those who did not, markedly many of the adherents of Islam and later of Catholicism and Judaism, found themselves in the lower brackets of the tsar's subjects, that is, some rungs below those of their class equivalents who were accepted as ethnically Russian. For a time, the Lutheran Germans of the Baltic provinces were an exception, that is, a favoured minority, but that disappeared during the xenophobic waves of the nineteenth century. By that time ethnic disprivilages were extended also to some of the non-Russian adherents of the Orthodox faith: the Ukrainians and the Armenians.

* * *

In the sixteenth century the tsardom proceeded to develop along the lines established already in the later period of Basil II's reign (1425–62) and under that of Ivan III (1462–1505). The Code of Law (*Sudebnik*) of 1497 related to Kiev but expressed the new political structures that were coming into being. Capital punishment (unknown under Kievian laws) was provided for 'state crimes' (para 9). Peasants were permitted to leave their masters only once a year (on St George's Day) and those of them who lived in landlord-built houses were made to pay for them before moving on, limiting considerably their potential mobility.[12] A complex system of courts was presided over by boyars and officials, all appointed by the grand duke.

The conquest of Great Novgorod meant the increase of the territories that Moscow controlled also in the north-east, extending as far as the Urals. Almost constant war, political subversion and diplomatic contests led to the absorption of the Tver's and Ryazan principalities, the Pskov city-state, and the Smolensk and Chernigov areas, conquered from Lithuania between 1500 and 1514. Tsar governors were appointed in the new provinces and new lands granted to the servitors. Conquest and the growing use of professional musketeers, artillery and foreign mercenaries enhanced the tsar's power – not only against external enemies but also against his own boyars and the lesser nobility. A major new component of the political situation of the sixteenth and seventeenth centuries was the extensive slave-taking raids of the Crimean Tatars to which the Italians and Turkish markets and merchants offered considerable inducement. The defence of the population, the constant building up of forts and defensive lines against the raiders, became a major long-term strategy and 'way of life' of the Muscovy State and its servitors' army. It also added considerable strength to the tsardom's popular appeal and substantive legitimation.

Under the rule of Ivan IV 'the Terrible' (1533–84) the struggle with Crimea (increasingly backed by Turkish might) went on, while the Tatar *khanates* of Kazan and Astrakhan were conquered and so was Siberia. The tsar's armies also advanced to the Baltic shore. Inside Muscovy, a massive attack on the privileges of the boyars, through radical land expropriations and the *oprichina* – a police army aiming at 'internal enemies of the Tsar' – advanced the tsar's omnipotence to a pitch never known before.[13]

In the late years of Ivan IV's rule it was as if Moscow reached the limits of its capacity for expansion. The growing brutality of oppression and the erratic rule of the tsar led to a sharp decline in the effectiveness of the state machinery. The never-ending wars, mounting taxation, executions and deportations, the new sack of Novgorod, etc. had depopulated the country and sapped its economy, its tax-producing ability and its military strength. The actual size of the servitors' army (*dvoryanskoe opolchenie*) dropped dramatically. By the 1580s Moscow had been defeated by the Swedes and the Poles, had lost its Baltic provinces and Siberian territories, and had its capital sacked and burned by the Crimean Tatars. Russian nobles were switching allegiance to foreign kings, while peasants increasingly fled to the wilderness in the south-east and north-east. For a while Boris Godunov, a courtier of Ivan IV, the chief boyar of his feeble-minded son and later himself a tsar, seemed to have arrested the decline of Moscow by a mixture of diplomatic compromises abroad and the appeasement of the servitors.[14] This included the consolidation of the bondage of their peasant dependants. The system of state administration was further enhanced and centralised, the army improved and western Siberia reconquered. At the turn of the sixteenth century Godunov's death, a civil war, a social revolt, dynastic squabbles and the foreign invasion combined in Russia's 'Time of Troubles' (*smutnoe vremya*) to lay Muscovy low, seemingly indicating its final decline and possible disintegration. That is when its sociopolitical system demonstrated an outstanding capacity for regeneration. Within two decades, under a new dynasty of Romanovs, the Moscow State had checked and defeated, one by one, its internal and external enemies. The tsar's government rapidly re-established its control over the 'serving' nobility and the rebellious peripheries, beating off at the same time foreign armies and a major attack by Muscovy's under-dogs. It proceeded directly to annex new areas in the south and south-east. By the mid-seventeenth century the new Legal Code of 1649 had formalised that reconsolidation, making any challenge to the tsar's will treasonable, and informing against his enemies the legal duty of every subject. The Code also finalised the bondage of the peasants to their communities and/or masters, abolishing the time limit that still existed under Godunov for the compulsory return of peasant runaways. It also extended the powers of the tsar's administration over the monasteries, increased state monopolies over the minting of money and alcohol production, etc.[15] The actual measure of state centralisation and control had rapidly outrun even the 1649 legal provisions. The *Zemskii Sobor* – a rather timid Russian version of a national conclave of representatives of different social estates known in Europe as the General Estates – which legislated the Code and helped the new dynasty to establish its rule, disappeared rapidly never to return, as did also the limited provisions for elected local authorities (the *guba*). Legislation by decree and appointed governors became universal.

Something more should be said about four major social factors in order to place the development of the state of Muscovy in context: the church, the peasants, the state economy and the plebeian dissent, that is, the churches' subservience, the peasants' enserfment, the state economy's strength and the popular rebels' defeat. The Orthodox church played an important role in delimiting and sustaining specific 'Russianness' within the Golden Horde, supported the extending power of Muscovite dukes and acted as the main apparatus of ethnic uniformity, assimilation and consolidation. The twelfth-century age of monastic advance in Europe had its thirteenth-/fourteenth-century equivalent in the Golden Horde when much wealth and its trappings was accumulated by the church. Later, in Muscovy, in the clerical factions' confrontation between the Trans-Volga Hermits who called for renunciation by the clergy of worldly riches and the Josephites who opposed them, the second group won by the grace of the tsar. A Yanov believes that it was their ideological plan and plot to claim unlimited religious mandate for the ruler that had underlaid the transformation of Muscovy under Ivan IV into new and terrorist despotism, which once established had eventually disposed also of the clergy's power.[16] Other historians doubt so dramatic a break and the 'putchist' social explanation. Either way, in contrast to the strong universalism and the territorial state power of the church of Rome, the Orthodox clergy was more parochial, state-bound and state-obedient. As in Byzantium of old, many of its Metropolitans were dismissed and replaced by men chosen by the tsar. The defeat of the political ambitions of Metropolitan Nikon in 1666 brought to an end any claims for the church's equal status with the state as representing the respective powers, spiritual and temporal. Even the stage-by-stage takeover of the lands of the church that began with Ivan III did not produce a rebellion of clerics.[17] When Peter I abolished the office of Metropolitan in 1700, it was accepted without a whimper. Later, when Archbishop Matseevich attempted to resist the massive closure and dispersion of monasteries by Catherine II, it was the churches' Synod that deprived him of his rank, declared him officially 'a liar' and imprisoned him for life. On the other hand, the main Russian religion of popular protest, the Old Believers who refused reforms of the liturgy and a state-bound clergy, were effectively marginalised without armed struggle (even though some Russian rebels used the Old Believers' arguments and secret brotherhoods, e.g. Pugachev). The whole dramatic experience of Reformation and the religious wars in Western and Central Europe was absent.

Second, the combined impact of growing autocratic power of the state and its system of 'service' led to a dramatic increase of peasant payments and their other obligations, especially the labour services.[18] The peasants' main reaction was flight to places 'where their struggle with nature was hard . . . but they evidently felt it was not as hard as the exactions and injustices imposed on them by the state'.[19] The squires acted also as the local judges on behalf of the state which meant further restriction of the peasant freedom of choice and movement. The right of peasants to move was legally restricted under Ivan III. Ivan IV suspended for a number of years peasant rights to leave their masters even once a year. In 1597 the tsar decree ordered further that 'to give justice to landlords', peasants who left their villages during the five years that preceded, should be forcefully returned to them. The Legal Code (*Ulozhenie*) of 1649, which was to last until 1830, had finalised the enserfment of Russian peasantry by turning them into 'movable property', that is, in addition to their now unlimited 'bondage', stripping them of legal competence.[20]

Third, the formation and consolidation of the Russian state was closely linked to the establishment of an extensive state economy. From catering for the requirements of the princely court and its retainers, the administration of the duke's domain had expanded into a complex machinery collecting tax and rents as well as tribute from the newly conquered lands, supplying a large army, monopolising and licensing whole branches of production of trade and of finance, and directly running mines, workshops and extensive landed estates. The 'state', intertwined with the tsar's court and his army, was Russia's largest single consumer as well as producer. The tsar's supreme rule, conceptualised as his personal patrimony of all lands and of all people was to play a considerable role in the deepening of state control in Russia. So did the expansion of the state's share in the country's produce – a massive state purse, used mostly for military purposes. The result of this process was well put by Klyuchevskii: 'The state swelled up [while] the people grew lean.'[21]

Finally, the gradual enserfment of the Russian peasants, the growing demands of the state, the famines and the ravages of war gave rise to the new phenomenon of plebeian rebellions which were to repeat themselves with fair continuity for two centuries. Peasant participation made them massive, the Cossacks of the frontier[22] brought military skills, and they were joined at times by non-Russian tribesman and, at the earlier stages, by some lesser nobles. These challenges to the tsarist state and army have often linked the social war of the underdogs to confrontation between the 'peripheries' and the 'centre', all of the dissenting forces defending 'the old rights' against the clerks, clerics, officers and squires of Moscow. Increasingly, these were class wars in which the state, its officers and its squires faced rebels consisting of the lowly social classes only. The movement of Khlopko in 1608 was followed by three larger-scale rebellions of Bolotnikov, Ryazin and of Pugachev, the last being crushed in 1775. The totality of the defeat of all those attempts and the disappearance of massive popular revolt in the late eighteenth and nineteenth centuries, on par with the vanquishing of all of the neighbouring states of Muscovy, were paramount to the making of the tsardom.[23]

* * *

Through the period of Russia's 'modernity' – its beginning usually associated with the rule of Peter I – and until as late as 1905, all the major changes in the political structure of the tsardom of the Romanovs were to come neither from 'below' nor from the 'outside' but from its very top, and were put to work by the state officialdom. Often the change 'from above' was the result of 'external' pressures, especially a political or a military defeat, but these were interpreted and the counter-measures were defined by the state dignitaries, with the tsar as the final arbiter. The whole epoch was to the Russian state one of 'Europeanisation', of conquest (actual or attempted), and of administrative reforms, in close association with each other. Military needs were paramount. Europeanisation meant first and foremost the adoption of European military techniques but the concepts of the well-ordered police state came also from 'the West', mainly from the small absolutist principalities of Germany. A centralised and painstaking control over the mass of the population was ever the focus of attention – a particularly difficult problem for a country with large territories, few 'natural borders' and constant colonisation of new lands. Autocracy and a highly centralised government explain the directness of association between any 'reforms' and particular rulers, for their individual tendencies and style of governing deeply influenced the way the state machinery was run. The most significant of state reforms were associated with the rule of Peter I (1682–1725), Catherine II (1762–96) and Alexander II (1855–81), always followed by spells of inertia or even by reversal of the reforms enacted previously.

Peter I brought the country into more direct contact with Europe than ever before.[24] His reforms introduced many European administrative and technological ideas that were used, interpreted and executed in ways often contrary to the conditions from which they were borrowed. What resulted was a peculiar mixture of 'Europeanism' hand in hand with the deepening of some of the major 'non-European' characteristics of the Russian state. It was that mixture which made them at times the more effective. The dual nature of those developments was well expressed by the fact that the title *imperator* adopted by Peter was simply added to that of the *avtokrat*, to make them one. Equally symbolically, a new 'Western' capital of St Petersburg was simply grafted on the body politic of Russia in addition to Moscow, which also proceeded to be treated as a capital city.

All this is not to belittle the extent of changes under Peter I, but rather to explain their nature, effect and ruthlessness of execution. These included reform of the whole system of social estates which was overhauled and reorganised into the categories of nobility, clergy, townsmen, state peasants and private peasants. The duty of every noblemen to serve in the army or in the officialdom and the exclusive rights of the urbanites to trade were formally legislated. Equally formally, the clergy was turned into a sub-strand of officialdom, under a lay minister of state. Serfdom was extended and consolidated by the fact that the 'state peasants', that is, peasants without a squire, were equated in their duties/disadvantages to 'private' serfs, with the state as their direct master. New decrees against peasant flight were enacted. The subject position of the 'tax-paying classes' was further reaffirmed by a per capita tax levied on them and the 'revisions' of population; that is, censuses of the 'taxable classes', introduced to secure the fulfilment of their duties to the state.

The whole of the Russian population was now divided into those who held state ranks or commissions and those who did not. A Table of Ranks was established to encompass all the 'serving' members of the society and was to stay unchanged as the backbone of the whole machinery of governing until 1917.[25] The officials were divided into a hierarchy of fourteen ranks: from the state chancellor to the scribe or non-commissioned officer, each with his specific uniform, title, salary and distinctions. Corresponding ranks pertained in the state administration, the tsar's court, the army and the navy, establishing the exact pecking order to which all officials belonged: an army colonel was below the court camerger but above the provincial secretary, and was to be addressed 'your superiority' by all and sundry. On his promotion to a general, the obligatory form of address changed (to 'your high-superiority') together with his salary, privileges, pensions and the colour of the trousers of his uniform. The top eight ranks of officials were to be automatically ennobled together with their offspring. The ninth rank received life nobility only. To put it in the words of Peter's crisp order, 'All senior officers who do not descend from nobility, they and their heirs, are nobles, and should be certified as such'.[26] The essence of the nobility–bureaucracy relation typical of the days of early Muscovy was formally stood on its head. It was not noble heritage that secured one's rank, but rank that was to provide the patent of nobility.

The strict hierarchy of ranks meant also that below the rank-holders, much, much lower, stood the 'taxable classes' – the fodder and the resource base of the grand imperial designs. Above it, at the top of the state structure of power and hierarchy of prestige stood the emperor, defined as 'an autocratic monarch' who 'is not answerable to anybody on earth' and who was expected to use his unlimited power to rule the state 'in a Christian manner'.[27] The *Duma* of the boyars and chief executives was abolished and replaced by a senate of tsar appointees,

carrying somewhat different functions, enacting legislation and directing the country in the tsar's absence. The old *Prikazy* were abolished,
their tasks consolidated and taken over by ministries.

The whole effort of reform was influenced by Peter's conceptions of
Russia's military needs and of *vernuft*, that is, 'reason', understood
mainly as an orderly administration in the sense adapted from Sweden and
from Germany's and Denmark's 'enlightened absolutism' of the day.[28] It
assumed the image of 'service' of everybody, the tsar himself included, to
'the state'. The military modernisation made its army new in structure
and for the first time fully able to confront the best of European
armies. To that purpose the old division between the 'servitors' and the
'tax-paying' producers was breached and once again 'stood on its head'.
Men of the 'tax-paying classes' were now massively drafted into the non-
commissioned ranks of Peter I's armies. The state economy, especially
the 'military–industrial complex' within it, was increasing by leaps and
bounds: a navy built from scratch, a new industrial region of mines and
factories based on serf labour developed in the Urals, etc.

After Peter's death and under a succession of 'weak' tsars and
tsarinas, state demands for the service of the nobility had lessened
considerably. Catherine II (1762–96)[29] consolidated the new trends in her
Charter of Nobility (1785) which freed nobles from the 'duty of service'.
Simultaneously, Catherine formalised their corporate being and turned
their land into private property. The serfdom of the peasants who
belonged to the nobles was made more absolute by state retreat from the
scene, as dramatically expressed by a new decree penalising serfs who
dared as much as to petition the monarch against their squire. While the
tsarina corresponded elegantly with Voltaire about the essence of
liberty, peasant serfs were officially turned into 'Christianised cattle'
which their masters were free to sell, buy or to punish at their pleasure.
Since Peter I the one remaining diversity between serfdom and slavery
expressed by the Russian peasant saying 'we belong to you [the squire]
but the land belongs to us' was being breached.[30] Peasants were being
moved from their land to become serf-miners, serf-workers or serf-
soldiers, at their master's or the government's wish. Under Catherine II
peasant families were often being divided while sold to new masters.
Hundreds of thousands of 'state peasants' were given in gifts to royal
favourites. The state, while renouncing supervision, was still ready to
support every squire fully, a simple request by him was sufficient for the
authorities to draft into the army or exile to Siberia a peasant
'troublemaker' and to put down any 'disorder'.[31] Yet, the remarkable
ascent of landed nobility, in the times of Catherine II had given them

neither a House of Lords nor *Estate Generale*. Also, the privileges were not won by the nobilities' collective action but granted by the autocrat's will. The autocracy stood firm against any devolution of its power, which rose to new heights.

Peter's Table of Ranks continued to apply under Catherine II and after, but fewer outsiders to the hereditary nobility found themselves now at the top of the administrative tree. Following the great scare of the Pugachev rebellion of Cossacks, peasants and tribesmen in 1773–5, the state administration was brought a step closer to localities and to the peripheries by the division of all European Russia into *guberniyas*, with a governor in charge of each. Associations of nobles were established in most of the ethnically Russian guberniyas and put under elected marshals to aid the governor and to promote the nobility's corporate interest. An attempt to establish effective city corporation was also made but with few results.

The policies of conquest proceeded and gained new momentum. In the south-west, Turkey was defeated in two successive wars and large new territories annexed, inclusive of Crimea. New parts of the Caucasus were made into a Russian province. The three successive partitions of Poland–Lithuania had destroyed Russia's once powerful neighbour and added massive new territories bringing the Russian frontier at the turn of the nineteenth-century deep into Europe. The Napoleonic Wars were eventually to bring the Russian soldiers as far as Paris and made their Tsar Alexander I (1801–25), Catherine's grandson, into the most powerful monarch of the 'Holy Alliance', which came to dominate Europe between 1815 and 1848. The frontier moved still further west. Under Alexander, as well as his brother and successor Nikolai I, the Russian army contributed to the stability of the reactionary regimes farther west, earning for the tsardom the nickname of the 'gendarme of Europe'.

The internal policies and the whole framework of state-and-society relations under Nikolai I (1825–55) were largely characteristic of tsardom during most of the nineteenth-century, through the reign of Catherine's descendants, from Paul I (1796–1801) to Alexander III (1881–94). Some historians have made considerable play of changes covertly taking shape under the conservative façade.[32] Related to the country's problems and the length of this period, what characterised its state machinery was those changes diminutive nature. The rule of Nikolai and the Russian nineteenth-century state in general, were marked by the totality of the tsars' power, the direct bureaucratic intervention into every aspect of life, the loyal servility of the nobles, the apathetic subservience of the peasants, the massive army and the

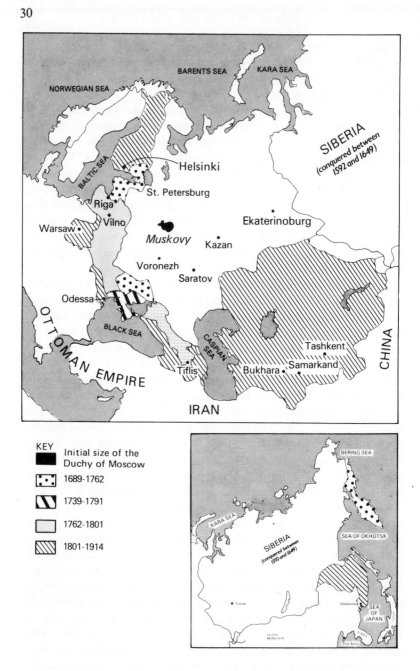

MAP 3 *Russian imperial conquests: eighteenth and nineteenth centuries*

sluggish economy.[33] Debate at the top concerning projects of reform was constant but mostly futile. The objections of the tsars, the bureaucrats and the nobles had effectively checked most of the suggested changes, immobilising and weeding out within the state administration the few active supporters of reform and suppressing such pressures as came from below.[34] The stirrings of open opposition were mostly limited to a thin layer of 'the educated public'. They were met by the dogged conservatism at the top well expressed by Uvarov (a Minister of Education of Nikolai I), as a credo of 'orthodoxy, autocracy and nationality'. Uvarov could have rightly added 'stolid brutality' of his triad of the tsardom's self-characterisation. The only immediate result of an attempt by young officers to force democratic changes by *coup d'etat* in 1825 was the gallows or exile for them, the establishment of a gendarmerie and the revamping of censorship and of political police. Local outbursts of peasant unrest and a 1830–01 struggle of the Poles for independence were suppressed by military force. Of the reforms suggested during the first sixty years of the century, only some of the changes in the organisation of the army and in the administration of the 'state peasants' were introduced and a State Council established to formalise legislation but given advisory powers only (even so, the monarchs proceeded to bypass it by the use of numerous 'secret committees').

The one exception to rule of the nineteenth-century was a major wave of reforms that carried the characteristics of its eighteenth-century predecessors: military couses (or at least 'triggering-off mechanisms'), a decision taken from above and the parallel reconstruction of the system of class privileges by the state bureaucracy. A defeat in the Crimean War in 1854–6 dramatically exposed Russia's growing weaknesses as against the Western-European powers. Russia's military supremacy in Europe was lost to a coalition of more 'modern' nations and armies. In what followed, and overriding the misgivings of the landed nobility, Alexander II (1855–81) ordered in 1861 the emancipation of the 'private' serfs.[35] A major part of the arable land was transferred into the hands of peasant communes and the squires were paid a considerable redemption fee. A parallel reform concerning the 'state peasants' followed in 1866 and 1867. Other reforms also attempted to 'bring Russia in line with Europe' as well as to pacify or incorporate the public opinion of the growing 'educated society'. The *Zemstvo* was established in most European *guberniyas* – Russia's first elected regional authority based on electoral colleges of different property groups. Modernised city authorities were established along similar lines. A new system of courts, autonomous of state administration, and a corporate autonomy of lawyers were enacted, and the autonomy of universities declared. Simultaneously, a major reorganisation took place in the army structure. The reform mood did not last, however, even through the period of Alexander II's rule. Ideas of a parliamentary rule were sternly rebuked and punished from the outset. The 'from above' nature of reforms drew growing dissent of a small but vocal opposition of liberals and radicals. Within a decade the pendulum began to swing back to the policies of containment and repression. It was met by revolt. Alexander II's killing by a bomb of a People's Will revolutionary brought the period to a suitably dramatic conclusion.

The rule of Alexander III (1881–94) and the first decade of Nicholas II who followed, were mostly defined by a powerful conservative backlash – the 'counter-reforms'. Their official ideology was once again that of the trinity of 'orthodoxy, autocracy and nationality' with the implicit addendum of brutal stolidity of administrative responses. Their essence was to 'tighten the screws' of the omnipotence of the tsar and his officialdom, establishing closer state control over the whole range of potential centres of autonomous power. An office of land chief (*zemskii nachal'nik*) was introduced to control the elected officers of the 'emancipated' peasant communes. *Zemstvos* were brought under tight supervision of the Ministry of Interior. The university autonomy was cancelled and professors dismissed in increasing numbers for political unreliability. The courts and the church functionaries were brought under closer ministerial supervision. There was also tightening of the reins over the non-Russian population and a policy of their Russification. The autonomy of the Duchy of Finland (secured by an international agreement when Finland was 'given' to Russia after the Napoleonic Wars) was curtailed. Repressions increased in Poland, the Ukraine, Armenia, etc. Non-Russian and non-assimilating ethnic groups were now being systematically stereotyped as a nuisance by the administration: Poles as rebels, Muslims as primitives, Ukrainians as illiterate peasants, Armenians as quarrelsome Orientals, Jews as despicable untouchables.

The counter-reforms also incorporated a systematic attempt to bring back the influence of the hereditary nobility as tsardom's solid conservative support and the country's 'first estate'. The land chiefs were to be selected from local nobility in a conscious effort to re-establish its political power in the countryside. The authority of the regional associations of nobility was enhanced, new resources for preferential loans poured into the Nobility Bank, and scholarships and exclusive institutions set up to promote the education of the noble youths (and hence to advance their future administrative or military careers). Steps were considered to limit the service-related entrance into the nobility 'estate' of the less desirable bureaucratic elements. In the long term these nobility rejuvenation programmes and the special State Council for Nobility Affairs proved of remarkably little consequence.[36]

On the whole, the 'period of reaction' in the late nineteenth-century in Russia was to prove in the long term of less substance than its perpetuators' aims and its critics' fears. Neither the reforms nor the counter-reforms did recover for the tsardom the international standing of 1815–48. The defeat in the Crimean War in 1854–5 under Nikolai I was followed by the diplomatic disaster of the 1878 Berlin conference of Alexander II's era, when Russia was made to disgorge most of its territorial gains against Turkey. Then, within a generation, came a shattering military defeat by Japan in 1904 followed by diplomatic reversals in the Balkans. Internally, the erosion of the 1860s reforms was partial only. Serfdom, decisive for the way of living of the massive majority of the Russians, could not be brought back. The new legal system and local authorities proceeded to operate despite growing restraints. Major social, demographic and economic processes had been modifying the face of Russia in ways that were increasingly beyond the control of the retrograde ideologies, conservative bureaucrats and reactionary monarchs. Also, since the middle of the nineteenth-century a new type of dissent by the Russian 'educated public' was being increasingly felt, its more radical representatives combining direct political challenge to the tsardom with repeated attempts to activate to that purpose the plebeian and ethnic underdogs of Russia. Defeated with the destruction of the People's Will Party in the early 1880s[37] and later checked as much by the apathy of the plebeian 'masses' as by police repressions, these attempts could not be outrooted altogether. By the end of the century, political dissent was coming to the fore again and with a vengeance. It was faced by the tsardom's 'state apparatus'.

C. THE STATE APPARATUS

The realism of the analytical division between *state* and the *civil society*, submerged though its usage became since the nineteenth-century, lay in the conceptual delimitation of the state as a distinct machinery of power controlling populations and territories. The linkage of this power structure with the 'private institutions' of the civil society was assumed to be mutual and central, but that did not nullify their discrete characteristics and dynamics or the need to study them distinctly.

The Russian tsardom was a state, that is, a system of sovereign power, monopolist within set territorial bounds. Coercion, the threat of force and a variety of manipulative and ideological devices were used to extort from its 'subjects' immense resources and utilise them according to the designs of the few. The state and 'its needs' were legitimated by a history of successful defence of the frontiers and fresh conquests establishing the tsar's control and order over extensive territory as well as by the historical myths of ethnic destiny, sacred statehood and natural loyalty to the state's metaphysical essence, personified in the tsar. Its size, multi-ethnicity and global claims made this state into an empire. Embedding it was a bureaucratic hierarchy of officials, who did the organising, the power monopolising, the pumping-out and the putting to use of the resources, as well as directing, conquering, suppressing, legitimating and mythologising. History, law and the social division of power have made the Russian bureaucrats mesh with squires and gentlemen of the nobility, and share with them the head-man and the fountain of loyalty, the empire's 'first nobleman' and its executive supremo: 'By The God's Will, The Emperor and Autocrat Of All Russias, Moscow, Kiev, Vladimir and Novgorod, Tsar of Kazan, Tsar of Poland, Tsar of Siberia, Tsar of Kherson in the Tavrida, Tsar of Georgia, Grand-Duke of Finland etc., etc., etc.'[1]

At the turn of the century the officialdom of Russia still lived by the Table of Ranks of Tsar Peter. A few changes occurred, the number of ranks was reduced from fourteen to twelve and 'hereditary nobility' was now granted to the top four ranks only (while only 'personal', that is, life nobility, was now given to the ranks five to nine). As in the army, 'rank' was by now separate from the actual job-description. Little had changed in essence, however. Generation succeeded generation along lines laid down strictly and uniformly by laws and regulations, providing for security, stability, and for unlimited obedience to those above, bound to the power (even if miniscule) over those below in rank and those outside of the ranking orders. Life was a career measured by promotions, punctuated by decorations, following its course towards one's pension (within which the rank and privileges were maintained). A man, well behaved towards his betters, could on the whole trust the clock-like precision of bureaucratic advance. For one who managed to impress those above and/or have the right connections in the tsar's own environment, gates could open to considerable wealth, power and renown. The stupid or apathetic were still rewarded for obedience.

Corruption was treated with licence, provided it was done in a decently covert way or under the powerful 'protection' of somebody high up. One did not easily rock the boat.

Russian regulations governing state service (*gosudarstvennaya sluzhba*) were initially shaped by the German and Danish examples, the *Polizeistaad* of the seventeenth and eighteenth centuries,[2] writ large by the size of the country and the power of its rulers. The connections between civil and military wings of the 'service' were closer than farther west. A civilian official was often an ex-army officer, who retained his rank in his transfer or a graduate of a military college. Both the civil and the military types of office were historically rooted in the functions of the royal servants, who were neither enserfed nor completely free but under direct orders of the state dignitaries and rewarded as such (*sluzhashchie, prikaznye lyudi*). The nineteenth-century authoritative text described their position in the state service as a 'legally defined relation of obedience, serving the needs and aimed to benefit the state'. It was accepted as a lifelong career, that is, neither 'a natural duty' (e.g. of all of the subjects to the tsar) nor a limited or temporary contractual arrangement (e.g. that of a state supplier, the *podryadchik*).[3] A career in the state service began with the taking of an oath of loyalty. The duties included zealous devotion (*userdie*),[4] secrecy, respect to those higher in rank, correct behaviour outside one's office, exclusivity of the functions performed (*nesovmestimost'*), that is, the duty not to engage simultaneously in certain other occupations proscribed for that purpose.[5] Special disciplinary courts punished offenders within the service. The rights that accompanied state service included salary and pension, but also considerable tokens of social standing and prestige: the uniform, the decorations, the official title and mode of address as well as extra legal protection (*usilennaya ugolovnaya okhrana*). Any attack on a rank-holder was punished in law more severely than similar offences against those outside the state service. More generally, the state uniform symbolised one's belonging to the exclusive body of those who personified and served the immense power of tsardom or, to use the spectacular term often repeated then and since, who were its 'organs'.[6]

It is the Prussian experience as distilled by Max Weber that has defined for social scientists the characteristics of bureaucracy as an 'ideal type' – a measuring rod for its more specific expressions. To Weber, the power of state bureaucracy (unavoidable in the modern world) resided in the routines of civil and military administration. Bureaucracy was characterised by formal employment, salary, pension, appointment and promotion by merit, functional division of labour, defined jurisdiction, documentary procedures and administrative hierarchy. A steady flow of resources to pay the officials salaries and pensions was implicit to this self-reproducing system. It was 'ideally' a factory-like machine, detachedly and effectively serving any master, with fixed norms securing predictability and the ordered usage of legitimate coercion at its disposal. Above it stood a necessarily non-bureaucratic stratum, that is, a group capable of decision-making, of the transformation and transgression of the system's rules of the game and not only of the execution of the orders from above. Weber had seen the historical origins of the modern European state bureaucracy in Byzantium (notice the significance of that point of entry for the Russian experience) transformed and developed further during its spread to Italy, then to France and finally to Germany, where it reached its most developed form. Its 'inescapable' nature was rooted in its effectiveness, as a most 'rational' system of administration.[7]

The Russian state bureaucracy was close enough in character to Weber's abstract model. It differed mostly in the extent of defencelessness of its 'cadre' as against its own superiors, in the more restrictive nature of its recruitment or promotion and in the extent to which petty corruption was endemic in it.

The Russian rank-holders (*chiny*) did not have the security of tenure that was built into the Prussian law[8] and they could be dismissed at a minute's notice without any explanation, severance pay or pension rights. There was no appeal from such a dismissal, no defence except by a petition to the tsar or his dignitaries. Second, selection and promotion by merit (be it intellectual capacity or the totality of obedience) was not the only consideration, even formally. Some of the ethnic groups were totally excluded from state service – for example, Jews, Asian 'natives' (*inorodtsy*) and, since the 1860s, Poles. In fact, the promotion of anybody but ethnic Russians of Orthodox faith was impeded. In particular, this was increasingly the case for the impoverished Baltic nobles, ethnically German and Lutheran by religion, who traditionally obtained a career in the Russian state service. Women were altogether excluded from state service. So were, in law, all of the 'tax-paying classes' save the sons of clergy, but the exceptions granted on the basis of education caused that rule practically to lapse. However, that regulation, still 'on the books', symbolised an important aspect of the Russian state service which remained true until the last days of the Romanovs: its particular relation to the 'social estate' of nobility.

Some division had always existed between the 'nobles' and the tsar's servants. Since the Charter of Nobility of 1780, even the idea of their being one, professed by Peter I, was formally disposed of. Yet that very break (which occurred in the conditions of increasing significance of state administration and of the growth of a massive infantry of serf-soldiers) turned the state service at its higher ranks from a consuming duty into a privilege that the nobles came to demand exclusively for themselves.[9] The state service gave income, power and prestige as well as command over soldiers or lesser clerks. Russian nobles felt increasingly the need for extra income, authority and honour. It was also natural for the noble dignitaries 'to keep the jobs for the boys', the more so since promotion would turn the incumbents of the top jobs into noblemen by law, and infest the ranks of true nobility by the *nouveau riche*. Russian nobility was never powerful enough to have its monopoly of service endorsed, even for the very top of the ranks, not least because of the increasing need of the tsar's administration for well-trained men which the nobility could not fully supply. As time went by and the state management and army command grew more complicated, university or advanced military training were increasingly considered necessary. These requirements could not be filled only by graduates of noble origin.[10] What resulted was a complex of partly informal arrangements, by which nobles were systematically preferred for appointments into state service but were not exclusive within it. A hereditary nobleman often began his service at a higher rank than a commoner and was promoted faster than a man without a title. A number of privileged educational institutions, to which only children of nobility were admitted, were set up to train the future senior civil and military officers of the realm – for example, the Tsarskosel'skii Lyceum, the Pazheskii korpus in Petersburg, etc. Their graduates were appointed to higher military and administrative posts, promoted at an accelerated rate and often reached ranks of generals and ministers.[11]

Russian nobility was thus divided into hereditary landowners, who could additionally join the ranking stratum for a career loaded in their favour, and the often landless 'nobility of service', that is, those whose claim to privileges was that of their or their not-far-removed ancestors' promotions within the army or the bureaucracy (and who usually proceeded with their family's traditional occupation). There were additionally the 'personal nobles' elevated from the 'tax-paying classes' by their rank within the state service. When particularly successful, they were promoted occasionally into the still higher ranks granting hereditary nobility. The tensions between the 'real', that is, hereditary and landowning nobility of long standing, and the 'serving' nobles and bureaucrats, were considerable. In the eyes of each other they were, on the one hand, incompetent and illiterate country bumpkins, ever asking for state handouts and, on the other hand, jumped-up clerks of no breeding, who were parasites on the tsar's majesty and pushed around 'real people'. A different confrontation was also taking place between the more enlightened leaders of the provincial nobility within some of the *zemstvos* and the provincial governors representing the Ministry of Interior. Those differences escalated every time the country faced a crisis: an economic reversal, a revolt or a war.

In the period discussed, the proportion of hereditary nobles within the top hierarchy of the state service and between the provincial governors was high, but in decline. It was much lower within the middle ranks and in some of the departments. The sons of the clerics (*popovichi*) were particularly important there in the middle of nineteenth-century but by its end, commoners with no kin in the state service or the church, no nobility status and owning no land were steadily increasing. There were very few nobles in the low 'ranks'. When the mass of 'Russian officialdom' is considered, it was 'in its essential part not of noble origin'.[12]

*   *   *

Marx has once specified the 'organs' of state as consisting of the 'standing army, police, bureaucracy, clergy and judiciary'.[13] To bring up to date that picture of the state apparatus as a bureaucratic structure of structures, and make it somewhat more precise, one should add or specify also the administrators in charge of education, of 'welfare', of state economy and, increasingly in our times, of the mass media.[14] The composition of the Russian officialdom can be categorised accordingly. The 1897 census, the general figures and categories of which are reviewed in addendum 1 at the end of this chapter, offered figures that may help us to establish or to approximate for that point in time the numbers of the 'state servants' within the population of the empire.[15] The relevant table is on p. 43.

The Russian army and navy consisted of two clearly distinct social categories, singled out in the census. On the one hand, stood the 43 779 'senior officers, generals and admirals', that is, career officers linked into the ranking system of state service. Army commissions were the major branch of the state service where hereditary nobles prevailed to the last, that is, until the First World War depleted their ranks to the point where a massive infusion of educated commoners into officers' ranks became a necessity. On the other side stood about 1 million of the 'other ranks', mostly army conscripts of peasant stock. In the middle were the junior officers, some at the beginning of a professional career but also those under conscription for a relatively short period. Also, there were the NCOs, not distinguished from the conscripts mass by their social origins (or by the official statistics), but 'professional' in terms of their career structure, if without the opportunities to aspire to a commission into officers' ranks (which were limited to the gentlemen and 'the educated' only). The sum total of all military personnel of Russia in 1897 was 1 133 000. Of the roughly 880 000 in the age cohort of those liable for conscription at the age of 21, only 225 000 were actually called up for service of one to four years.[16] (The percentage was to increase considerably as from 1904.) The army's share of the state budget was about one-quarter, made to look smaller by the very substantial size of the non-military items.

Within the army, the officer ranks of the Guard regiment stationed in Petersburg were mostly a fief of the noble families, especially of the hereditary nobles. To hold a commission there was to serve close to the centre of power and the eyes of the tsar and his ministers, providing possibilities for an illustrious career. On the other hand, to have a son serve as an officer in the Guards was an expensive honour kept within a fairly narrow circle of those who were not only 'noble' but also influencial and wealthy.

Police formed the second category of the 'state organs' of Marx's designations. In Russia, they were part of the civilian administration, and employed 105 000 men in 1897 and provided for nearly half of those in employment by the general state administration, as listed. There was additionally an unknown number of paid informers. At the core stood the combined organisation of the uniformed Corps of Gendarmes and the plain-clothed *Okhrana*, both under the Vice Minister of Interior as their *ex officio* chief. The central organisation of police also supervised regional and local organisations of police, rural guards, etc. The official police structure blended into the half-official vigilantes, for example, the gate-keepers (*dvorniki*) of the large houses of Petersburg and the *sotskie* elected in every peasant *volost'* for unpaid police duties.[17] The gendarmes formed an autonomous hierarchy, with representatives in every region who, while closely co-operating with its governor, had the duty to report 'over his head' directly to their superiors about any possible lapses of the local administration. Since their inception in 1836, the Corps of Gendarmes offered high salaries, considerable privileges and extensive rights to attract into their officers' ranks loyal and capable administrators, and often competed effectively in recruitment with the army (many of the top gendarmes officers had military training or military careers before joining the corps).[18]

It is important to note that the brief and the self-image of the Russian police exceeded that of its western neighbours. It was an image of a moral physician or guardian of population, the evil tendencies within which and whose essential infantility were assumed. Related to this was the task of the social observer and analyst, the surveys of public opinion by the gendarmerie being often of very high quality. By the beginning of the twentieth-century there were also attempts at police-directed organisation of political movements, labour unions and welfare institutions.

The general 'civilian' wing of the *state* administration formed the core of the category of officialdom (*chinovniki*, used in Russian common parlance). In addition to the police, the 'state administration and judiciary' category of the 1897 census had 95 577 employees of whom 44 481 were defined as non-ranking clerical staff. The central Ministry in that field was that of the Interior, with its many supervisory networks, provincial governors, officials etc. and including the police and the gendarmerie. Its task was to secure 'law and order', which meant the execution of the flood of general demands and instructions coming from the top, the repression of any dissent to it (or any 'slackness' in its execution) and the reporting of anything that might be of interest to the government or pose a threat to it. Its top local representatives, the governors of provinces, were under law the most senior state officials there. In every region and in the country, general administration intertwined with the specific hierarchies of the other main ministries, for example, a finance, justice, transport, etc. and with the local, part-official organisations. What resulted was a fairly effective network of control, despite the conflicts usually produced by its heterogeneity. The constant struggle for resources and power between the competing bureaucracies, the different 'satrapies' as the Russian opposition was to call them, was part of the daily life of Russian administration.

The education and welfare services were to a major degree in the hands of the *zemstvo* regional authorities and of the church (in roughly 2:1 proportion within the primary schooling). Some of these institutions were controlled by the state directly, while the facilities of the local authorities were supervised by a variety of state inspectors. Within the government in Petersburg there were two relevant ministries in charge: that of Education and that of 'The Institutions of Empress Maria' (a rough equivalent of 'Ministry of Welfare'). Through its direct and indirect controls, the network extended to a considerable number of employees, most of whom were non-ranking, but at their top inevitably stood those with official ranks within the state administration. The general number of school teachers and schoolmasters of Russia was recorded in 1897 as about 80 000 men and women. (It would be more if one is to believe the Ministry of Education figures which differed from those of the census and which probably included part-timers.)[19] There is no way to ascertain the numbers of those whose functions would be defined nowadays in Western Europe as those of paid 'social workers', but there would not be less than 10 000 of them.

The reform of 1863 introduced the concept of an independent 'legal profession' and in 1897 there were about 9000 men whose occupation was described as that of a 'lawyer'. Considerably larger than that was the figure of the graduates in law in state employment. The judges were state officials appointed for life. Their supervision came from the Ministry of Justice and from the Senate (the main function of which was at that stage to act as the High Court of Appeals). The Ministry of Justice has controlled directly a network of 'state prosecutors' (*prokuror*). The Prosecutor's Office held considerable powers and was closely linked in execution of its duties with the police.

In the face of the 'counter-reforms' that attempted to curtail their autonomy in the 1880s and 1890s, the legal profession has shown increasingly dissenting moods. Many of the luminaries of the liberal movement and some socialists were Russia's practising lawyers, using the courtroom and the legal debate to defend their political stance. They faced in the courtrooms a stratum of legally trained, ranking state officials, uniformed and bound by the oath of loyalty to uphold unlimited state power. As in the case of the lawyers, the medical doctors, scientists, technologists, etc. (that is, what was customarily described as the 'free' or 'liberal' professions) were incorporated to a much larger extent than in Western Europe into the state 'salariat'.[20]

Formally outside the ranking state service, but in fact very much a part of it, stood the 63 000 priests of the Orthodox established church of Russia (the 'white' clergy). There were also 21 000 senior monks and nuns and 64 000 junior part-servants (*poslushniki*), that is, altogether 85 000 of the 'black' clergy – that is, monastic orders (of those, three-quarters were women). The church was led by more than 100 bishops and by the abbots and abbesses of about 900 monasteries and convents. Since the time when the Metropolitan's office was abolished by Peter I, the Orthodox church was directed by the Synod of its senior clergy with the tsar's appointee at its head – a layman with ministerial status. For all practical purposes the activities of the church were directed as a ministry of the government. There were no salaries or automatic rank promotions within the church, however. A rural priest had to fend for himself and make a living from the dues collected from his parishioners, which often meant relative poverty – that is, an income not much above that of his peasant flock, possibly supplemented by part-time farming.[21] Some of the clergymen managed much better than that. In particular, at the top of the church hierarchy were the bishops and the senior monks of the famous and wealthy monasteries, who lived a life of relative luxury and of considerable power and prestige.

The Orthodox church hierarchy closely controlled the lower priesthood. Ecclesiastic courts were available to deal with those who had offended against church discipline. With much of the liturgy and prayer focused on tsarist mystique and on total obedience to the legitimate powers, temporal and spiritual, the clergy acted as a major prop of order and as a rural network of unpaid informers about dissent of any type. It was also in the forefront of loyalist campaigns for 'autocracy, orthodoxy and nationality' and engaged in its own proselytising activities aimed to extend the loyalist camp and the Russian ethnos.[22]

The Russian tsardom did not possess a specific ministry for propaganda, information or ideological training. The Orthodox church was the arm expected to provide ideological guidance as well as vigilance against possible offenders against the moral duties to support the powers that be, the unity of the Russian state and the exalted standing of its ruler. The other branch of state administration that handled problems of ideology was that of state censorship, a department within the Ministry of Education eventually taken over by the Ministry of Interior.

Finally, the actual figures of Russian 'technocrats', that is, executives and specialists in technology, in charge of the state economy and its productive enterprises, were never singled out with precision. The most numerous group within the 'economic' branch of the state employees were the railwaymen, about 262 000 of them, mostly manual workers. They manned what had by that time become Russia's main means of public transportation, its largest single enterprise and a powerful economic tool of the state. The number of administrators, conductors and clerks within the railway system was 81 000. The state also employed 49 000 men and women within its post offices, an unknown but substantial figure in the state factories (the *kazennye zavody*, often of armaments industry), as well as more men and women within the state farms and forestry. There were also the extensive and part-bureaucratic networks of supply and provision of 'state needs', usually attached to the different ministries. The superintendents of those activities were usually ranking officials – 'technocrats', possibly with technological and managerial training and/or university degrees but these activities involved also many outsiders to the ranking system, that is, non-ranking employees, part-independent enterpreneurs, etc. who lived on the margins of officialdom and the state economy and off it.

A combined statistical picture of the tsardom as a bureaucracy can be drawn accordingly (Table 1.1). It would show, as indicated, con-

TABLE 1.1   *The 'state servants' of Russia in 1897*

(A) *The bureaucratic 'core'*	
1. Civil administrators, judiciary, police[a]	202 000
(of those, civilian rank-holders and officers of the police 64 000)	
2. Senior officers of the army, navy and the border-guards[b]	49 000
3. Junior army officers and professional NCO (estimated)[c]	147 000
Together (A)	398 000
(B) *The 'margins' of the state bureaucracy*	
4. Municipal employees (other than teachers and 'professionals')	46 000
5. The elected officers of local and 'estate' authorities[d]	14 000
6. The officiating 'white' and the senior monastic ('black') clergy of the Orthodox church	84 000
7. Teachers	79 000
8. The state-employed members of 'free professions' (estimated)[e]	16 000
9. Administrators and executives of the state economy (railways, factories, etc.)[f]	148 000
Together (B)	387 000
Total (A + B)	785 000
% of the working population[g]	
The bureaucractic core	0.65 % (if males only 1.23 %)
The 'core' and the margins	1.29 %

Source:
OSPN, vol. 2, pp. 356–79.
Notes:
[a] The employees of state administration less the porters and office-servants (*sluzhiteli*).
[b] Inclusive of the civilian rank-holders within the Ministries of Army and Navy.
[c] Estimated as three times the number of senior officers.
[d] That is, nobility associations and peasant *volost'*.
[e] Estimated as two-thirds of the Russian medical doctors plus half of its 'engineers and technologists, scientists and writers' and employees of scientific and artistic institutions. For substantiation of the figure for medical doctors, see ES, vol. 13, pp. 894–5. State-employed lawyers appear mostly in section 1 above.
[f] The figure is that of appropriate groups employed within railways and the post office, etc., plus a token 20 000 to represent the state industries (*kazennye zavody*) and farms – probably an understatement.
[g] The working population of Russia was roughly estimated as 61 million by accounting for the population age 15 to 60 and decreasing the result by the figures of those estimated to be handicapped, idle or engaged in studies plus women not involved in paid work or farming for social reasons. It therefore included 95 per cent of men and 80 per cent of women within those age groups.

siderable 'grey' areas and other shortcomings, usual when an approximation takes place of the exact figures. None the less, it helps to consider the picture of state and society in Russia at the turn of the nineteenth century.

The first impression of such summation of figures is the surprising small size of the Russian state service, but then only 30 000 Chinese mandarins have ruled in the nineteenth century the Celestial Empire. There were 116 000 senior rank-holders, both military and civilian, at the bureaucratic core of the state apparatus, that is, about 0.002 (one-fifth of 1 percent) of its working population. Even if we add to it all of the administrative 'margins' of the 'state apparatus' (some of whom were in open political opposition like many of the Russian rural teachers and *zemstvo* employees), we are still speaking of less than 2 per cent of the Russian working population. Another estimate of 385 000 given by Zaionchkovskii for all of the rank-holders within the civilian wing of the state officialdom in 1902 (of which only 1 per cent belonged to the top four ranks) would make them slightly more than 1 per cent of mature male population and the 'top group' 0.01 per cent of it.[23] The ability of the state 'organs' described to perform effectively their tasks was necessarily based on the passive compliance of the great majority of people as well as the selective harshness towards any dissenting minority.

*   *   *

An alternative way to look at the Russian 'state apparatus' is to follow its hierarchy from the top down, proceeding along one of its strands. At the top of the bureaucratic structure of structures of the state service and 'above it' in the Weberian sense of exercising sovereignty, stood the tsar and the two basic categories of his closest collaborators and aides, who also formed his immediate social environment: the tsar's court and 'circle of courtiers' (*tsarskii dvor, krug pridvornykh*).[24] The first of those categories comprised of official heads of the main bureaucratic hierarchies: the ministers of state, the army chiefs, the leading members of the state council, the Senate and Synod (*sanovniki* in Russian common parlance). The second category within the tsar's 'circle' was that of his kinsmen (the princes of royal blood, that is, the 'grand dukes' by their official title) and the heterogeneous crowd of personal servants, childhood friends, tsar's mistresses, favoured clergy and journalists, all those who unofficially had the tsar's ear. Some of them were the smart and the well-connected Petersburg men-about-town, sons of the old nobility, officers of the privileged Guard regiments, and 'lobbyists' trading in 'connections' in high places. In the middle, linking the heads of state service and the tsar's favourites, stood the 'official courtiers', that is, men with a particular 'court rank' (in the Table of Ranks) and a specific task to perform – for example, the highly influential Minister of the Tsar's Court, who saw to the tsar's family's well-being, and often acted as royalty's confidant. Hereditary nobility with long pedigrees of court service provided a major part of the tsar's personal aides.

A minister of state was, within this context, not a politician in the West European sense, but 'tsar's servant' – a high-ranking official in charge of a specific office, staff and line of command. He was selected and 'fired' personally by the tsar. He reported back to his 'boss', who personally authorised every substantive initiative. The tsar was also the government's only co-ordinator. There was no collective responsibility of ministers or 'cabinet policy'. The Council of Ministers discussed some matters and then passed on all of the views expressed to the tsar. The decision was his, the support of a project by ministerial majority meant nothing, unless the tsar has chosen to adopt it. The same held for all substantive matters considered by the State Council, the Senate and the Synod. The never-ending chain of reports going up to his majesty's desk from the heads of the branches of the government and bureaucratic committees, the royal scribble on the margin ('yes', 'no', 'should be promoted', 'stupid excuses', etc.) and the subsequent comment at an audience or an instruction passed via the royal chancellery, were decisive for the processes by which Russia was administered. The usual way to take a major political decision was for the tsar to closet himself with a few aides chosen for the occasion. The final word was of the tsar, not only formally but substantively. This gave exceptional powers to the informal wing of the tsar's aides, the *coterie* of tsar's kinsmen and favourites. It was their influence that reflected in the appointment and dismissals of ministers and officials as well as in the choice of the advice the tsar received or was ready to adopt. The power of the *camarillia*, their never-ending squabbles and their requests for favours addressed directly to the tsar, were well known through rumours and deeply resented by the Russian 'educated classes', including many within the top bureaucracy and nobility, especially the 'nobility of service'.[25]

The Ministry of Interior was traditionally a senior branch of the Russian government.[26] During the last hundred years of Romanov's rule, there were no less than four men at its helm who became the tsar's most influential advisers, each of them with almost dictatorial powers for a while: M. Loris-Melikov in 1880–1, D. Tolstoi in the later 1880s, V. Pleve in 1903–4 and P. Stolypin in 1906–10. In the constant ministerial struggle for power, prestige, resources and the 'tsar's ear', it was usually either the Minister of Interior or the Minister of Finance who jostled for it most effectively and came out on top. At times they have represented the division of views between the 'Westernising' supporters of reforms and the conservatives, but that was not always the case. The wars between the two bureaucratic elephants filled much of the Russian administrative history. In what follows the Ministry of Interior will be used to exemplify a strand of the state bureaucratic hierarchy.

By the turn of the century the functions and the specific departments of the Ministry of Interior (the MVD) included the appointment and supervision of the provincial governors, the control of police, colonisation activities, aspects of public health and welfare, food provision in the time of famine, censorship and the national statistical bureau. The MVD supervised the work of the Land Chiefs (and through them, of the peasant 'elders' and communities), the Associations of Nobility and the regional and municipal authorities. The ministry organised those electoral processes that were taking place and since 1905 took charge of the election to the state parliament (the *Duma*).

A study of the incubents of the top five 'ranks' within the MVD in 1905 offered a panoramic view of 'the top brass' closely corresponding to the results of other studies of the Russian civil administration at large (and with remarkably little difference between the middle of the nineteenth and the beginning of the twentieth centuries).[27] Of the 101 listed, 83 per cent were 'hereditary nobles', that is, came from the stratum representing less than 1 per cent of the country's population. Only 37 per cent of them owned landed estates, however, and this figure was declining (it was 27 per cent in 1916). More than 88 per cent of their wives were themselves daughters of nobility or of state officialdom, consolidating the picture of a closely knit and self-reproducing social group. About 92 per cent of 'the five ranks' were of Orthodox religion (a major badge of ethnic Russianness), while the 'others by religion' consisted of six Lutherans and two Catholics (i.e. most probably Germans and Poles respectively). Not less than 77 per cent of the whole group were university graduates and some of the others came from the privileged military colleges. Their average salary was 6000 roubles per annum, ranging from the 26 000 for the minister himself to about 3000 in the lower parts of this bracket. On average, those involved had thirty years of state service, indicating promotion by seniority and 'proper' bureaucratic careers.

This picture is in fact somewhat misleading in understating the actual income of Russia's top bureaucrats. An official career record (*posluzhnyi spisok*) chosen by as at random can supplement some of the missing details. It belonged to G. S. Kovalev, 48, nobleman, Orthodox, Russian, of the fifth rank, graduate in law of Moscow University, and with four orders for excellent service – slightly above the average for his stratum.[28] In 1915 he was governor of a not very important province with a salary of 5000 roubles, but the record also reports a supplementary salary of 800 roubles and a lodging grant of 5000 roubles, that is, altogether 10 800 roubles annually, and more than twice the nominal salary. It was also more than twenty times the per family annual national income in Russia while still disregarding considerable non-monetary privileges of economic value (e.g. human service, transportation, etc.) and, in at least in some cases, income from bribes.[29]

The List of Ranks of the Department of Police can give us a parallel picture of the lower ranks within the Russian officialdom.[30] The Department of Police was part of the Ministry of Interior and fifteen of the senior five ranks of the MVD reviewed above were assigned to it. At the bottom of the list stood thirty-five men of the lowest twelfth rank (the *gubernskii sekretar'*). None of them was an 'hereditary noble' and most of them did not receive secondary education of any description. None of them owned landed property. All of them were of 'orthodox' religion. Their average annual salary was 988 roubles, and their average length of service was seven years.

The information concerning the work-loads of the Russian state bureaucracy indicates strenuous efforts and a virtual avalanche of paperwork, streaming down and up the official channels. Particularly at the bottom of the hierarchy, it resulted in harsh conditions, and long hours of work linked with very low pay. At the top, the conscientious fulfilment of one's duties was fairly difficult too. The evidence is mostly anecdotal but a provincial governor whose routine included signing 270 papers daily and a typical policeman of Kiev who (in the admittedly 'difficult' year of 1907) worked an average of sixteen hours every day inclusive of holidays,[31] are indicative of the type of demands Russian state service made upon its members. Yet, figures for 1906 show that four-fifths of the state officials received an annual wage of less than 1000 roubles (i.e. roughly $500).[32] At times, especially for non-ranking clerks, the salary was 500 roubles or even less than that.[33] To the low strata within the state service, it meant the cheerless life of 'little folk', the humiliated petty officials the description of whom made Gogol, Dostoyevski and Chekhov famous in world literature. It also meant the 'passing on' of humiliation to those lower down, especially to the peasants and of the non-Russian populations, and a particularly strong inducement for petty bribe-taking, to supplement the inadequate pay.

For those in the higher ranks it often meant turning a blind eye to corrupt practices below, as it was the only way to make one's department run. If corruption is to be defined as promoting private gain as opposed to gain by 'the state', most of the top ranks were engaged in it also, on par with the collective jostling for power and resources of the bureaucratic cliques to which they belonged.[34]

Finally, the regional division of the state officialdom centred on the provincial governors and general governors of the ninety main subdivisions of Russia, the *guberniyas* and *krais*. The powers of a governor were extensive. He had to supervise and/or authorise much of what was happening within different local branches of the state authorities, the municipal authorities and the specific organisations of the 'social estates' in his province. (The rest was his own staff of senior officials and officers, aides, assessors, inspectors, etc. and numerous junior clerks and policemen.) In every *guberniya* there was a separate office of the Ministry of Finance (*kazennaya palata*), of the Department of State Control and of the Ministry of War. The governor's office had its own departments concerned with factory and industrial affairs, peasant affairs, municipal affairs, etc. Each *guberniya* was divided in turn into *uezds* each run by a coalition of ranking officials taking orders from the governor's office. Below the top officials stood, once again, the lower ranks and the unranked members of the state service.

There were two major types of differently constituted authorities in each province: the elected *zemstvos* or municipal authorities and the specific organisations of the 'social estates'. The *zemstvo* and the large city municipalities were elected by 'electoral colleges' which offered privileged positions to the large landowners and owners of estate in towns. Within thirty-four *guberniyas* in which they were constituted, and in their *uezds*, the *zemstvo* offered public services in education, medicine, agricultural extension, welfare, road building, mail, insurance of properties, etc.[35] In addition to those who were state appointed and to those elected (often consisting of publicly spirited and liberal nobles), it introduced into the countryside the 'professionals' employed by the *zemstvo*: the agronomists, the medical doctors, the teachers, etc. Since the 1890s the rights of the *zemstvo* to increase their budgets and thereby services were harshly restricted at the request of the Ministry of Finance (opposing anybody who could compete with government over resources). The sum total of Russia's local budgets was in those days 14 per cent of those of the government, as against 38 per cent in France and 73 per cent in Great Britain.[36] Also, the activities of *zemstvos* were closely supervised by the governors, and their more outspoken leaders time and time again dismissed from office.[37]

Last, the officially constituted 'social estate' institutions related exclusively to the nobles and to the peasants. The provincial Associations of Nobility were created under Catherine II and had fulfilled since a variety of formal and informal functions, representing the nobility before the state authorities and, up to a point, representing the state within each province. A marshal of nobility, elected by the nobles of each *guberniya* and *uezd* was authorised by the state and carried a variety of functions and privileges of a ranking official, for example, each conference of the *zemstvo* was chaired *ex officio* by the provincial marshal of nobility. The emancipation of serfs led to the creating of specific peasant organisations, the commune and the *volost'*, which formed a tier of local government below the level of *guberniya* and *uezd* at which the state and the *zemstvo* authorities operated. The elected officers of the peasant authorities acted as a *de facto* lowest ring of officialdom, executing its orders. We shall discuss this in Chapter 2. First, though, let us return to the general characteristics of the Russian state.

D. STATE VERSUS SOCIETY

A major tradition within historical and analytical writings has tended to equate society with state, by reducing the first to the second. The history of a 'nation' was, by that viewpoint, the history of its kings, palaces and wars to which the massive majority of people provided a scenic decoration and the (seldom mentioned) resources, a view well expressed in the Brechtian jingle: 'Alexander of Macedon conquered the world, was he alone?' A critical reaction to this approach was offered by the nineteenth-century social and economic history and political economy which usually 'bent the stick the other way'. The state was being reduced to 'society', that is, was treated as a vector of extra-state 'social forces', be it the growth of rationalism, the interests of the ruling class or the natural and necessary patterns of economic evolution. It has been argued above that to grasp contemporary history one may do well to restore and keep the nineteenth-century conceptual polarity of 'state and civil society', explicating the parallel and often contradictory developments at both sides of this relationship. Far from providing an 'either/or' alternative to the types of analysis that explicated the political expressions and determinations of the 'civil society', it can and should supplement them by focusing on the specific dynamics and personnel of 'the state'. The contemporary Russian usually assumed and explored the civil society/state disjunction and their analysts did often move a step further to analyse the state v. society dynamics, or the systematic assault by the 'state apparatus' upon all other social entities, aiming at their total control.

One way to bring out the general characteristics of the Russian state is to link the above discussion of its origins and of its functioning to the 'state v. society' issue and to the major paradox of tsardom's durability as against the ease of its eventual collapse. We shall begin by specifying the main 'institutional bricks' from which the Russian state was constructed. As to the 'dual parentage' of the Russian state, Byzantine and Mongol,[1] we are indeed addressing 'ideas, institutions and methods of government . . . unfamiliar and puzzling to the modern Western observer'.[2] The impact of Byzantium, especially during its last period of flourishing under the Macedonian dynasty, was transferred to Russia via the world outlook, the canonic law, the liturgy and the administrative structures of the Orthodox church. It provided for a heritage linking the Hellenistic political philosophy and statecraft of the fourth century, the Byzantine images of the universal Christian empire and the 'Third Rome' of Ivan III. It promoted the concept of the emperor as the living law – the 'autocrator' – and images of a rule which was the earthly awesome reflection of God in heaven. It united in one person military high command, secular power, and the authority of the 'guardian of true faith', expressed in the practice of appointing and of deposing patriarchs, metropolitans and bishops.[3] The titles, heraldry and ceremonial taken over from Byzantium by Muscovy were both symbols and ideological reinforcements of those claims on behalf of the tsar, as was the church liturgy, especially for the plebeian masses. The complex legal system of the Russian empire incorporated major elements of Byzantine law and administrative experience.[4]

The Mongol impact had established in the Russian provinces of the Golden Horde all-inclusive taxation and recruitment for military service, with the whole population divided accordingly (into *t'my*, 'hundreds' etc.). Russian dukes became tax collectors for the khans while Russian–Cuman army units served as far away as Peking. Since 1245 there were repetitive censuses for the purpose of the allocation of duties (*chislo*).[5] The Mongol law (the *Yasa*) with its inbuilt assumption of the *Kogan* as head of a conquering army, focus of total obedience and owner of all lands claiming world-imperial rule (exercised regionally by his governors) had met and reinforced the Byzantine prescriptions. It added the concept of universal obligatory service and military organisation overriding family and tribal loyalties. The introduction of the death penalty and of juridical torture, date from the Mongol period when they came to serve the common interests of the Russian princes and their Tatar overlords. The decline of the cities' self-rule, central to the political system of the Kievian Rus', reflected once again the common interests of the Khan of the Golden Horde and his Russian vassals.[6]

The victory of Muscovy in the 'competition of the three models' meant that the heritage of Byzantium and of the Golden Horde was greater in significance for the future of the Russian state than other impacts, and in particular much stronger than the influence of Scandinavia and hence the West European feudalism (claimed as decisive since the eighteenth century by the so-called 'Normanist' School). Two points must be kept in mind here, however. The foreign 'ideas, institutions and methods of government' were not simply copied, but used, that is, adjusted to the conditions of Russia and often restructured. Second, the knowledge of origins cannot substitute for an explanation of the way political systems operate and of their durability. The Russian tsardom was shaped by the dual task to which the energies of its rulers and administrators were mostly devoted: a constant military struggle at the 'open frontiers' and the extortion of resources from a population prone to move on when pressurised. The size and the 'wildness' of the territory involved added to the difficulty of carrying it out. The Byzantine and Mongolian political experience and expertise plus a considerable measure of ingenuity were put to use in the constructing of a distinctive legal, administrative, political and military structure of domination with a discrete history of its own.

The rule of Peter I had symbolised and dramatised new elements which had entered Russian political processes even before his times and were there to stay. Their essence was the combination of struggle, competition and learning derived from the contacts with Russia's Western, mostly Protestant neighbours, and expressed as 'modernisation' or 'Europeanisation'. Particular stress was laid on the military and the administrative practices of absolutism, especially that of the 'well-ordered police state'.[7] The clear discrepancy between Western Europe and the socio-political context in Russia was the lack of established burghers supporting the king's power against 'feudal anarchy'. That did not preclude the process of learning and transfer of patterns of state organisation. On the other hand, the West was not simply 'aped' despite the many anecdotes to the contrary. The substantial results were not a replication of the European absolutism but a complex political structure in which new methods of government intertwined with Russian past practices and current administrative invention to solve the problems of establishing a social and technological base for a 'modern' – that is, Europe-like – army of a rapidly growing superpower. Rather than to dissolve past forms of political organisation many of them were refitted for new use within a new context and serving new immediate goals. The most important of these were the serfdom and the 'service'.

To those who faced tsardom and tried to comprehend it at the turn of the twentieth century, the durability of it, its immensity and the seemingly total grip of its bureaucracy, often made it look eternal and overpowering. The nationalist press of Western Europe in addition to the writing of the liberals and radicals, there and in Russia, bear evidence to the extent to which the Russian tsardom was feared as well as hated. Since the mid-nineteenth century it had increasingly been said with what looked like wishful thinking that the Russian empire was a 'Colossus with feet of clay'. Its collapse was confidently predicted by its enemies, not least because it offered impediments to the 'natural road of progress'. There were also dark forebodings expressed by many of the tsardom's most faithful supporters. But tsardom did not collapse under the Crimean defeat by the armies of Europe in 1855, nor under the attack of the revolutionary People's Will Party in 1879–84, nor in face of the vicious famine and its own incompetence to prevent mass starvation in 1891–2. Between 1900 and 1907 it had outlasted the combined threat of economic crisis, military defeat by Japan and a revolution. Those who attacked it from the inside and those who watched such attacks sympathetically, had been often enough left with a feeling of the hopelessness of any head-on challenge of the tsardom. It was as if to take on a medieval siege tower, crude and immense. It dwarfed opposition and seemed to roll over it by sheer weight.

Metaphors about the 'feet of clay' of the colossus, about the 'shackles to progress' which history is to break, about the 'waning of medievalism' and siege towers as well as the many *ex post factum* explanations of the collapse of the tsardom, pointed to contradictions between its character and that of Russian society at large. There have been two lines of argument there, often combined. First, the tsardom was seen as a particularly parasitic growth on Russian society, an extension of the Mongol conquest and as exploitative and alien. By its very nature it was no more than a thin layer of henchmen and their flunkies, due to be eventually destroyed by the joint effort of the oppressed, that is, the massive majority of the Russians. Second, rooted in the West European historiography was the liberal–Marxist view that tsardom is but a case of a belated 'feudal state', lingering behind a society that has already left this 'stage' of socio-economic progress. The consequent state v. (civil) society contradiction would necessarily tear the tsardom apart. Indeed, it seemed surprising that such a state could 'still' exist at all. Plekhanov has combined both views in his concept of the Russian 'Oriental Despotism' which since Peter I was gradually giving way to capitalism.

As an explanation of the Russian tsardom's nature and eventual collapse, the register of *state* v. *society* contradictions is highly relevant without being sufficient. An image of it as being epiphenomenal to the feudal or capitalist class system, that is, simply a tool in the hands of the squiredom or of the bourgeoisie, is neither sufficient nor realistic, despite the state apparatus links to the nobility. The tsardom was also anything but the liberal/Functionalist ideal of a computer-like class-neutral management for the benefit of 'the society' in toto, but, in its unevenly repressive functioning, it was autonomous in goals, structure and personnel ('semi-autonomous' for those who like semantic gymnastics – all autonomy is 'semi' in social context). That is why the state must be studied also as such.

To consider the tsardom, one must first leave behind assumptions about abstract justice or the will of the majority which *must* prevail and about the 'stage of socio-economic development' which by 'contradicting' a political system *must* dissolve it or explode it. A tendency, a conflict or a crisis of social structure does not result in a single necessary resolution. Power-holders have the potential ability to learn to reform and to defeat challenges, while holding on to what matters most: power and privilege. Also, political and social change are not necessarily introduced by forces of progress as designated by the liberal and Marxist theories of the nineteenth century. Bureaucratic state organisations with army and police forces and 'ideological' manipulative devices at their command can usually defeat 'their' people in open confrontation and may transform society 'from above'. If Franco could survive in the Spain of 1971 and Khomeinie prosper in the Iran of 1980, so could have the Tsar of All Russias in 1917 and indeed in the 1930s. Neither *Zeitgeist* nor 'contradictions' explain by themselves the decline of an empire unless we establish the dynamics of it more specifically than at the level of philosophy of history.

To understand why the tsardom was destroyed we must look not only at the social crisis of Russian society and its class-related and ideological expressions, but also at the 'weak joints' of the state machinery that made it fail in the containing of those who challenged it. To function and to 'reproduce itself', the tsardom had to discipline, 'squeeze' and control a massive majority of the plebeian classes and ethnic 'minorities', mostly peasants 'stirred up' by the new dynamics of capitalism. It had also to check a small but increasingly vocal and hostile 'educated stratum' and the growing international pressures. To do so, it utilised the administrative power of a fairly small 'state apparatus'. To a decisive degree its operation was an exercise in the systematic political demobilisation of the prevailing majority of the people, to secure the passive acceptance of the political *status quo*.

The essential weaknesses of the Russian state apparatus were inbuilt into its nature, and linked with its strength. The effective way it depoliticised the Russians for centuries had left the tsar's social environment and the officialdom in the 'sole possession' of actual state power. The lay and military officials and officers were bound as much by the executive hierarchy as by similarities of background, outlook, trained preference, prejudice and manners. As with every design of management, in addition to its structure, its personnel and its resources, the Russian state bureaucracy was characterised by its specific style of management, that is, typical and general key models of preferred solutions in proceeding towards its goals. Conceptually, this particular style of political management and the related insights were best expressed in Italy, the European country of the most prominent tradition of discrete political analysis, by the man chiefly responsible for its marriage with Marxist thought: Antonio Gramsci. It came in his discussion of 'domination' v. 'hegemony' as models of political rule.[8]

It was the Russian example that Gramsci used as generic for the state executive exercising its power by direct or threatened coercion – the form he called 'domination'. Much of what had been happening in Russia within the nineteenth century and the first quarter of the twentieth century (inclusive of the ways adopted by the Russian revolutionaries) was to him determined by that general characteristic of Russia's political organisation. The alternative way by which the bourgeoisie has chiefly exercised its power in Western Europe was typified by Gramsci as control of cognition, which he termed 'hegemony'. Another way suggested by Gramsci to typify state power, once again relevantly for Russia, was to consider on par with the rule by coercion and the rule by manipulation also the rule by explicit consent of those who are ruled, and whose interests are partly met by the rulers. It goes without saying that we are talking here of 'general types', while the actual political structures would display significantly different mixtures of the major 'styles' in question.

Gramsci's insight from an Italian prison was remarkably apt for the understanding of the general nature of the tsardom. Similar views were also often expressed, if less clearly, by Russia's own theorists and eulogists. To the officialdom the totality and rigidity of tsardom's rule was not a matter of implicit preference but of declared wish, proudly displayed. Any initiative was permitted only 'from above', via the 'proper channels' of the state bureaucracy. The subjects' loyalty was considered best expressed in political apathy, he or she were simply to obey the tsar's will as declared by his officials. The official political philosophy gave it some coherence by assuming a Hobbsian nature of humans.[9] For their own sake, their many weaknesses were to be constantly curbed and restrained by men of experience, serving the one annointed by God. It is not an accident that the police force has played so major a role in the general administration, political analysis and moral guidance within Russia.

In the second half of the nineteenth century the tsardom faced the challenge of being overtaken militarily and technologically by the Western powers and a corresponding decline in its international position combined with the new internal threats to the *status quo*: the spontaneous social and economic processes triggered off by capitalist industrialisation and the conscious defiance by revolutionary underground and literate public opinion. The defeat in the Crimean War signalled to those in power the severity of Russia's international decline. The following era of reforms attempted to 'untie the bundle' of 'European' characteristics, adopting selectively its technical and administrative achievements but refusing parliamentarism and any fundamental reforms of the state apparatus. The emancipation of the serfs brought further rural extension of its power. As time went by the counter-reforms increased once again the power of official intervention. Yet the attempt to adjust and use the state apparatus to 'modernise' Russia looked unlikely to succeed. Two generations later Paul Baran put it well concerning the rulers of the 'developing societies': 'the keepers of the past cannot be the builders of future'.[10]

Any extension of the tsardom's socio-political base and support was checked by the nature of its bureaucratic system. Not only dissent was harshly suppressed but even the attempts to serve the tsar by actively building up monarchist 'ideology' or movements were suspect.[11] The 'rule by political immobilisation' and by administrative command extended also to the dominant class. A petition for a mild reform by a nobility-led *zemstvo* usually resulted in repressions against its high-born officers. The very idea of autonomous initiative by the elected *zemstvos* was defined as unreconcilable (*nesovmestimo*) with orderly government by the then tsar's Minister of Finance. (He suggested instead the *zemstvo*'s 'statisation', i.e. turning over their functions to appointed state officials.) Totality of control and 'domination' as the overriding style of state management meant limited ability to manipulate, to compromise and/or to confront hostile ideologies on their own grounds. Immediate challenges were usually crushed with ease – too easily, one might say, for tsardom's long-term survival. There was, in fact, a strong tendency for massive administrative over-kill of 'nuts' being crushed by 'hammers' where much less pressure would do. Large-scale and long-term challenges that could not be effectively resisted by the old means or by simple displays of brutality, have thrown the system into disarray. Their historical experience, their social characteristics and their arrogance made the state bureaucracy slow in picking up warnings about major long-term dangers, and ineffectual in dissipating them. The unity of purpose and behavioural patterns made it more able to concentrate resources but also much less responsive to local and/or new conditions.

The military origins and legitimation of the tsardom have introduced another strength — which was also a weakness. The state could call on the nationalistic loyalties of most of the Russians and, up to a point, substitute imperialism for reforms. The centuries-long squeeze of resources from all and sundry (once again inclusive of the 'dominant class' of the noble landowners) was justified by the tsardom's ability to stop foreign invasion and to provide 'order' as against the well-rooted fear of anarchy and foreign raids at the inception of the Russian state. The consent of the ruled was secured by that 'need' being met (realistic or unrealistic, as those fears and anticipations may be). But in such an ideological context a military defeat shook the state to its core, making its apparatus lose its unity, its confidence and its ability to 'demobilise' effectively its subjects. Even the loyalty of the monarchistic nobility and of its army officers' segment was in doubt once the basic legitimation of the tsardom was shaken.

A final characteristic point of strengths and weaknesses alike and a major piece of 'past within the present', were the administrative and social arrangements for officialdom's self-perpetuation. The ladder of promotion did not advance men of imagination. The other side of the coin was the promotion of the stolid, pliant and obedient within the ranks. The 'ideological line' offered to the rank-holders, the nobility and the populus alike was well expressed in the dictum: 'All evil comes from opinions.'[12] Those who attempted to reform the state service from the inside, usually the tsardom's most able loyalists of broader vision, were 'thrown to the wolves' of gut-conservatism within the tsar's environment and paid with their careers. Memoirs of the brightest of the tsar's ministers and dignitaries, 'liberal' as well as 'conservative', are full of growing despair, and of a feeling expressed by a recent reviewer as 'the conclusion that . . . one can only serve the Romanovs in spite of them'.[13] While in line with Lenin's certification, the Russian officialdom was 'exceptionally well organised', and 'ideologically united'; it was also 'traditionally enclosed' and structurally immobile. Worse, its structural dynamics made its efficiency decline in face of the new types of challenge to it. A crisis of goals and administrative means was rapidly building up at the turn of the century with the very strength of the Russian state apparatus increasingly showing its inbuilt weakness. This was to become a major element of the revolutionary situations in 1905 and 1917.[14]

ADDENDUM 1   A SOCIETY: A SNAPSHOT OF RUSSIA

In 1897 Russia underwent its first "all-inclusive' (*vseobshchii*) population census. The adjective came to signify a new departure. The experience of population recording was not utterly new to Russia but in the past it was selective in scope. The Mongol conquerors had carried out some regional censuses of the tributary Russian populations (*Chisla*). Peter I had ordered in 1718 a national census which came to be eventually called a 'revision of the population' and subsequently Russia underwent nine more of them, the last in 1857. These 'revisions' aimed to secure the payment of the taxes, army recruitment, etc. and, consistent with this function, registered only the mature males of the 'tax-paying' social estates. The 1897 census differed in that it was directed at every single individual present on the territories of the Russian empire on 28 January 1897.

In view of the size of the country, the illiteracy of most of its inhabitants and the general complexity of the matter, this census proved a resounding success. The restrictions came later. Because of the miserly attitude of the authorities, a budget was granted insufficient to analyse and publish much of the evidence collected. Only twenty-five tables in all were compiled and put in print in 1905. These two volumes present the most significant reservoir of population data concerning pre-revolutionary Russia: a collective snapshot of its people at the turn of the century.[1]

The census has shown the total population of the Russian empire (exclusive of the Duchy of Finland and the protectorates of Bukhara and Khiva) to consist of 125 680 682 men and women.[2] The findings were subdivided by ninety *guberniya* or *krai* i.e. the provinces which formed the main territorial divisions of the Russian state administration, and presented also within five larger regions: European Russia (fifty provinces), the Visla region (i.e. the mainly Polish ten provinces), the Caucasus (twelve provinces), Siberia (nine provinces) and Russian Central Asia (nine provinces). The population of European Russia's 'fiftee guberniyas' – traditionally treated as the core of Russia proper, held 74.3 per cent of the total population (72 per cent if Finland and the Asian protectorates of Bukhara and Khiva were also taken into consideration).

The categories employed by the census have laid out a social map of Russian society and its major dimensions of diversity as understood by those who conducted the study. In this sense, besides the information provided by its figures, the census carried the evidence of the self-understanding and/or ideological tendencies of a generation of Russian social scientists. The analytical divisions anticipated the shapes to come of the inter-group conflicts within Russia. It happened that within a few months of their publication these assumptions came under the scorching verification of the revolution of 1905–7. On that evidence, the categories chosen by the Russian social statisticians proved remarkably apt.[3]

The presentation of the census applied itself mainly to three fundamental diversities of population: ethnicity, education and social 'estate'/class, relating them to territory, age, gender, marital patterns and geographical mobility. Ethnic awareness was high in Russia with most of its ethnic groups self-enclosed to a considerable degree in terms of the language spoken, religion, intermarriage, etc. Ethnicity directly affected personal and public rights, privileges and limitations of every subject of the realm: a Jew could not settle in some areas, a Pole would be 'naturally' passed over in promotions or appointments to some of the administrative posts, the western areas of the empire (in which Russians formed a minority) did not elect the *Zemstvo* regional authorities, and so on. The state policy of russification intensified those tendencies, generating in many regions growing ethnic awareness. Despite these accentuations of ethnic identity, the task of defining precisely who is what was at times far from simple. The main 'grey' areas of uncertainty were a number of groups in the process of assimilation. The solution adopted by the census was to identify ethnicity by 'language spoken', a procedure that overstated the numbers of the Russians, clearly in line with government preferences.

Reflecting these preferences, the presentation of the ethnic composition of Russia by the 1897 census began with a manifest lie. It stated that Russians formed 66.8 per cent of the population of the empire. The way that the ideologically proper Russian majority was constructed was through adding the Ukrainians (officially named *Maloros*, i.e. Small-Russians) and the *Beloruss* (White-Russians) to the Russians proper (who, by orders of the authorities, came to be defined from the nineteenth century as *Velikoros*, i.e. Great-Russians). The census registered 56 million Russians within the empire (44.3 per cent of the total population, while a more recent estimate of ethnic Russians as against the Russian language speakers has dropped the first figure still further to 41 per cent).[4] There were 22 million Ukrainians (17.8 per cent) and 6 million Beloruss (4.7 per cent). The three groups formed a distinctive ethnic division of the Eastern Slavs with some historic, social, linguistic and religious similarities between them but with undeniable dissimilarities.

Altogether the census recognised 146 ethnic–linguistic groups within the population of the empire. In order of size, the Russians and the Ukranians were followed by 8 million Poles, 6 million Beloruss, 5 million Jews, 4 million 'Kirgiz' (renamed Kazakh under the Soviet rule), 3.7 million Tatars, about 2 million each of Latvians, Lithuanians and Germans, about 1 million each of Moldavians,

Armenians and the Ugro-Finnish Mordva and Ests, and so on, down to the smallest ethnic groups of Aleuts and Chuvans in the Far East, their populations 584 and 506 respectively. In terms of the supra-ethnic categories used, there were 92 million Slavs, 40 million Turki and a number of much smaller groupings, that is, Jews, Germans, Romanians, etc. The distribution by religion closely followed, clearly reinforced and at times surpassed in political significance and identification the ethnic division of the country. The Catholic was more often than not a Pole, a Lutheran was German, etc.[5]

Important to the life of the empire was the territorial spread of the ethnic groups. The Russians proper formed a clear, often very high, majority of population in twenty-eight out of the fifty *guberniyas* of European Russia and also in nearly all of Siberia and in the Stavropol gub. of the Caucasus – the major areas of Cossack and peasant colonisations. Ethnically Russian territories stretched from Smolensk in the west to the Amur River flowing into the Pacific and from the Far North (where Russians coexisted with the native hunters) to Voronezh, and to the Cossack frontier on the rivers Don and Kuban and Ural, where the lands of the Kalmyk and Kazakh tribes and of Caucasian hillmen began. At the periphery of the Russian population to its south, south-west and north-west, intermixing with them on the borders and in the areas of colonisation, lived the Ukrainians and Beloruss who formed the majority in twelve more of the gubs. of European Russia. At the further periphery lived the officially admitted ethnic minorities – usually majorities within their own region. The four Baltic and one Romanian gubs. belonged to that category. In the midst of Russia proper, two more gubs. of Ufa and Kazan (in what used to be the centre of the Golden Horde) had only one-third of their population Russian while the Tatars provided the bulk of the rest. There were five more European gubs. without a clear ethnic majority in them. Also in Europe there were the nine mostly Polish gubs. of the ten singled out officially from 'European Russia' as the 'Visla region'. Finland was autonomous, with a clear ethnic majority of Finns. If one adds to it the mainly non-Russian Central Asia, the mosaic of ethnic grouping on the Caucasus, and the Jews spread between different gubs. (but settled mostly at the western and southern peripheries), one can see how complex the ethnic map of Russia was. It held, of course, an historical and political logic of its own. The ethnic map of the 1897 census portrayed a long history of colonisation and conquest. The empire consisted of a multiplicity of ethnic minorities of which the 'proper Russians' formed but the largest one.

The second major parameter considered by the census was that of education.[6] These findings presented a scale but also a division, a major breach between an elite, schooled by the best European standards, and the mass of the population for whom simple literacy was the upper reach of any schooling, and even that was not achieved by most.

The national literacy rate of the population of the empire above the age of 4 was registered in 1897 to be 29 per cent for men and 13 per cent for women, an average of 21 per cent. Related to the 'social estate' of those considered, the figures have shown that even for the members of the nobility there was a staggering 28.8 per cent rate of illiteracy and a more-than-primary education of only 40 per cent of its males. The equivalent figures for the 'peasant estate' were

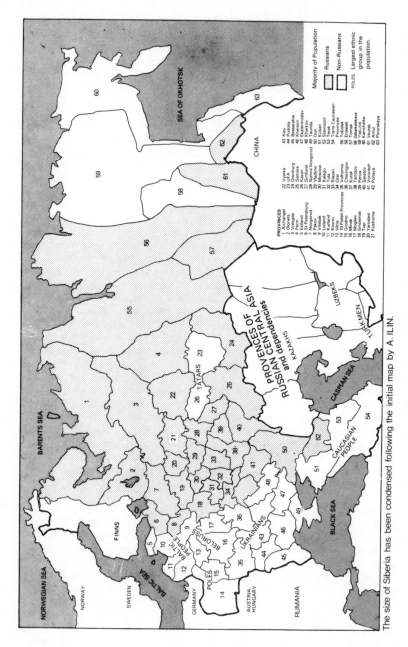

The size of Siberia has been condensed following the initial map by A. ILIN.

MAP 4   Russia's ethnic map, 1897

72 per cent and 0.1 per cent. However, at the other end of the educational scale, 10 per cent of all of the nobles received higher education, while the corresponding figures for the 'urban estate' were 0.4 per cent and of the peasants 0.0 per cent. Looked at 'the other way round', about 71 per cent of the Russians who benefited by 1897 from higher education were nobles by social estate, a group that accounted for 1.5 per cent only of the total population. (One must remember here, that many of the 'students of noble origin' were children of the 'service' or 'life' nobility, i.e. of the officialdom and army officers who carried nobility status following their administrative rank and to whom higher education was the usual way to transfer their social position to their children.)

On evidence of the census, schooling in Russia was clearly being transformed. The education reforms of the 1870s and 1880s were reflected in the fact that the literacy rate rose to about one-third (45 per cent for men and 19 per cent for women) in the age group 20–29. More than half of Russia's children were receiving by that time some type of schooling, even though mostly within the single-class rural establishments.[7] Significant in its immediate impact was to be the fact that while only 0.2 per cent of the population had 'higher education', that group amounted numerically to the substantial figure of 238 000 (of which 7000 were women). The country had 1 245 000 more men and women who received full secondary education, which in the Russian context has partly substituted for a university. A specific study of the university population of Russia undertaken in 1902 has shown 1420 members of academic staff and 24 000 students within thirteen universities or 'equivalent institutions', which had established by that time a considerable international reputation and acted as major centres of cultural life even as far as the Siberian city of Tomsk (the 'Athens of the North' to its eulogists).[8] An important next line of tertiary institutions for 'advanced professional training' – pedagogic, legal, medical, agricultural and military – can be properly added to that list. Together, the total number of students in Russia was 43 000 at the time of the 1902 survey.

The figures concerning education depicted therefore a major duality: on one hand, the massive illiteracy or negligible education of the bulk of the population, while on the other hand an illustrious group of those well-schooled by best West European standards, small in percentage but fairly large in number. It was this split between 'the educated' and all others as well as the deep ambivalence of being placed between the Western culture and the 'native backwardness' without fully belonging to either, that provided the context and the self-images of the peculiar social entity defined in the Russian concept of *Intelligentsia*.

Last of the central categories of findings of the census was the information concerning the related socio-legal and socio-economic diversity within Russia. The legal structure of the empire enabled and indeed necessitated the consideration of the 'social estate' (*soslovie*) of those accounted for by the census (see Table 1.2).[9] Every Russian had his assignment to a specific estate endlessly drummed into him – officially stamped on him, one may say. In every document, passport, petition and police dossier one's 'estate' came directly after one's name, preceding questions about age, occupation, ethnicity, etc. One's 'estate' defined a variety of rights and limitations: legal, electoral, fiscal. While showing a clear correlation with one's occupation, wealth and income, the hierarchy of social estates did not fully match any of them. All the same, to the officers of the census it offered a considerable boon, for it was clearly documented and

TABLE 1.2   *The 'social estates' of Russia in 1897* (% of population)

The social estate	The empire	European Russia	Russian Poland	Central Asia	Siberia
Nobles (hereditary)	0.97	0.95	1.44	0.15	0.29
Nobles (of service)[a]	0.50	0.52	0.47	0.20	0.51
Clergy	0.47	0.54	0.08	0.04	0.34
Merchants and 'honoured citizens'[b]	0.49	0.58	0.14	0.09	0.32
Urbanites (*meshchane*)	10.66	10.65	23.53	1.95	5.62
Peasants	77.12	84.16	72.98	4.98	70.87
Cossacks	2.3	1.54	0.11	3.28	4.46
Aliens (*Inorodtsy*)[c]	6.61	0.45	0.00	88.97	14.64
Foreigners	0.48	0.27	1.15	0.29	1.08

Source:
OSPN, vol. I, p. xiii.
Notes:
[a] That is, enobled as the consequence of their rank in state or military administration (see Chapter 1, p. 27).
[b] Since 1832 a title of 'honoured citizen' (*pochetnyi grazhdanin*) was established to be granted for achievements in arts, science, trade or industry to these who did not qualify for an enoblement. It exempted its possessors from some of the legal limitations of the 'tax-paying classes', e.g. corporal punishment, the pole-tax, etc. The actual numbers of 'honoured citizens' was very small.
[c] A number of ethnic groups considered 'uncivilised' to the point of inability to exercise fully their legal rights, i.e. most of the aboriginal population of Russian Asia: the Kazakh, Tunguz, etc.

therefore simple to define for each person. It was also at the top of the list of questions the administrators of the empire asked and first on the list of the answers offered by the publication, once the purely demographic details were done with.

A number of conclusions from this evidence was drawn directly by the editors of the census. About $1\frac{1}{2}$ per cent of the population consisting of nobles, both 'hereditary' and 'of service', was collectively referred to by them as the 'privileged classes'. Their territorial dispersion (and their schooling as discussed above) indicated their clear links with the state administration. The 'density' of the nobles within the general population differed considerably, centring around the capitals and declining sharply as one moves away from them. The share of nobles within the population for St Petersburg gub. was 7.16 per cent, that is, five times the national average. There were barely any of them in the north and in

Asian Russia. For historical reasons, Poland and the Caucasus had a more than usual share of nobles 'by origin' – ethnically non-Russian and often landless and/or impoverished.

Of the 'peasants by estate', 6.7 per cent in 1897 actually lived in towns, forming the majority of the populations of St Petersburg and Moscow.[10] At the same time the editors of the census declared that about half of the 'urban estate' (*meshchane*) should be realistically treated as peasant.[11] The actually urban part of the 'urban estate', together with 'merchants' and 'honorary citizens', accounted for about 7 per cent of the total population and about half of the urbanites. (A much larger share of the 'urban estate' was reported in the ten Polish gubs., about 23 per cent in all, the Jews forming one-third of the urban population of Polish Russia.)

Listing the population in accordance with the 'occupation of the main bread-winner' of each family provided direct evidence of the socio-economic divisions.[12] It was, of course, more real in social terms than figures concerning 'social estates' but also more open to error and doubt. The 'grey areas' were fairly broad: people of dual occupation, engagement in the 'informal econ-omies', etc. The resulting ambivalence of evidence was not made any easier by its ideological significance; these figures were treated as major tests of substanti-ation for political ideas and strategies. The interpretation of these figures was the focus of a constant debate, often misinformed. The actual figures of the census were as shown in Table 1.3.

The census was not designed to specify income, wealth or ownership of land and capital. There is no way therefore to determine directly through its findings presented by the Tables 1.2 and 1.3 the composition and size of the actual 'social classes' of Russia. Such an analysis would necessitate further work on the qualitative substance of those figures, which will be partly undertaken in the text below. A few conclusions can already be drawn at this stage. As a very rough indication and using some sources drawn from outside the census, the top echelon of the administration, army, landed nobility, the 'free professions', clergy and the merchants, can be estimated as about 1 per cent of the total population.[13] This stratum was well endowed with political privileges and income, and the security of both. Statistically speaking, they have blended imperceptibly into the 'middle strata'. Families that controlled major parts of the country's wealth and industrial muscle and power easily disappeared into general categories like that of 'honoured citizens', or 'merchants', that would incorporate also impoverished small shopkeepers, etc.

At the lower end stood those marked as manual labourer, that is, the country's 'plebeian classes'. Their main category was that of the three-quarters of the population who 'lived off agriculture' (land husbandry was the main occupation of 70.3 per cent of the national total while the rest made their living as stock breeders, fishermen, foresters and hunters). They blended into manual labourers of other trades and designations. The census has registered one-fifth of the 'heads of rural households' as deriving some supplementary income from 'crafts and trade' – a considerable figure that included part-time wage labour and was still probably understated. On the other hand, of those defined as industrial 'wage workers' within mining, transport, industry and crafts, about half resided in what was 'statistically speaking' the countryside – that is, the industrial or the farming villages. A major part of the urban wage labourers were

TABLE 1.3   *Sources of income of the main breadwinner in 1897* (% of population)

Employment in public administration[a]	0.75
Army and navy	0.99
Medicine, education, science, literature and legal practice[b]	0.61
Religious institutions or employment[b]	0.63
Living on capital income	0.72
Servants and daily manual workers	4.61
Mining	0.44
Transport and communications[c]	1.55
Manufacturing and crafts[d]	9.34
Commerce	3.99
Agriculture[e]	74.57
Others[f]	1.80
	100.00

Source:
OSPN, vol. II, pp. 256–67.
Notes:
[a] That is, state, local authorities and those organisations of the 'social estates' which formed part of the Russian state bureaucracy.
[b] Low technical staff, e.g. clerks and janitors were included, accounting for a considerable part of the category.
[c] Horse and cart drivers, mostly of peasant stock, formed nearly half of this category *(izvoz)*.
[d] Craftsmen and employees of small establishments formed the majority of this category. The branches ordered by the size of employment were: dressmaking, construction, metal, textile and woodwork. For discussion of the wage labour, see Chapter 3.
[e] Including livestock production, fishing and forestry.
[f] The largest single component of that category were 'family servants'.

the mostly female house servants of peasant stock and peasant workers, returning seasonally to the village to help with harvesting.

For the urban/rural division, the 1897 census showed the urbanites of Russia to reside in 932 localities defined as 'towns' by the state administration. Urban population was roughly 13 per cent of the total, representing 16.2 million of men and women in 1897. Its percentage in European Russia was closely similar, that is, 12.9 per cent. It was estimated to have risen to 15.3 per cent by 1914 but some figures are higher by up to 2 per cent.[14] While the population of European Russia doubled between 1861 and 1914, its urban population roughly trebled during the period, a fairly small increase considering the circumstances.

As an index of territorial mobility the census had used the percentage rate of people resident outside the areas of their birth. It showed the Russian population to be static but with some important exceptions. Of all those registered by the census, 90 per cent lived in the gub. they were born in, 9 per cent in another gub. of Russia, while less than 0.5 per cent were foreign born. Large cities had clearly absorbed considerable rural migration. The city of St. Petersburg recorded 69 per cent and the city of Moscow 74 per cent of their inhabitants to be born outside the city boundaries.[15] Exceptionally high territorial mobility was recorded in a few of the regions, for example, Siberia (with 24 per cent of its population born elsewhere in Russia, and described as 'mostly colonists and exiles'). The same could be said about the 'privileged classes', that is, nobility, of which 36 per cent resided outside the *guberniyas* of their birth. The census has shown also that despite the essentially even general distribution of the population between genders, there were within the urban population eighty-nine females to every one hundred males. The census editors had interpreted it as an expression of the selective and partly transitory migration to the urban centres of young rural males and by the mostly urban placement of military units.[16]

Finally, the census has presented some general demographic evidence concerning age and marriage. The findings have shown the Russian population to be young, high in its rates of marriage and low on divorce.[17] Its average age was 25. The percentage of people married within the 'marriageable age' (i.e. above the age of 15) was 64. As shown by other demographic sources, that did not result in particularly high natural growth. The birth rates were high but so was mortality, with a resulting annual increase of about 1.7 per cent.[18]

To conclude, the 1897 census has recorded considerable and significant diversities between the subjects of the Tsar of All Russias: ethnic, educational, legal, occupational, territorial, etc. It has also carried one overriding message of similarity. In the words of the editors of the census, peasants in the social sense of that term, together with those who 'in their way of living and occupation differ but little from the peasant' were 'nearly 90 per cent of all mass of the population'.[19]

The 1897 census had the virtues of a well-executed snapshot of Russian society. Considerable care was taken to secure the reliability of data despite difficult circumstances. The census stands out as an important achievement of Russian scholarship. A comparsion to a snapshot is however valid in yet another sense. The census carried the limitations of a snapshot – it was a collection of features at a single point in time, that is, a static picture of a changing reality. At the turn of the century the Russian analysts were deeply divided as to their outlook, preferences and predictions but most of them would accept that the country was proceeding through a crucial process of social transformation and economic change which had at its core the development of capitalism in Russia, often treated as its advancing 'Europeanisation'. Focusing on the quantitative representations of population at a given moment and disregarding the indices of wealth, the census could only indicate indirectly the fundamental social structures, dynamics and discrete histories of the major components of Russia's actuality and change, that is, of capitalism, peasantry and of the tsarist state.

2 Russian Peasants: Household, Community and Society

The peasantry, the key toward understanding of China, is a way of living.
Fei Hsiu Tung

A. THE PEASANT HOUSEHOLD

Peasant households form the nuclei of peasant society. The nature of the peasant household constitutes the most significant single characteristic of the peasantry as a specific social phenomenon and gives rise to the generic features displayed by peasantries all over the world. A peasant household is characterised by the extent of integration of the peasant family's life with its farming enterprise. The family provides the essential work team of the farm, while the farm's activities are geared mainly to production of the basic needs of the family and the dues enforced by the holders of political and economic power. The vast diversities between and within the peasantries do not obliterate the insights of this classification.[1]

The Russian peasant household (*dvor*) at the turn of the century corresponded very closely to the general type depicted. 'The family and the farm appear as almost synonymous', testified Mukhin in his compilation on peasant legal customs at the end of the nineteenth century.[2] A volume of a Russian encyclopaedia published in 1913 described the bulk of peasant households as 'consumer–labour enterprises, with the consumer needs of the family as their main aim and the labour force of the family as their means, with no or very little use of wage labour'.[3]

A Russian peasant household consisted typically of blood relatives spanning two or three generations and their spouses. However, the basic determinant of household membership was not actual kinship but the total participation in the life of the household or, as the Russian peasants put it, 'eating from the common pot'. This unity implied living together under the authority of a patriarchal head, close co-operation in day-to-day labour, a 'common purse', and the basic identification of a member with the household. Consequently, one who joined the household through marriage or adoption (*primaka, vlazen'*) was considered its full member, inclusive of all property rights, while a son of the family who set up a household on his own was viewed as an outsider (*otrezannyi lomot'*).

The peasant household operated as a highly cohesive unit of social organisation, with basic divisions of labour, authority and prestige along traditionally prescribed family lines. Generally, the head of the household was the father of the family or its oldest male member. His authority over other members and over household affairs implied both autocratic rights and extensive duties of care and protection. The household was the basic unit of production, consumption, ownership, political alliances, socialisation, sociability, moral support and mutual help. The social prestige and the self-esteem of a peasant within his community were defined by the social standing of the household he belonged to and his position in it, as were his loyalties and self-identification.

Women, in spite of their heavy burden of labour (both housework and fieldwork), and their functional importance in a peasant household, were considered second-class members of it, and nearly always placed under the authority of a male.[4] The exceptions were represented mainly by widows with small children to sustain (these could usually head a household and hold land directly). Even the full rights of the male members should be considered, however, in the framework of a patriarchal structure involving extensive powers of the head over his household. The cohesion of the family and the way family property operated meant submission and lack of tangible property for its junior male members. The policy of the Russian state before 1906 (and to a lesser degree, later on) supported the stability and cohesion of the peasant household by imposing collective family responsibility for the payment of dues and for the 'good behaviour' of its members. Up to 1906, it also legally confirmed the head of the household's wide disciplinary powers over its members.[5]

'The life of a family is the life of a farm'.[6] A typical peasant farm in Russia in the period under consideration was a small agricultural enterprise based on centuries-old agricultural techniques and types of equipment, communal crop rotation, family labour and the horse-drawn wooden *sokha*, slowly being replaced by an iron plough.[7] Grain-growing dominated peasant field production and diet.[8] Peasant family life and labour offered the main form of occupational training for the younger generation, while tradition acted as the main occupational guide. The scope of market and money relations was limited by the extent of the consumption-determined production, low rates of surplus, and a low level of professional specialisation and diversification of the rural population. It was, on the other hand, gradually enhanced by the pressure of taxes and rents, the penetration of industrial produce into the countryside, and the supplementary employment in crafts and trades (*promysly*), made increasingly necessary as additional or alternative sources of peasant income. Growth of production and markets of the agricultural goods led to similar results.

The household's production activities and plans consisted primarily of strenuous efforts to make ends meet – that is, to feed the family and to pay dues and taxes. Heavy rural underemployment, both total and seasonal, was partly tempered by peasants' supplementary employment. Competition with growing industry and with the use of machinery was made possible by desperately low rural earnings. 'When the brief agricultural season did not yield a living for the peasant family, work for less than subsistence through the long winter months was better than to be altogether idle – and perhaps to be buried in the spring.'[9] The Russian peasant usage of the term *promysly*, which puzzled economists and led their figures astray, was indicative of the way such tasks integrated into the peasant economy. As used by the peasants, it comprised a single category of activities that could appear as quite diverse: domestic industry, off-farm wage work in agriculture, off-farm non-agricultural work (at times as part of a traditional co-operative – the *artel*'). The logic of such an all-embracing term was simple enough to the peasants, for these activities formed the residuum of their occupations over and above the peasants' 'proper' task, that is, family farming on their own farms. The main occupation of Russian peasants consisted both ideally (i.e. in normative terms of preference) and in reality, of performing a wide variety of tasks combined to make a coherent whole of land and animal husbandry. Yet the *promysly* formed an important and increasingly necessary part of their occupation and income, especially so in the poorer strata.[10]

The massive use of family labour, the high levels of home consumption, the 'traditional' methods of production, the relatively low marketability and the lack of book-keeping in generalised money terms made the peasant household into a production unit very different from a capitalist enterprise. Production strategies and economic solutions differed consistently and considerably, – for example, the 'non-profitable' land renting that made excellent economic sense within the specifically peasant economy, to be discussed below in Chapter 3. Also, the influence of nature upon the peasant economy was powerful and direct; the smallness of peasant resources magnified its impact. The difference between a good agricultural year and a very bad one was the difference between prosperity and famine, if not death and the extinction of a family. The demographic cycles of family history determined to a considerable extent the functioning of the farms while the needs and seasons of traditional farming prescribed the patterns of everyday life. Nature and the typical family history made for a peculiarly deep-rooted cyclical rhythm of daily, annual and multi-annual stages of life on the peasant family farms which were often of more immediate significance than the grand flows of national and international markets of goods and labour.

The longest of the cycles was usually biographical in its major determinants. Within the established division of labour only a male–female team could make the farm fully functional and effective. The dominance of the male has defined typical family-farm histories in essentially masculine terms. A peasant male normally proceeded through the prescribed stages: childhood, premarital adolescence, marriage, a headship of his own household, and eventually, retirement and death. Only by becoming the head of a household could he rise to the full status of a man within the peasant community. (The only alternative road to self-emancipation involved his leaving the peasant community altogether.) Marriage was thereby 'an absolute postulate'[11] – a crucial precondition of social maturity necessitated by the character of farming. The second parallel condition was the availability of a farm, that is, a holding of land and equipment. Its passing from one generation into the next was a decisive issue of peasant life.

Family property was a major legal reflection of the character of the Russian peasant household. So far as peasants were concerned, Russian legislation since 1861 had left these matters to the customs of the locality as understood by its elected magistrates. The latter codifications have shown that peasant customs concerning property were remarkably uniform all over Russia, despite the fact that until 1921 no unifying legislation was passed on that matter.[12] Unlike *private property* defined in the Legal Code of the Russian empire by which the non-peasant Russians lived, *family property* limited to a considerable degree the rights of the formal 'owner' (*khozyain*); he acted as the administrator of the property (*bol'shak*) rather than its exclusive proprietor in the sense current outside peasant society. (An extreme expression of this feature was the legal possibility and actual practice of removing the head of a household from his position by an order of the peasant commune in some cases of 'mismanagement' or 'wastefulness' and of the appointment of another member of the household in his place.) On the other hand, and in contrast to *collective property*, that is, a partnership or a shareholding company, the participation in family property did not entail any specific and definable share in the property or the profits that an individual member could claim at his choice, except of the general right of each to share in the collective consumption.

Within the legal customary framework of 'family property', the very notion of *inheritance*, as developed and enacted in non-peasant Russia, failed to appear. The passing of property from generation to generation did not usually await the death of a parent and was legally treated as *partitioning* of family property between its members. Partitioning (or apportionment, to set up a junior male) corresponded to a considerable extent with the growth of nuclear families and their requests for independence. The head of the household took the decision (partly defined by custom) as to when exactly to partition his farm or when to make apportionment to a son, and when to retire. His refusal to do so could be, and at times was, challenged before the communal assembly or peasant magistrates. The whole issue was treated not just as a problem of economic expedience but also as one of social living and 'maturation' in its broadest sense.

Partitioning meant, on the whole, equal division of household property between all its male members. A somewhat larger share was at times granted to the son who was to look after the aged parents or the unmarried sisters. The peasant customary law made an exception of 'female's property', which included cutlery, cloth, etc. The 'female's property' was within the peasant household the only private property in the 'urban' sense and could be consequently left by will and/or unequally divided. In cases of the death of all members of a household (*vymorochnost'*), the property was generally taken over by the peasant commune.[13]

A typical new household would begin as a young couple with a few young children on a smallholding. Such a farm would usually consist of a limited amount of land, little equipment and possibly one or two horses shared out from the original unit in the process of partitioning. It would benefit also from some communal rights – for example, to grazing land. The growing children provided additional labour on the farm but also created new consumption needs and problems of employment. Children also posed the problem of providing a dowry for daughters and equipment for setting up new farms for sons, which required apportionment.

In the times of serfdom, the peasant family often consisted of several nuclear families, that is, family couples and their children.[14] The post-1861 decline of the squire's control over the day-to-day life of the peasants led to 'nuclearisation' of the peasant households – when left to themselves, the Russian peasants tended to synchronise the nuclear family and the farm while the number of households grew accordingly. Government 'educational efforts' and decrees that attempted to preach and to legislate some minimal size for an 'efficient' farm, were consistently defeated by the peasant way of living – the patterns of social reproduction and customs of social 'maturing' prevalent within the Russian countryside.

Budget Studies – a major Russian contribution to the advanced methodology of peasant studies – came into their own at the turn of the century and provided a store of additional knowledge concerning the ways peasant household economies operated.[15] The essence of this methodology lay in the detailed presentation and analysis of input/output relations within selected peasant households during a whole agricultural cycle/year. The Budget Studies have presented and quantified with increasing clarity the complex yet closely knit picture of production patterns involving husbandry (of land and animals), gathering and manufacturing on the farm, as well as wage labour elsewhere.[16] Their findings have consistently substantiated the massive reliance on family labour within the peasant economy and a strong tendency for actual physical division of the sources of income into consumption-directed farming versus the cash-directed activities that were specific to each region (e.g. rye for home consumption and wheat or hemp for sale in the Black-earth area, flax and, alternatively, engagement in crafts to secure the necessary money income in the northern areas, etc.). The relation between wealth differentiation and the economic strategy of the households was explicated as a *u* curve, expressing the tendency for a higher share of income coming from wage employment for the poorest, the concentration on one's own farm by the majority at the middle range, the higher extra-farming (mostly 'enterpreneurial') income of the well-to-do. Monetisation followed a similar distribution but; less than half the average peasant income came from wages or sale of produce.[17] The consumption side of these accounts showed a large share of food (especially grain and potatoes), a small share of expenses on textiles, tea or oil, practically nothing for 'culture' (e.g. books), and very little investment in equipment. It also showed an extensive similarity of the types of goods used by the different strata of peasants.

The Budget Studies and the parallel investigations of rural migration have indicated also how often the seasonal and even permanent jobs in town fitted closely into the operation of the Russian peasant household and were determined by its needs. The same man could be a farmer in spring and autumn, an urban carpenter in summer and a lumberjack elsewhere in winter. Russia, however, knew much less flexibility of rural labour than, say, Latin America of today. The majority of its peasants were farmers only and consistently so.

Of those who left the village, quite a number were peasants' sons collecting money to facilitate the setting up of a household of their own, or else poor householders attempting to save money for a horse or an urgent due – an emigration aimed at underpinning of the peasant economy and/or re-peasantisation.[18] Male and female workers coming directly from the villages provided much of the permanent labour engaged in the urban construction, industry and services. Even when settled in town, many of them returned seasonally to the village and 'kept their roots' there, that is, contributed financially to the upkeep of their farming household, held on to their rights within it and often left their children, wives and elderly in its care. The significance of the peasant-workers in Russian towns was very considerable, both actually and potentially (one should remember that even one peasant per village per annum could swamp the urban labour markets).

The studies of the Russian peasant households have specified, beside structural similarities, some major dimensions of difference and discontinuity, without which any generalisation about 'the peasants' would easily mislead and mystify. Two of these discontinuities were particularly pertinent to the life of the peasants, that is, the socio-economic and the regional diversities. Both meant systematic differences in the livelihood, in typical productive 'packages' and strategies, etc., both between the peasant communities and in each of them. We shall specify this issue in Addendum 2. Also, the character of the peasant households can be fully understood only in its broader societal setting. The most immediate link between the peasant households and the Russian society at large was provided by the peasant commune. We shall proceed to it directly.

B. THE PEASANT COMMUNE

Rural communities display some manifest similarities all over the world. These general traits have been brought out conceptually in a variety of definitions which speak of territorially based human groups united by ties of direct social interaction by an integrated system of accepted norms and by the consciousness of being distinct from other groups delineated on similar lines.[1] Considerable socio-economic interdependency dictated by the 'traditional' agriculture, for example, the 'three-field system' of crop rotation in Europe, provided another dimension in the defining of localised peasant groups.[2] Unity of descent and relatively low territorial mobility, 'primary' (i.e. face-to-face) personal contact and lack of anonymity, low division of labour and direct co-operation result in high 'social cohesion' and a specific world-view. Pitt-Rivers's classical description of 'the closed community' as based on habitual personal contact, extensive endogamy, homogeneity of values, emphasis on strict conformity, intense group solidarity, marked ideological egalitarianism, etc., is a fair generalisation of those cultural traits or, at least, persistent tendencies.[3] Common political and economic interests find their usual expression in at least rudimentary communal authority, administering local affairs of neighbourly small producers and representing them before the outsiders. It was the peasant community (often sentimentalised) that provided fodder for the 'ideal type' dualities prominent in the social sciences at their nineteenth-century inception, offering the main antonym of urban, industrial, changing, conflict-ridden and diverse.[4]

Actual village life is far from being the rustic haven of equality, stability and brotherly love that its models often used to imply. Redfield's classical and influential descriptions of a conflict-free village of Tepoztlan was badly ravaged by Lewis's re-study of it, and many further demystifications followed.[5] Village communities show homogeneity but, at the same time, are split into conflicting strata, groups and factions. These divisions in no sense express temporary social pathology; rather, they play a vital part in village life and are decisive for understanding its social structure and dynamism. Also, the relative stability does not preclude change and transformation as the results of 'internal' and 'external' forces. The rural community must be treated in its historical and societal setting.

Rural communities are usually more specific to their ethnic and regional characteristics than the peasant households of diverse cultures and societies. This was also the case with the peasant commune which in the nineteenth century became the specifically Russian feature of the countryside best known to foreign and local students and analysts.[6]

From the 1860s a typical Russian peasant commune (*mir, obshchina*) was a self-governing territorial community and the main legal owner of land held by its households. The primary extra-farm social organisation of the Russian peasantry was thereby not a village or a parish but the commune: a local authority, an economic entity, a collective landowner, a jury-like court and a policing organ, all in one. Its membership consisted not only of those in actual residence but of all those born or accepted into it and thereby rightful claimants on its services and land.[7] Both the right and the duty to belong to a commune were restricted to peasants alone, thus making it an essential element of membership of the peasant 'social estate' (*soslovie*).

The legislators had intended that on the abolition of serfdom a commune would consist of all the peasants in one village and those only. However, in actual fact, communes were constituted also of peasants who used to belong to the same master. This varied genesis gave rise to different relations between the actual localities and the communes. Some settlements found themselves split between different communes, while some communes consisted of a number of villages or even of segments of a number of different villages.[8] All the same, the peasant communes of pre-revolutionary Russia were clearly localised and usually displayed the general characteristics of a rural community. Rural censuses published in 1902 and 1905 indicated that in European Russia a typical commune averaged three to five 'settlements', that is, clusters of houses, and about 100 households which collectively held about 750 des. (2000 acres) of land.[9] The figures of households-per-commune increased as one moved from the north-west to the south-east of European Russia.

The self-government of a Russian peasant commune was embodied in the communal assembly (*skhod, mir*) which consisted of the heads of all of its landholding households or their representatives.[10] The wide functions of the commune made this assembly into a most powerful body, at least potentially. The actual process of decision-making in it was far removed from the formally democratic proceedings laid down by law.[11] The decisions were typically unanimous, that is, by a consensus rather than by a majority vote, with the actual power in the hands of the more active and often, but far from always, the more wealthy members of the community, who took the lead.[12] Conformity and inertia coloured such processes. The landless and non-peasant families of the locality were excluded from representation. Their combined numbers were small, however – as documented below.

The executive authority of the commune rested in the hands of an 'elder' (*starosta*) who was elected for three years. The gathering also elected officers in charge of land-use, tax collection, welfare, etc. The commune offices were, in many cases, a heavy burden to their holders.

Their appointment was treated as compulsory and refusal to accept office was punishable under the pre-revolutionary law.

Functions of the peasant commune as the lowest rung of administrative authority included maintenance of roads and bridges, care for the welfare of the orphans, the lonely aged and the handicapped, the provision of education facilities, the accommodation of travelling officials, help in drafting of recruits, and so on. It fulfilled, moreover, basic police, judicial and fiscal functions. Officers of the commune were held responsible for the registration of residents and for law enforcement; they also had the right to arrest and to impose small fines. For a time, the Emancipation had left the commune with the collective duty of ensuring the payment of the redemption fees, to which taxes were added (*krugovaya poruka*). Even after the general moratorium of debts and the legal abolition of the communes' 'collective responsibility' for taxes in 1906, the commune authorities were still used by the state officials to ensure the payment of taxes by their members. The various duties undertaken by the commune required funds and these were raised by the imposition of commune dues (*mirskie sbory*), fixed by the communal gathering. This money was supplemented by compulsory services (*naturalnye povinnosti*), for example, the duty to provide labour for various needs of the commune.[13] The apparent injustice of an arrangement whereby the expenses of the rural administration were shouldered by the peasantry alone via its communes was frequently discussed before the revolution, but left at that.

A number of communes formed a *volost'* – an administrative unit that was since 1861 the highest echelon of specifically peasant local organisation. The *volost'* was administered by an executive (*uprava*) which consisted of the elders and their aides of constituent communes and headed by a *volost'* elder (*volostnoi starshina*) assisted by a clerk (*pisar'*), the last often the most central figure in the life of the *volost'*. A court of elected peasant magistrates operated in each *volost'* with the right to hear, in accordance with local custom, cases involving civil and petty criminal offences. It also held police and fiscal powers. The *volost'* and communal authorities were tightly controlled by the state administration, since the 1880s via the Land Chief (*zemskii nachal'nik*), a state official appointed from the ranks of the local nobility. The land chief had the final say in authorising peasant elections (or else made the final choice from among the candidates suggested by the peasants). He also had the statutory right to overrule any decision taken by peasant electees, to arrest them, and until 1905 to have them flogged for failures in the performance of their duty.[14]

Turning to the economic sphere, the large majority of the communes were legal owners of the main part of peasant land. A peasant household would usually keep on a hereditary basis only the small plot round the house (*usad'ba*). The bulk of arable land was held by the household in strips as an allotment (*nadel*) granted by the commune. Another section of commune land was reserved for collective use, that is, pasture and, possibly, forest. In some provinces like Voronezh and Saratov some of the arables were also put to collective cultivation by the communes (*obshchestvennye zapashki*). Peasant households and communes were free to buy private land from non-commune sources. This privately owned land was of little importance to the great majority of Russian peasants but offered a form of accumulation of wealth to some in the richer stratum.

The communal character of landownership found its fullest expression in the land-redivision. Even lands that had been held for generations and redeemed by the post-emancipation payments of a specific peasant household could (and were) taken away and reallocated by the commune assembly. The frequency and character of land-redivision varied a great deal, according to local conditions (e.g. the availability of land, problems of taxation, the power of various interested groups, etc.). Each commune was free to set standards of land-redistribution but was bound to relate it to some egalitarian principle – such as, for example, division by the number of consumers or the labour power in each household.[15] It was estimated that two-thirds to four-fifths of communes underwent at least one full-scale redivision of land between the 1861 Emancipation and the end of the nineteenth century. However, a full-scale redivision of the land was only the extreme case of a commune-induced change of land holding. The communes have engaged much more often in partial redistribution of communal land by dividing the holdings of households that had emigrated or become extinct, reallocating strips of land of some of the resident households to others (*skidka/nakidka*), etc.

Land-redivision, which caught the eye of outsiders because of its lack of accord with the social and economic structure of urban society or Russia's contemporary neighbours, fell far short of expressing fully the economic functions of the peasant commune. The prevailing open-field system, inclusive of crop-rotation cycles and the division of land into strips, made agricultural co-operation of all the members of the commune mandatory.[16] The communes took care of grazing the local livestock and often organised larger collective tasks, for example, the building or maintenance of collective services as well as renting additional lands, owning or administering workshops and mills, etc. The administrative and the economic activities of the peasant commune formed a closely integrated complex providing an inclusive social and economic organisation.

The main rural alternative to the communal system described was provided by the 'non-repartitional communes' which in 1905 held 19 per cent of the pesant lands of European Russia.[17] In these communes, the arable hands were held by the households 'in permanent possession' – that is, owned, some restrictions accepted. The geographical distribution indicated a genesis of the non-repartitional communes; they have clustered in the west and north-west regions, that is, in the areas that previously had been under Polish or Baltic–German rule. Even the non-repartitional communes usually engaged in an annual repartition of meadows supervised by the communal assembly, used forests in common, etc. Close communal links were imposed usually by a three-field rotation in farming, the common village services, common grazing, etc. Land was rarely sold and outsiders to the neighbourhood were kept at arm's length – a major restriction specific to the whole of peasant landownership. To an extent that was often missed by the onlookers, the non-repartitional commune operated thereby in a way resembling that of the repartitional one. The fundamental uniformity of legal, administrative and welfare duties, of the state legislation, demands and controls and the general context of peasant life enhanced these similarities. Even more generally, the peculiarity of the Russian repartitional commune is often overstated. Many of its characteristics were dictated by fundamental characteristics of smallholder agriculture and of rural communality that can be observed the world over.[18]

The countryside of the period discussed showed a high degree of homogeneity of its occupational divisions. Non-peasant inhabitants were few: some teachers and clergy, a number of petty officials and a few craftsmen, publicans or traders, of whom many farmed in a supplementary way. Smallholders who held enclosed lands outside the commune (*khutora*) were once again few, and concentrated before 1906 in Russia's west and north-west. With the exception of the Baltic provinces, landless wage labourers were less than one-tenth of the ruralities, often only 2–3 percent of the population of a village. All this did not mean, of course, that the communal system of land-redivision, even when fully operative, provided economic equality in the rural areas. Major factors of production were outside its scope, that is, horses, cows, lands privately owned and rented, extra agricultural income, etc. In all of its known past history, the Russian peasant commune was clearly differentiated in wealth but there were some levelling mechanisms inbuilt into it and the pre-eminent dimension of rural inequality was that of the peasant householders as against those outside the peasant commune: the noble landlords, the merchants and the state with its officials. The post-1861 decrease in the local power of the squires corresponded with the rise of those who represented the market and the state.

*   *   *

The origin of the Russian repartitional commune provided a major field for everlasting debate. To begin with, and to the fury of the local nationalists, its very existence was first noticed and signalled by Augustus Haxthausen, a German tourist-official.[19] A dispute began at once between the Slavophiles – who declared the commune to be an ever-present and exclusively Slav way of life – and those who tended to treat it as a fiscal invention of the tsarist state. The broader implications of the debate determined its character: it was the issue of Russian exceptionality, or its reverse, that was indirectly argued.[20] A third tradition critical of Slavophiles as well as of the 'state school' of liberal 'Westerners' was developed by the theorists of revolutionary populism from Hertzen and Chernyshevskii to the People's Will Party, whose analysis was adopted also by Marx in the last decade of his work.[21] In that view there was nothing exceptional about rural communes (and nothing 'to take pride of'). It used to exist all through Europe and lingered in Russia simply because of the country's sluggish development. That is not, however, necessarily a reason to wish to dispose of it now. On the contrary, for the post-capitalist society would resemble dialectically the communalism of capitalism's predecessors. Also, the peasant commune can and should be used in revolutionary struggle. The future may link the available social structures and traditions with suitable reforms and with mechanisation to make the peasant communes into major components of the new, post-tsarist socialist Russia.

At the turn of the century the question was still hotly debated. The 'Western' and 'statist' view was presented with particular strength by G. Milyukov who was to lead the liberals, and on the other hand, by some disciples of S. Plekhanov who specialised in the studies of rural Russia. I. Chernyshev, the most active among them, developed the view that the repartitional commune (described by him as taxation–directed *tyag-lovay*, an instrument of state) was imposed in the sixteenth century in the teeth of peasant opposition, to secure the fulfilment of duties to their lords.[22] By that historiography the repartitional commune, spread with the serfdom, was used as a model in the later 'regulation' of the 'state peasants' and, afterwards, in the legislation concerned with the 1861 emancipation of serfs. The view of N. Chernyshevskii and K. Marx, who assumed the historical continuity of the Russian peasant commune was simply wrong, because the Russian 'primitive commune' was left somewhere very far behind, while the state-imposed *obshchina* of the sixteenth to nineteenth century was a different thing altogether. It was, therefore, by its genesis and design, socially reactionary and politically counter-revolutionary. That view was directly related to prediction and prescription for the future. Peasant communes had to disappear, the sooner the better, to give way to healthy capitalist growth and Russia's proletarisation.

A major breakthrough in the studies of the origin and character of the Russian peasant commune resulted from a different approach to the very way the issue was considered. The new method was pioneered by A. Efimenko and F. Shcherbina and reached its full expression in the work of A. Kaufman.[23] In a major deviation from the strongly deductive flavour of the mainstream of the debate, Kaufman turned his attention to the processes of spontaneous creation of communes actually taking place in his time within the colonisation areas of Siberia (in his words, looking at the 'living history' as against the 'frozen history' that treats social institutions as given). He established that the institutionalisation of peasant communal land-use in Siberia proceeded under an increasing population/land pressure, from the initial squatter holdings (*zaimka*) determined solely by the labour invested in them, towards the increasing redivision of land between the rural neighbours. It was, therefore, not the commune that in his view determined the land-redivision, but rather the development of land-redivision between neighbours which promoted the formal establishment of a commune. Once the land became scarcer the power of the rural neighbourhood with the full scope of its sanctions (from the pressure of simple non-co-operation up to arson and murder) brought to heel households that refused to become part of a redistributional system. The 'state' was distant and essentially disinterested, the outsiders and the environment were hostile or considered as such, one's neighbours and family were all one could call on for support. A measure of egalitarianism in land-usage was the price of it. The redivision of land usually began with the meadows but spread to the arable lands. Later, the state officialdom simply registered the fact.

The debate concerning the peasant communes is still very much alive, those claiming the generic nature of rural communes drawing new evidence from European history and current 'developing societies'.[24] A contemporary version of the State School views is in evidence also.

Recent analysis by Russian scholars has added substance to the assumption of the generic nature of the Russian communal organisation. An important study of the manorial economy in the seventeen-century has offered new important pointers to the issue of the peasant communes' historical roots, generality and consistency. In the seventeenth and eighteenth centuries the power of the squires over their peasants was unlimited in law, as was made dramatically clear by Catherine II's decree forbidding peasants even to petition the tsar against the squires. Yet, V. Aleksandrov has shown how much the actuality of rural Russia differed from a simple rule 'from above', and it was the commune that constituted the core of this difference. The study has shown that in actual fact, only seldom were the demands of the all-powerful squire simply imposed without considerable 'give and take' with the communes' elders. Aleksandrov summarised his findings by stating that: 'At all stages of its history, it [the commune] remained an organisation of the small producer-peasant, limiting by the very fact of its existence the more extreme expression of feudal role'. Moreover, 'its existence and traditionality all through rural Russia is doubtless' and despite the ups and downs in its activities, the long-term view of the communes showed that they 'did not decline' (*ne zatukhayut*).[25] Communal organisation of different areas and under different squires showed 'remarkable similarity.[26] One can add that this consistency and generality would be even more pronounced with respect to the 'state peasants'[27] where the whims of the particular squire did not influence matters.

Whatever its historiography and genesis, a central additional point concerning the existence of peasant commune in Russia was well made by the pragmatic and politically engaged statement of N. Ogarev, Chernyshevskii's closest collaborator in the mid-nineteenth century: 'It is all the same to society if the commune existed since Rurik or was established by Peter I. The commune in Russia is a fact, and the problem is if it should be destroyed.'[28] *Ex post factum*, one should add: 'and what role would the commune play in the political struggles of the forthcoming Russian revolutionary century'. In the period we are interested in, the commune was a major factor of peasant life in Russia. It proceeded to play that role until the early 1930s to the unending surprise of many peasants-watchers. It was the persistence of the commune and the way it could drop out of sight only to resurface later on, that puzzled most of the non-peasants looking at it. The informal functions and unexpected uses to which the commune was put by its members added to the puzzlement and the debate.

Central to its continuity, its generic nature, its flexibility, and its ambivalence, was a fundamental duality of the commune functions and a third capacity, hidden for a time. The communal system served both peasants and their masters, exploiters and potential foes. The commune assured economic services, some collective security and welfare (e.g. care of orphans and the aged) as well as a measure of defence for its members. It also provided an administrative device for tax collection and local policing, etc., which served the state administrators. In the face of the agrarian crisis and external demands of the 1880s and 1890s, the peasant communes showed also a considerable ability to shield their hard-pressed members by sabotaging the payment-collecting measures of the state. That was not the only expression of a third, latent function of the commune in the organisation of peasant self-defence and defiance. In the 1905–7 revolution, the Russian peasant commune was dramatically to reveal its characteristics as a unit of class organisation, a generator of egalitarian ideology and a school for collective action of the kind capable of turning into well-organised revolt overnight. As a result, the following decade witnessed a major effort by the government to destroy peasant communes – a major objective of the so-called Stolypins Reforms. Successes were reported and such reports challenged. We shall return to this question elsewhere. The speed, the extent and way in which peasant communes revived in the next revolutionary period, initiated in 1917, showed how deeply the commune was still rooted in the structure of the peasant society and in the peasant collective consciousness of Russia.[29]

C. PEASANTRY: MODELS AND HISTORY

Turning from the discussion of the peasant household and peasant commune to that of peasantry as such, we proceed to a phenomenon different in kind. The peasant household and peasant community are definable in terms of personal participation and direct, face-to-face social interaction. Peasantry can be defined on the whole only in analytical terms. Indeed, the very segmentation of the peasantry, that is, the lack of constant and necessary social interaction among its units, is one of its essential characteristics. Political action has brought peasants together at times on a broad regional or national scale, that is, made peasantry 'real' not only analytically but also as a coherent and self-conscious entity – a 'class for itself' in Marxist parlance. The particular socio-legal structure of the Russian empire has provided an additional dimension that made peasantry stand out as an enclosed group. Since the 1860s the membership in peasant 'estate' (*soslovie*) has not only defined a variety of exclusive duties and rights but also meant belonging to and meeting within officially recognised groups which consisted of peasants only: a commune, a *volost'*, an electoral college. At the turn of the century discrepancies between the 'estate' and the social class were increasingly evident, that is, there were 'peasants' by estate who were actually urban merchants, and 'townsmen' by estate who were peasant in actuality, but the division into 'estates' still matched fairly closely social reality in rural Russia.

'Peasant society and culture has something generic about it. It is a kind of arrangement of humanity with some similarities all over the world.'[1] The danger of over-generalising accepted, this summation by Redfield and the description of the Chinese peasantry by Fei as 'a way of living'[2] have made considerable sense to the majority of those who studied and compared peasantries of different periods and countries. The term 'peasantry' is a generalisation, both pragmatic and scholarly, which expresses the actual experience of what was described by E. Wolf as a 'recurrent syndrome'.[3] It is also an analytical concept that forms a link within general theoretical structures set to explain how societies *in toto* work and change. Much of the classical sociology was constructed in the nineteenth century in Europe and the USA around models or polarities that were based, explicitly or implicitly, on the actual differences between the peasant and urban societies: Durkheim's notions of 'mechanical' v. 'organic' solidarity, Tönnies's 'community' v. 'society', Cooley's 'primary' v. 'secondary' relations, etc. The same held true for much of contemporary historiography.

Peasants can be defined as small producers on land who, with the help of simple equipment and the labour of their families, produce mainly for their own consumption and for meeting obligations to the holders of political and economic power. A wider definition would consider and extend those features: the functioning of the family production unit, the 'traditional' agriculture as main occupation, the life of small rural communities, the specific social relations and political economy attached to the under-dog position in society. It assumes, therefore character-istic units of social organisation as well as specific economic, political and cultural traits. Peasanthood would reflect an interdependence of these characteristics and cannot simply be reduced to either one of them. More is implied, however, than a list of linked features. First, the list has a hierarchy of its own and the social and economic characteristics of the peasant family farm have been usually treated as decisive in the delimiting of peasanthood. Second, the concept assumes continuity rooted in characteristic patterns of social reproduction as well as some specific roads of social transformation from it. Put another way, peasantry is a social (sub)system, perpetuating its own structure. The way this 'system' works does not assume, of course, immutable presence but limits change, slows it down and circumscribes its patterns, frustrating the ability of reformers to transform peasantries at will.[4]

As with every conceptualisation, the process of defining is bound to strip reality of some of its uniqueness and mutability. That should not be read as a claim for peasantry's uniformity or constancy. Peasants differ between villages, regions and countries and within every village too. Peasantries change constantly and ever interact with non-peasants. To bring out their general characteristics and the systems of their social reproduction is not to contradict but to see in greater depth (and to 'measure') their diversity, 'external' interdependencies and change.

During the period discussed, Russian peasantry has displayed the major traits that have appeared in different peasant taxonomies elsewhere and since. This statement carries in fact a measure of circularity, for the extensive studies of Russian peasantry have played a considerable role in the theorising of what peasants are, or are not. More than a simple tautology is implied, however. Peasant economy and society in Russia closely resembled social structures and patterns of reproduction and change in countries otherwise very distinct (especially so, within Euro-Asia), making the cross-use of models and theories instructive. Which is, of course, the point of the generalisation.

Extensive homogeneity in the *economic* sphere has been shown within studies of Russian peasants: the ways peasant households operated, peasant property customs, peasant agriculture and diet, the economic functions of the peasant community, etc. These similarities are remarkable if one remembers how large and diverse the country was. The similarities refer not only to the 'objective' economic conditions and problems, for example, the ecology of rye production or the rural 'over-population', but also to their typical resolution, social and technical, within the scope of the peasant economies – for example, the 'three-field' system of rotation and the 'under-valuation' of family labour (to be discussed in Chapters 3 and 4).[5]

In the *political* sphere the Russian peasants have ordinarily displayed factionality side by side with considerable unity against 'outsiders'. This unity, cross-cutting different economic strata, is known and was named and documented for peasantries elsewhere as 'vertical segmentation'. It was accentuated and reinforced by the peasant legal handicaps in

Russia; members of the peasant 'social estate' were singled out as late as the twentieth century by specific taxes and duties as much as by juridical flogging as punishment for petty infringements of the regulations. As against all others, peasants were exceedingly lowly in their social status with only some despised non-Russians and the beasts beneath them (it goes without saying that simultaneously, within the official ideology, the peasants were ever referred to as 'the salt of the Russian earth'). The entrenched peasant tactics of avoidance and external servility were ways to 'handle' political powerlessness and so were the many forms of active peasant resistance through sabotage, arson and riot (*bunt*).[6]

Russian peasant communities showed distinct *cultural patterns of cognition*[7] – both the results and the determinants of other peasant characteristics. In this sense of specifically linked and mutually reinforcing political economy and consciousness, the description of peasanthood as a 'way of living' makes considerable sense. *Traditionalism*, that is, justification of action in terms of past, *conformism*, that is, justification of action in terms of the will of the community, formal *egalitarianism*, high normative value placed on land holding and on the family, are available as examples and played a major role in the peasant interpretations of the present and in the shaping of dreams about a better future. Conformity and a tendency to justify action in terms of the communal will (*po vole mira*) was reinforced by the Russian form of communal organisation and supported it in turn. The attitude to the land as serving essentially consumption purposes (*kormitel'*) was reinforced by the land-redivision customs and was to become particularly important in the agrarian revolution. Social reproduction, that is, the production of the material necessities bound with the reproduction of the human actors and of the whole system of social relations, was tied to relatively low mobility, the occupational training within a family farm and the 'family property' as well as the specific inheritance customs. Attitudes to justice, as often expressed in the decisions of peasant magistrates, were determined by an overriding concern for communal cohesion: the maintenance of good neighbourly relations was valued more highly than impartiality.[8] The image of the peasant millennium of a just society appeared, if at all, as a 'black repartition' (*chernyi peredel*), that is, an equal division of land between all of its tillers, or else as *Vselenskii mir* – a grandiose peasant commune of communes, embracing all of the people of Russia or of the entire universe.

In the mid-nineteenth century, Hertzen spoke of 'two Russias which had come into hostile opposition from the beginning of the eighteenth century'. He enlarged: 'On the one hand there was governmental, imperial, aristocratic Russia, rich in money, armed not only with bayonets but with all the bureaucratic and political techniques taken from Germany; on the other hand there was the Russia of the people shrouded in darkness, poor, agricultural, communal, democratic, helpless, taken by surprise, conquered as it were without battle'.[9] By the end of nineteenth century, the 'upper' Russia was undergoing rapid change, incorporating new social strata and ways, called into being by industrialisation, educational reforms and the growth of capitalism. The Russian cities were the focus of this change. The 'lower', mostly peasant, Russia was probably never as communal and democratic as the Russian radicals would have liked to have it. Changes were occurring there also. Yet a major split between the two Russias was marked and there to stay for the decades to come. In an economic, political, legal, cultural and even visual and linguistic sense (i.e. in dress and idiom) the Russian peasants have varied consistently from the non-peasant sections of society. Existentially, every Russian would recognise nearly every peasant at a glance, and adjust his behaviour accordingly.

A number of peasant/non-peasant continuums have been rightly claimed (e.g. that of income). There were important divisions cross-cutting that of 'towns v. peasantry'. Those linked with the differentiation with the village processes leading to the decline of the urban/rural diversity were under way. The development of market, of money economy and of wage labour market played an important role here. Some of the state administrative measures acted alike; the military service and the educational network has advanced the integration of the peasants into the 'wider society'. But prognosis of the future and knowledge of the processes cannot substitute for actuality.

The persistence of the peasant/non-peasant social diversity was such that even those who invaded the 'other world' by the fact of residence, for example, the peasant-workers in town and the rural intelligentsia in the villages, tended to establish socially separated 'enclaves' rather than 'bridges' over the societal split. Nor could it be treated simply as a matter of 'cultural inertia', that is, a gap in time between a new reality and the awareness of it. The 'enclave' tendencies in Russia were based on very real economic ties and interests. To exemplify, the 1908 investigation of members of the Printers' Union in Moscow has shown that about half of them kept their families in the villages and returned there consistently every summer to engage in farming. Those links were still stronger in the smaller towns of Russia.[10] On the other hand, rural teachers, agronomists, doctors, etc., relatively few as they were, have clustered in the larger villages interacting mostly with each other while relating through the patterns of employment, supervision and expectations of promotion to the urban-centred networks of dependence and interaction.

The related processes of social reproduction *and* fundamental transformation of the Russian peasantry, all at once, led to a constant and angry debate. The question was mostly that of the results anticipated, and in particular of peasantry's possible disappearance – of what the peasants themselves called 'depeasantation' (*raskrest'yanivanie*). The ideological consequences of the argument provided fuel for its 'heat'. Ideologies apart, the most significant of the processes in question were socio-economic mobility, the actual extent of socio-economic differentiation, the agrarian 'vicious circle', the development of capitalism, and some characteristics of what we would call today the 'dependent development' at the peripheries of industrial capitalism. A specific study was devoted to the first of these issues.[11] The others will be discussed in the text to follow. To lay foundation and make clear the approach adopted, two points concerning peasantry will be made directly: a preliminary comment concerning the conceptualisation of peasantry in the broader societal setting and a word about the immediate historical background to the period under consideration.

*   *   *

All through the world the terminology of the peasant 'embedding' within society has been at issue since the time when industry, the city and/or capitalism came to form the major axis of social change. The debate has grown with time. Kroeber spoke of peasants as 'part society and part culture' and Redfield elaborated it further in an imaginative description which, however, offered little analytical explanation, especially because of the ambivalences concerning the concept of 'culture'.[12] In an attempt to categorise it for Russia, the term 'dualism' understood in Hertzen's way, that is, stressing the power relations and inequalities, comes easily to one's tongue. The association of the word with the later work of J. Boeke makes its usage ambivalent and possibly misleading.[13] Boeke has offered a typology delimiting two parallel sectors of Western-colonising and Eastern–rural economy and society in Indonesia. He saw the division as essentially static and its root in the incompatibility of the 'mental attitudes' along lines expressed by Kipling and duly quoted as saying: 'East is East and West is West, and never the twain shall meet'.[14] The fact of structurally different economies operating territorially side-by-side and connected along 'a narrow front' was well documented in this work. Boeke's exploration of the different logics of their combined operations is also important but the explanation attached cannot be accepted. Such phenomena have appeared also in ethnically homogeneous environments and not only in colonial societies.[15] The assumption of rigid stability of such a division, postulated by Boeke, was not sustained either. A considerable amount of evidence has shown rapid 'de-dualisation' in societies in which socio-economic and/or political conditions facilitated such change. It is the specific rationale of different economies, rather than intrinsic mental attitudes and ethnic rationalities, which seems to underlie the differences between peasants and non-peasants in Indonesia as well as in Russia, China or India.

The position polarly opposed to that of Boeke took two forms, the institutionalised view of Structural Functionalism and of the Neoclassical school (in sociology and economics respectively), and a theoretically parallel, if socially critical, functionalist tendency within Marxism.[16] All these views share the assumptions that the totality of the social system (to the functionalists – its 'needs') define fully the nature of all of its components – a 'holist' view bound to an over-integrated model of social reality. The methodological conclusion is that once you had understood the general laws or the 'core' element of 'the system', you could deduce the rest. As for the peasants, what they are or will become is fully defined by the broader social system or the political economy into which they are linked. Their specificity and/or its exploration are spurious or secondary.

We shall return to the general issue after considering Russian capitalism and rural political economy. For the moment let us simply state that, during the epoch in which we are interested, Russian peasant and non-peasant social and economic 'systems' have operated side by side, ever related and never 'equal' but with the peasantry also never simply mirroring the impact or the 'needs' of 'the other side'. To put a terminology to it, one can call it 'dualistic' while relating the term to political economy (as was done by T. McGee) or else to accept the terms 'articulation' or 'subsumption', as long as those are clearly separated not only from the ideas of immutable diversity between parallel social organisations but also from the presumptions of total assimilation of the 'subsumed' system to the logic of the one that dominates it. Or we can plunge for another term altogether. What is mostly at issue is not terminology, however, though a concept named can offer to reality a clue and an approach to explanation. In the last decades many students of peasantry, often deriving from different theoretical traditions, moved closer in their general position concerning peasants and society. That view, adopted also in the text to follow, dismisses the possibility of studying peasants separately but also rejects as reductionist the idea of a supra-structure whose supra-logic dictates absolutely and explains totally the nature and dynamics of its peasant 'component' (e.g. peasants are creatures of feudalism while outside its confines there can be no peasants but should it not work, peasants become creatures of capitalism, imperialism or of 'the society' *in toto*, fully explained by its 'needs'). Put positively, this approach assumes broad societal determination, as well as distinctive dynamics of peasantry and resulting contradictions, leaving space, within limits, for various outcomes of the political battles. History is not 'free' but nor is it prefigured, and this holds true also for the social phenomenon called peasantry. Peasantry is not, and never was, a-societal, but nor is it thereby epiphenomenal.

A different duality implicit in Marx's definition of the peasants in early capitalist France may offer here a suggestive and historically informed set of questions and a point of entry into the problem. To wit, 'in so far as millions of families live under economic conditions of existence that separate their mode of life, their interests and their culture from those of other classes, and put them in hostile opposition to the latter, they form a class. In so far as there is merely a local interconnection amongst these smallholding peasants and the identity of their interests begets no community, no national bond and no political organisation among them, they do not form a class.'[17] Which leaves us with a question and a riddle. An elaboration is called for the class nature of peasantry. A riddle is left with us: in so far as peasantry is not a class, what (else) is it?

By social class the Marxist tradition (of a decisive impact for the whole of European political sociology) meant a group with common interests within a unified structure of political economy. That common interest finds its expression in group consciousness and group action, shaped by the conflict-relations with other classes. Peasants have acted often enough as 'a class for itself' within the contemporary 'developing societies' and in the historical context of 'modernisation', facing landlords, exploitative urbanites and oppressive state apparatus, possibly foreign or foreign backed. The class conflict and social position of the peasants, their resulting action or the lack of it, played a major role at the crucial junction of world history in the last century: in Russia, China, Vietnam, Mexico, Algeria, Mozambique, Portugal, Hungary or India. However, a simple designation of peasants as 'a class' in the sense implied suffers badly from the theoretical difficulty establishing the type of political economy to which it is to be related. Is it capitalism? Can it be feudalism? What else can it be? The twentieth-century peasants 'on the marsh' often acted as a 'class for itself', blissfully oblivious of the fact that heir 'class in itself' status is doubted by many Marxist theorists. We shall consider it all in the companion volume *Russia 1905–07: Revolution as a Moment of Truth* after discussing the facts and characteristics of the peasant 'class war' of 1905–7. As to the riddle, the duality expressed in Marx seems to recognise the fact that peasants can be meaningfully analysed not only as a class (of a particular 'classness') but also as a distinctive system of production, which would explain the passage about 'the economic conditions of existence which separate their mode of life and, less directly, their culture'. The 'riddle' can be solved therefore only through the explication and further analysis of peasant economy *vis-à-vis* societal and inter-societal systems of political economy. We shall proceed to it in Chapter 4.

The West European experience has produced a fundamental historiography that came into extensive use also in the Russian interpretations of the rural data. It relates to the peasant/non-peasant division, offering the model of its disappearance. In its essence, it is an image of static peasantry gradually devoured and eventually assimilated through commercialisation, marginalisation, etc. by the urban capitalist economy. Some typical stages (or 'laws') of that development expressed it. For example, the early result of the commercialisation of the villages was usually their 'agriculturalisation', that is, the non-agricultural tasks being specialised-out and taken over by industrial production with the peasant labour increasingly used in land and animal husbandry. Experiments with agrarian reforms since the 1920s and even more since the 1960s introduced as an alternative model the state-induced modernisation of the peasants. The capital v. peasantry image of social transformation usually disregarded the discrete impact of the policies of state on the peasantry's structural stability, destabilisation and, at times, restabilisation. Marxist works of that inclination tended to leave out also the contradiction between the state managers and the capitalists and/or large landowners. The 'other side' proceeded to do the reverse: to talk of state policies or reforms and to disregard capitalism. Both tended to detract from the fact that peasants do not always passively accept depeasantisation (and/or pauperisation). Peasant counter-action, in a violent confrontation as well as by passive resistance or 'walking away', has determined much of rural and 'national' history. Even reaction to political defeat by this bulk of the population plays a major role in influencing the character of peasant, peasant-related and post-peasant societies.[18] The neat simplicity of capitalism-devours-peasants scheme or its state-reforms-peasants alternative are bound to mislead when used singly or simply, at least so far as the long-term processes are concerned. When evidence concerning the transformation of peasantry is looked at, one must transgress both and clarify in one's mind a *rural triangle of social determination.* (A 'pyramid' if big landlords proceeds to play a major and independent role.) One must also accept the *mutual* nature of those impacts. To do so is to expose it to the weight of fundamental contradictions and to the possible multiplicity of 'roads' of social change, and thereby make it far more realistic.

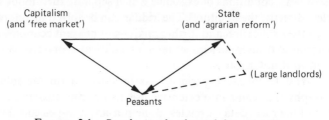

FIGURE 2.1   *Rural triangle of social determination*

In the second half of the nineteenth century, rural Russia came under the combined impact of major state-induced reform and of advancing commercialisation and industrialisation. In 1861 'the right of bondage over the peasants settled upon landlord's estates and over domestic serfs was forever abolished'.[19] The 'private serfs' were emancipated and the scene set for a new stage in the history of Russia. The ex-serfs were granted a major part of the land they traditionally held, subject to payment of a 'redemption fee' over the next forty-nine years. After having it ordered, the state administration proceeded to act as the chief managing agent of reform: establishing which lands were to be transferred in cases of disagreement, paying out at once 80 per cent of the sums due to the squires (minus their very substantial debts to the state banks) and collecting those monies from the peasant communes. About 1200 state officials (*mirskie posredniki*) were appointed to secure and settle the new land division. The laws as set and the interdependence of the state administrators with the nobility had worsened the deal for the peasants, who overpaid for some of their land, often got the 'worse pick' of it, and had to give up the use of some of the commons, forests and meadows. Robinson estimated that 4 per cent of the arables, farmed by the peasants before the Emancipation, were added to nobility's private lands (the so-called 'cut-offs').[20] (Larger figures ranging as high as 15 per cent were suggested elsewhere.) On the other hand, the Russian squires did not get what most of them wanted either. The redemption payment had sweetened the pill but the squires would rather have had all of the land and a rural proletariat of ex-peasants to work it (as when serfdom was abolished for the 400 000 souls in the Baltic provinces of Russia in the years 1816–19). The whole operation in 1861 and after was shaped by the strategies, prejudices and conveniences of officialdom, which sharply opposed 'proletarisation'. The new rural system of administration was initially experimented with on the 'state peasants' land and even earlier on the tsar's own estates (*udel*). Apart from land, most of the earlier legal powers and responsibilities of the landlords were transferred now to the peasant commune, the *volost'* and the elected 'elders', under the direct control of the state much enhanced thereby.

In 1866 Emancipation had been extended along similar lines, to the 'state peasants' but with land allotments considerably larger than those granted to the private serfs. Out of the variants rooted in the past, a single peasant 'social estate' was now moulded by the state administration, with similarities in circumstances and way of life reinforced by specific 'peasant legislation', distinct from the 'national' law.[21]

Dramatic as all these changes were, 'the great reform did not effect a revolutionary change in the internal organisation of the peasantry', concluded G. T. Robinson in his unsurpassed history of the Emancipation of the Russian serfs.[22] What he meant and extensively documented for the period of 1861–1916 was the extent to which the essential features of peasant social structure have endured and reproduced, defying, time and time again, reforms, legislation and administrative pressures. Robinson's view can be extended still further in time, for while the 1917–20 period of revolutions followed by the civil war represented a most dramatic watershed in the life of the Russian society, the specific characteristics of peasantry were maintained and magnified by the disappearance of the nobles and the revitalisation of the communes.[23] The works by R. E. F. Smith and A. Alexandrov, referred to above, extended these characteristics also back in time, into the seventeenth century and further still.[24]

As for state adminstration within the new post-emancipation rural world, it had clearly first intended to perform the role assigned to God by some of the modern theologians, that is, to let the peasantry proceed by its own motion, with daily offerings of incense and prayer, soldiers and taxes, to 'those above' assumed and accepted. The formal aims of the state policy were mostly 'defensive', that is, to defend the peasants from proletarisation and the squires from disappearance, to keep order and to receive the recruits and the financial dues. The legislation of 1891–3, and the appointment of land chiefs, tightened the police controls over the peasants, but the essence of peasant–state interaction changed but little. The peasants were milked, while the statesmen dealt mostly with matters more important than rustics. International politics of the empire occupied much of the attention 'at the very top'. The economic strategies of the government centred on financial reforms and deals, the construction of railways and on industrialisation, the impact of which on peasant agriculture was considerable but indirect. The social characteristics of peasantry were reinforced by the exploitative removal of economic 'surplus' from the countryside as well as by the conserving policies of the state administration.

None the less, Russia's policy-makers came increasingly to understand that some changes in the social structure of peasant society were taking place, and would have to be taken account of or even initiated. In the long term, policies of rapid industrialisation necessitated the mobilisation and/or suppression, or at least the neutralisation, of the peasantry in what would inevitably amount to its deepest crisis. There were also major economic implications to them. That is why the alternatives of Russian general policies could be and increasingly were formulated in terms of a changing social placement of the peasantry in the wider society, and patterns of its transformation. As years went by, the rural policies of Witte, Stolypin, Lenin and Stalin represented also set theoretical assumptions and conscious choices concerning different roads towards industrialisation and general strategies of the social transformation of Russia.

At the Russian rural scene, restructured by the abolition of serfdom, the initial peasant reactions to the hardships and opportunities of industrialisation, capitalism and more autonomous farming were limited. Some riots concerning land demands in the early period of uncertainty were put down by force. The amount of grain sold by the peasants increased but the use of new technology had grown but little. There was growing village-to-town migration, which even at its peak took only a part of the natural population growth, while many of the migrants returned. The famine of 1891 produced apathy rather than revolt or technological change. Yet the long-term results of those developments were nothing like stagnation. By the beginning of the new century the grand rural reforms of 1861–7, the spread of market relations and the exploitative political economy caused a stagnant rural society dominated by a conservative government to produce a radical political response and a violent revolution. Then, once the certainties of peasant docility disappeared, the rural and agrarian policies moved decisively to the fore, to be recognised as the major determinant of Russia's future, and resulted in a sequence of radical reforms aiming to de-peasantise Russia.

ADDENDUM 2   RUSSIAN PEASANTS: AVERAGES,
DIVERSITIES, SOCIO-ECONOMIC DIFFERENTIATION

This may be the place to supplement the 'statistical snapshot' of the Russian
society presented in Addendum 1 by saying something more about rural Russia.
As stated, the villagers consisted in 1897 of 108.8 million men and women, that
is, 86.6 per cent of the population of the empire. The subsequent figures for
European Russia were 81.4 million and 87.1 per cent.[1] Further information
about the population outside of European Russia was scarce and often less
reliable. For European Russia only, where three-quarters of the population
lived, studies have shown about 110 000 rural communes in existence, divided
into roughly 500 000 settlements (*poselenie*, i.e. a village or a hamlet, often a
territorially separated subdivision of a larger community).[2] That made for an
average twenty-one households per settlement and ninety-six households per
commune, with 168 peasant 'souls' per settlement, or 745 per commune.

Two basic categories of diversity must be taken into account, when turning
from such statistical 'averages' towards the actual picture of rural Russia: the
regional specialisms and the socio-economic differentiation. We shall introduce
them in the shortest possible way.

Ecology, ethnicity and history have underscored the diverse regional
characteristics of the countryside. We shall present it in qualitative terms,
leaving the rest to the sources given in the notes. From west to east run the major
zones of the (i) frozen and essentially empty tundra, followed by (ii) a broad
band of poorer land (*podzol*) often covered by forest and with a fairly cold
climate, and then (iii) the more fertile 'black soil' turn thin and the warmer
climate, turning hot and dry as one moves to the south and south-east. History
and ethnic specificity interposed their own pattern in the way the density of
'repartitional' communes prevailed in central Russia, the Ukraine and Siberia,
declined as one moved to the north-west and disappeared in the Polish and
Baltic gubs.[3] There were none in the Caucasian and Muslim districts of Asiatic
Asia. The different form of emancipation from serfdom has meant that the
German nobles of Latvia and Estonia owned most of the arable lands there and
faced a mass of Latvian and Est landless workers (there were also some non-
German landowning family farmers). In the Ukraine and Belorussia, Polish
squires often faced non-Polish peasants and tenants (possibly with Jewish
intermediaries as the sub-holders). In ethnic Russia the large holdings and the
squires became less frequent as one moved east, to disappear completely in the
inhospitable north-east, in Siberia and major parts of the Cossack areas.
(There the bulk of the land conquered from the native population was granted to
settlers—soldiers of the 'Cossack armies', subdivided to the Cossack *stanitsy* and
then into the family holdings of the individual Cossack households.)

For reasons that linked ecology with the history of the colonisation, in
European Russia the size of the villages increased, moving from north-west
towards the south-east. So did the distance between the peasant house and his
lands and his water supply. Correspondingly, the average number of the strips of
arable land per household dropped and so did the percentage of peasants
engaged in non-agricultural work. The population per land density has followed
a different pattern. The north of European Russia was thinly populated. Farther
south came the central agricultural zone – the major colonisation areas of the

seventeenth and eighteenth centuries – with an extremely dense rural population. It was followed by the newly colonised areas of New Russia, with a relatively low density of rural population settled on good soil, much of it virgin or newly put to use. The worst rural poverty was consistently reported from the zone of highest rural density of population, that is, the so-called Central Agricultural Region, the West-bank (of Dnieper), Ukraine and some of the Volga areas. Up to 2 million seasonal workers trekked every summer from those districts, hundreds of miles to the New Russia with its richer farming and better developed market production of grain to bring back the wages of harvesting there. Others went to the mines and formed the core of the peasant colonisation of the Asian parts. As to the peasant emigrants into towns, permanent and seasonal, the majority of them came from a relatively restricted 'catchment area'. The northern zone supplied most of the rural migration into Petersburg and Moscow.

The farming patterns offered a central dimension of regional specificity. While grain production formed the core of the land husbandry all over the empire, the type of grain produced differed roughly following the climatic conditions: wheat in the south, rye to the north, barley and oats in the far north. The extent of cash crops offered another possible division defining the usage of the peasant 'surplus labour', sources of money income and market links to the extra-village world: flax was used in this way in the north, hemp and sugar beet in the south, potatoes in the gub. of Vladimir, etc. So was the supplementary wage employments. All of those patterns changed with the passage of time, for example, wheat production advanced north, butter became the major peasant commodity-production of Western Siberia, etc. Russian scholars considered different approaches to region-building, focusing on different aspects or 'packages' of characteristics: geography, production, marketing, etc.[4] We shall return to some consequences of these regional divisions in Chapter 3.

*   *   *

The economic divisions within the Russian peasantry have been anxiously studied by Russian administrators, social scientists and revolutionaries. The reason for their interest lay in the rural socio-economic differentiation, which was accepted as the most significant index of the development of capitalism and of the related class formation.[5] It was treated subsequently as the test of the major theories of social development of the day: Marxist, populist, liberal and the modernising monarchist, it was the major way to substantiate such theories or to put them at doubt. The record of socio-economic differentiation was to define the direction of the transformation of rural Russia, and/or to 'measure' the stage already reached in the process of its 'modernisation'. While the local evidence collected by the *zemstvos* was often very sophisticated, relevant national data were scarce. Not surprisingly, estimates swayed wildly under the impact of hot-blooded ideological debate.

The more advanced evidence, relevant to the latter period of the 1917 revolution and the first decade of the Soviet rule, has been presented elsewhere, together with an argument why a fundamental change in methodology is necessary to relate more adequately the argument and the 'snapshot-like' static data to differentiation *processes* i.e. polarisation and levelling).[6] In what follows we shall centre on the quantitative and static evidence available at the turn of the century and on its interpretations.

By the end of the first decade of the twentieth century only two relevant pieces of evidence on a national scale came out in print: the population census of 1897 and the landownership census of 1905, published within a year of each other.[7] We shall discuss the three most influential attempts to put that data to use in establishing the socio-economic differentiation of the Russian peasants. We shall then suggest an alternative set of figures – a reinterpretation. All of the figures are for European Russia only, but experience has shown that the percentage's divisions were roughly similar for the empire at large.

(A) The editors of *Statistika zemlevladeniya 1905 g.* presented a reasoned estimate as to why, in their view, the 90.5 million members of the 'peasant estate' in European Russia were divided as shown in Table 2.1.

TABLE 2.1   *Peasant differentiation(A)*

Sub-categories of 'peasants by social estate'	European Russia 1905	
	Number of families	Size of population
a. Farming on own land	12.5 million	62.5 million
b. Landless	2.2 million	11.0 million
c. Occupied outside agriculture	3.4 million	17.0 million
Total	18.1 million	90.5 million

Source:
Statistika zemlevladeniya 1905 g. (St Petersburg, 1907) p. 197.

These estimates are inadequate so far as the second and third categories are concerned, on grounds that were recognised in part by the authors themselves. To begin with the category of those 'occupied outside agriculture', the editors assumed the average size of peasant family to consist of five members. The 'peasants' occupied outside of agriculture (group c.) were then treated as the residuum of the total population of the 'peasant estate' as recorded, minus those households that were actually accounted for in the countryside and multiplied by five. The actual figure of the average family size within the rural population of European Russia at the turn of the century was 5.7. Even if a drop of, say, 0.2 per cent is assumed, that is, the average size of a rural household to be 5.5 in 1905, the population of 'peasants by social estate' engaged in agriculture (categories a. and b.) would be not less than 81 million. The number of the 'peasant estate' population outside agriculture (i.e. category c.) would accordingly drop from 17 to 9.5 million.[8]

Turning to category b., the authors themselves have pointed out that the figure of 11 million landless peasants, that is, the equivalent of 12 per cent of those who farmed, must be scaled down to take account of those holding private lands via peasant partnerships, etc. One must scale down further the size of that population in view of the fact, disregarded by the authors, that the family size of the poorer and landless families in Russia was universally lower by not less than one-third than the averages shown for the peasant population of those times.[9]

These amendments combined would put the population in question at less than 7 per cent. Of this, some would be tenants with the whole of their land rented, blending into those poor peasant households in which a slice of one's 'own', that is, mostly held from the commune was supplemented by land that was rented. In the south-east, or Siberia, such tenants could at times be better off than a poor peasant landholder elsewhere. Others would be rural proletarians in the true sense of that term, that is, living on their wage work.

(B)　The second pre-revolutionary evaluation of the classes within the countryside (and in the whole of Russia) was proposed by A. Lositskii and based on the national census of 1897. The author carried out a seemingly straightforward operation of relating the 2.4 million permanent 'workers and servants' recorded within the rural areas to the 16.2 million of the other ruralites recorded as engaged in agriculture. He concluded that the rural proletariat consisted, therefore, of 14.6 per cent of the rural labour force. He proceeded to say that peasants 'in the economic sense' have therefore constituted no more than 55 per cent of the total population of Russia (64 per cent of the population if their families are included) as against 17 per cent for the urban and rural proletariat. To wit, 'the scheme of Marx as related to Russia has proven itself with absolute exactitude'.[10]

Leaving aside the crescendo of the conclusion (and remembering what Marx said on a somewhat similar occasion about himself 'not being a Marxist'), a closer look at the division by gender within the figures of the census makes it clear where the error lies. The number given by the census for men 'independently occupied' in agriculture and in related professions is 14.3 million. The equivalent number for women is given as 1.9 million only. There can be little doubt what those figures represent. In most of the areas in which the information was collected, peasant women were not recorded as 'independent agricultural labour' for reasons that have to do with the images and presumptions of the recorders, but not at all with the realities of Russian rural life. The Russian peasant woman played as much of a role in the labour input of the family as the man would. Indeed, the Time Budget Studies have consistently shown her to work many more hours than he, that is, to roughly match men's labour in farming but to add to this extensive housewifely duties. While the female wage-labour figures were realistic, most of the rural 'housewives' were simply left out and then the figures related.

Once we accept the facts of the Russian peasant life and adjust the statistics accordingly, that is, assume the number of the recorded males engaged in agriculture on their own farms to be roughly equalled by the number of women so engaged, the percentage of wage labour in agriculture drops to 8.3 per cent of the rural labour, which indeed brings it within the range of figures suggested by the other estimates. The percentages assumed by Lositskii for the Russian proletariat will also drop accordingly. The figures are as in Table 2.2.

Many of the early Soviet studies since have simply chosen to repeat Lositskii's figures. On the other hand, Anfimov's calculation in 1969 based on the same source, that is, the 1897 census, has put the agricultural wage workers of European Russia at 2.3 per cent of the total farming population, that is, roughly 4.6 per cent of its mature labourers' component.[11] That is clearly much closer to the mark.

(C)　On the basis of the 1905 census of landownership in European Russia

TABLE 2.2   *Peasant differentiation (B)*

Category	1897 Lositskii figures			Amended figures		
	Men	Women	Total	Men	Women	Total
Farming ('000) on one's own farm	14 273	1932	16 205	14 273	14 273	28 546[a]
Rural wage labour etc. ('000)	1709	659	2368	1709	659	2363
The % of wage labour in farming	12.0	34.1	14.6	12.0	4.6	8.3

Source:
A. Bol'shakov and N. Rozhkov, *Istoriya khozyaistva rossii* (Leningrad, 1925) vol. 2, pp. 267–71.
Note:
The figure is still understated because many youngsters involved in agriculture were not considered on par with the rest of the farmers. A closer estimate (by the method used in Table 1.1 above) would increase this figure farther still to 34 million.

referred to above, Lenin built his own stratification chart, incorporated in his 'The Agrarian Programme of Social Democracy in the First Russian Revolution 1905–1907' published in 1908.[12] His categories and figures were as in Table 2.3.

The table is inadequate on several grounds. To begin with, Lenin's own theoretical position makes insufficient the delimitation of 'capitalist' farming (category c.) and /or of bourgeoisie purely on the grounds of land holding, even if one adds a proviso claiming it to be an approximation only. Lenin himself said that much in 1915. A farm of above 25 desyatin size could be, and often was, worked exclusively by family labour. A much smaller unit, benefiting from

TABLE 2.3   *Peasant differentiation (C1)*

Social stratum	European Russia 1905 Land per holding (des.)		Holdings	
	Range	Average	Mill.	%
a. Ruined feudal peasantry crused by exploitation	0.15	7.0	10.5	80.6
b. Middle peasantry	15.20	15.0	1.0	7.7
c. Peasant bourgeoisie and capitalist landed proprietors	20–500	46.7	1.5	11.5
d. Feudal latifundia	500+	2333.0	0.03	0.2
All strata	0–500+	21.4	13.3	100.0

Source:
V. I. Lenin, PSS, vol. 16, p. 203.

massive investment and/or closeness to an urban market, could be run as a capitalist farm. More importantly, the suggested categories of land holding are extremely vague. What does one mean by 'ruined, etc.'? If it means 'poor', it could be extended even further. If, on the other hand, it is to be related to the contemporary estimates of what constituted peasant well-being, relative as these were, it will have to be considered anew. Let us try to do it.

The house-to-house rural census and the Budget Studies of Kaluga gub. in the late 1890s can provide us here with a realistic set of empirical categories offered by practising rural researchers.[13] The study itself is one of the most acclaimed surveys of its type undertaken by the *zemstvo* statisticians and was often used as a model and as an example elsewhere and since. The Kaluga gub. was located in the centre of European Russia and was close in its most relevant social and economic parameters to the known averages for rural Russia *in toto*. The study of Kaluga gub. established a scale of six socio-economic strata of peasants in accordance with the land sown per household. The 'middle peasants' were defined as the categories with an area of land sown of 3 to 9 des. per household and systematic justification was given for that choice in terms of the actual operation of the peasant households. The arable land holding estimated as typical for this group was 7–16 des. Interestingly, as late as 1927 a study carried out by the Communist Academy in the fairly close gub. of Saratov (differences in the quality of land accepted), and using a completely different approach (i.e. Marxist class analysis operationalised via 'indices of exploitation') has concluded the middle peasant stratum to have typically an arable land holding of between 6.1 and 17 des., that is, as close a match to the Kaluga figures as one can ever expect.[14] The same applies to the study of Penza referred to in note 21 to follow. It is clearly the common perception of Russian rural specialists.

If we adopt the Kaluga figures, relate them to the table concerning the communal allotments of land in the source used by Lenin, and assume an average of one des. per household of private (i.e. non-communal) land to be owned in the middle peasant stratum, the results for the peasant households are as in Table 2.4.[15]

TABLE 2.4   *Peasant differentiation (C2)*

	European Russia 1905 Land allotment size	% of households
a. Well-to-do peasants	15 + des.	15.8
b. Middle peasants	7–15 des.	51.8
c. Poor peasants	–7 des.	32.4

Sources:
Statistika zemledeliya 1905 g. (St Petersburg, 1907) pp. 128–9; *Statisticheskoe opisanie kaluzhskoi gubernii* (Kaluga, 1897–8) vols I and II.

These amended figures give a rough but realistic idea of the actual socio-economic differentation within the Russian countryside. Their limitations for the consideration of class division and its transformations (as well as of the political potentials of the peasantry) would be still considerable because of (i) the static character of these figures, that is, the lack of attached indicators of socio-economic mobility, (ii) what was termed the 'optical illusion' by Oganovskii, resulting from the unifying of differentiation data coming from different regions, that is, when large discrepancies between regions would exaggerate the evidence of actual differentiation within each of them,[16] (iii) the need to relate these figures to the usage of labour, especially in an analysis contextualised within the classical or the Marxist traditions of political economy.

In conclusion, in so far as Lenin tried to express in his table the general poverty of the Russian peasantry, the fact of diversity within it and the difference between the typical land holdings of the peasants and the nobility of Russia, his point is well taken. However, his over-narrow mid-category, contradicted by the conclusions of the contemporary rural specialists, Marxist and non-Marxist alike, resulted in a sharply over-polarised picture. In particular, his bourgeois—capitalist stratum was a conjecture and a strongly overstated conjecture at that, as Lenin was to learn and to admit in the period of the revolution and of civil war in 1917–21.

(D) The figures suggested in Table 2.4 can be advanced further if one takes into account and relates to the data already discussed a major piece of evidence and an alternative dimension of analysis neglected in the above considerations. The 1897 census has recorded 18.4 million 'rural families' defined as units of at least two persons with a 'common roof' and 'common pot' (plus 740 000 single persons residing on their own). A 'wage worker or servant employed' was reported for 867 000 of those families (4.7 per cent) while a further 318 000 families (1.7 per cent) had at least two such 'workers or servants'.[17] The parallel figures for European Russia, probably somewhat more exact, were 13.0 million families, 867 000 of them with one permanent employee (6.7 per cent) and 225 000 (1.7 per cent) with two or more of them. Part of the 'rural employers', especially the larger ones, were the landed estates or the enterprises of the nobles, the merchants, the church and the state. Some of the 'workers and servants' performed actual personal service for the non-peasant residents (who accounted for less than 5 per cent of the population registered as rural). Assuming that one-third of the units with one 'worker-or-servant', and half of the more-than-one ones, represented the non-peasant rural employers – a realistic scenario – one can proceed to estimate on that basis the actual class division within the peasantry. By those figures, less than 1 per cent of the peasant farms would have employed permanent wage workers *on par* or in excess of their family labour, that is, two or more (plus seasonal labour), and less than 3 per cent would have a single full-time wage labourer (*batrak*). To remain on the side of caution, we can also consider these figures increased by half (with the rural employees of the non-peasants decreased accordingly). The figures would be still 1.2 per cent and 3.9 per cent only, that is, altogether one-twentieth of the total.

The fact that the 1897 census was taken in winter must put the wage-labour figures below the annual averages but that applies mainly to seasonal labour.

Looked at 'the other way round', the actual number of rural proletarians accounted for by the census was 2.4 million (i.e. roughly 4.5 per cent of the mature rural population of the empire). The figure for European Russia referred to was 4.6 per cent and for male rural wage labourers 1.8 million or 6.7 per cent of the total.[18] A Soviet demographer has estimated the wage workers to be about 5 per cent of the total rural population in 1913.[19] The wage labourers represented in the countryside smaller-than-average families and a considerable number of them were solitary males or females (*bobyli*). With all that in mind, the households of the rural proletarians would have accounted for 6–8 per cent of the total in European Russia, with 4–6 per cent as their share in rural population.

The peasant households of European Russia in 1897 could be therefore divided as in Table 2.5 in accordance with the use or offer of wage labour.

TABLE 2.5   *Peasant households and wage-labour in European Russia* (D)

Peasant households	Nos. (millions)	%
Capitalist farmers[a]	0.10–0.15	0.8(1.2)
Peasant employers[b]	0.34–0.51	2.6(3.9)
Family farmers	11.77–11.13	90.6(86.9)
Rural proletarians	0.78–1.04	6.0(8.0)
	13.00	100.0

Source:
Obshchii svod po imperii resultatov razrabotki dannykh pervoi vseobshchei perepisi naseleniya (St Petersburg, 1905) vol. I, pp. v–viii and 16–17.
Notes:
[a] Operationalised as employing two or more wage labourers, that is, potentially as much as the family labour used with the additional use of seasonal labour assumed. The second figure adds 50 per cent to the computation based on the census, accounting for possible over estimation of rural wage labour engaged outside peasant economy.
[b] Employing consistently one wage labourer (additional use of seasonal labour assumed). The second figure adds 50 per cent to the computation based on the census for reasons mentioned in note[a] .

(E)   Suggesting an alternative and a reinterpretation, one must state clearly that *as with all of the other figures*, these are and can be approximations only. The statistical data available for the pre-1917 period do not permit one to draw unequivocal conclusions concerning the socio-economic differentiation of the peasantry of Russia. A new attempt in this direction has its uses all the same, particularly in view of the fact that estimates which seem even less adequate, have acquired by default and endless repetition the status of established truth to be then uncritically presented as substantiation for a variety of deductions.

Table 2.4 offered figures that are less in doubt, their main limitation being methodological, that is, the rough nature of such an exercise, made worse by the differences between a general picture and the actual divisions between and within each region, district and village. Also, the amount of land held is far from ideal as the single index of rural wealth, for reasons that were often enough stated.[20] It is still the best we can do or was done. Derived from the 1905 census of landownership and related to the empirically drawn categories argued, the figures show that by land held peasants were divided into well-to-do, middling and poor (inclusive of the rural proletariat) in a rough proportion of 1:4:2.

We can divide these figures further by cross-relating them to the pattern of rural employment in 1897 as presented in Table 2.6 (which combines Tables 2.4 and 2.5). The assumption adopted is that the difference of seven years would have not produced a large discrepancy in *proportions* and that all of the employers of permanent wage labour are well off in terms of land-use.

TABLE 2.6   *The socio-economic differentiation of Russian peasantry: an alternative table*[a] (E)

Categories[b]	European Russia 1897–1905 Peasant households %	Population[c] %
Capitalist farmers	0.8(1.2)	1.2 –1.8
Peasant family farmers:		
rich	2.6(3.9)	
well-to-do	12.4(10.7)	94.2–95.8
middling	51.8	
poor	24.4(26.4)	
Rural proletarians	8.0(6.0)	3.0–4.0[d]

Sources:
Obshchii svod po imperii resul'tatov razrabotki dannykh pervoi vseobshchei perepisi naseleniya (St Petersburg, 1905) vol. I; *Statistika zemledel'ya 1905 g.* (St Petersburg, 1907); *Statisticheskoe opisanie kaluzhskoi gubernii* (Kaluga, 1897–8) vols I and II.
Notes:
[a] For initial data and analysis, see Tables 2.4 and 2.5. It was assumed that all of the peasant employers are 'well-to-do' in terms of land holding and all of their permanent wage workers and servants came from the peasant or 'rural proletarian' households.
[b] Capitalist farmers (potential) were defined as households employing two or more permanent wage workers. 'Rich' were delimited as those who while holding more than 15 des. employed one permanent labourer (i.e. used more family labour than permanent wage labour on their farms). The categories 'poor' and 'well-to-do' are the residuum, once the figures of employees and employers are subtracted from those in Table 2.4.
[c] We assume the size of the family in the rich strata to be higher by half than average and those of the 'rural proletarians' to be half of it. In both cases the adjustment underestimates, if any, the extent of discrepancies in the typical household family size of the different strata. The population size of family farmer is the residuum.
[d] This figure matches closely the 7 per cent share of resident landless households as estimated for the 1890s by A. Chelintsev, 'Pomeshchich'e khozyaistvo v Rossii pered revolyutsiei', *Zapiski Instituta izucheniya Rossii*, vol. I, 1925, p. 75.

Translation of percentages of the households into general population figures would increase the share of the wealthier groups and decrease it for the rural poor and proletarians. We used notional 1:2:3 proportions to represent it.

Despite the broad margins of error, a fairly consistent picture of the Russian countryside emerges. About 4 per cent of the peasant households would have been the more prosperous ones who employed permanent wage labour, but only about 1 per cent were wage-labour employers with enough employees for them to be possibly designated as capitalist farmers. Some 6–8 per cent of the 'rural households' were those of the wage labourers, but only 3–4 per cent if the total population is considered. (If we try to put some figures also to Lenin's concept of *batrak s nadelom*, i.e. a *de facto* rural worker who supplements his wages by supplementary farming, the share of households with up to one des. of communal land was 1.9 per cent, which would alter our conclusions but little.)

Those figures are remarkably close to the conclusions of the most significant *zemstvo* study of a fairly typical *guberniya* in central Russia on the eve of the First World War by a major Marxist economist, V. Groman (a 'left-wing' Menshevik and the man who was to direct *de facto* the preparation of the first Five-Year Plan of the USSR).[21] The picture is mainly that of a mass of family farms in which nine-tenths of the rural population lived and produced. These social boundaries were anything but static because different strata of the peasants underwent constant and massive processes of socio-economic mobility. Their diversity would be therefore a matter of scale *as well as* of the dynamics operating.

Russian peasants and rural proletarians shared space with non-farming rural residents. The rural employees of state administration and police, the clergy, the medics, the teachers and the *zemstvo* employees amounted in 1897 to 384 000, that is, about 1 per cent of the full-time rural labour force. The number of 'nobles by birth' and their families residing 'in the country' was about 650 000 that is, 0.6 per cent of the population total. The specialised merchants and craftsmen, that is, those not engaged in the ordinary peasant mixture of farming and other activities, would account for not more than 3 per cent, probably less. We are talking therefore of less than 5 per cent of the rural non-peasant population. The 'craftsmen villages' (e.g. in Tula gub.) would offer here some regional variations.[22]

To recapitulate, any realistic analysis of the Russian peasantry must take account of socio-economic differentiation and of regional diversities. It should not overstate them, however. The main message of the population figures was that at the turn of the nineteenth century and until fairly late into the twentieth century, two-thirds of the people of Russia were peasants and nine-tenths of them would be of peasant stock; the same held for the Russian army and the Russian industrial working class. In the rural areas where 85 per cent of the Russians lived, nearly nine-tenths of the population was peasant by the strictest definition of the term. The editors of the 1897 census of population were right in the essence of their summation.[23] Numerically speaking, peasants were Russia.

3 The Development of Capitalism in Russia

You are destitute
Yet full of riches
You are all-powerful
Yet helpless,
Mother Russia.
                    Nikolai Nekrasov, 1877

On your wild expanses, My Russia
Now the same, now different seems
For she turns a new face upon the world
And the heart beats with quick changing dreams . . .
. . . and I see over the boundless steppe rising
The new America's star.
                    Aleksander Blok, 1913

A. THE NEW AMERICA'S STAR

The riches of Russia were as impressive as its size. By the turn of the century the dukedom of Moscow had grown into an empire of 26.5 million square kilometres – more than a hundred times the size of Great Britain, nearly three times that of the USA, one-sixth of the world's land surface. Its population topped 125 million.[1] The resources of soil, forest, minerals and human labour made Russia's productive potential fabulous. The actual production figures show Russia to be second in the world in grain production and first in exports. The indices of industrial advance, for example, of the production of steel and textiles, use of mechanical power, etc., put Russia among the top five world powers – very substantial, if never heading that list.[2]

When related to the size of the population, to the territory and to the labour force, these huge absolute figures reveal abject poverty and technological backwardness as against Europe and the USA. In 1900 the income per capita in Russia was three times lower than in Germany, four times below the UK, one-third lower than even the Balkans.[3] Because of the extreme diversity between the very rich and the very poor these

103

average figures still understate the poverty of Russia's poor.[4] As to the production per capita the Russian figures for 1898 were 8 per cent of the comparable British figures for iron, 2 per cent for coal and 10 per cent for textiles, while the similar comparison with Germany has shown 13 per cent, 4 per cent and 36 per cent respectively. The Russian production of iron *per worker* was half that recorded in Western Europe. The production of grain *per unit of land* was less than one-third of that of Germany or Great Britain. The second largest railway network in the world was, at the same time, the smallest in Europe in relation to the area and the population it served.[5] A prominent Russian economist of those times summed it up by saying, 'we are the poorest of the cultured countries'.[6] Notice both the statement and the point of comparison.

While manifestly 'backward' as against 'the cultured countries', the contemporary Russian economy was showing signs of rapid ascent and transformation. During the decade that preceded the 1897 population census, the production of iron trebled while that of coal and textiles doubled. The rate of increase in production of the Russian industry was growing also and reached in the 1893–7 period an impressive annual average of 15.9 per cent, treble the percentage of the annual production increases recorded for the 1878–87 decade.[7] Outside agriculture the nature of production processes was changing, with the heavy industry and the large-scale enterprises increasingly taking pride of place as against the craftsmen and the small workshops.

The agricultural production was increasing but at a much less spectacular speed than that of industry.[8]

Changes in production figures corresponded with broader social and political motions. The rate of natural growth of the population was estimated to have doubled since the first half of the nineteenth century.[9] Migration had grown rapidly and at its centre extensive processes of urbanisation and colonisation occurred. During the period 1900–13 up to 4 million peasants settled in towns and an additional 2½ million had made their way to the areas of colonisation in the Asiatic parts of Russia.[10] Two-thirds of Russia's population over the age of 10 was illiterate in 1897, but the educational facilities were spreading and by 1913 more than half of the appropriate age group was attending primary schools.[11] State administrators also tried to come to grips with some other 'social ills' and 'pockets of backwardness': reforms of peasant agriculture, of the labour conditions, of the army, etc. were enacted or considered. A major outburst of political activity outside the 'official circle' of top bureaucrats heralded new times: new demands of the *zemstvo* local authorities, the establishment of two socialist and a constitutionalist party were followed by the revolution of 1905–7, the proclamation of a parliament (*Duma*) in 1905 and by the victory of the opposition to it in two elections.[12]

How was one to make sense of those simultaneous strands and determinants of Russia's history and political economy, its riches and its poverty, its technological backwardness and its economic ascent, its acclaimed conservatism and its revolutionary flair? Most of the Russians to whom such 'making sense' was a preoccupation, a passion or a duty, looked for illumination to Europe's past, be it England, France or Germany: industry, revolution or empire. Questions concerning the nature of Russian society were related directly to those concerning the possibilities of its transformation and social change. At the earlier stage of the nineteenth century such 'Western' anticipations and yardsticks of advance were opposed by a current that assumed Russia's near-Messianic exceptionality, and looked for its roots in the depths of the Slavonic soul, tsardom, Orthodoxy or, more sociologically, in the eternal unchangeability of the Russian communal sense (*sobornost'*) expressed in the peasant commune. At the extreme wing of that tendency, a few romantics scandalised everybody by claiming Russia's Asiatic nature and heritage, deriving this from the times when Scythians or the Cumans roamed the Steppe. A major attempt to work out a third view of Russia that refuted both the 'Westerners' and the Slavophile position went under with the physical destruction of the revolutionary populists of the People's Will Party.[13]

The view that Russia would follow the inevitable road mapped out by the West European societies was contested also by some of the Russian economists who could not see how the relative poverty and the massive 'peasantness' of Russia, its limited market and surpluses available for investment, could provide a starting point for the development of its economy along West European lines. During the last decade of the nineteenth century this debate seemed to be rapidly running out of steam. The dramatic rise of industry, railways and mining and their share in the national economy, the growth of towns and of the urban working class, the rapid increase of trade, vivacious speculation, expanding banking etc., offered evidence that the 'Westerners' had won the debate conclusively, on the strength of the predictions they offered. Those who doubted them were reduced to silence or to defensive postures, at least for the moment. Sharply in focus for 'the educated' and the politically active, a dramatic social transformation was taking place and was recognised increasingly as the development of capitalism in Russia.

To those Russians who systematically set out to understand the working of their society, mostly out of a wish to see it changed, capitalism offered the paramount conceptual model of Russia's present and future. The model was descriptive as well as prescriptive, that is, it offered analysis and prediction while at the same time explaining why the advance of capitalism was to provide the conditions for Russia's bright future. Europe and the USA offered a theory, an imagery, a historiography and a language of experience that Marx's genius helped to name *Das Kapital*. Others would simply (and vaguely) call it 'progress'. The model's plausibility rested on a powerful meta-theory of evolution and of its immanent social laws as understood and supported by the whole authority of Western scholarship: the British classical political economy, the French rationalist political theory, the German idealist philosophy, the Marxist interpretations of the 2nd International and the political creed of nineteenth-century liberalism. The experience of the West and its best theoretical summations, as much as the growing evidence of industrialisation in Russia, had given credence to the profound hope of the Russian intellectuals to see Russia rapidly overcome the morass and the shame of poverty and slavishness of the majority of its people, and to join the civilised nations at the world centres of wealth, power and culture: to 'see over the boundless steppes rising the new America's star'.[14]

*   *   *

Capitalism signified *a type of political economy* that interlinks with a broader social structure and is definable as an historical epoch. At the core of this socio-economic system and its conceptual model lies the linked phenomenon of a highly advanced division of labour and of commodity production. The advanced character of the division of labour is expressed in mechanisation and the systematic use of science within the process of production, as dramatised by the term 'industrial revolution'. The advanced character of commodity production is expressed in the profit-directed commodisation of the major 'inputs' of production, inclusive of labour power and of the use of land. Consequent on it is the centrality and the extensive nature of the 'free' market as a social institution through which prices are adjusted, defining the flow of goods, wage labour and land usage as well as of credit, of technological know-how and of legitimate coercion.[15]

Capitalist enterprise acts as the basic unit of capitalist economy, relating private ownership of basic equipment and of raw materials to the use of labour. Free ownership of goods as well as free contractual wage labour must be understood within a system of political economy in which the direct producers do not own the means of production. The process of production is subject to massive investment and the competition dictates most of the investment choices. 'Capital' is thereby not just an accumulated lump of goods or of money but a self-reproducing, market-regulated social system of commodity production. A powerful and never-ending drive of every capitalist enterprise and of capitalism *in toto* is determined by the combinations of profit motive, competition and the necessity for capital accumulation. The way to maximise profit and to win in the depersonalised, merciless and endless competitive struggle within the market is constantly to improve technology and the organisation of production, to make input less expensive and/or to control distribution or else to go under. Careful cost-accountancy, elaborate credit systems, struggles for new markets and constant increases in productivity follow as a matter of course. The general advance of such types of economy is cyclical, with periods of 'boom' regularly followed by periods of depression.

The advance of capitalist economy is linked to a variety of necessary social conditions, interdependent institutions and social consequences. A new hierarchy of social power and a new major dimension of social conflict becomes decisive: the big capitalist at the top and the propertiless producer at the bottom are locked in constant conflict over wages. A new class system and typical patterns of class struggle come into being. The place of the peasants in the pre-capitalist era, as the major producers of material goods (and of the surplus on which the well-being of the rulers rested), is being taken over by the industrial working class. The control of the crucial components of economy shifts from the rent-absorbing landowners to the profit-making bourgeoisie. The 'industrial revolution' led to rapid urbanisation and to a related change in the countryside: its mechanisation and capitalisation. While agriculture is being technologically transformed and reorganised into capitalist enterprises, its share in production declines as against that of industry. The accumulation of capital and the struggle for markets restructure both inter-state and intra-state relations. On the world scene it establishes new types of dependency, promoting colonialism and imperialism. The extending market, transport and communications make large-scale social entities (e.g. nations) 'real' for the first time in terms of actual and constant interdependence. The population rapidly increases. In the political sphere the matrix and the needs of the free market world result in enhanced social mobility, parliamentarian rule and the extension of democratic rights, curtailing the old ruling classes that based their strength on the royal court, landownership, the army and the church.[16]

The transition from feudalism to capitalism would be an offensive of the forces of progress against the institutional arrangement of the past: rural latifundias, absolutist empires, the privileges of 'social estates', the 'rural cretinism' of the peasants' way of living under domination of the landlords. Every aspect of social and personal life is penetrated, influenced and transformed by the establishment of capitalism: the family, education, the legal system (especially the civil law), etc. The very nature of the human mind changes by reflecting the new world: competitiveness and 'adjustability' as much as scientific procedures or the use of mathematics, are increasingly fed into human consciousness by the very working of capitalism. So are new types of 'fetishism'. Capitalism is a new civilisation, a new way of living.

A common theoretical ancestry of rationalism and classical political economy and the close study of the British industrial experience produced all through Europe two major party-political strands. The liberals accepted capitalism and free market as the ultimate form of economy and society (admittedly, due for some limited amendments following the evolution of human rationality, scholarship and good reason). The socialists aimed at a revolutionary disalienation of humanity, which would mean a new post-capitalist political economy and social structure, established and dominated by the proletariat.

This concept of capitalism has carried two consequent historiographies. Capitalism has its predecessor in the feudal 'mode of production' or else in 'backwardness'. Both the liberals of the nineteenth century and the Marxists of the 2nd International accepted England as the genesis and the 'classical' case of capitalism, due to spread globally. To the liberals the establishment of capitalism was essentially the discovery by mankind of the one rational way to live in optimal wealth and liberty. To Marx, while some elements of it could have occurred at any stage, the inception of capitalism begins with the times of vicious repressions which he described as 'the so-called primary accumulation'. The concentration and the productive investment of riches by the few meets then the alienation from the means of production, that is, mostly land, of the mass of the producers. These are thrown thereby on to the labour market, both as employees and as the unemployed and ever-ready 'reserve army' of labour. That is when and how capitalism rises in the context of growing commodity production to be eventually defeated and eradicated by the proletariat.

As to the immediate facts and anticipations concerning capitalism, both liberals and Marxists agreed fully in those days. Capitalism comes to dominate production and exchange, beginning with industry, but eventually transforms society *in toto*. Its capacity to penetrate, dissolve and transform after its own image other economic and social forms explains its rapid extension and its eventual global mastery. Furthermore, capitalism as a socio-economic system reproduces itself while 'deepening' its characteristics. The process of accumulation and concentration of capital does not stop with the non-capitalist producers dispossessed; the smaller capitalist enterprises are being devoured by the larger ones.

All that was seen as a matter of necessities, definable (and to be defined) by science of society as laws of accumulation of capital or of progress, *on par* with the laws of nature. On the other hand, the adoption and usage of the model of capitalism was never simply a detached summation of the West European experience of industrialisation. We have already stressed the way it was written into political thought about the future in Russia. To the liberals, the essential rationality of capitalism and parliamentary rule were to be fought for and, once established, defended against reactionaries and utopians. To Marx and even more so to his followers of the 2nd International, capitalism was a necessary stage on the road to socialism. It was historically progressive, to begin with, promoting the unheard-of growth of forces of production necessary for the advance of the well-being of mankind and establishing the material base for a future socialist society. It was also a new system of exploitation which, besides the flow of goods, produced the conditions of its own destruction, that is, a working class in opposition to it and critical social science challenging it. In the historical process the new most progressive social class of the modern proletariat and the most advanced social theorists adopt each other, establishing a revolutionary camp able to challenge, to defeat, and to substitute the capitalist 'establishment'.

With the essential nature of Russia's development seemingly established in that light, to those who took as given the theory of progress and/or the model of the development of capitalism in Russia three more specific questions followed. First, where exactly did Russia stand on the developmental ladder of advance? How far had the manifest industrial development transformed Russian economy and society and, in particular, how deeply did it penetrate the massive majority of population within rural Russia? Also, when was it to reach the new political stage that was assumed necessarily to follow economic advances, for example, as in France of 1848 or Germany of 1871. The second question was one of action, that is, would it all proceed spontaneously or must one try to force the pace of the inevitable processes and 'unfetter' them, by removing major obstacles from their path? Also, should one try to moderate their harshness? Third and last, those who opted for action had to choose between the specific political models made available by Europe – England, France or Germany; liberalism, revolutionary republicanism or a monarchism with a 'modernising' and imperialist bent. They had consequently to decide also on the political forces, alliances and strategies that would bring their goals to fruition.

B. INDUSTRY, CAPITAL AND 'UNEVEN DEVELOPMENT'

The mainstream of Russia's economic history during the period of our particular interest underwent a double cycle in which the 'low' of 1891 was followed by an economic boom in the second half of the 1890s, a recession in the years 1900–9 and a new boom in 1910–13.[1] The political and social history of the period was clearly linked with the patterns of economic growth. To present Russian economic history with the full weight of the social drama involved, it went from the Great Famine of 1891/3 via the industrial 'economic miracle' of the 1890s to the 1899 financial crash and steep industrial decline of 1900/3, followed directly by war, revolution and heavy repressions. It then proceeded through an economic boom in 1910–13, towards the First World War, the revolutions of 1917 and the civil war of 1918–21. The very nature of the 'economic cycle' seemed to change. The desperate straits in which Russian economy and society found themselves at the beginning of the 1890s were clearly determined by a natural disaster – the failure of crops and the resulting famine in 1891–2. The next economic downturn corresponded and was related to the crisis of industrial profits and investments in Western Europe (indeed, signalled it for the whole of Europe), even though the 'natural' drop in agricultural production especially in 1905–6) played a role in it.[2] Russian industry missed its share in the European upturn of 1905–8 – the consequence of war and of revolution.[3] By 1910 Russia had 'rejoined' the All-European economic cycle and was going 'up'.

There exists a broad consensus of scholarly opinion on the immediate causes of the post-1893 industrial 'leap forward' in Russia. An economic boom was triggered off in the 1890s by an extensive programme of state-generated railway construction and the consequent large-scale orders for industrial goods, by the harshly protectionist state policies promoting industrialisation and, to a lesser degree, by the increase in the export of Russia's grain.[4] By the twentieth century, the impact of the railway construction had slackened, but the Russian government continued its policies of state intervention and investment, as well as of high protective tariffs on manufactured goods to the benefit of home industries. The rates of profit in Russia, which were much higher than those in Western Europe, as well as massive government-guaranteed loans, encouraged foreign investment, which brought an average of 200 000 000 roubles' worth (roughly $100 000 000 in values of the day) of foreign capital into Russia each year.[5] A sharp drop in foreign investment in the 1904–7 period of the war and the revolution 'levelled out' by 1909. The resumption of massive foreign investments, the extension of the internal market and the rapid increase in state expenditures offered major stimuli for the further leap in industrial growth and capital accumulation recorded in 1910–13.

The development of capitalism in Russia, that is, the 'stage' it reached, was usually 'measured' by the growth of the manufacturing industries, by the expansion of markets, the movements of capital, the development of the industrial working class and the extent of urbanisation. Since the time when the 'anti-industrial' policies of Nikolai I ended and the emancipation of the serfs removed the legal bondage from most of the labour, industrialisation proceeded with alacrity.[6] This development was uneven, but the long-term trend was 'up', and at considerable speed. The same held true for the number of workers per factory, the top enterprises of Russia often becoming the largest in Europe. Table 3.1, published in 1906, offers an indication of this trend.

TABLE 3.1   *The industrialisation of Russia, 1887–97*

Year	Number of factories	Number of workers
1887	30 888	1 318 000
1890	32 254	1 425 000
1897	39 029	2 098 000

Source:
A. Pogozharev, *Uchet chislennosti i sostava rabochikh Rossii* (St. Petersburg, 1906) p.6.

In 1900 the country's foremost statistician of industry, V. Varzar, produced a combined picture of the 'registered' factories and mines of Russia. It accounted for 38 041 enterprises with 2 373 400 workers, an annual production value of 3440 million roubles and a wage-bill of 477 million roubles.[7] The share of mining in it was about one-tenth of the workforce and one-seventh of the production value. While half of the

Russian factory labour force was engaged in the very large units of more than 1000 workers, an average enterprise would still have sixty-two workers only, using 38 h.p. of mechanical power.[8] These figures indicate the extensive small-scale production, yet still overestimate its 'technical base' and the typical sizes. They did not include enterprises with less than ten to fifteen workers and/or the 'handicraft and cottage industries' (*kustarnichestvo*) which, using simple tools in small, often family-based units, manufactured much of Russia's consumer goods. There is no reliable information about them but they employed (often seasonally or part time) millions of labourers. They worked not only for consumers but also secured higher profits of the larger-scale industry and of the merchants who often subcontracted labour-intensive work at incredibly low rates. In 1900 there were in Moscow 190 000 'non-factory' small enterprise labourers as against 180 000 factory workers. These figures increased in the provinces, for example, in Kostroma and its *guberniya* the ratio was 149 000 and 23 000.[9]

The rapidly improving work of the Russian social scientists put to use new forms of tabulation and indices of the economic growth. In 1906 Prokopovich produced the first estimate of Russia's national income, which enabled systematic comparison with the rest of Europe.[10] These figures have since been considered anew but all those who revised them accepted their essential soundness.[11] More importantly for our purpose, Prokopovich used similar methods to establish figures for 1900 and 1913 which provided for a fair estimate of the basic economic trends (see Table 3.2). During the 1900–13 period, the Russian national income increased by three-quarters but only by a quarter if per capita production in constant prices is considered. The value of agricultural production was 45.2 per cent of the total in 1900 and 47.7 per cent in 1913. The increase of agricultural production in constant prices was in fact less than half of that in manufacturing, but that was more than compensated by the substantial increase of the international prices of foodstuff. As a result, the proportion of manufactured products in the total national income was 21.2 per cent in 1900 and 21.7 per cent in 1913. The total annual growth of the national income was about 5 per cent but less than $1\frac{1}{2}$ per cent in constant prices and per capita. The gap between the per capita national income of Russia and that of Germany and France was, by 1913, exactly the same as in 1900 – Russian figures were one-third of those of Germany and France and the gap had even slightly increased as against Britain, from 1:4 to 1:4.5.[12]

Other figures for the period (Table 3.3) show even more clearly that despite the crisis of 1899–1909, manufacturing and mining were expanding at a considerable rate while the agriculture fared less well.

TABLE 3.2   *National income of European Russia, 1900 and 1913*[a]

	1900	1913 Figures	Per cent of 1900
Total income (roub.)	6600	11 800	178.8
Total income (roub. in 1900 prices)[b]		9170	138.9
Total argicultural production (roub).	2985	5630	188.6
Total agricultural production (roub. in 1900 prices)[b]		3995	133.8
Total manufactured production (roub.)	1402	2567	183.0
Total manufactured production (roub. in 1900 prices)[b]		2282	162.3
National income per capita (roub.)	63	101	160.0
National income per capita (roub. in 1900 prices)[b]		79	125.4

Source:
S. Prokopovich, *Opyt izucheniya narodnogo dokhoda 50 gub evropeiskoi Rossii* (Moscow, 1918) pp. 67–70.
Notes:
[a] The figures were given for the fifty gubs. of European Russia where three-quarters of the population of the empire lived. It excluded, therefore, the Asian, Polish and Caucasian areas. Only the flow of goods (and not of 'services') was accounted for. All the basic studies of the post-revolutionary period, inclusive of those of the Soviet Central Statistical Board (TsSu), are based on this pioneering work of Prokopovich.
In 1931, Prokopovich revised some of these figures, by increasing them, especially in so far as agriculture and small-scale manufacturing were concerned. For discussion, see M. Falkus, 'Russia's National Income, 1913: A Revaluation', *Economics*, vol. XXXV, nos. 137–40 1968, and A. Vainshtein, *Narodnyi dokhod Rossii* (Moscow, 1969). Both seemed to doubt Prokopovich's new version and suggested some revisions of their own that were not substative, however.
[b] The general increase in prices during the 1900–13 period was estimated by Prokopovich to be 27 per cent (40.9 per cent for agriculture and 12.5 per cent for the products of the manufacturing industries). Prokopovich, op. cit., p. 69.

(The generally used single index of grain production overstated agriculture's achievements because animal husbandry was doing much worse than corn.)[13] The nominal value of exports doubled; all through the period half of its value was derived from grain and one-quarter more from the other agricultural products. The capital accumulation was high and banking as well as markets of goods registered considerable growth. Between 1900 and the First World War, the nominal value of capital and the turnover of industrial enterprises had nearly doubled while the state expenditure had increased more than twofold.

The long-term aggregate output of Russian manufacturing and mining was considered anew by the 1960s work of Goldsmith, who based his work on Kondrat ev's pioneer effort in the 1920s.[14] According

TABLE 3.3 *Indicators of Russian economic development, 1900 and 1913*

Indicator	1900	1913 Figures	Per cent of 1900
(A) *Population* total (million)[a]	131.6	161.3	122.3
of which urban (%)	13	17	—
Production			
(B) Grain (million metric tonnes)[b]	59.0	74.6	126
(B) Iron and steel (million metric tonnes)	2.7	4.0	148
(B) Coal (million metric tonnes)	16.4	36.3	221
(B) Cotton consumed by industry (million metric tonnes)	0.262	0.424	162
(B) *Exports* total (million roubles)	716	1520	212 (164)[c]
Industrial enterprises			
(B) Capital (million roubles)	2032	3900	192 (171)[d]
(B) Turnover (million roubles)	3761	6882	183 (163)[d]
(C) *State Expenditure* (million roubles)	1464[e]	3094	211

Sources:

(A) V. Den, *Kurs ekonomicheskoi geografii* (Lenigrad, 1924) p. 9.

(B) P. Lyashchenko, *Istoriya narodnogo khozyaistva SSSR* (Moscow, 1952) vol. II, pp. 395 and 414–15.

(C) A. Finn-Enotaevskii, *Kapitalizm v Rossii (1890–1917 gg.)* (Moscow, 1952) vol. I, pp. 179, 185 and 189.

Notes:

[a] Excluding Finland and estimated by extrapolation.

[b] For grain production, the averages for 1899–1901 and 1911–13 were used rather than data for 1900 and 1913 in view of the distortion sometimes engendered by the use of individual years, particularly in view of the atypically good harvest in 1913 (see text). Lyashchenko figure (relating 1899 and 1913) is given in brackets.

[c] The general rise in prices during the period of 1900–13 was estimated by the author as 29 per cent (Lyashchenko, op. cit., pp. 350–1). The figure in brackets indicates the consequent increase in exports in constant 1900 prices. Prokopovich suggested the price rise to be 27 per cent (see Table 3.2).

[d] Figures in brackets are amended by 12.5% i.e. the increase in prices of industrial products as suggested by Prokopovich in Table 3.2

[e] An average of the figures available on state expenditure for 1899 and 1901.

to those figures the output doubled during the 1890–1900 decade and increased by a further three-fifths in 1900–13 (all of it in the second half of that period).[15] It would have averaged thereby $5\frac{1}{2}$ per cent per annum for the period of 1861–1913. The much less reliable estimates of the handicraft and cottage industries assumed their increase also. Their share in the value of manufactured production was said by Goldsmith to have declined from about half the total in 1861 to one-fifth in 1913 – a probable overestimation of rightly identified trends. In mining, especially of coal and oil, the overall rate of increase of production was higher than that in the manufacturing industries.[16]

Turning to the accumulation of capital, its advance expressed and underlay Russia's industrialisation. To a considerable degree this was based on foreign investments. Within the joint-stock companies in manufacturing, mining and banking, foreign capital had quadrupled in 1890–1900 and multiplied a further two and a half times during the 1900–13 period. Its share of the total had increased during the twenty-three years from 25 per cent to 41 per cent. (Once capital other than shareholding is also considered, the foreign investment and ownership figures decline by about one-third.)[17] Its characteristics were authoritatively defined by Eventov as (i) being involved with '. . . large and concentrated industries while avoiding completely small industries and crafts', (ii) playing a '. . . limited role . . . in branches unrelated to the state economy and state finances', (iii) acting as the senior partner 'and the chief midwife' of the Russian mining industry (see Figure 3.1).[18]

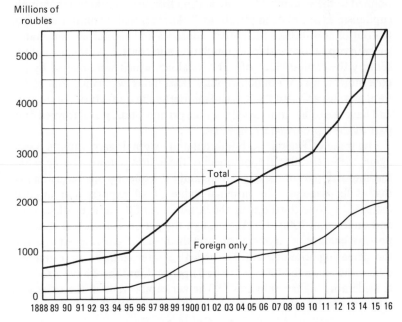

FIGURE 3.1   *Capital investments in Russia: total and foreign*[a] *(shareholding companies in manufacturing, trade and banking)*

Sources:
L. Eventev, *Inostrennye Kapitaly v Russkoi promyshlennosti*, (Moscow, 1931) based on P. OL' *Inostrannye Kapitaly v Rossii* (Moscow, 1925).

Note:
[a] The percentage of foreign-owned shareholding capital in Russia grew from 17 percent 1880 to 26 percent in 1890 and 45 percent in 1900. It then remained stationary until 1914 (47 percent) and dropped during the First World War. It was 38 percent in 1916.

Importantly, a large share of the foreign capital was invested in banking and/or crediting the Russian government and major municipalities.[19] During the whole period the internal divisions between foreign investments were changing. The relative role of the German capital declined, the French surged, the British and Belgian proceeded steadily.

Russian economists have also considered the build up of the native private capital within the Russian industries. It increased at a considerable rate but there is no reliable way to estimate it fully. The investment scene was often secretive and complex: many of the native capitalists have operated in partnership with foreign ones, while others ran their own factories via family ties, or with the help of 'hidden' sponsors as well as on credit provided by private banking. A number of Russian economic historians have argued that the significance of the native capital accumulation was major (and understated). They also pointed to the structural transformation from free market to monopoly capitalism as one of its implications.[20] Another major component often left out of accounts of the native industries and capital was the state's share in capital ownership accumulation and control. At the turn of the century the capital value of railways alone, which were owned by the government, was 3.5 billion roubles. This figure was twice that of the total private capital in the Russian mining and manufacturing industries and have the total estimate value of the private lands. It still formed only part of the state-owned properties.

The trade of Russia, both internal and external, grew rapidly. Once again, the international component of the figures is more reliable, while the 'internal' part of them is less so (and subsequently open to estimates that differ widely). The nominal value of all exports and imports increased by one-third during the last decade of the nineteenth century and doubled in 1900–13. All through the period Russia had shown a positive balance of payments, mostly the result of growing exports and the increasing price of grain. The growth of internal trade was estimated by Lyashchenko for 1900–13 to be 31 per cent, but there have also been considerably higher estimates.[21] The per capita trade in the cities was estimated to be twenty times higher than in the rural areas.[22]

*   *   *

As anticipated by the 'models' of capitalism, the advance of large-scale and highly mechanised industry, the accumulation of capital, the growing integration of economy, and the development of trade were aspects of one major process. The other side of that coin was 'the making of' a new map of social classes. Contemporary attention was drawn particularly to the advance of wage labour and at its centre of a semi-skilled industrial working class. Once again, we are short of 'hard' evidence prior to the census of 1897. Tugan-Baranovskii's pioneering work has assessed the industrial working force to have been 1.3 million in 1887 with a growth rate of about 6 per cent per annum during the decade that followed.[23]

The Russian Ministry of Finance carried out its own further analysis of the data collected by the 1897 census, concentrating on wage labour only.[24] According to these findings, wage labourers, engaged in manufacturing, mining, transport, construction and trade, numbered 3 222 000. Its largest occupational subcategories were those in textiles (16.5 per cent), metal (11.5 per cent), construction (10.8 per cent) and the garment industry (10.2 per cent) followed by food industry processing (6.6 per cent), railways (5.4 per cent), mining (5.1 per cent) and horse-carting (*izvoz*) (3.6 per cent).[25] A number of general social characteristics were established by that study, offering a rough composite picture of the Russian contemporary working class. About 80 per cent of them were peasants by 'social estate'. Women provided 13.9 per cent of it but their percentage varied considerably, from nearly half of the working force in the textile industry to next to none in the metal industry and transport. Related to national averages the group was higher in literacy (about three-fifth of its males), and younger – very few in it were above the age of 40. A clear majority of 58.5 per cent of the men were single or lived separately from their families. At the same time, 27 per cent of them were defined as heads of 'large families' (with more than six members each), indicating a large proportion of 'bread-winners away from their families'.[26]

As indicated thereby, many of the urban wage labourers were peasant-workers with connections to the countryside that ranged from seasonal work in towns, to the definitely urban way of life and employment, at times coupled with a seasonal return to the village to help with harvesting and/or to hold on to the 'communal rights' to land. Many kept their families in the village, possibly aiming to return to farming at some later stage. Quite a number of the wage workers were peasants' sons who went to town for a period, to save money or to buy horses before a partition or to get married and pay off taxes. There was also a considerable group of peasants-craftsmen, especially in the construction trades, often within labour gangs recruited from the same village, sharing expenses and operating under an elected 'elder' – the *artel'*. Most of these went back to the village for ploughing, harvesting, holiday and rest (which explained why the mid-winter date of the 1897 census has doubtlessly underestimated their figures).

Because of ideological reasons the actual extent of the rural connections of the urban labour was often sharply disputed. According to Dementev, much quoted by liberals and Marxists, these links were limited and mostly formal.[27] On the other hand, the study of different industrial areas carried out at the beginning of the 1890s has shown that while in the factories of the province of Moscow about 80 per cent of the labour force 'stayed in town the whole year round' (i.e. did not depart to their villages for every farming season), in the factories of Kharkov, Kiev and Voronezh in the south that percentage dropped to 49, 42 and 24 respectively.[28] When in 1908 a much more precise study of the Printers' Union of Moscow looked at members of this highly skilled occupation, (and often the 'political vanguard' of the city's working force), it showed that 46 per cent of them were personally involved in part-time farming. About 52 per cent of the printers kept their families in the village and 89.6 per cent systematically sent money contributions to their relatives in the countryside. An average sum of these contributions was 100 roubles per man per annum (i.e. the equivalent of about three months' wages).[29]

The 3.2 million workers in manufacturing, mines and railways were usually considered the hard core of the Russian working class. Its 'fringe' was formed in 1897 by the 5.9 million other wage workers. Of those, 2.7 million were engaged in agriculture. This social stratum was partly discussed in Chapter 2 and Addendum 2 and we shall return to it in the text to follow. Of the other wage workers, 1.1 million were described as non-permanent and unskilled manual labourers employed on a 'daily' basis and 2.8 million were servants, mostly personal servants (82 per cent of those were women). Lositskii has estimated therefore the 'proletarian part of the population' of Russia to be 9.2 million (i.e. 17 per cent of the total). If we take the available labour of Russia in 1897 to consist of 61.8 million men and women, the actual share of the wage workers would be 14.9 per cent of the total labour force of Russia with an industry, railways and mining 'core group' amounting to 5.2 per cent in all.[30]

The conceptual counterpart of wage labour within the models of capitalism were its employers and capitalists, the owners of means of production who drew their profits accordingly. The correspondence of the actual 'moneyed classes' of Russia with that concept and with the bourgeoisie of the West European conditions that informed it, was very limited. Historically speaking, neither the proud burgers of the European medieval municipalities whose 'air made one free', nor the sophisticated 'merchant culture', came into being in Muscovy or in the Russian tsardom.[31] Nor did the smart engineer-turned-enterpreneur of industrialising England define Russia's productive scene. The major characteristics of the Russian bourgeoisie as broadly agreed by those who studied it, were (i) its relatively small size, (ii) the clear supremacy of traders over industrialists within it, (iii) 'provincial' narrow-mindedness, 'backward' business practices and extreme despotism towards the employees as well as towards the members of their own families, (iv) the political indifference of the majority coupled with monarchist, xenophobic and anti-liberal political tendencies of most of those who were ready to commit themselves.[32] The very few collective organisations of the Russian bourgeosie, for example, the managing committees of the bourse, some clubs, associations and specific newspapers, were loyally subservient to the government yet still more radical than their 'constituency'. At the turn of the twentieth century and despite the considerable economic advance of Russia's capitalist economy, what was striking in its absence was the Russian bourgeoisie as a 'class for itself' – an organised, self-conscious group united by common interests, dominating the social processes of production and in pursuit of state power to serve its specific ends.

Some figures may make this picture more specific. Russia's businessmen, both the more sizeable merchants and the industrial entrepreneurs, were officially licensed into two 'merchant guilds'. In 1881 there were 5755 who qualified by size of their operation as members of the first, that is, the 'top' guild and their number grew very slowly (it was 7220 in 1907).[33] For 1905, Dyakin has estimated the elite of the profit-makers in industrial enterprises, financial operations and urban properties defined by him as those with a 20 000 rouble ($10 000) annual income to consist of 5739 men and 1595 partnerships or shareholding companies.[34] He has also shown that in accordance with the licences issued, 87 per cent of the business enterprises were issued to merchants, 11 per cent to craftsmen and 2 per cent only to the factory owners. The municipal census of Moscow in 1902 supported this picture, showing that only 5 per cent of property owners residing in the city were factory owners, 1600 in all. The figures of the Minister of the Interior introduced indirectly an interesting dimension of historical origins, by indicating the social estate of the Russian businessmen. Of those registered, 81.6 per cent were members of the 'urban estates', 2.2 per cent were nobles, 10.2 per cent were peasants, and 5.9 per cent 'others'.[35]

The 1897 census of population gave the figures of those 'living from commerce' and of 'merchants and honorary citizens' by social estate as about 5 million (3.99 per cent) and 0.6 million (0.49 per cent) respectively. The first of those categories included the very sizeable group of shop assistants (*prikazchiki*) – the census failed to single them out from their employers. About 677000 (i.e. 0.54 per cent) were defined by the census as those 'living on capital income' and their families which would have included some 'gentile poverty' of declining old fortunes, etc. In the light of all that, the figure often used by the Soviet scholars, estimating Russian 'big bourgeoisie' as 1.5 million,[36] seems to overstate it many times over. Those who could be so defined with their kinsmen and immediate dependants, were probably not more than 100 000. Between that stratum and the manual labourers of Russia stretched a much larger group of middle and poor tradesmen, publicans, small craftsmen and so on, then the shop and bar assistants all the way down to what in the contemporary 'developing societies' came to be called the 'lumpen bourgeoisie', the petty 'go-betweens', pedlars, etc. with an income that could be lower than that of the manual workers. In Russia, this social category, consisting mostly of 'urbanites' (*meshchane*) by their social estate and by residence, who were often divided from the workers', the servants and even some peasants by aspiration and pretence rather than by actual wealth and income. Too heterogeneous to be described as 'a social class', they produced at times in Central Russia sporadic 'political action', mostly loyalist and/or xenophobic. There were about 5000000 of them in the population, the vagueness of their delimitation expressed in the rough nature of this estimate. In the west of the country their share increased and their ethnic composition changed; Jews there formed a disproportionately large part of that social category.

The arts have provided important testimony concerning the main capitalism-bound classes of Russia. Novelists in particular have described vividly the harsh lives of workers' compounds and barracks, the squalor, the poverty, the repression by petty officials, the constant insecurity. They also offered colourful descriptions of the typical rich merchants' milieu: rigid patriarchialism, avarice coupled with an extravagant display of squandering (when cigars were lit by 100 rouble banknotes), drunken orgies and religious sanctimony.[37] There were also those few who stood in marked contrast. The 'conscious workers' striving for education, often political activists in the condition of heavy political repression, were matched by publicly spirited and enlightened merchants of Moscow who spent lavishly on paintings, philanthropy and literature, or even for ethical reasons supported political dissent to the point of financing the revolutionary underground like the famous Savva Morozov. A major arts museum of Moscow, endowed by a merchant of cultural attainment and still carrying his name – the

Tretyakov Gallery – stands as a memorial to them. Their names are the better known because there were so few of them.

*   *   *

Finally, the main territorial expression of the development of capitalism in Russia was urbanisation, its nature and its speed. The populations involved in wage labour, industry, capitalist economy and in urban living were not similar. Residents in the areas defined as 'rural' included more than half of the countries industrial labour force (much of it in 'industrial villages' around factories and mines). On the other hand, the main occupation of 9.4 per cent of the 'urban dwellers' in the 1897 census was defined as farming mostly peasant in type.[38] All the same, the correlation of city with industry was important and growing.

The population defined as urban by the 1897 census was 16.8 million (i.e. 13.4 per cent of the total). In this, 30.9 per cent were those who made their living in industry, 5.9 per cent in transport, 17.0 per cent in commerce. Estimates differ but between 1897 and the eve of the First World War, the urban population rose by anything between 2 per cent and $4\frac{1}{2}$ per cent of the total. It was to drop in the 1917–20 period of war and revolution and to rise again later but stayed within 5 per cent of the 1897 proportions for nearly four decades.[39]

The cities of Russia varied considerably in their social composition – those that functioned mainly as administrative centres, those that mostly offered services and trading to the neighbouring ruralites and those that were centres of manufacturing industry and rapid industrial growth.[40] At the top, the two capitals of Moscow and Petersburg with more than 1 million people residing in each, were multifunctional centres of administration, manufacturing, commerce, education and communications. In the next category by size, there were the seventeen large cities with populations of between 100 000 and 1 million each. Of those not less than twelve (i.e. three-quarters) were at the non-Russian ethnic periphery in the west and in the south.[41] On the whole, less of their workers worked in factories and more were engaged in small work-shops, in trade and in service. With the exception of the two conurbations around the two capitals, the density of the urban population decreased steadily as one moved from west to east: it was 23 per cent in the Polish provinces of Russia and less than 8.5 per cent in Siberia.

A 1904 study of Russian cities supplemented the information gathered in 1897.[42] It offers a glimpse of the actual urban life of Russia of those times. Despite the rapid increase in the population of the capitals and of the large industrial or trading cities, two-thirds of the Russian urbanites still lived in two towns described as 'small' or 'medium' (i.e. with less

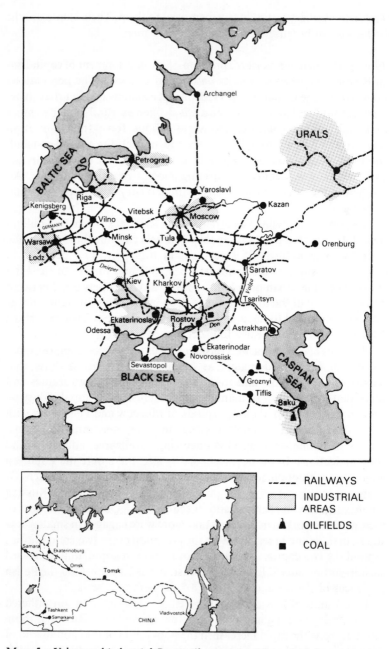

MAP 5 *Urban and industrial Russia (beginning of the twentieth century)*

than 100 000 residents in each). The picture that emerged of many of those smaller Russian towns would not easily qualify as 'urban' nowadays: two-thirds of the total city dwellings were wooden, most of the streets unpaved, and usually without piped water or a sewage system. The great majority of the 932 Russian towns, and even most of the *guberniya* towns, that is, towns where a *gubernator* and his staff resided, had no factories whatever and no railway station. On the other hand, the same survey reported public libraries in all but one of the *guberniya* towns and local newspapers, museums or theatres in most of them. It was the city of Warsaw that actually led the Russian empire in the number of locally published newspapers and journals, twenty-one and ninety-nine respectively, followed by Moscow with thirteen newspapers and sixty-nine journals. Even Tomsk, the sole university city of Siberia with population of 52 000, had eleven local newspapers and journals. Libraries and/or reading rooms were reported in three-quarters of all of the cities of the empire.

* * *

To recapitulate, during the period discussed, Russian economic development has substantiated some of the major anticipations of those who look at it in the light of the models of capitalist development, based on the experience and the social analysis of Western and Central Europe. Manufacturing, mining and transport have grown considerably with the heavy industries and large enterprises at the forefront of that ascent. Commodity production and export were growing too, and so was, very sharply, the capital invested in trading, banking and industry. The urban industrial working class had expanded and so did the urban population.

One possible conclusion is to assume Russia was undergoing the process of development of capitalism already accomplished in Western Europe, some steps behind it on the ladder of universal advance. To be sure, if so treated Russia would have to be placed quite far behind the forerunners of capitalism. Witte's 1899 report to the tsar[43] described the period when the 'agricultural classes of the principal European state' were at the currently Russian stage as the 'end of the former [eighteenth century] to middle of present century'. To quantify it (and it is the quantitative aspect that matters most if that view is adopted), the contemporary census of Great Britain has shown 57 per cent of its labour force to be employed in manufacturing and mining and 10 per cent in agriculture. The parallel figures for Russia were 5 per cent and 74 per cent.[44]

Not only a difference of stage along the ladder has been at stake when such comparisons were made, however. The complexity and multi-directionality of the processes involved was increasingly considered via the concept of 'uneven development' assuming 'different roads', as first suggested by the Russian social theorists of the nineteenth century.[45] Much poorer than Western Europe, Russia was not actually 'catching up' in terms of the aggregate income per capita, productivity or consumption.[46] While within industry and mining capital accumulation was considerable, much of it was increasingly controlled by foreign capital and/or by the state economy. What did all this mean in terms of the characterisation of Russian economy and of the predictions concerning its future? Also, what conclusion could one draw from the growing gap between the pace of Russian agriculture, in which the majority of the labour force was engaged, and that of industry – Russia's main focus of capitalist advance? The increase in the production of Russian industry was by Kondrat'ev/Goldsmith's figures fairly high when compared to those of West European industrial societies but the increase in agricultural production was only slightly ahead of the rise in population.[46] 'The gap between the development of agriculture and of industry', mentioned by Lyaschenko, the 'discrepancy between the industrial segment of the economy which was forging ahead and the relatively stagnant agricultural segment', spoken of by Gerschenkron, represented a crucial characteristic of Russia's economic development.[47] Russian economic transformation differed from the 'model' of capitalism in terms of its extra-economic characteristics, as well as intra-national. Particularly, the power of the tsardom, the exploitative properties and the extent of repressions built into the system played a major role in the political economy of Russia.

We shall go somewhat farther into the issues of the state economy and the rural economy before proceeding to the general problem that presents itself here, that is, that of the fundamental character of the development of the Russian society *vis-à-vis* the most influential model that came to clarify it to its contemporaries.

C. THE STATE AS AN ECONOMY

Strict divisions between the 'political' and the 'economic' belong to the world of conceptual abstractions. It has its analytical uses that should not be mistaken for reality. So does the division between state and economy. Yet simply to declare that is to say but little, for it is not the fact of the matter (trivial to all but some professional economists), but the nature and the extent of that linkage that is fundamental for the understanding of the way a society works. It is also central to our analysis.

The textbooks of economic history offer an invariable model, according to which during the last four centuries the European states passed through three major stages of economic policy and of explanatory models attached: mercantilism, liberalism and neo-protectionism of sorts. Between the sixteenth and eighteenth centuries, systematic state intervention was aimed at a positive balance of foreign trade and the advance of local manufacture. The economy of the state and its subjects was treated as a whole, the way a king's private manor would be. This entailed state supervision and state regulation of major branches of the economy, especially of foreign trade, aiming at a 'positive balance'. This period was followed by one in which, while the explanatory doctrines differed, their conclusions as well as the actual state policies followed *laissez-faire*, that is, the diminution of state intervention and a free market of produce and resources; policies assumed to be the best way to promote the coveted 'economic growth'. At the third stage, protectionist tariffs and state intervention in the economy increased once more but were understood and justified in new ways. From 1945 onwards, one can more or less take one's pick; the state economic policies were sufficiently ambivalent to provide evidence for those who see it as the next swing of the pendulum back to liberalisation, for those who see it as the climax of state intervention and for those who see it, differently again, as the superseding of the state-size economies by a new multinational capitalist oligarchy.[1]

The relevant parts of the economic history of pre-1917 Russia went through a consistently skewed version of the European three-stage cycle described. The difference concerned the extent of state power and state economy within Russia. While repeating the essentials of the West European periodicity, the Russian economy was more state-bound at every one of its stages. Russian mercantilist policies reached their peak during the long reign of Peter I (1682–1725). They were associated with the systematic policies of 'Westernisation', the nearly constant war effort and the extensive reconstruction of the state machinery and the army. They were aggressive to the point of vicious brutality in the destroying of the ancient rights and in attacking the livelihood of all the established classes and groups of Russian society: the peasants, the urban craftsmen-soldiers, the Cossacks, the nobility of old. Its contemporary, Pososhkov, the first theorist of Russian mercantilism, was also an apologist for the tsar's unlimited rule over everybody and everything.[2] The period of Catherine II's rule (1762–96) saw the rapid spread of the ideas of the Physiocrats – supporters of *laissez-faire*. In close relation to the increasing privileges of the landed nobility, manorial agriculture came to be seen as the essence of the Russian economy and any limitation of foreign trade as counter-productive. A few turns and twists excepted (e.g. Tsar Paul I paying in 1801 with his life for an attempt to challenge head on the interests of his nobles in joining the Napoleonic blockade of England), the images and policies of 'free trade' were dominant until the second half of the nineteenth century. Yet the extent of political control of tsardom over the inhabitants of Russia, the enserfment of the peasant majority of its population, the extensive state monopolies, state mines and state factories as well as the direct state control/ownership of half of Russia's serfs (the 'state peasants'), resulted in an economy that caricatured rather than repeated the West European economic liberalism of the eighteenth and nineteenth centuries.

By the end of the 1870s, neo-protectionist theories and prescriptions came to guide Russia's official policies. Beginning with Bunge's appointment in 1881 to the Ministry of Finance, that strategy was consistently and increasingly followed by all of his successors in office who, within the Russian system of government, were the supreme controllers of the state economic policies. It was the next in line, Vishnegradskii, who from 1887 onwards came to establish and symbolise some of the basic characteristics of the policies and the men most suitable for the new times. Policies of harsh taxation, forcing grain sales by increasingly impoverished villagers, and the world's highest protectionist tariff on industrial goods, were administered by a financial maverick with engineering training, deeply involved in private speculative business and making money hand over fist for himself and his kind.[3] It was during the ministry of his successor, Witte (1892–1903), that the whole strategy approached its fullest development, found its explicit conceptualisation and underwent its harshest test of a massive crisis, followed directly by the 1904 war and the 1905–7 revolution.

Russia's state economy under Witte welded together components representing different periods and conditions. It inherited the direct state ownership of much of Russia's land, forest and minerals.[4] On the production side, the Russian state was for centuries directly engaged in mining and manufacturing – a large-scale economy in itself, referred to by many as 'state capitalism'.[5] These state-owned enterprises were being extended still further under Witte. On the other side of the balance sheet the tsar's court, bureaucracy and army constituted by far the largest single consumer of the country with the consequent massive ability of influencing its markets, prices, profits and 'private enterpreneurs'. The state expenditure amounted in 1900 to a quarter of the estimated national income, with the state share of the national income on the increase. In 1900, half of Russia's iron production was directly used by the 'state treasury' (*kazna*), while the share of 'the population' totalled only 14 per cent.[6] The legacies of old also included close administrative control of labour and of migration (through a system of passports), a system of state monopolies and the close police supervision of every public and private organisation and enterprise in the land.

The rapid increase in the *custom duties* was the signal of the new stage of the Russian economic history (i.e. of the increase in the state intervention in the economy). The estimated average of duties on foreign-made goods went up from 13 per cent of the imports value in 1868 to 33 per cent in 1900 and threefold for iron (to which the duties on agricultural machinery were directly related).[7] The increase in duties was to facilitate the 'growth' of the local industries but also a form of indirect taxation, highly selective of its payees (these were mostly ruralities who paid it). The so-called 'Mandeleev tariff' of 1891 constituted a decisive step in the transformation of custom duties listing all but fourteen of the categories of the items imported, and trebling the tax on many of them. Contemporaries have rightly described this tariff as prohibitive rather than protective.

Banking and *credit* provided a further dimension of state intervention in Russia. Once again, it is the extent of state involvement that made it different from Western Europe. The development of industry and trade was powerfully influenced by the Russian State Bank, which 'differed from European banks by being financed mainly by government sources'[8] and operated under the direct control of the Ministry of Finance. Land transactions, land mortgage and agricultural credit were mostly in the hands of two more state banks: the Peasant Bank, created in 1882 to facilitate the buying of land by peasant households or communes, and its counterpart, the Nobility Land Bank, established in 1885 to offer privileged and preferential credit aiming 'to facilitate residence of nobles within their own estates, to whom attention should be given in accordance with the duties of their status'.[9] Both the land banks acted as a direct tool of government policy (i.e. exceeded purely economic and monetary functions); they propped up the declining agriculture of the nobility, financed state agrarian reforms, facilitated colonisation programmes, issued loans 'to enable Russian hereditary nobility to acquire land from non-Russian owners within the Western provinces' (i.e. to dispossess Poles), etc.[10] Other *de facto* state banks carried out aggressive economic policies in countries their names testified to: The Russo-Chinese Bank, the Discount Bank of Persia, the Mongolian Bank.

The *emission of banknotes* and the over-supply of printed money offered a steady source of state extra income in the first half of the nineteenth century. It led to inflation. At a later stage, it came into conflict with the state policies of industrialisation, especially the attempt to attract foreign capital into the country. Under Bunge, the aim of the monetary policies became therefore the 'establishment of a gold standard' (i.e. direct convertibility of the Russian rouble into gold). Witte had achieved this by 1897, amid an increasing influx of foreign investment into industry and mining (estimated by Witte himself as half the total addition to the commercial, industrial and banking capital in 1900).[11] Whatever the value of such estimates, the massive nature of foreign capital investment and its impact on Russia's industrial development was indubitable. So was the significance of the state in these advancements. Central to it was the increase in the 'national debt' described by one of the major texts as the source 'of financial well-being at the roots of the development of industrial capitalism'.[12] The state was underwriting major parts of Russia's investments and trade, both foreign and internal. Placement of Russian shares and loan certificates on foreign markets became a major aspect of Russia's foreign policies of the period, linking once more 'the political' and 'the economic', the 'international' and the 'internal' into a single whole.

On the eve of the 1905–7 revolution, the annual figures for 1903 showed that 635 million roubles (i.e. one-third of the state income) came directly from its properties, capitals and service enterprises, a sum that compares with the nominal total of the entire French, English and German shareholding capital in the Russia of those times.[13] By 1913 the share of income from properties, productive capital and services of the state within the total state income had increased to 60 per cent.[14] A major upturn in state economic activities resulted from the 1890s decision to take over the Russian railways (i.e. to make them state owned through gradual buying-out of the privately owned lines and direct construction of new ones). For more than a decade, the creation of the Russian railway system was to form the backbone of the economic development of the country. It became the major category of capital formation and changed the nature of the local agricultural markets and exports. Its 'spin-off' effect was also considerable; Russia came to produce on the spot most of what was needed for the grandiose railways construction programme. By the end of the century, the state owned two-thirds of Russia's railways, and increasingly used them as a major tool of economic policy through differential tariffs promoting grain export abroad, by offering privileged building contracts, and so on.

Economic historians have often compared this phase in Russia's economic development to that of Japan. This is true up to a point when state intervention is considered, but wrong in an important sense. The government of Japan systematically privatised state enterprises and by selling them facilitated the expansion of 'national' industrial capitalism of large private monopolies. The Russian state bought rather than sold economic enterprises. It also build new ones and kept them.

The total scope of the state economy, its incomes and expenditures had been increasing rapidly. The nominal value of the annual state income doubled during the period of Witte's stewardship (i.e. between 1892 and 1903) and more than doubled again by 1913.[15] By 1913 it was close to the estimated sum total of the country's industrial capital, or, to take another comparison, to the total annual value of all the grain produced in Russia.[16] Its major components, the indirect taxation and the profits from state properties and enterprises, doubled and trebled respectively under Witte. The indirect taxes that reached by 1903 the sum of 1000 million roubles, took their pound of flesh from every consumer and from nearly every manufactured product of day-to-day use: salt, lamp oil, sugar, tobacco and alcohol. These taxes, as well as the 'skimming' of agriculture for the sake of industry, were highly regressive (i.e. came down hardest on the poorest groups within the Russian population).[17]

The story of the 'state vodka' can exemplify and indeed symbolise these characteristics of the Russian fiscal and economic policies during the period reviewed. A liquor monopoly, which commenced partially and experimentally in 1895, was established in 1901 all through the empire. It consisted of a scheme by which much of the country's vodka was produced by the state-run factories, while production quotas were also offered to private owners of distilleries, often built on large landed estates from whom the vodka was bought at a price offering very generous profit margins. A state monopoly of sale was put into operation and prices that incorporated high indirect taxation were collected, mostly from the poor. The 'monopoly vodka' figured increasingly on the workers' and peasants' budgets of expenses. Eventually Russia led the world in the industrial production of strong liquor and the vodka monopoly came to secure one-third of the state income. Nor were the Russians spared a suitable dose of hypocrisy in the explanation of why a paternalistic government was the main beneficiary of liquor ever condemned and preached against by its church. Witte, who took particular pride in introducing the scheme of 'monopoly vodka', offered also the explanation for it: it was introduced to control drunkenness and to advance public health – the state-bottled 'scourge of the Russian people' was simply more hygienic. He also set aside a small fund to support an organisation devoted to the 'struggle against alcoholism' – a committee of bishops, high-bred ladies, toothless professors and, of course, Witte himself.[18]

The Russian state was a massive economy in two distinct senses. It was a gigantic enterprise *sensu strictu* and at the same time a powerful system of political and administrative intervention, penetrating every aspect of Russia's economy and society. These categories were closely interlinked: Russia's largest single enterpreneur had at its service the tax-and-spending capacity of the state budget, a variety of methods of state interventions (e.g. the establishment of a sugar cartel along German lines, etc.). One should also mention in this context the paternalistic labour legislation – somewhat of a caricature of the German government's idea of 'state socialism', once removed in the direction of what can be termed 'police socialism'. These diverse elements were united by a strategy, defined by the Imperial Minister of Finance. Its fundamental assumptions, adhered to since the 1880s, were spelt out with particular clarity by the most talkative of them. Reporting to his tsar in the year in which the century commenced, Witte stated that Russia was still a 'predominantly agrarian country' and 'foreign industries can break through our custom barriers and take root in our motherland'. As long as this was the case, 'Russia cannot consider its political might unassailable'. That is why 'international rivalry would not wait. . . . It would be a fatal mistake to assume that . . . we can wait . . . for the (spontaneous TS) creation of a broad and many-sided industry'.[19] To Witte, at stake was the very existence of Russia's imperial power which could be saved from political decline only by rapid industrialisation. A massive state intervention into the economy was seen as a necessary link of a giant 'feedback system': the state economic intervention – the industrialisation – the power of the state – back to the state economic intervention. This was Witte's choice – the road along which Russia was to move forward to catch up with, if not to outrun, the 'Englands' and the 'Germanys' of the world.

The concept of 'triple alliance' coined for Brazil of the 1970s to define the complex relations between local capitalists, the foreign capital and the state economy was remarkably apt for Russia of the period described. Despite considerable dependency on foreign credits and investments, the Russian state administrators were able to face major Western financiers from a position of strength, using as much the state's own riches as the monopoly of politico-territorial control and the ability to play the foreign capitals one against the other. When the German politicians or bankers tried in the 1880s to use the lever of extensive German investment and credit to force a change in the Russian customs policies, they lost.[20] The politically inspired *Finanzkrieg* ended by a rapid increase in the involvement of French capital, replacing in part the Germans both as a creditor of the Russian state and as an investor in Russian private enterprises.[21] On the other hand, much of the Russian capital was linked with the foreign owners and investors, often playing the field together against the state controls, tax officers and declared policies. Mutual dependency as well as clear contradiction between the three distinct sectors can be distinguished all through the period. Moreover, that division was not exclusive and each 'camp' acquired agents and collaborators in the other two: the local 'comprador', the official due for a cushioned job in the 'private sector', and so on. Russia's major road to quick riches was for centuries that of a supplier of the court, the army or the ministries. Local services to foreign capital and foreign investment in Russia could now be added.

The many mystifications of that state of affairs offered then and since, shared the tendency to reduce that picture to one that is simpler but wrong. In pre-revolutionary Russia, much was said on the political right about the 'national interest' facing 'foreign capital' while its 'local' partners and alliances were disregarded. On the left, the Russian state was often treated as non-existent economically speaking, reducing its image to that of the executive agency of the 'capital' (at its most abstract) or else to a vector of the confrontations between foreign and local capitalist factions, disregarding its specific organisation, resources, power, interest and strategies. Correspondingly, some of the liberals treated the Russian state as the 'policeman on the beat', which in its 'backwardness' had somewhat overstepped its duties and was to be called to order (by pointing out the fine Western, preferably British, examples of progress). This analytical blind spot was and still is a major reason why scholars and laymen have consistently misunderstood the nature of the political economies of the type discussed.

The Russian state economy, and in particular the 'Witte system', suffered from a number of inbuilt structural weaknesses and contradictions, both political and ideological. Some of these were defined by the general nature of officialdom, others were specific to the field of state-directed economic action. The awareness of them had been growing for some time. These weak points concerned in particular problems concerning bureaucratic incompetence, foreign capital, the heavy emphasis of industrialisation strategies and the political results of exploitation under which the majority of Russians lived (i.e. the problem of class, state and revolution).

Russia's officialdom was by its nature selectivity, employing and promoting personnel both ineffectual in the running of the economy and corrupt in its contacts with the 'private sectors'. At the very top, there were often a few very able and fairly honest men. The general run-of-the-mill supervisors of the state's affairs were very much typical participants of networks of patronage and sinecures, in which promotion was secured by 'influence' with the tsar's courtiers or else age-in-service and blind loyalty to superiors. Nothing could better promote inefficiency, 'red tape' and lack of initiative. The whole network of state contracts and monopolies granted through the 'connections in the right places', set a premium on all the wrong qualities, human and institutional, in so far as the aims of the state programmes were concerned. It promoted speculative cartels in the private economy and bribe-taking in the administration.

Second, the nationalist promise and self-image of the industrialisation programme stood in sharp contrast to the state promotion of the flow of foreign capital into Russia. Witte himself had no doubts: Russia was short of capital, capital was urgently needed and one should acquire it wherever it could be found. The influx of foreign capital was to be encouraged and the foreign debts extended. Also the resident, but ethnically 'non-Russian', capital (especially of the Jews) was to be drawn in through the abolition of the legal restrictions on its owners. The nationalist objections were faced squarely by Witte's claim that 'in nearly no country did industry develop without foreign capital . . . while the political power of those countries led to this capital nationalisation and assimilation . . . doubtlessly typical of every healthy political organism'.[22] The Italian traders and the Huguenot manufacturers at the starting point of the capitalist breakthrough in England were quoted as examples. Looking backward and with the experience of the 'developing societies' of today in mind, this comparison appears less realistic. The contemporary critiques of the Modernisation Theories made clear why the metaphor of the 'healthy body' assimilating foreign capital was misleading; it was rather the foreign capital that often 'assimilated', incorporated and subjected local economies and societies. Also, with the capacity of the Russian officialdom to control local capitalists much in excess of its ability to interfere with the foreign ones (usually energetically backed by their own governments), the picture of the power relations in the economy could be usually expressed as a formula combining two relatively 'independent' and one considerably more 'dependent' variable. The negotiations and confrontations of these interests would have often resembled a round table with two chairs and a stool.

Third, the way Witte's policies of intense 'protectionist' support of industrialisation were carried out in a predominantly agricultural society meant the sacrifice of the second for the first. The rural/urban terms of trade and the Russian fiscal policies made this dramatically clear. Yet, the impoverishment of the Russian rural majority severely curtailed the internal market deemed necessary for the 'healthy' development of the industry. Furthermore, the constant 'squeeze' of agriculture led to low investment in it, both limiting the internal market of means of production and enhancing low productivity. To recall, despite its industrial advance, Russia was a predominantly rural society. Agriculture provided in 1913 more than half the estimated national income, engaged three-quarters of the national labour force and accounted for 84 per cent of the national exports (the respective figures for industry were 21, 5 and 9 per cent).[23] The fact that the majority of Russians were peasants meant also that the deficiencies of Russian agriculture and its unequal standing have perpetuated and deepened the poverty of the Russian people as a whole.

Finally, at the turn of the century, the economic intervention of the Russian state was massively and manifestly serving the privileged and moneyed classes, while the bill was footed by the poor in direct proportion to their poverty that is, it was openly, indeed brazenly, unjust. The manifest and growing inequality within Russia was bound, at least in the moments of general crisis, to elicit a mass political challenge aiming at the privileged classes as much as at the machinery of oppression and the country's largest single employer and property owner rolled in one – that is, the tsardom itself. In the long run, the results of the stategies of economic intervention were to be determined by a confrontation in the political sphere.

D. RURAL ECONOMY: LAND AND LABOUR

Agriculture was the main branch of Russia's production and employment. It was also the major economic sector where neither the state nor foreign capital were substantive entrepreneurs or even the major suppliers of technology and inputs. The same was essentially true for the Russian private 'entrepreneurial capital'. Grain production by 'traditional' means, mostly within a variety of three-field land-rotation systems, formed the base of the Russian agriculture of the period (and, indeed, as late as the 1940s). To put it in figures, at the turn of the century, grain was produced on about 90 per cent of Russia's agricultural lands and more than one-fifth was subsequently left fallow in any single year.[1] The main fertiliser was manure and most of the agricultural equipment was locally or self-made and primitive to an extreme.[2] Animal husbandry played a fairly important but subsidiary role, the estimates of its contribution range from 10–25 per cent of the total value of agricultural produce.[3] It was mostly the requirements of grain production that made horses central to Russian animal husbandry. Milk, dairy produce, some pork and vegetables, fresh and salted, were the main dietary supplements. Diversification within agriculture involved mainly the labour-intensive and cash-producing crops specific to some of the regions: flax in the north-west, sugar beet and oilseed sunflower in the Ukraine, potatoes in the Vladimir gub., butter production in West Siberia and cotton production in central Asia.[4] But once again, these branches of production were mostly subsidiary in scale and in economic significance. Grain was the staple diet of the rural population of Russia, the main produce of its agriculture and the main item of the country's export.

Farming (i.e. land and animal husbandry) did not express the full scope of the rural economy. We have already mentioned industrial and craftsmen's villages as well as the non-farming ruralities. Even if concentrating on the 'farming population' only, farming did not exhaust its productive activities. The Budget Studies, mentioned earlier, of the Russian peasant households have shown them from the vantage point of the smallholder units of production. There was considerable consistency of patterns: farming was supplemented by a measure of gathering, that is, direct use of nature (e.g. fishing, mushrooms, grass off the meadows, manure) and by what peasants called 'craft and trades' (*promysly*), of which a major part was given to part-time manual labour in the village alternating with craftsmanship and wage labour elsewhere. Vainshtein has estimated the average *promysly* income to be 17 per cent of the peasant budgets on the eve of the First World War and there were some claims, probably over-stated by a regional bias, of its being as much as 32 per cent of the total.[5] It was agreed by all that the extent of the non-farming income and its content was significantly related to the well-being of peasant households, the mid-group devolving its labour least, while the poorest provided the main pool of manual wage labour. The richer households were engaged more in entrepreneurship and/or hired themselves out together with their horses (and were at times registered thereby, paradoxically, as the wage labourers of their poorer and horseless neighbours). [6] While the specific composition of peasant income has changed in relation to the region, the socio-economic stratum as well as historically, lack of specialisation was ever the rule and not an exception. During the period discussed, the majority of households had grain farming as their main source of income, with the whole economic strategy of the peasant families shaped accordingly.

An important way to look at the Russian grain production is to consider the composition of its inputs. S. Strumilin has estimated that in 1887–8 labour accounted for 61.2 per cent (of which two-thirds was 'human' and one-third 'by animals') of the value of the input in the grain production of European Russia. It was closely similar in 1912–14 but the value of the animal–labour component increased to two-fifths. The parallel figures for the usage of tools and equipment were 5.8 per cent in 1887–8 and 7.8 per cent in 1912–14. [7] The message of those figures is clear, and would be even more pronounced if the price of land-use was introduced (other estimates indicate that average rental value would have represented 27 per cent of Strumilin's total figures, which excluded land for conceptual reasons). Consideration of the nature of the peasant crafts and trades would have strengthened it still further. The bulk of the inputs in the Russian rural economy was manual labour and land, its chief supplement was horse power and manure for fertilisation.

Labour and land, their availability, control and use were therefore at the core of the fundamental economic equations of rural life. While labour was mostly that of the peasant smallholders, their families and their beasts, the land belonged in part to non-peasant owners, mostly to the landed nobility. A dual structure of land ownership was established in law during the 1861 Emancipation. On the one hand, was the land of the peasant communes that could not be sold and that was to be held and used as peasant family parcels and commons. On the other hand, there were the private lands, mostly in much larger units and owned by the squires. The state, and the other institutional land property, were of relatively limited significance to farming. A major part of these lands were forested. (Russia's timber, the main local material for construction and heating, was on the whole kept out of the peasants' hands, i.e. was state or privately owned. [8]) Those state lands that could be used for farming were rented out to peasants or else were run along lines similar to those of the private manorial estates, and blended into them.

The figures of landownership for European Russia gathered by the Land Census of 1905 (with the non-agricultural far-north excluded) have shown that 47.2 per cent of the farming land was in peasant or Cossack communal ownership, 35.9 per cent was private and 16.9 per cent belonged to the state or to other 'institutions of the realm' (i.e. church, local authorities, etc.).[9] The subcategorisation of private lands, in accordance to the 'social estate' of their owners, showed that 61.9 per cent of it belonged to nobles, 15.4 per cent to peasants 15 per cent to members of the 'merchant estate' with other social groups holding the rest.[10] Within European Russia in 1905 the ratio of the peasant and Cossack land (both communal and 'privately owned') to that owned by the nobility and the 'merchant estate' was 10:3:1 respectively. The comparison of the landownership records has shown a rapid process of change, with much of the land being bought or sold. In result the nobility had lost 27 per cent of its lands during the 1877–1905 period, half of which was purchased by peasants. The peasant share in land purchases was on the increase (see Table 3.4).[11]

The most striking characteristic of agriculture within the lands owned by the nobles was the extent to which its use by its owners was indirect (i.e. through renting it out to peasants and simply pocketing the proceeds). In 1903 about 30 million des. of land were estimated to belong to this category (i.e. nearly half of the total of the non-peasant land) and an equivalent of nearly one-fifth of those owned by the peasant communes.[12] As to land in direct productive use by the nobility, the masterly work of A. Anfimov clearly shows that despite the massive redemption fees received after the 1861 emancipation (partly wiped out, admittedly, by the nobility's pre-emancipation debts), the rents and the moneys for the lands sold since, the generous state support and constant appeals, little advanced agriculture was in evidence there.[13] Capital investments in large-scale agriculture were remarkably limited. With few exceptions the technology and the methods of production on the noble estates closely resembled those of the neighbouring peasantry: a three-field system, horse ploughing, little if any chemical fertiliser. The neighbouring peasantry not only purchased or rented much of the nobility's land but they also worked much of the rest, acting as the main source of 'wage labour'. Such work was often done under an agreement by which a peasant was contracted with his own horse, equipment and the help of his family to work the land of the squire and to be paid for it either in actual wages or else by the use of another strip of land.[14] A consistent

TABLE 3.4   *The landownership of the 'social estates' in European Russia, 1877 and 1905*[a] *(in 000 000 des. and %)*

Social estate	Total land				Changes in land ownership 1877–1905 (des.)	
	1877		1905			
	des.	%	des.	%	Private	Communal[b]
Peasants and Cossacks	123.3	58.5	163.4	67.9	+ 18.2[c]	+ 22.1
Nobles	73.1	34.7	53.2	22.1	− 19.9	
Merchants and indust-rial co.	11.5	5.6	16.7	6.9	+ 5.2	
Others	2.8	1.3	7.2	3.1	+ 4.4	
Total	210.7	100	240.5[d]	100	+ 7.9	

Source:
Statistika zemlevladenia 1905 (St Petersburg, 1907) pp. 188–9.
Notes:
[a] State lands were excluded and only lands in agricultural use were accounted for. The difference between the total lands in 1887 and 1905 was partly a matter of changes in the system of accounting, but was mostly the result of actual increases in lands in use.
[b] All Cossack lands were treated as communal.
[c] The category incorporates the lands owned by the peasant 'partnerships' as well as single peasant families.
[d] The 14 per cent increase in arable lands between 1877 and 1905 for reasons discussed on pp. 143, 147.

15–18 per cent superiority of yield on the 'private' lands (both peasant and non-peasant) as against those on the 'communal' lands was reported during the whole of the period.[15] Under the circumstances it seems to represent mostly the 'pick of the best land' by the nobility during the 1861 emancipation and the impact of selective sale of the worse lands afterwards, while peasants were increasingly ploughing up 'marginal lands' of lesser productivity. There is little evidence of superiority of techniques or of 'benefits of scale' on the larger estates. Significantly, the peasants owned a much higher share of Russia's horses, ploughs and other agricultural implements than of land and this share was on the increase.[16]

Something more should be said about the diversity within the landed nobility itself. Russia was famed for the manorial estates of its princes and their size. The largest of them could compete in size with any latifundia of the world – the lands of Count Stroganov spread over

1 465 000 des. (i.e. more than 10 million acres). About 70 per cent of the land of the nobility was held in what was considered as large units (i.e. units of above 1000 des. of land des.). Yet, at the other extreme, often forgotten behind the glitter of the princely wealth, was a stratum of not-so-well-to-do squires. The average size of a nobility-owned landholding was about 500 des., but 57 per cent of them were in units of less than 100 des. Some such pieces would be parts of a larger fortune but many of them represented the total holding of a family. The constant cry about the 'impoverishment of the landed nobility', the claim of mounting debts, the increasing mortgages and land sales, was particularly true for this group.[17]

Reports published by the Russian income tax department offer an interesting insight into the place of agriculture at the top of the income league of Russia (Table 3.5). The report for 1905 has shown a total of about 400 000 Russians with an annual income of at least 1000 roubles. The size of this group in 1909–10 was about 700 000. The annual income of 1000 roubles was fairly modest by European standards but much above that of the Russian manual workers, middling

TABLE 3.5   *Income and its sources: Russia 1905 and 1909–10 (only those with incomes of 1000 roubles per annum or more[a])*

Sources of incomes	No. of payees 1905	Per Payee[b] (roubles) 1905	Total income (million roubles) 1905	Total income (million roubles) 1909–10
Land	59.700	4791	286.0	412.4
Urban real estate	57.900	3622	209.7	275.5
Industry and trade	83.600	7732	646.4	856.6
Financial capital	55.200	4331	239.1	339.8
Salaries and fees	148.300	2310	342.6	760.3
Total	404.700	4250[c]	1723.8	2644.6

Source:
A. Vainshtein, *Narodnyi dokhod Rossii i SSSR* (Moscow, 1969) pp. 58–9.
Notes:
[a] Based on the income tax return of the Ministry of Finance. Such figures are necessarily understated but their mutual proportions offered a reasonable guide.
[b] An actual payee could appear more than once (i.e. as a house-owing urban firm and as a land-holding squire). The number of payees in 1909–10 is not available.
[c] Considerable differentiation of the income-holders by the size of the income was also recorded. They have ranged from a top stratum of those who earned 50 000 roubles and above (2800 payees 0.7 per cent of the list) to those who earned 1000–2000 roubles (220 500 payees, 18.4 per cent of the list).

peasant households and petty officials. The tax department report
showed that in 1905, 51.3 per cent of this income went to the owners of
financial capital, commercial establishments and industry (45.1 per cent
in 1909–10), 10.4 per cent to the owners of urban properties, 19.9 per
cent to the highest paid officials and to members of the 'professions'
(to increase to 28.7 per cent in 1909–10) and only 16.6 per cent in 1905
and 15.6 per cent in 1909–10 to the landowners in respect of their land
property.[18] As a source of profits, landownership was strongly out-
classed by others, at least for those outside the narrow circle of the
owners of the great latifundia, who did, of course, appear at the very top
of any list of incomes. There were in the 1890s some nobles who
'went back to the land', modernised their estates and made a go of
effective profit-producing farming. For the general run of the nobles, the
principal opportunities for larger incomes seemed to lie within the top
bureaucracy-cum-army (to which the nobility had privileged access),
within urban real-estate operations (where the holdings of some nobles
were considerable) and to a much lesser degree, within banking and
industry, in which some of them had started to engage.[19]

Two conclusions follow, both of considerable significance to the
shaping of Russian rural economy and society. First, the squires of
Russia, both the largest landowners and the many owners of the small
estates, were very often 'absentees', attempting to squeeze out of the
land as much income as quickly as possible and with as little investment
and attention as feasible. Their consumption and most of the possible
further investments were viewed very much in urban terms. Second, the
explicitly parasitic nature of such a social setting was related to the
squandering and wastage of incomes and goods for which Russia's
nobles became famous, as much in Petersburg as throughout Europe. It
has also provided for a particular negative self-selection of many of those
who did stay on in their own mortgaged and remortgaged estates. Those
were, in the words of a contemporary, 'people not able enough for state
administration, the rejects of the bureaucratic system'. A considerable
number of outstandingly incompetent and/or corrupt estate managers
stood in for the 'absentees'.[20]

All of this underlay the general characteristics of Russian nobility's
engagement with agriculture. As pointed out by Anfimov, their
landownership has differed from both the British total alienation of the
landowners from farming and from the Prussian large-scale units of
production. Put otherwise by another author, 'Russian agriculture . . .
combined in many parts of the country and in several of its important
branches, the disadvantages of small scale operation and of the large-

scale and often absentee ownership; and showed at the same time the low yields per acre of new settled countries and low output per man-hour of the densely populated regions of the old.'[21] The extent of direct farming by the squires was declining to reach by 1913 the low of about 10 per cent of the arable lands. Figures for the livestock have shown similar changes in the nobility/peasantry ratio.

Of the lands classified by the Land Census of 1905 as belonging to the 'merchant estate' and to private companies, very few were used for industry-related production, or for types of farming more intensive than that typical for the peasant majority in Russia. Land was often bought-up by the merchants simply to strip it of timber. Otherwise (or, subsequently) land was invested in, or retained for security or prestige. The use and management of most of those lands were similar to those owned by the nobles from whom they were acquired, i.e. either rented out or else worked by peasant labour. Only in the sugar beet areas of the Ukraine were some of such lands used 'industrially', i.e. worked by wage labour to produce the inputs for the mills, once again not unlike the estates of the local nobility and linked to extensive use of peasant labour and peasant share-cropping. Even in this particular branch of agriculture not only labour but the majority of produce came from the family farms.

*   *   *

On the other side of the rural fence stood the peasants. The poverty of the mass of them was the major characteristic of the Russian economy. In a country intrinsically poor, half of the Russian national income was produced by an agriculture which engaged three-quarters of the national labour force. Exclusion of the landed nobility and of the thin upper crust of richest peasants would lower still further the average income of the peasant majority of the Russians. In the eyes of the peasants themselves, but also to a major group of Russian scholars, the plight of the majority of peasants was in considerable part that of a growing discrepancy between the land and the labour they dispensed with. One way to quantify the poverty of the Russian peasants was to put it in terms of 'surplus population' – a measure of the underemployed labour force and underfed humans. The 'surplus rural population' was estimated by Vorontsov as 5 out of 24 million of mature male workers in European Russia of 1897, and in 1907 by Neferov as 42 per cent of the total, while only in ten out of fifty gubs. of peasant communal allotments in European Russia were considered sufficient to feed the peasant population that worked them.[22] The three-times larger annual variations of yields observed in Russia as against those in Germany and Great Britain has also meant frequent years of famine, when even the normal poverty levels could not any longer be sustained. The shortage of 'production factors' as against the availability of labour was clearly not limited to that of the land only. The 1910 census of rural equipment reported a lack of basic farming implements in 34 per cent of peasant households and no horses in 30 per cent of them.[23] 'In this grain-growing country', commented G. T. Robinson, 'the existence of millions of farms without work animals is a fact which assaults the imagination with suggestions of every sort of hardship'.[24]

Despite the purchases of arable and grazing land, the rates of land per capita and horses per capita within the Russian peasantry was rapidly declining. Between 1862 and 1879 the Russian natural growth nearly doubled and the rural population increased by an estimated 23 million.[25] The average land unit per peasant male was estimated as 5.1 des. in 1861, 3.8 des. in 1880 and 2.6 des. in 1900. (Kaufman later suggested the slightly lower respective figures of 4.8 des., 3.5 des. and 2.6 des. He has also evaluated that figure for 1917 at 1.8 des.)[26] The proportion of horse-less families increased. Payment arrears (*nedoimki*) mounted despite 'tax amnesties' and brutal methods used to collect rural taxes and dues. The size of the territory where famine appeared was growing also.[27] The average size of the peasant allotment in Russia at the turn of the century was still not much lower than a typical smallholder farm in Germany or France, it was rather the 'pre-scientific and pre-mechanical level of agriculture' that led to the 'acute sense of population surplus and land hunger'.[28] One should add to this the prevailing feeling of insecurity. An image of a 'vicious circle', in which poverty breeds more poverty, was increasingly on the mind of the Russians with regard to the bulk of the rural areas. The Russian ruralites seemed caught in a 'Malthusian cycle' of more and more population chasing after produce, and productivity that increased at too slow a rate to satisfy their needs. We are not dealing here, of course, with natural laws or unavoidable necessities; but the potential for improvement through the introduction of technically more advanced (and more costly) methods of farming, would not make its actual characteristics any less pertinent to those who faced deepening poverty.

How far was the image of the 'Malthusian cycle' realistic? The answer lies in the production figures for agriculture, but their message is ambivalent in a number of ways. It is also highly uneven: different regions and different groups of producers have shown differences of production patterns, productivity, extent of cash production, etc. Between 1881 and 1889 the land on which grain was sown in European

Russia increased by 8.7 per cent and 14.2 per cent more was added to that by 1913. The figures for the whole of the empire grew during the latter period by 23.1 per cent to a grand total of 92.6 million of des., expressing in part the result of the colonisation of Asiatic Russia. The increase in grain production in European Russia, both as the result of the increases in arable land and in productivity, was by 21.9 per cent for the annual average of 1896–1900, by 42.9 per cent for 1901–5, and by 43.1 per cent for 1906–10, if we use the average for 1886–90 as a base.[29] The corresponding average annual increase of production would be 2.2 per cent for the earlier period and 1.8 per cent for the first decade of the twentieth century. On the other hand, figures arrived at more recently by Nifontov have shown a larger increase (by about half during the last two decades of the nineteenth century).[30]

Looked at in relation to the Russian population and rural labour, these general figures were not very impressive. By the usually accepted figures, grain production per capita would have increased barely at all, while the higher figures suggested by Nifontov would mean a per capita increase of about 0.6 per cent per annum (rising to 0.8 per cent in the last decade of the nineteenth century when grain exports were rising very steeply). Significantly, most of the absolute increases came in the particularly favoured regions where land was still plentiful, population pressure low and the farming 'predatory' (i.e. based on the ploughing-up of virgin lands, little fertiliser, short span of high yields usually followed by rapid deterioration of land productivity). In no place did the increases result from substantial capital investment.

The development of productivity within grain production is still debated. An authoritative article in the contemporary Russian encyclopaedia at the beginning of the century summed up the changes in agricultural production to say: 'There was no particular change in yields. As in the old times the yields depend nearly entirely on nature . . . in this sense "private lands" do not differ from the peasant ones'.[31] The 'as in the old times' character of agriculture could be quantified by the fact that the capital per worker investment in rural Russia is shown as one-tenth only of that reported for rural Germany of the day, and two-fifths of its yields in wheat.[32] As against that stand, once again, the views of Nifontov about the fairly rapid and accelerating increase of productivity of grain, coupled with the spread of potato production, the peasant alternative crop for diet and vodka distillation. Nifontov's explanation of his evidence was 'the restructuring of the post-emancipation agriculture of Russia on a capitalist base'.[33]

We shall return in the next section to the issue of the possible

capitalism-induced productivity within rural Russia. Less controversi-
ally, in connection with the regional division there was a steep rise in
production and land-usage within the sparsely populated regions of the
south-east, etc., an average increase in the more northern *podzol* soil
areas, little growth on the Volga and in the Ukraine and an actual
decline in the central agricultural region.[34] The general message was
that of growing discrepancy between land and peasant family labour,
the land-usage increasing where such labour was scarcer and the
potential labour increasing where the shortage of land was particularly
acute. Uncontroversial also is the fact that the composition of field
production was changing. Rye – the peasants' staple diet – was declining, while wheat, the preferred item of export, was taking over. The
production of sugar beet, cotton and potatoes had increased much faster
than that of grain, the flax production oscillated while the production of
some non-grain products (e.g. hemp) declined. In all these cases we are
dealing with highly labour-absorbing methods of agriculture, the
advance of which was based on extremely cheap labour. To keep these
changes in the right perspective, the sum total of income from Russian
field-produce other than grain was estimated in 1913 as 9 per cent only of
the total income of the Russian agriculture.[35]

The branch of Russian agriculture second in importance and the
principal mode of peasant capital accumulation was livestock, especially
horses. More than four-fifths of the livestock was owned by peasants.
The growth of the number of livestock was slow. The figures for horses
in relation to rural population and for land were getting steadily
worse.[36] Lands with natural fodder, and meadows, were being ploughed
up for grain, while oats were displaced by wheat or else exported. The
other side of the coin of the increase in the staple food production and of
grain export was the relative decline of livestock as against the size of the
population.

Important for the national budget as much as for the budget and diet
of most of the Russians, was the fact that during the whole of the period
reviewed the grain export stood at 16–20 per cent of the national
product.[37] The increase in grain exports had reached by the turn of the
century the annual total of about 10 million tons, more than five times
the size of Russia's grain export in the early 1860s. Since then wheat and
barley had been taking over from rye and oats.[38] Russia's consistently
positive 'balance of payment' was very much the result of massive and
increasing grain export, which made up about half of the total export of
the country. (The other-than-grain 'agricultural exports' accounted for
a further quarter of the national total.) More than three-quarters of the

grain for the international as well as the internal markets came from the peasant households. They also played a decisive role so far as Russia's 'other' agricultural export was concerned: flax, and animal produce, etc. The increase in commercial agricultural exports in the twentieth century was clearly stimulated by the ascending prices of grain on the international market, but (an important point to keep in mind) it was taking place at a time when international prices for grain were dropping sharply during the 1890s.

*   *   *

Under all those circumstances the consideration of peasant economic strategies of survival, of 'crisis management' and advance, must play a central role in any attempt at understanding the Russian rural economy of the period. They cannot explain it exclusively, for what happened was not simply the sum total of choices and actions by its many composite units. Major structural and extra-peasant determinations played their role: national and international markets, capitalist industrialisation, state policies. All the same, besides the 'imperatives' and pressures of political economy and state intervention, the parameters of the peasants' choice (i.e. what they wanted, what they actually did and the expected and unexpected results of both) were to play a major role in the development of the Russian economy.

The possible solutions for peasants facing poverty and precarious existence, ever in fear of the 'vicious circle' of poverty breeding still more poverty, were capital investment to intensify the agriculture, emigration to remove 'surplus labour' or else an extension of land-usage. Other methods, if available to increase productivity, could be substituted for capital investment. Emigration could be replaced by crafts or by local wage labour outside one's own farm. It did not take sophisticated book-keeping, university business-schooling or even simple literacy for a peasant householder of Russia to understand the nature and the limits of that equation.

A small number of manorial estates and peasant farms were beginning to put to use technology developed in Western Europe. Some regions with extensive virgin lands and/or easy access to local or international markets and availability of credits (e.g. the New Russia in the south-east) began to engage new machinery and to extend the use of wage labour. For the rest, the actual rural 'accumulation of capital' and investment in equipment stayed very low. The percentage increase in the use of agricultural machinery and chemical fertilisers was often misleadingly high, given its low take-off point. To the core of the peasant economy, conceived nationally as well as regionally, such solutions were not usually available. There was very little capital investment there and no capital from the 'outside' was forthcoming as far as agriculture was concerned. Indeed, the exact opposite was happening, with nobles, urban merchants and the state sharing in and pumping out the peasantry's produce and possible profits. Redemption payments and taxes, together with payments for land bought and rented, drained the pool of potential peasant investments. Banking credit for the improvement of peasant agriculture was very limited (not so, one should add, for mortgages related to the buying of land). Capital formation in agriculture and investment in its improvement was kept in check by the general poverty of the peasantry, diluted by population growth and skimmed off by those in power in the Russian countryside and the Russian state.

The recorded increase of productivity per unit of land proceeded mostly by the shifting of Russian agriculture to more fertile 'colonisation' areas, changing methods of farming and increasing intensity of labour usage rather than new investments and machinery. The areas where natural fertilizer was systematically used had been increasing. Improved systems of land-rotation and the growth of grass were introduced by some peasant communities (acting on the advice of the regional agronomists attached to the *zemstvos* etc.).[39] The potential for improvement without further investment was clearly not exhausted.

Emigration into towns or else into the regions of colonisation, mostly in Asian Russia, was to the peasant a second possible 'way out'. Its parameters were limited by the availability of working places in towns and of land and the necessary capital to settle and succeed in the areas of colonisation. The poverty of the majority of Russian peasants restricted emigration. So did the legal and financial ties to the peasant commune, the right to land in one's own village that a rural 'permanent emigrant' had to forgo, etc. Considerable numbers of rural migrants returned to their villages after a time. Some came back as initially planned (e.g. a peasant's son returning to settle as a householder) others following a disastrous failure as a 'colonist' and having lost the little they possessed. Actual emigration figures must be treated as the differential between those going away and those coming back. During the half-century that followed the 1861 Emancipation, rural natural growth doubled to reach 1.8 per cent per annum. At the end of that time the net emigration from the villages was taking away less than one-third of the natural population growth.[40] There was consequently little 'drainage' of rural population

and, especially its poor, which decisively contributed to the transformation of the countryside elsewhere. The population of villages proceeded
to increase.

With the roads of investment-bound intensification practically closed
and that of emigration restricted, the peasants reacted by a rushing,
often desperately, in the few directions still open to them. To begin with,
they starved themselves to meet their dues, rents and financial obligations. While the production figures of grain have shown that Russia
produced only about three-quarters of the per capita ration considered
sufficient by its medics, the figures for the export of grain went up by half
between the 1880s and the end of the century.[41] Something similar if less
drastic in scale was happening with milk and butter (and the related diet
of the peasant children). The internal logic of such forced sales was well
captured by the comment of Vishnegradskii (the then Minister of
Finance): 'We shall under-eat, but we will export.' Under the Russian
conditions that meant, of course, under-eating by peasants and
exporting by profiteers.

The second method of the peasant 'crisis management' through 'self-
exploitation' was to undervalue their own labour. Work at 'negative
profit' (i.e. use of family labour to a point when its per hour return is
much below average wages but the total return increases) was a usual
strategy of peasant farm management.[42] Elsewhere, the labour of the
peasants (man and his beasts) has competed successfully with wage
labourers or sophisticated machinery, often freezing the agriculture of
the large estates at their pre-mechanical state. To stay 'primitive' (i.e.
unmechanised) was often more profitable. (One is reminded of the fact
that no cranes were introduced until late into the twentieth century
within the harbour of Shanghai. The coolie labour was too cheap to
make it profitable.) The 'marginalist' economists of those times were
bewildered, if not scandalised, by the fact that, contrary to 'the laws of
economics', a sharp increase in the price of grain was regularly followed
by a decrease in rural wages. The secret of the economic curve that
misbehaved was well known to every Russian peasant and employer
alike: the hungrier the peasant, the more ready was he to offer his
services for practically any pay. The peasant engagement in crafts
(especially its female sector) was often similar in nature. In many
branches of peasant handiwork manufacturing it was the desperately
low rate of return that made it able to hold its own against the machine-
produce. The lower the income from farming, the stronger the tendency
for the broad range of rural supplementary 'crafts and trades' (*promysly*), that is, actual small-scale manufacturing, seasonal migration to

engage in harvesting, seasonal wage labour in construction work, etc., possibly merging more constant migration into towns. By the turn of the century 'supplementory' occupations were a necessary part of the peasant income and in some cases (especially in the poorer households) offered the largest part of the income of their males. Opportunity for such engagements was limited, however.[43]

The third 'way' was to get hold of more land, whatever its price. The results were manifest. Prices of land rose threefold between 1860 and 1900 and continued to rise thereafter. The rents rose even faster to multiply more than seven times during the 1861–1901 period.[44] The fact that some of the nobles were, since the mid-1890s, returning to direct farming,[45] increased the prevailing feeling of land shortage. Rents and prices of land, together with taxes and redemption payments, often took away not only any savings and potential investments the majority of peasants could possibly make, but also much of what was their most basic necessities. All the same, peasants (and by no means only rich peasants) proceeded to acquire land and to increase the extent of lands in their usage.[46] At the turn of the century, the squires were receiving much more in rent than two decades earlier, when they possessed and rented-out much more land. Russian peasants increasingly rented land at prices that exceeded any estimated 'profit' (i.e. the price of its produce less the market price of the inputs). To the peasant that was, of course, rational enough, for it increased the total results of his labour (while decreasing the peasant income per hour for his work and that of his family). To the noble landowners it meant that renting out of land could bring higher benefits than direct farming.

This may be the time to emphasise a point that could be lost in an avalanche of facts and figures. The conditions discussed cannot be treated simply as a case of shortage of resources, even if the 'cumulative' tendency of such shortages is stipulated. Russian peasant economy was powerfully influenced not only by the abject poverty of the peasants, but by their power situation *vis-à-vis* other social actors. That was the essence of what land tenure, redemption payments, state policies, etc. were all about. During the years 1861–1901 Russian peasants paid to the nobles and the state about 1 billion roubles in redemption fees. Reports of Russia's Minister of Finance were adamant that these were not 'his' taxes that led to the destitution of the peasants but admitted that 'terms of land redemption were settled without the paying capacity of peasantry being sufficiently taken into account'.[47] The taxes and rents paid by the peasant households were still estimated by 1913 (i.e. after the 'redemption payments' came to an end) as 18 per cent of their total income.[48] Terms of trade disadvantagous to the peasants were taking from the Russian peasantry yet another slice of it. To drive home the class aspect of it all in the countryside, the peasant paid seven times more than a noble in state and local tax per the same amount of land.[49] The political economy of the countryside *in toto* has in fact acted as an exploitative system-within-a-system. While the noble landlords engaged in the appropriation, transfer (mostly into towns) and usage (mainly for consumption) of peasant surpluses, the 'national' and the 'international' economy, acted in a similarly exploitative manner towards the whole of the Russian agricultural economy (admittedly followed by the partial 'redistribution' of the state income via the state bureaucracy to the noble land holders). The peasantry carried the burdens of the nobility dues, the state expenditure and the forced capitalist development of industry and the foreign debts, while participating to a very limited extent in the benefits of the Russian industrial 'economic miracle' of the 1890s. Russian peasantry was not only poor, but was also the exploited class who footed the major part of the bill of the upper classes' consumption, the 'needs of the state' and the development of the extra-agricultural economy.

One can present therefore the essential tenets of the Russian rural economy and its dynamics as a 'positive feedback model'. An agrarian system of political economy was reproducing itself, providing a stream of income to landlords and to the 'state apparatus' and contributing 'surplus' for extra-rural capital formation. It had also provided growing amounts of wheat, flax and butter for national and international markets, their production increase centered mostly in a few regions at Russia's territorial peripheries. It provided massive, cheap and pliable labour, both rural and urban. While securing all that, the system was advancing its own destruction through the gradual dissolution of some of its basic premises. Despite the massive transfer of wealth from the peasants to the nobility through dues, under-valued labour, over-taxation and state handouts, the noble landlords were being 'bought out' by their poorer peasant neighbours. The agriculture of the noble 'social estate' was 'folding' both in the size of the land it farmed and of the overall share of the production on it.[50] Peasant households did not disappear but grew in numbers. But by bringing under cultivation marginal lands and grasslands, peasants undercut their own animal husbandry (i.e. the main source of mechanical power, of fertilisers and of fats and proteins within their diets). Forests were rapidly cut down, leaving peasants without the timber necessary for setting up new households as well as their chief fuel and major source of work in winter.

On the freshly colonised virgin lands the use of 'predatory' methods meant rapid gains, but in the long term led to the decline in productivity. Massive land erosions were indeed reported throughout Russia.[51] The amount of land sown in some of the provinces in the overpopulated central Russia was actually declining. In major parts of agricultural Russia, especially in its hungriest parts, the very farming was put in jeopardy with no effective alternatives with which to supplement it.

It is often best to express such matters in the peasants' own words rather than second-hand, via the perceptions and words of 'the educated', however conscientious. What follows will dramatise it but would not represent an exception for the main areas of densely settled peasant populations. In the revolutionary years to follow shortly (and due to be discussed in this book's companion volume, *Russia 1905–07, Revolution as a Moment of Truth*), the peasants of the village Volchinets in Besarabskaya gub. on the western tip of the central agricultural zone of European Russia, were moved to address the freshly created and short-lived parliament – the second *Duma*. In the heavy rhythm of the prayer chant of a peasant congregation, their letter, preserved in the parliamentary archives, spoke as follows: 'We have only three *desiatin* of poor land giving very little income. We have nowhere to graze our livestock and many do not possess any of it. The local squires do not show us mercy and claim rent of 40 roubles for each *desyatina* of land.[52] We are therefore ever in debt for the payments of which our last possessions are sold by the bailiffs. Our distress is indescribable. Our poverty is total. The *Duma* is our last hope. We beg and cry out for the quickest solution to the land problem. Those with 8 or 10 children are dying of hunger.'[53]

4 The Peasant Economy: Semi-feudalist, Semi-capitalist or What's-Its-Name?

In so far as millions of families live under economic conditions of existence that separate their mode of life, their interest and their culture from those of the other classes and put them in hostile opposition to the latter, they form a class. In so far as there is only local interconnection among these small-holding peasants – they do not form a class.

Karl Marx

. . . which leaves us with a question and a riddle.

Chapter 2 above

A. CAPITALISM, RURAL PROLETARIANS, KULAKS

The discussion of capitalism in Russian agriculture forms a major and necessary step towards the more general debate of the impact and development of capitalism in Russia. Current arguments indicate that much of the discussion is still topical and controversial, both for the understanding of Russian history at the turn of the century and in the appreciation of the conditions in other countries and times. For reasons already mentioned, and to which we shall return, Russian agriculture has been used extensively as the substantiation and the testing ground for general theories and strategies of social transformation.[1]

To recollect the facts, the most fundamental change in the Russian rural economy of the period was its 'peasantisation', which was taking place within the context of the advancing commercialisation of rural society and of industrialisation on a national scale.[2] It meant that the large landed properties of nobles were being transferred through purchase and rent to family-labour and smallholder peasant production units, while hardly any of the big landlords or merchants of Russia had transformed their estates into capitalist enterprises and/or put to use capital-intensive technology – nor had the overwhelming part of the wealthier peasants. Also, with few regional exceptions, such as the Russian south-east and the non-Russian north-west of the empire, the percentage of permanent wage labourers used in farming was low and remained so. Most of the wage labour used was not 'proletarian' in the usual sense (i.e. it had more often than not represented the part-time work of peasant family farmers or a transitional period of pre-marriage wage work by their sons and daughters). The poorer strata engaged in it more but it was found also among the wealthier peasants (the category of 'wage worker' could be particularly deceptive there, as when referring to a horse-owner who was paid for ploughing the land of a poor horseless neighbour).

The 'peasantation' described did not mean, of course, regression to eighteenth-century Russia. The rural involvement in markets, especially grain markets, and in money economy continued to increase even though Prokopovich's first account of the Russian national income for 1913 estimated the 'marketability' of peasant produce at only 32 per cent.[3] As against the enserfment of the past there were now the relative freedom of movement and sovereignty over the production processes for the peasant householder. New and more effective methods of farming were spreading, albeit slowly. Also to recap, the rural world of Russian family farms was not some Rousseauesque ideal of altruistic co-operation between brothers; neighbourly exploitation was rife as were social tension dramatised by the extreme poverty and new financial pressures felt by many of those involved. Nevertheless, the decisive fact remains that in the most inhabited rural areas of Russia, family farming was massively and increasingly the rule, often caught within pauperisation processes which the much later classification of 'agricultural involution' would have fitted well.[4] In the Central Agricultural Zone stretching across the centre of European Russia and where the bulk of the peasants lived, the land per capita rapidly declined and the growth of population surpassed the increase in agricultural production.

Moreover, the prevalence and gradual increase in the proportion of family farms was true not only in terms of land-use, equipment and produce, where it came to amount, within the first decade of the twentieth century, to nearly nine-tenths of each, but also for the commodities production and exports. The international agricultural crisis of the 1880s and the 1890s had intensified those characteristics. While in Germany the big landlords responded to the fall in agricultural prices by a steep increase in capital investment, their Russian counterparts reacted by stopping investment altogether, and by the further increase of land sales, and the proportion of their land that was rented out or share-cropped.[5] The rise in prices and export opportunities after 1896 did not fundamentally reverse these patterns. As for the Russian peasants, they reacted by increasingly renting land at a 'negative profit', that is, put to use their 'surplus labour' by its heavy under-valuation – Chayanov's 'self-exploitation', Kautsky's 'under-consumption', Lenin's 'plunder of labour'.[6] At the same time, they systematically split further their meagre possessions within 'partitioning' dictated mostly by demographic changes and family biographies and proceeded to 'equalise' land holdings in their communes. Through the markets of labour and produce they were increasingly drawn into circuits of capitalism, becoming neither capitalist nor proletarian in most cases. The peasants generated also a steady stream of money earned in town which they sent or brought back to their families in the villages to meet consumption needs and taxes but also to be spent on re-peasantation through the buying of horses, extending the land the households tilled and the setting up of new farms. While making good enough sense to the peasants, to most of the economists steeped in the end-of-the-nineteenth-century models and images of capitalist progress, all this appeared as irritatingly irrational as clocks moving backwards. As to those who 'took the peasant side' and rejected the West European experience, they often did it by assuming the eternal stability of smallholder economy, explained by the intrinsically 'irrational' qualities of the Russian peasants' souls (e.g. the attachment to land, to the Orthodox religion etc.). Yet, as the rural conditions changed, the peasants did react to it, and, souls or not souls, did it consistently and with a fine feeling for their best economic interest.

This has been subsequently the field where generation after generation of Russia's scholars and/or radicals have crossed swords with particular fury. The question was whether the Russian rural economy was capitalist ('already'), or was it ('still') on its way to becoming so, or else, would it never become capitalist because of the fundamental impossibility of such developments within rural Russia. Was Russian peasant economy capitalist-rational but poor, peasant-irrational, or was it structured by the specific rationality of family production units? The political relevance of the alternative views heavily coloured this debate. Its main questions (and types of evidence drawn in support of the alternative views) concerned, in the first place, the extent of rural wage labour and of the production by capitalist farmers (i.e. what was universally accepted as direct evidence of capitalism). This was supplemented by questions concerning the extent, nature and significance of market relations and of the increases in production. Another type of questioning considered the advance of capitalism in the light of its political expression within the rural class struggle. We shall devote the remainder of this section and the next to the review of the first and the second of these questions and proceed to consider some alternatives in the final section of this chapter. The issue of the political expression of capitalism will be briefly referred to, but is discussed fully in another volume of this two-volume series: *Russia 1905–07: Revolution as a Moment of Truth*.

*   *   *

As to the characterisation of the rural economy of Russia, in the early days of the debate the Slavophiles simply refused to accept a 'materialist' and commercial determination of the life of the Russian peasants, save for some pathological occurrences or as an imposition. Later, some of the 'legal populists' argued on the basis of their economic analysis that capitalism could not penetrate Russia (or at least rural Russia) for reasons concerning its natural economy and poverty which circum- scribed commercialisation. No market – no capitalism. It was this view that was tackled with particular vehemence by the early Marxist writers. Young Struve and young Lenin proved convincingly enough that 'natural' economy could and did self-generate market relations and was not merely 'penetrated' by them.[7] Many have proceeded to document accordingly the fact of increasing market involvement of the Russian peasant households, interpreting it often as a sufficient proof of their being but a sector of a capitalist economy. As a second string to his bow, Lenin used the plentiful evidence of socio-economic differentiation within Russian villages, interpreting it as an advanced stage in a polarisation process splitting peasants into landless proletarians and rural employers (i.e. of peasantry 'not only differentiating' but 'being completely dissolved . . . ceasing to exist . . . being ousted by ab- solutely new type of rural inhabitants . . . the rural bourgeoisie . . . and the rural proletariat').[8] Still, it was the actual extent of wage labour that was the decisive index of capitalism, especially for the Marxist economists. On that score, a very young Lenin endorsed on behalf of the whole of the Russian Social Democratic movement the classification of European Russia in accordance with the prelevant type of labour usage on the large landed estates, as suggested by N. Annenskii – a leading economist of the day.[9] This analysis equated capitalism with the predominance of wage labour on them as against the 'feudalist remnants' expressed as share-cropping and *corvee*. By these standards, of the forty-three *guberniyas* of European Russia studied by Annenskii for 1883–7, the 'capitalist system' of landlord farming was said to have predominated in nineteen, the non-capitalist in seventeen, while seven were in a transitory position.

The consequent 'mostly capitalist' image of Russian agriculture dominated the writings of the Russian liberal economists as well as the initial general programme of the first congress of the Russian Social Democracy, written by Struve in 1899, and its first agrarian programme delivered by Lenin and adopted by the second congress in 1903, (at which the party was actually inaugurated and split down the middle).

The 1890s industrialisation wave demolished the stand of the conservative 'legal populists' as effectively as the experience of the 1905–7 revolution was to undermine, at least among the Bolsheviks of 1906–7, the purely 'capitalist' image of rural Russia. Little more was heard in the twentieth century of the fundamental impossibility of Russian capitalism (or even the intrinsic refusal by true Russians to engage in 'German-style' behaviour). On the other hand, by 1906, arguing from the new political experience towards socio-economic characterisation, Lenin declared his early estimate of capitalist development within agriculture to have been 'overstated'. He proceeded to argue for a new agrarian programme that manifestly recognised the existence of peasantry as a class of cohesion and revolutionary potential, within a countryside which by that very token could not be capitalist, at least not to an 'orthodox' Marxist. The way Lenin now defended his case was explicit enough in that sense. 'On the whole the contemporary manorial economy of Russia is based on an enserfing (*krepostnicheski-kabal'noi*), rather than on a capitalist system of economy. Those who refuse to admit this cannot explain the current broad and deep peasant revolutionary movement in Russia.'[10] A more recent comparison between Russia and Germany made by a leading Soviet scholar brought out more fully the general significance of that line of argument. At the turn of the century, Germany had seen the rapid development of elements of agrarian capitalism: massive wage labour, new technology, high productivity, rural depopulation. It had not produced peasant political movements of class autonomy and strength, let alone of radical and revolutionary potential. In Russia, the reverse all along had taken place.[11]

It took two more generations for a Russian Marxist to abandon the simple repetition of Lenin's 1899 text and to proceed with the analysis of the actual evidence and issues Lenin studied. In 1961 A. Anfimov published an article in which he considered how Annenskii's division of Russian *guberniyas* would fare if *not only* landlords' farming were taken into account, but *also* the peasants.[12] Accepting with the Lenin of 1910 the premise that it is the use of wage labour that offers 'the decisive characteristic of any advance of capitalist agriculture',[13] Anfimov added the lands of peasant households that engaged wage labour (any degree of it, i.e. explicitly overstating the case for capitalism) to Annenski's figures referred to above and which concerned the landed estates only. Summing up the total of land on which wage labour was used, Anfimov concluded that out of the five gubs. of European Russia for which such evidence was available, only in one could the claim of prevailing capitalist agriculture be sustained in this way. This *guberniya* was that of Stavropol at the newly colonised south-west with the neighbouring Tavrida following it closely (i.e. the manifest regional exception within rural Russia referred to often as its 'New America'). By reckoning only the cases where wage labour *prevailed over family labour* the amount of land involved would drop dramatically even there. More importantly, the Yaroslavl gub., typical of the provinces in which agriculture was defined as capitalist by Annenskii's account, has shown that once peasant holdings are added, only about 10 percent of total land was worked by enterprise or farms employing any extent of wage labour.[14] That is confirmed by the work of Chernyshev published in 1927 which has shown that in pre-revolutionary Russia peasant households using permanent wage labour held only 10.7 per cent of total arable land, 5.2 per cent of horses and 5.8 per cent of cows.[15]

Anfimov's conclusions about the limited use of wage labour within agriculture and the consequent limited advance of capitalism within it if Lenins own methods are consistently used are also supported by other types of findings. The reviewed figures of the 1897 census (Addendum 2 above) have shown how limited, on a national scale, was the permanent wage labour in Russian agriculture. As presented elsewhere, the extent and nature of socio-economic mobility within the Russian rural areas has challenged the accepted explanation of 'differentiation' as a self-evident 'stage' along the necessary road towards rapid entrenchment of capitalist farming.[16] Even the evidence of the decline of land holdings and horses in the hands of the poorer peasants did not always spell growing polarisation and consequent 'proletarianisation'. It often represented an 'aggregate shift downward' (i.e. the impoverishment and 'involution' of peasant communities *in toto*).[17] As put by M. Simonova in her discussion of the Central Agricultural Region, 'rather than being proletarianised, the peasantry has shown impoverishment, was turning into paupers'.[18] We have learned since the nineteenth century that throughout the world pauperisation does not necessarily result in 'proletarisation', if understood as the formation of an industrial or rural class of wage-earners. It was admittedly less clear in the Russia of the 1890s but as true.

Turning to the 'other side of the coin' of the classical model of capitalism, that of 'capitalist enterprises', the accumulation of land in the hands of the few and the spread of large-scale units of production was confidently expected by the early liberal and Marxist analysis in Europe. The fact that this did not happen was already noticed by Kautsky, who then proceeded to defend his assumption concerning the necessary 'capitalist accumulation' in agriculture by pointing to the possibility that intensification could have taken the place of the expected extension of the size of land-units (i.e. a small land holding could still express capitalist development via investment-bound technological advance).[19] Later Lenin came to belabour the same point.[20] What it meant in the first place was the acceptance of the fact that, contrary to earlier expectations, a concentration of landownership on par with the accumulation of capital within the capitalist industries was not coming about and that the opposite was in fact being documented. Also the advance of capital-intensive technology was very limited in Russia, as was its role as a determinant of agricultural production. With the declining role of the 'noble' estates the case for capitalist advance must hang either on the nature and the impact of the so-called 'kulaks' or on some claims defining it *via* the 'general nature of the economy'.

It is important to clarify first the meaning of the Russian word 'kulak' – a major concept and mystifactory device, often replicated with an air of deep sociological wisdom in 'second-hand' debates whose Marxist and non-Marxist participants know as little Russian as they know of rural Russia. The word 'kulak' ('a fist' derived from the Turki *kul* – i.e. 'a hand') was a peasant term of abuse aimed at 'smart alecs' who prospered not by the sweat and slog of peasant farming but by usury, go-between activities, shoddy deals, etc., mostly at the expense of the communities they belonged to. In its usage the word was often coupled with *miroed*, that is, the commune's 'eater-up' (i.e. its parasitic destroyer). It also defined some negative traits of personality: avarice, meanness and unneighbourly behaviour. This mixture of meanings sheds light on the norms and precepts of the Russian peasants of the period as authoritatively documented by the linguists who studied the peasant vernacular. The etymological dictionary of 1903 has given as synonyms of the term kulak: 'shoddy wheeler-and-dealer' (*vorotila*), a 'go-between' (*maklak*), a niggard (*skryaga*) and the *miroed*.[21] As late as 1934, another Russian etymological dictionary understood it to mean a 'rich peasant exploiting his neighbours', a 'buyer-up' (*skupshchik*) and a skin-flint (*skupets*).[22] This was also the image presented by the most influential, if overdrawn, pre-revolutionary description by Gvozdev who spoke of that 'figure which enslaved the Russian existence . . . and whom you will necessarily meet in the city and the village . . . ever changing its forms'.[23] The 'forms' of economic exploitation he actually listed as typical of 'kulaks' were usury, renting for the purpose of sub-renting, marketing, directing craftsmen's *artel*'s, buying-up peasant produce, and the type of shop-owning that 'tied-up' its customers through the advancing of credit. Gvozdev concluded that 'kulak-usurers are a general term for all of the exploiters spread over the Russian land'.[24]

The point emerging is not a linguistic one but of major importance to rural economy. Not 'all' exploitation is actually included in all of these descriptions. In particular, the typically capitalist exploitation through the use of wage labour is consistently absent. Nor was the term a simple synonym of peasant wealth – a peasant could be rich or a farmer–employer without being a 'kulak'. On the other hand, a 'kulak' did not need to be outstandingly rich nor an employer of wage labour, for indeed, as pointed out by a major Soviet historian, Tarnovskii, 'A kulak's economy, based on commercial-usurious form and method of exploitation is not farmers' economy.'[25] What is more, to use one's resources in a kulak way restricted rather than advanced capitalist enterprises within peasant farming, as noticed already in Marx's *Capital*, a point taken up later by P. Baran in his pioneering work on the political economy of the 'developing societies'.[26] In his 1899 study, Lenin had shown himself well aware of this, distinguishing between 'kulaks' and 'enterprising muzhiks'. (His point was that, as opposed to what he claimed to be the populist view, these were not 'totally unconnected and opposite phenomena' but 'two forms of the same phenomenon'.[27] Quite.).

Needs of legitimation and propaganda led the Bolshevik state to adopt the peasant abuse attached to the term 'kulak' and use it to delimit farmer–employers and, eventually, in the late 1920s, even peasants who were simply better-off (e.g. 'all those with more than 10 des. of land and two horses or cows') or simply those who objected to government decrees concerning collectivisation.[28] It was these deeply misleading reinterpretations of the term that came to be adopted unwittingly into languages, conditions and theoretical structures far removed from its origin. In such usage the term loses the meaning Russian peasants have given to it and the illuminations of its actual social contexts. This also renders unintelligible the important analytical distinction drawn by Russian scholars between productive and non-productive profit-making in smallholder farming. From a pejorative image rooted in the Russian peasant's communal life, values and codes of honour and from a specific illuminating term used by the Russian rural specialists at the turn of the century, a bastard concept evolved which is as weak analytically (for how many cows make a peasant into an exploiter?) as it is open to glib propaganda or ritual abuse against any peasant opposition to the officialdoms pursuing contrasting goals, as much in Tanzania as in Peru, in Eastern Europe as in South Asia of today.

To recapitulate, the 'kulaks' as understood by the Russian peasants and indeed by everybody with sufficient knowledge of the Russian countryside before the propaganda exercise took its toll, cannot be equated with capitalist entrepreneurship. Arguably, the opposite holds true, that is, the 'kulaks' hampered rather than advanced the development of capitalist farming. While 'kulaks' flourished in the Russian countryside there were no signs of grain or meat or milk-producing 'factory equivalents' nor a concomitant rise in the numbers of wage labourers engaged in agriculture. Moreover, the political behaviour of peasants in the 1905–7 revolution, as noted by the more perceptive of the revolutionaries, has supported the non-capitalist (or not yet capitalist) image of rural Russia. The argument in favour of capitalist interpretation has increasingly taken alternative routes. This became apparent in the debate between Soviet historians during the 1960s and 1970s. The review of it will necessarily grow more technical and abstract. A 'lay' or impatient reader may wish to leap to p. 172 to pick up there the thread of discussion concerning Russia's rural history rather than its historians and other social scientists arguing about their trade.

B. CAPITALISM, AGRARIAN MARKETS, PRODUCTIVITY

In the USSR of the last generation, the debate about capitalism within the Russian pre-revolutionary agriculture has often taken the form of Leninocitology. In that spirit two opposing views were argued, both supported by batteries of quotations drawn from Lenin's writings. (Lenin's works are of course an interesting contribution to the issue, but that is not quite the way they were usually treated.) On the one hand stood those for whom Russian agriculture was fully capitalist by the end of the nineteenth century. Their citations came mostly from Lenin's writings of the 1890s. On the other hand stood those who concluded that the capitalist advance in Russian agriculture was limited and chose their quotations particularly from Lenin's writings in the period of the 1905–7 revolution and the 1920s.

The first view followed the tradition relating Plekhanov's anti-populist crusade and the parallel views of the Russian liberal academic establishment to those of the young Lenin. Rural Russia was capitalist in its essential characteristics. The advance of capitalism was progressive (i.e. good whatever its blemishes). The division of ruralites into a bourgeoisie and proletariat had made peasants not a class but a notion. In so far as no re-counting of the numbers of the rural proletariat could make them sufficiently high for that purpose, Lenin's conception of 'disguised proletarians', i.e. *batrak s nadelom* – cottagers to whom farming was but a supplement to wage labour (and due rapidly to proletarianise entirely) was being liberally used in substitution. This paradigm became less fashionable in the revolutionary days of 1905–7 and again in 1919–21 but grew in impact in the post-revolutionary periods of 'Stolypin's reforms' of 1907–13 as much as during late NEP of 1925–8. It was imposed at its crudest in the 1930s as a major legitimation of Stalin's collectivisation drive.

The late 1950s saw the resumption of the argument that stressed the non-capitalist characteristics of pre-revolutionary Russian agriculture and of the consequent debate.[1] Extensive new evidence concerning units of production, wage labour, capital investment etc. was brought into play. K. Tarnovskii related it to the biography of Lenin, by suggesting two distinct periods in Lenin's didactic approach.[2] Until 1905 Lenin's attention was seen to have been centred on the general laws of capitalism in agriculture as part of the confrontation of the 'orthodox' Marxists with the 'legal populists' of Russia and the 'revisionists' of Germany. As from 1905, Lenin would have concentrated upon specific impediments that slowed down the general process of capitalist development and subsequently taken greater account of Russia's particularities and the consequent revoltionary capacity of the Russian peasantry – understated until then.

This general conclusion was expressed on the scale of historical progress, understood as the transition from feudalism to capitalism. The claim of the not-quite-capitalist nature of Russian rural economy at the turn of the century would place it in between feudalism and capitalism, with descriptions like 'semi-feudal' or 'semi-capitalist' used to pin it down. Lenin's reference to the Russian rural economy as 'medieval' (in his 1906 argument for a new agrarian programme of the RSDWP) and his related demand for reassessment of the 'stage of history' at which rural Russia found itself then,[3] was used as the major legitimation for that approach. So was Lenin's comment in 1917 that the repeated demands of the Russian peasants for the nationalisation of all lands must be explained by the fact that 'all Russian landholdings, peasant as well as manorial, within communes as well as on the homesteads, are fully permeated (*propitany*) with the old semi-feudalism'.[4] The conclusion put at its clearest was that 'within the agriculture of European Russia half-feudalism (half-enserfment?) was prevailing over the capitalism'. Moreover, 'half-feudalism' (*polukrepostnichestvo*) was not to be understood as equivalent to 'half-bourgeois'. Those were feudal relations, modified to be sure by capitalism, but significant to the extent that they limited and chained capitalist relations.[5] One Soviet analyst went even further, moving away from Lenin's assessment of rural Russia's next stage of capitalism as that of 'two possible roads', that is, the 'American' (smallholder based and radical) or the 'Prussian' (manorial and conservative), to a view that both models were insufficient and should be superseded by a designation of a specific type corresponding to the actual and distinctive conditions of Russia.[6]

The counter-offensive of the supporters of a capitalist designation of rural Russia was not slow to materialise. In part, they argued their case through the old evolutionist argument used by some Russian writers of the 1920s, for example, Shestakov and Geister on the Bolsheviks' side or Kosinskii of those who opposed them,[7] supplementing it by new evidence (e.g. the reanalysis of peasant political behaviour in 1905–7 in the books of Dubrovskii and Tropin).[8] A different line of argument was put forward in the work of Koval'chenko and Milov, closely linked with a more overtly ideological position presented by the writings of a senior party official.[9] The crux of that line of analysis was that at the turn of the century rural Russia was capitalist as assumed by Lenin in 1899 for reasons related to the *general nature of the economy* expressed in the rural markets. (Indeed, reading those texts closely, one must suspect that Lenin erred still in underestimating the extent of capitalist transformation).[10]

The massive econometric work presented by Koval'chenko and Milov in substantiation of that view has documented a decline in the variations between the major agricultural regions of Russia in so far as prices of agricultural produce, land, horses and rural labour as well as land rents were concerned. The establishment of a national market was clearly taking place. Such a trend would have been stipulated, no doubt, by every student of rural Russia but the regionalised figures and the determinants of production and profit are of considerable interest. The main significance of the book lies, however, in its historiography and conclusions. It offered a periodisation by which there was first a slow and ambivalent formation of a national market of agricultural produce, mostly grain, which was accomplished by the 1880s. This was followed by the rapid formation of a specifically capitalist market, that is, the national market of factors of production: land, horses and wage labour. It would have also induced a universal 'rate of profit' with the poorer households supplementing the intensity of labour self-usage for capital investment. (The authors admitted that all this was never accomplished for land, much of which could not be purchased and in relation to which the rent was consistently and considerably higher than the estimated 'capitalised rent'.)[11] The book concluded that regardless of any contrary evidence, by the beginning of the twentieth century rural Russia was 'bourgeois capitalist. . . by its objective economic content, and consequently, its socio-class structure' or, put otherwise, 'the formation of the agrarian-capitalist market proves the fact that the development of agrarian capitalism in Russia has achieved its highest stage . . . the turning of agricultural production into a mere sector of a general system of capitalist production'.[12]

The authors have shown awareness of some of the difficulties their analytical stance produced when related to the work of Marx. In particular, they have had to dismiss 'primitive accumulation' as the necessary precondition of the development of capitalism and did so by pointing to the fact that Lenin did not mention this concept at all in his 1899 study of capitalism in Russia. (Indeed, he did not – an interesting point to ponder.) They also spoke of 'feudal remnants' still in evidence, for example, the peasant commune, and of 'different forms' of capitalism, but at once circumscribed the term 'forms' to express 'subjective side of the process' only, making it secondary and epiphenominal as against the objectivity of the 'bourgeois–capitalist' substance of the rural economy of Russia.[13] That is why, while the book presented itself as a 'middle-road position' between the views that assumed rural Russia's semi-feudal/semi-capitalist economy and between those who (like N. Rozhkov in the first quarter of the century) treated the Russian countryside as simply capitalist, the claim of 'even-handedness' is mostly tactical. The substantial view is a major defence of a fully fledged 'capitalist already' image of rural Russia in the 1890s or earlier still.

A supplementary line of this argument equated the rapid growth of the production of Russian agriculture in the 1890s, documented by Nifontov, with capitalist advance.[14] This supplement is particularly unsatisfactory for reasons already discussed in Section 3D and can be dismissed at the outset. Russian agricultural production did rise, there is no doubt about that, but the view that rising productivity definitely indicates the rise of capitalism could only be tenable should (at least) a proof be offered that capital investment and/or capital-intensive technology and/or an extension of wage labour lay at the root of that advance. Even then, the argument would have to be carefully scrutinised for its analytical meaning and might still be rejected (as indeed it was, by quite a number of recent studies we shall turn to presently).[15] There is no need to go that far, however, when all of the evidence points in the other direction. Subject to a few regional exceptions, the increase of production within rural Russia, however significant, was not the result of substantial new technology, capital accumulation, capitalist investment and/or of structural change of the prevailing 'relations of *production*'. Nor was it related to an extension of wage labour in farming.

* * *

The issue of the classification of the economic structure of Russia appears on two related levels: intra-national and international. As a 'junior', dominated and exploited component, Russian peasant economy (and arguably the whole of the agricultural sector) was linked with the capitalist and the state industry, within a national market delimited and strongly coloured by the intervention of the Russian state. Simultaneously, Russia and its economy were linked as a junior and 'less developed' (i.e. less capitalist) poorer and weaker partner, to the world centres of financial and industrial capitalism (often supported by 'their' governments), and to international markets. On both levels of generalisation the question is that of defining, characterising and considering the *dynamics of the counterpart* to the definitely capitalist side of the equation. Should it be analytically assimilated under the 'laws of motion of capitalism' and treated as simple reflections of the interests or 'needs' of the 'core economy' and of those who rule it? Should it be, alternatively, singled out as a discrete social form(s) with capacity to reproduce which resists and modifies up to a point 'external' determinations and/or dictate? Moving from the 'systems' to the linked but not identical question of historiography, were the Western Europe and the capitalist industries of Russia subsequently showing the 'image of their future' to Russia as a whole and the Russian rural economy? Or, on the contrary, did the evidence indicate distinct 'roads', despite or indeed because of the linkage of the 'components' on a global and national scale? We shall discuss it in the subsequent parts of this Chapter and the preliminary sections of Chapter 5.

To begin with the rural economy, an initial approach to it was made in the review of social 'embedding' of the Russian peasantry in Chapter 2. We can advance it now by focusing on political economy and relating it to the 'circulationist' and 'productivist' argument hotly debated by those Western social scientists who were critical of the Modernisation Theory of the 1950s. For, interestingly, the argument offered by Koval'chenko and Milov corresponds closely to the view about the Latin America of the 1950s advanced by A. G. Frank, even though an exactly opposite conclusion was being reached as to the developmental potentials of the situations considered. In his discussion of Latin American findings, Frank has delimited and treated as synonymous the development of the (unequal) world market relations and that of capitalism.[16] His conclusions were deeply pessimistic: the structural and exploitative 'dependency' of the Latin American 'periphery' precluded industrialisation, economic growth and, by these tokens, 'proper capitalism' in it. The problem was seen not any more as that of pockets of feudalism interfering with progress, but of a capitalism-generated deterioration of the peripheries brought about by their assimilation into global capitalism and thereby of 'development of underdevelopment'. Similar models have been offered since for other regions and in relation to the rural versus urban sectors of the Third World.

In the debate that followed, the critics of that view objected both to the equation of commodity-production with capitalism and to the 'structural holism' which treats every section of the market-related social whole as determined utterly by the 'general structure' or by its controlling 'core', while disregarding discrete characteristics and processes within the 'peripheries'.[17] Much of this counter-argument is well taken in terms of theory as well as of empirical substantiation and prediction. While offering a relevant critique of 'methodological individualism' (by which social reality is not more than a sum total of its constituent units), Frank's 'holist' tendency appeared as unrealistic in 'falling over backwards'. Also, to equate capitalism with market relations would extend the bounds of capitalism so far and so wide, into past history as well as globally, as to make the concept vague and diminish its illuminations. To those who have argued against Frank, his view was also fundamentally non-Marxist, because to Marx, even though capitalism is ever bound to commodity production, not every commodity production would be capitalist even when 'factors of production' do enter markets.[18] A parallel view of contemporary farming at its most technologically advanced was taken to task in a recent study of US grain farming. It warned against a 'focus on commodity production' which 'collapsed the distinction between commercial household production and capitalist production'.[19]

The interpretation of Koval'chenko concluding about the capitalist nature of rural Russia at the turn of the century (and which gained, at least for the moment, the upper hand in Soviet scholarly institutions) raises analytical misgivings similar to those concerning the views reviewed above. Defining capitalism via market relations is doubtful in its analytical results while the 'holist' model of a 'general system' of capitalist production was usually overdrawn and 'over-integrated'. Empirically, the lack of fit between land market and profits makes the Koval'chenko and Milov case for the 'capitalism already' school of thought deficient and so does the presentation of much of its evidence. The mathematics of the tables looks impressive but the sources for the econometric computations are not open to inspection and possible reconsideration by its critics – a major shortcoming, particularly since other types of evidence stand in direct contradiction to that of the political experience of the 1905–7 revolution (as explicated also by Lenin, regarded as the supreme theoretical authority by the authors). We now know that the large figures for grain marketing by capitalist producers of pre-revolutionary Russia, unveiled by Stalin in 1928 to justify collectivisation, and still often used, were a fake. Those figures were: squires 21.6 per cent, 'kulaks' 50 per cent, 'middle and poor peasants' 28.4 per cent, that is, nearly three-quarters of Russia's marketed grain coming from 'capitalist producers'.[20] The true author of these figures, V. Nemchinov, admitted to the 'trick' and even explained how it was done – he simply extrapolated to the whole of Russia figures from the south-eastern region of New Russia, where extensive commodity production was indeed taking place.[21] (Needless to say, Stalin-cum-Nemchinov have also used the expression 'kulak' in an explicitly misleading way.) It is amusing to note that an empirical study by Koval'chenko was said by the author 'to show results which are close to those of V. Nemchinov' (while leaving out the peasant/'kulak' divisions of them).[22]

A brief aside, before leaving the 'circulationist' line of argument (i.e. the view that bases its definition and analysis of capitalism on market relations or a sub-category of their advanced version). The 'Western' studies of commodity production within a rural context and the consideration of its meaning were often bedevilled by a particular misinterpretation of the increasingly influential work of Chayanov and his friends (i.e. the way the Russian peasant households were defined or rather misdefined on their behalf). The 'model' or 'ideal type' of a market-free peasant family farm was used by Chayanov as a major heuristic device.[23] It has been treated by some of Chayanov's critics as a claim or a description of a set of actual characteristics of the Russian peasant scene. Chayanov knew, investigated and stated the exact opposite,[24] but once a silly assumption equating analytical tools with actuality has been made, the next step is the exposition of Chayanov's lack of realism. Pure non-market and 'natural' peasantries have been an exception or a figment of imagination in all ages, at least in Euro-Asia. As a model such a view offers some interesting insights. In assuming it to be 'reality' one activates the particular blinds of this model. It also (or else) by default overstates changes. The natural next step of such a conceptual operation tends to transform terminologically an actually existing peasant economy into a 'commercialised petty-bourgeoisie' – an undistinguishable sector of capitalism.[25] The alternative to such a deductive exercise is to consider specifically the nature of peasant economy within its broader context. It is also the best way to state directly the view that our own study represents.

C. PEASANT ECONOMY: 'MODES', PRODUCTION AND HISTORY

What is 'peasant economy'? Common speech that equates it usually with agriculture and/or the life of the rural localities tends to mislead us here. Farming can be undertaken in a variety of alternative ways, only one of which is 'peasant'.[1] Peasants do not solely farm for their living, and they share the rural environment with other social groups engaged in economies differently structured. Another conceptual cul-de-sac is to assign it all to the realm of consumption and exchange. That would mean the delimiting of peasant economy as market-free ('natural'), or else as exclusively oriented towards consumption needs.[2] By heavily overstating the significant self-consumption element of the peasant budgets and the peasant tactics of making a living, this makes it into a caricature, or else implicitly removes the whole issue into the long-lost past. One more path to frustration is the attempt to establish the nature of peasant economy as representing specific psychology, for example, peasant irrationality, understood as a mysterious attachment to land, that is, a tendency to react differently from the theorising observer to economic stimuli. Peasants have left their land frequently enough so long as it made sense to them, be it contemporary Sicily or Russia under Ivan IV. Peasants have often enough 'out-rationalised' PhD-holding advisers where long-term farming and their own well-being were concerned. Their conservatism, suspicion of outsiders, refusal to adopt 'national goals', etc. that have been the constant reason for complaints of officialdom and of the university trained, are usually well grounded in actual peasant experience of production, taxation and exchange.[3] The biases and prejudices of their perception do not necessarily surpass those of other groups in any population.

The main alternative route is to define peasant economy in terms of production processes. That can use as a starting point either societal political economy or the peasant farm. Much of the current debate attempting to characterise peasant economy belongs to the first category and was carried out in Marxist language relating it to the concept of 'modes of production', even though the actual issue and its resolutions have clearly cross-cut Marxist/non-Marxist dichotomies. The peasant component of the 'developing societies' has been approached accordingly in four different ways, none of which is fully satisfactory. First, it was said to be capitalist throughout, because the poor peasants, who mostly engaged in wage labour, are not more than a disguised form of proletariat. Second, such rural societies would represent a feudal 'mode of production' – a backward remnant in a rapidly changing world. The third is like the second but it was supplemented by the idea of the 'articulation' of the rural–feudal and the dominant–capitalist 'modes of production'. The peasant 'mode of production' is subsequently left undissolved but is being socially reproduced because of its functionality for the accumulation of capital and profits elsewhere via cheap food, the 'reserve army of labour', etc. Finally, the overwhelming logic of capitalist core economy is assumed, but it is 'articulated' with a specifically peasant 'subsidiary mode of production'.[4]

For our specific purpose, that of characterising rural Russia at the turn of the twentieth century, the evidence presented above seems to invalidate the first of these approaches at the onset. Not only the rural proletariat, but also those peasants to whom the income from farming was secondary as against wages, were a fairly small group in most of the Russian villages. Peasants provided much of Russia's wage labour but the bulk of it came from family farms, the operational logic of which was neither that of capitalist enterprises nor that of wage-working families in a capitalist industry. Capitalist enterprises farmed a small minority of Russia's lands.

The ways in which Russian peasant economy of the day did not operate as a capitalist 'mode of production' did not 'therefore' made it into a feudal one. The relative sovereignty that the Russian peasants exercised over their family labour and production units makes spurious the description of their post-emancipation economy as 'feudal' i.e. a 'mode of production' delimited in all Marxist designation by coercive rather than economic extraction of surpluses by the landlords.[5] (A parallel argument is also true for much of the non-Marxist historiography of feudalism.) 'Feudal remnants' can reasonably be claimed but even their characterisation as 'remnants' is often doubtful. Much of these arrangements was fairly recent, responding to social and economic process or to state policies, often by an original social restructuring. All of this holds true also for the idea of a feudal or 'semi-feudal' peasantry 'articulated' into the capitalist mode of production, which reproduces it for its own needs. As put succinctly by H. Bernstein: 'It is not capitalism nor imperialism which reproduces the peasantry – the peasantry reproduce themselves through their own labour.'[6] An inbuilt functionalism-for-the-strong bias of the 'articulation' models limits the recognition of inherent conflicts, different outcomes and the abilities of peasant production units to choose, to act and to oppose within limits pressures of market and nature, capital and state.

Finally, the conceptual solution of designing a subsidiary and specifically 'peasant' or 'simple commodity' mode of production that is 'articulated' to capitalism (or even to both capitalism and 'semi-feudalism'[7]), has the virtue of enabling the systematic discussion of specific characteristics of peasant economy, its societal structure and constraints. The limitations of that usage are considerable, however. In particular, the use of the concept of 'mode of production' that places the main dimension of exploitation and conflict between rather than within the 'modes of production', deprives the concept of its most substantive illumination. The heuristic 'gain' seems lesser than the 'loss' incurred.

To define specific peasant economy as well as 'peasanthood' as a conceptual entity in ways that can stand the test of validity and of realism in the contemporary world, we must begin from the units and the processes of production but not leave it at that. This has indeed been the position adopted by a long line of otherwise unlikely partners: Marx (but not necessarily the 'Marxists'[8]), Znaniecki, Chayanov, Sorokin, Firth or Thorner. The refusal to admit (or the ambivalence about) such delimitation of peasant economy has inevitably turned it from a 'tight' concept into an unspecific figure of speech. The way a family farm operates, and at its structural core, the productive use of family labour under 'self-management', provided the crux of that approach. A variety of specific and typical consequences follow: a characteristic division of labour, discrete economic strategies (e.g. the 'self-exploitation' and the 'irrational diversification' of crops), the 'telescoped' occupational skills and the family-bound occupational training,[9] the interlinked life/farming rhythms, the 'packages' of different categories of employment, i.e.

gathering, husbandry and manufacturing, family employment, wage labour and crafts.[10] It is this focus and framework of social relations of production that gives sense to the land-husbandry and self-consumption aspects of peasant lives, which cannot be understood otherwise. The same obtains for the particularities of the use of arable land as the major 'means of production'. The argument about the specific peasant rationality may make sense thereby, which is however not psychological but socio-structural (as explored by Chayanov and a just reason for his recent analytical impact and fame). Peasant households operating at 'negative profit' offer a good example here. Essentially, it expresses the way family farms operate within a context of exploitative political economy and relative deprivation. It meshes with what is usually treated as extra-economic aspects of social living into a distinctly peasant 'way of life', with continuity, consistency and meanings.

To avoid misunderstanding and to reiterate a point already made, the acceptance of the economic specificity of peasant production units does not equal an 'essentialist' view by which 'homogeneous "interests" or "laws of motion" of peasantry . . . serve as predicates from which all else follows'[11] even though such readings of it were at times made. Nor is it to accept in entirety Chayanov or Thorner, especially where the issues of social transformation and of capitalism are concerned. It is the *specificity of the reaction to the 'broader' intra and inter-national political economy* (the significance of which is not in doubt) that must be understood and analysed in this way (i.e. in discrete analytical terms). This claim of specificity does not assume peasant economies' eternal presence, but it helps to explicate its stability as against the many failed predictions of its imminent demise. It also helps to see more clearly and to typologise the *distinct* ways peasant economies have reacted to and changed under the impact of capitalism. The generalisations concerning what came to be referred to as 'blocked', 'deformed' or 'impure' capitalist penetration as well as of the peasantry's disappearance as a distinguishable social entity can be presented more clearly as a specific taxonomy of patterns of transformation of the peasant economies: differentiation, pauperisation and marginalisation.[12] The significance of such 'sorting out' for the better understanding of the fundamental socio-economic processes of the 'developing societies' of today is considerable.

More generally, to conceptualise peasant economy of the modern world one must admit, theorise and 'model' different, parallel and (unequally) related socio-economic structures and operational logics that do not 'fit' but rather contradict and confront each other within systems of political economy. Another side of the same conceptual coin is acceptance of discrete if related patterns of historiography with different determining power. Peasant economy is definable as a combined social structure, operational logic and transformation pattern. It is neither separate nor static; the image of 'dualism', if so interpreted, would not do. It is 'subsumed' in the sense of being dominated and exploited *on par* with other plebeian classes, but this term must be put in contradistinction to supra-functionalist views that reduce it simply to 'laws of capitalism' and its 'needs'. The peasant hold on fundamental 'means of production' means that the impact of the logic of profit-maximisation of capitalist enterprise can up to a point be held at bay, qualified or inverted by a peasant economic logic, rooted in the structure of the family farms.[13] The fact that the concept of 'mode of production' as used in the mainstream of Marxist analysis did not fully fit contemporary capitalism-related peasants is not a reflection on the legitimacy of the concept of peasant economy, but on the lexicon that fails to specify it. It is the lexicon that has to adjust.

It is when we turn to motion, transformations and historiography that the theoretical problems of peasant economy stand out fully. To begin, in so far as it is the peasant family farm that delimits the peasant economy, the question is if every family farm is *ex definitio* peasant or put historiographically, is there a stage of development when a family farm cannot be seen any longer as belonging to peasant economy? If so, can it be defined by the characteristics of the family farm? The major Soviet historian of contemporary peasantry, V. Danilov, has offered here an elegant Marxist solution.[14] He suggested that not only the relations of production expressed in the structuring of the family farm but also the forces of production shall be brought into the taxonomy. The 'forces of production' consist of natural ones (land, labour, etc.) and the man-made ones (i.e. the 'capital' of Marxist terminology). To Danilov it is the prevalence of the first over the second that is typical of peasanthood. Depeasantisation may be expressed by the disintegration of the family farms as the basic units of production. A second way to depeasantisation would be when the prevalent 'factors of production' of the family farms become extra-natural (i.e. highly mechanised and capital-bound grain farms of Utah, USA, or meat farms of Holland). Danilov's approach relates well to the contemporary studies of the gradual subversion of the autonomy of management and production of the USA and West European family farmers by agro-business. High technology, mortgage and the contract make the family farmer move into the position of a 'surplus value' producer. (Interestingly, this point was anticipated by *both* Kautsky *and* Chayanov.)[15] Even then there is of course no place 'to collapse the distinction' between commercialised household production and capitalist production. The quadruple division of economic forms (i.e. manorial, peasant, farmer and capitalist) is necessary for the clear understanding of the socio-economic structure of agriculture. In the case of our specific interest, the adoption of such a conceptual division would stress the peasant nature of the Russian rural economy at the turn of the century.

Once we admit the possibility of parallel and 'uneven' histories of different social components, linked in diverse and contradictory ways, the broad historiography to follow comes to accentuate differently 'facts' and conclusions. Central to it is the fact of the existence of substantively similar peasant social structures and, in particular, the peasant economy expressed in peasant production units, in other ways different, i.e. slave-owning, feudal and capitalist societies. To resolve this analytical issue by noticing that 'it is not the same thing' once the circumstances change, is true, trivial and irrelevant. Nobody ever tried to claim the lack of difference between the members of a Germanic Mark of the late Middle Ages and the tractor-owning Punjabi Jats of today. The question is that of the similarities that lie beside the differences and of what we may learn from them. The suggestive argument of R. Brener about peasant resistance as the possible reasons for the diverse developments in European agriculture may add some important points here.[16]

Still concerning historiography, there remains the question to what extent its fundamental axis adopted as a 'social law' by both 'camps' of the Soviet scholars (i.e. the 'capitalism-already' and the 'capitalism-not-yet') is equal to the task of adequately conceptualising Russian agriculture. The second of these views is more realistic on the evidence shown, but is it sufficient? When neither 'capitalism' nor 'feudalism' fit fully, what is it? The over-exposed prefix 'semi' became a favourite hiding place here but offers little illumination to what *it* is we are talking about. For what does 'semi-feudalism'/'semi-capitalism' imply precisely, except as a statement of taxonomic confusion, or else, the truistic declaration that social forms do mix and do change? The neat sequence of unilinear 'transformation' from 'feudalism' to 'capitalism' (even when enlivened by 'sub-stages') has since the 1960s increasingly exhausted its power to explain in West European terms realities known only too well to the 'developing societies'. The same seems to hold for rural economies treated separately. Is it not time to draw conclusions concerning Russia?

To advance and supersede the debate between the 'capitalism-already' and 'capitalism-not-yet' schools of thought, one must begin not with the question, 'how far did capitalism advance and feudalism retreat and therefore how "semi" was its "semi-capitalism"', but to explore first if it was 'capitalism' which was advancing and/or what do we mean by that term in Russia at the turn of the century. To recall, Russian villages were never economically equal but the relations of production for the massive majorities in them was based on family labour and family production units. Nor were these in decline, which would make the issue largely one of time. On the contrary, the family farms' share in production was increasing. Elements of 'agro-business' were very limited and so was the capital accumulation and the banking credit extended to peasants (with the exception of the state Peasant Bank loans for the buying of land but land only). Nor could Russian peasant economy be defined as feudal while peasants made their own economic choices, the peasant grain was increasingly reaching international markets and peasant labour was often directly engaged in most advanced capitalist factories (with alternatives like wage labour v. farming actively considered by many of the family farmers).

A crucial general insight of the last generation was well summed up by E. Hobsbawm's reference in 1976 to the 1950s debate about the social transition from feudalism to capitalism. He said:

> It is very doubtful whether we can speak of universal tendency of feudalism to develop into capitalism. In fact, of course, it did so only in one region of the world, namely Western Europe and part of the Mediterranean area. There is room for argument whether in certain other areas (e.g. Japan and parts of India) such an evolution would have eventually been completed, by purely internal forces, had not the historical development been interrupted by the intrusion of Western capitalism and imperialist powers.[17]

We shall return to the inter-societal consequences of it presently, but the logic of this analysis extends clearly also to the intra-societal capitalism v. rural economy issues. More specifically for the rural economy-and-society component, the West European experience was producing parallel reconsiderations. For example, a recent study by G. Djurfeld concluded that the long-term agrarian crises led to a 'flow of capital out of agriculture and into agro-industry, as increasingly the most profitable strategy'. This, it is said further, went hand in hand with and facilitated in most of Western Europe the stability of 'middle size' peasant farms to an extent that made then into a 'general form of capitalist development in relation to agriculture'. Simultaneously, the actual and potential 'rural proletarians' have disappeared into the cities and industries of those countries or overseas. The study concluded that where capitalism is concerned, even in the Western Europe of today 'we cannot say "in agriculture" because we know that the capitalist mode of production has developed outside agriculture, in agro-industry' and also, 'it must be wrong therefore to call this a "modification" of the capitalist pattern of development; it should rather be seen as foreboding of a shift in developmental tendencies'.[18] One can add: 'and, belatedly, of its theories also'. As to the roads of depeasantisation the question is increasingly and rightly not of capitalism and/or 'modernisation', but of different capitalisms and of other social forms and transformational roads besides, a reality too rich to be squeezed into unilinear historiography of any type.

*   *   *

Russians faced these current dilemmas earlier. In this sense, theirs was the more difficult task and there is no accident in the primacy and strength of the impact of the different facets of their analysis of problems of 'growth' as transformed elsewhere via the work of scholars who were pathbreakers as much as cultural messengers, like P. Baran, P. Sorokin, and A. Gerschenkron in the USA. Much time has passed, however, since the turn of the century and we possess enough comparative evidence to look at the issue anew, for Russia also. While the theorising of this field is still unsatisfactory, the insights to be drawn from the rural and general history, especially the experience of 'developing societies' and their register of doubts, should by now help to move out of the 'either feudalism or capitalism' terminological trap and the clap-trap to follow, while ideas and things are mummified and transported a hundred years and ten thousand miles. The problem is not how to insert Russian evidence into a general historiography (or, vice versa, how to call distinct developments elsewhere by Russian names, often misconceived) deftly manipulating an empty prefix 'semi', but how to establish the nature and the development of specific rural societies and to construct realistic conceptual models reflecting their similarities and dissimilarities.

To sum up finally, the peasant agriculture of Russia was different in structure, functioning, logic of response and patterns of change from the 'model' by which classical capitalism was defined as well as from the actuality of the Russian town and industry. These different social economies were increasingly linked but that did not promote specifically capitalist agriculture – facts that would not greatly surprise students of the recent rural scene, the more so in the 'developing societies'. The character and change of the Russian peasant economy can be satisfactorily explained neither as capitalism *sensu strictu* nor as feudalism, nor else simply as 'something in between', for in a number of ways it obeyed (and reacted to 'external' impacts through) its discrete operational logic. Simply to recognise this is insufficient for the understanding of the working of Russian rural economy – it did not stand alone and must be understood in its relation to the capitalist production and market as well as to the state impact on it. But not to recognise peasant specificity obscures reality as much. The way to approach the problem is to *begin* by the accepting of an historical complex and contradictory 'triangle' of interdependence between the discrete structure/dynamics of peasantry, those of the state and those of capitalism, both 'national' and international. It calls for a complicated conceptual model but, once again, so is social life, often reflecting in concepts that best illuminate it.

When considering the relation between Russian peasant agriculture and the political economy of the country at large, one should reaffirm also the impact of the sheer size of peasantry within the total Russian population. A quotation from M. Dobb sums it up well: 'The basic reason for the lowness of the average standard of living in tsarist Russia was the low production of agriculture which consituted the livelihood of four-fifths of the population.'[19] The national indices of socio-economic growth and the project of development had to be set in Russia against the overwhelming peasant numbers. Even the doubling of wages of all industrial workers would have influenced average per capita income relatively little. Even total literacy in towns could have left three quarters of the nation illiterate. And so on. The impact and indexes of the most spectacular achievement of urban and/or industrial economy was diluted, often to the extent of one-sixth. The per capita production growth of the Russian industries was fairly high by both international and European standards, yet, despite this, Russia was not competing well because of the significance of agriculture ('which', as Goldsmith has put it, 'in virtually every other country grew much less rapidly than the rest of the economy').[20] A Russian contemporary would probably add here the word 'peasant' before the word 'agriculture'. At the turn of the century, it was peasant economy that was increasingly being seen as the metaphorical 'ballast' or 'bottleneck' of Russia's social and economic development. In a major sense this perception was true, but that was not the whole of the story. Following the already quoted dictum of Bloch about the 'knowledge of fragments' being subject to 'their reintegration . . . [and] the knowledge of whole',[21] we shall proceed now to the larger 'whole', that is, to the characterisation of Russia as a system and a process of political economy and to the social and political conclusions that can be drawn from it.

5 The Russia's Morphology of Backwardness: Present and Future

China, India, Turkey, Persia and Latin America are politically feeble in direct proportion to their economic dependency on foreign industry. In our times the political might of the great states called upon to play a role in history is based not only on the spirit of its people but in its economic system. . . . The international rivalry would not wait and if immediate, decisive and energetic steps are not taken. . . .

Sergei Witte

Under our regime of absolute despotism and denial of the rights and the will of the people, reform can be only achieved by a revolution.

The Executive Committee of the People's Will Party

A. A TYPE OF 'DEVELOPMENT': THE 'GROWTH' AND THE 'GAP'

In 1946 Timasheff published in London an extensive treatment of Russia's development patterns. In a 'mental experiment', he extrapolated forward the major trends of the Russian economic and social history between the 1890s and 1913. He concluded that 'if undisturbed', Russia would have reached by 1940 levels of industrialisation, income and education similar if not higher than those actually achieved under the Soviet rule, a rule that simultaneously 'threw back Russian philosophy and arts at least a century'.[1] Far from being a necessary removal of the obstacles to development, 'the communist revolution has been a dangerous illness, but the Russians possess enough vital energy to overcome it'.[2] Central to this argument, the economic growth of pre-revolutionary Russia at the rates recorded in 1909–13 was assumed to be self-perpetuating into the future – a 'take off' to join 'the West' (i.e. the club of the countries of well-being, advanced technology, international power, high educational attainment and further continuous ascent).

The time that has elapsed has not diminished the appeal of

Timasheff's way of thinking. In fact, quite a number of more recent studies have echoed directly his argument without referring to him or enriching on his analysis.[3] A further twist to this was given by a variety of convergency theories, which extended the argument forward by assuming that whatever the rhetorics or the crudities of Russia's socialist experiment, it has been not much more than a gigantic exercise in 'belated industrialisation'. Stalin was necessary, explicable (and essentially justifiable) as an economic 'take-off' device. Now, with the industrialisation targets essentially met, the USSR is converging towards the one and only known and possible 'advanced world' of univeralised electronics and bureaucratised plenty, mapped out by the way in which we ourselves thrive (see the most recent indexes of GNP, cars, or plastic bags per capita).

None the less, the prospect of universal economic growth and social ascent closing 'the gap' between Western Europe or the USA and the rest of the globe is very far removed from the evidence of the world we live in. There have been rapid and deep changes all over the world but the division into 'three worlds' first debated in the 1950s still applies in its essential outline. Despite some appearances, the Second World ('centrally planned', 'socialist') was not really turning into First ('developed', 'advanced capitalist'), but it is the Third World that interests us here. Since the early 1950s, when a non-problematic modernisation theory offered all round the ex-colonial world optimistic predictions and do-it-yourself kits for 'take-off' towards a US-like modernity, both the official reports and the explanatory theories have grown increasingly alarming.[4] The basic parameter of the issue was well stated by A. G. Frank as that of 'thirty developed countries having less than 30% of the current population and foreseeably only 20% of the world population in the year 2000, which now account for approximately 90% of the world's income, financial resources and steel production . . . 95% of the world scientific and technological production . . . consume over 60% of the worlds food'[5] and what such figures mean for 'the rest'. More decisive is the record of the 'catching-up' processes. During the four decades that followed the Second World War, despite clear diversification among them none of the major 'developing societies' of the 1950s and 1960s came to resemble Western Europe or the USA. That includes those 'developing societies' that benefited from the oil windfall (and whose GNP rocketed accordingly) as well as those who have shown rapid industrialisation and/or urbanisation. Time and time again optimistic frenzy, based on hastily read indices of 'economic growth', has swept the press, which declared yet another candidate for the closing of 'the gap' or even for the rapid overtaking of 'the West': Brazil, Mexico, Iran, India, Nigeria, etc. It usually ended up with yet another national bankruptcy, military *coup d'état* or revolt of the poor. The economics of different countries change rapidly but one clearly cannot understand and predict major processes by comparing the GNPs, and extrapolating elements of 'economic growth' into the future. Moreover, the diversity is not only 'economic'. The global map of diseases, illiteracy or of military dictatorship and of systematic use of torture, and their correlations with the GNPs, bear testimony to the combined nature of the phenomena. So does the comparison of those indices and socio-economic polarisation within the countries, which consistently demonstrated a particularly steep contrast in income as typical of the 'developing societies'. A long-term multiple and substantively growing 'gap' between the 'West' and the bulk of the 'developing' societies (i.e. the countries at the 'top' and the 'bottom' of the UN global scale) has been documented.[6] The 'gap' forms one of the decisive characteristics of the present stage of global history, arguably the most decisive one.

It is this experience, central to the realities of power and of economy as well as to the self-images, theories and ideologies of our own generation, that should be related to Russia at the turn of the century. Was the Russian development different in kind from that of the recent experience of the 'developing societies' (i.e. was Timasheff's projection into the future valid for pre-revolutionary Russia)? Alternatively, was Russia, a 'developing society' in the sense we attach nowadays to this term (i.e. a society that is not only poor and/or 'backward' but that shows a major gap-sustaining or gap-generating tendency of its economy and social structure)? To put this in the words of a recent Soviet writer, is it true that 'catastrophe nearly met Russia . . . which was saved [from] national destruction [and] the grip of backwardness . . . by the great October socialist revolution'?[7] Whichever our answer, what do we learn from it?

*   *   *

To place Russia in those terms, a detour is necessary to specify what is meant by the category of societies, even the very name of which has shifted puzzlingly every few years since the 1950s: 'backward', 'under-developed', 'emerging', 'developing', LDS, etc.[8] Quantitative desig-nations aside (e.g. 'all the countries with less than $400 GNP per capita') there are essentially two ways to delimit such entities structurally. The first treats 'developing societies' as backward, that is, as societies proceeding towards modernity along the necessary scale of social and economic advance but for some reasons (to be filled in) not yet 'there' or else moving 'there' too slowly (the impediment to be ascertained and rectified). The second approach assumes different venues of 'development', with the 'developing societies' representing a category of this. In many ways this division parallels the above debate concerning the 'agricultural sector' of the 'national' economies. This fundamental division in the logic of analysis has cross-cut specific topics, different levels of generalisation as well as major ideological camps. Moreover, this particular piece of diverse theorising has been playing a major role in the structuring of political strategies and confrontations. We shall begin by a short sketch of its intellectual history.

The model of industrial capitalism based on nineteenth-century England has offered considerable illumination but has also exercised a somewhat hypnotic impact on scholars and laymen alike. The roots of that fascination are deep and carry considerable conviction. Despite the human misery and the new problems it produced, industrial capitalism has 'delivered the goods' of material abundance on a scale never before known, and did it at breakneck speed. It put science to direct day-to-day use, both in a technological permanent revolution and in the opening up for quantification of major spheres of social analysis. It offered new experience and hope of material well-being to masses of humans and of the rational resolution of mankind's major ills. It acted as a global unifying and transforming force, to become in the eyes of many the contemporary Midas myth and the Bible's book of Genesis rolled into one – what it touched turned into gold, what it produced or socially constructed took on its own likeness.

Timasheff's view of Russia and the Convergency Theory are particular cases of the Modernisation Theory, reflecting directly those illuminations and fascinations. This paradigm posited the global inevitability, the unilinear nature and the fundamental merit of 'progress' (i.e. of advance along the axis of development marked out by the capitalist industrial societies).[9] Its conceptual parentage lies with nineteenth century evolutionism and classical economics – as much a philosophy and a science of the new world as an apotheosis of capitalism. Its essence has been the interpretation of history *via* the advancing social division of labour related to the rise of new technologies and the transformation of social institutions.[10] The twentieth-century neoclassical school in economics and Functionalism within sociology have continued that line of thought, accentuating and/or building into it a particular dimension of optimism concerning the mechanisms for the resolution of social problems – the assumption and the metaphor of 'social balance'. Any distortion of equilibrium and of homogeneity would produce rectifying forces, the larger the distortion the stronger the rectifying force. The fact of a 'social gap', international and intra-national, would have produced thereby its own remedies. The evolutionism of the left, associated particularly with the theories developed by the 'orthodox' wing of the 2nd International, accepted all this but went a step further by placing socialism as the next-to-capitalism, necessary and final 'stage'.[11] Socialism was the ultimate 'mode of production' and of equilibrium due to convert the material breakthrough of capitalism to the use of the collective producers. Witte's dream of the Russian tsardom as the new industrial giant, the books of Plekhanov (and in particular the twist given to them by the 'legal Marxists' of Russia), Stalin's manner of executing Lenin's unfortunate slogan about communism being 'Soviet rule plus the electrification of the whole country' and Warren's recent posthumous book published in London, differ radically from each other, but are of a kind in being impregnated by the essential unilinearism and the idea of 'progress' implied by it.[12] It is in that context that the *Oxford Dictionary*'s description of 'developing society' should be read, as a testimony of West European common sense entrenched by its media. A 'developing society' is 'a poor or primitive country which is developing higher economic and social conditions'.[13]

In fact, images of progress seen mainly as the industrialisation of backward hinterlands, carry considerable ambivalence, especially for socialists and liberals faced with colonialism. Capitalism has been progressive but also repressive and regressive even on its own terms. Capitalism-related colonialism has transformed 'native' societies but has also suppressed their industries and popular will while twisting objectionably the metropolitan societies and economies. Hobson's *Imperialism* published in 1902 had followed critically that lead. Within the councils of the 2nd International, Marxist social critique and analysis had also increasingly taken a global form, beginning with the works of Hilferding and Rosa Luxemburg followed by Bukharin and Lenin.[14] A Marxist theory of imperialism came to analyse the exploitation of colonies and its place within the metropolitan economies.[15] It said little of the colonised societies.

Shifting the scene by two generations, the aftermath of the Second World War saw the appearance of new post-colonial world, while the UN and television ensured that the consciousness of a 'Third World' spread widely. As the modernisation theory and policies guided by it in the 1950s and 1960s failed to deliver the goods, new explanation was needed to throw light on its main failure (i.e. on the 'gap' which refused to decline and on the armed struggle growing in the colonies and ex-colonies: Algeria, Vietnam, Cuba, Angola, etc.). The attempt to make sense of the political economies of the ex-colonial countries has produced several new beginnings to which, the differences accepted, the works of Myrdal, Prebish and Baran have been the milestones.

The different 'father figures' of the onslaught against modernisation theories have personified its diverse prongs. Myrdal and Prebish were senior advisers to the UN, originating from Sweden and a 'developing society' (Argentine) respectively, Baran was the Russian-educated and the only Marxist professor of economics in the US universities of the 1950s. The remedies suggested ranged accordingly: a call for an assumption of moral responsibility by the West from Myrdal (to be expressed in massive charitable aid), the demand for industrialisation policies and for state control of foreign trade from Prebish, the demand for revolutionary reassertion of sovereignty followed by the restructuring of society from Baran. The Modernisation Theory was dismissed by all of them as inadequate, over-optimistic and ideologically Western-centred.

Myrdal's notion of 'circular causation' and of 'cumulation of advantages and disadvantages' has challenged the 'equilibrium' model of economic growth by identifying at least one of the resulting issues.[16] In a 'free market' economy, it is the accumulated investments that tend to produce further accumulation of investments; accumulated ability to produce determines the further increases in productivity; the better the educational facilities the better the conditions for the growth of new educational facilities, and so on. Conversely, shortage of capital, low productivity, limited access to educational facilities, and also political feebleness and massive poverty, will tend to 'accumulate' at the underprivileged pole of society, in a sequence of 'vicious circles'. There is no 'natural' flow towards equilibrium. The question is not why the 'gaps' do not close, it is rather, how could it happen that some countries of the globe (e.g. Japan) have 'caught-up' with the first-comers?

In Latin America the criticism of modernisation theory was voiced by the Structuralists school – a first reconceptualisation of 'developing societies' in the UN era, coming from those societies themselves. At its centre stood the work of Prebish who challenged the Neo-classical assumption of natural and mutual advantages of international trade by evidence of terms of trade consistently disadvantageous for the 'developing societies'.[17] Prebish and the UN Economic Commission for Latin America (ECLA) have drawn social and political conclusions from the analysis of unequal exchange which became part of a credo and vocabulary of the 'dependency theory'. Of those the industrialisation strategy of 'import substitution' is the best known.

Paul Baran's pioneering work reasserted the stress on broad aspects of political economy rather than on the 'free market' mechanisms of either equilibrium or inequality and cumulation. He proceeded from the view voiced already in the late 1920s by the 3rd International about the overwhelmingly regressive impact of imperialism on the economies of the colonial societies. A Marxist paradigm and terminology were extended by Baran to the inter-state dependencies, suggesting ways the capitalist 'laws of motion' and the existing relations of power, interest and exploitation operate at the lower pole of the global society.[18] International patterns of exploitation would explain the 'blocked' development of the 'underdeveloped regions' (he used the comparison of the deficient economic growth of colonial India, as against the successes of Japan which locked itself up against the Western impacts and the 'open market'). The industries of the 'developing societies' are strangled as much by the cheaper mass-production of well-established industrial complexes as by the conscious policies of the major powers. Monopolistic controls purposefully drag down the prices of most of the products traditionally exported by the 'developing societies', securing uneven exchange to the advantage of those most powerful. Nor is it a matter of economics only. Rule by parasitic and oppressive elites is conserved at the 'underdeveloped' pole of the world by the nature of the imperialist impact. It helps to keep those regions 'underdeveloped'.[19] It is the capitalist centre of the 'advanced' world with its accumulated and accumulating advantages and bullying power and its local agents-'compradors' that stand in the way of the 'developing societies'. That is the rationale of a growing 'gap'.

At the turn of the 1970s, after two decades of predominance of Modernisation Theory, the Dependency Theory came for a time to dominate the field of 'development studies'. It has drawn on the critical analysis referred to. In Anglo-Saxon literature it was most influentially expressed in a book of A. G. Frank published in 1967.[20] It was also most clearly challenged in the debate that followed it. The events of 1968 in Vietnam, the USA, Latin America, France, China and Czechoslovakia offered an immediate background of political crisis and anticipation of dramatic changes. The book presented a view of unequal international division of markets and labour, 'syphoning away' the wealth of its Latin American 'periphery' and leading to stagnation there. It dismissed the earlier images of a (semi?) feudal society or else as a region littered with feudal 'pockets of backwardness' which slowly dissolve under the impact of capitalism and/or progress. The capitalist world market transformed it centuries ago into a part of the global capitalist economy. It also provided for the diverse dynamics of the different areas on the globe leading to the necessary and deepening decline of countries where the majority of mankind's poor lived. Frank summed up his pessimistic conclusions in the dramatic image of the 'development of underdevelopment' at the peripheries of capitalism.

For a short time a new dual concept of *centre/periphery* took the place of the universal master-key of explanation, reserved before for the chief polarity of the Modernisation Theory: the *backward/modern* division (and sequence). In what followed, much of the 'dependency theory' was rapidly trivialised or taken over. The concept of centre/periphery, used loosely, became merely another word for rich/poor with a critical undertone of voice added – a verbal substitute for analysis of complex reality. The World Bank analysts and civil servants were utilising it increasingly to sharpen and to legitimate their employers' strategies. But even the genuinely critical and sophisticated versions of the dependency theory displayed serious limitations, gradually acknowledged by its authors. Theoretically, the difficulty lay with the 'holist' structural assumptions, already discussed above, an overkill, one may say, of Baran's line of reasoning and of the older theories of imperialism. World capitalism and/or the international market and/or the multinational companies (or, more general still, the 'laws of accumulation of capital') were being treated as the sole determinants of history. The 'peripheries' and the human collectivities there became thereby by default mere 'carriers' or puppets of the characteristics of the international social matrix. Politically the only consequent choice became that of 'either fascism or socialism'. Evidence of complex diversification of the 'developing societies' and of rapid industrialisation in some of them undercut these analyses. So has the evidence of political struggles and dramatic shifts in policies. The fact that world market was used by Frank as a synonym for capitalism has added to the theoretical argument.[21] Importantly, the 'export substitution' programmes, when adopted, were not doing very well either. New types of penetration and safer ways for the skimming of super-profits by the multinationals followed their application. Yet, on the other hand, the 'gap' did not disappear. The fundamental image of global grip by the 'core' of capitalism and of a consequent world division of 'statics' as well as of 'dynamics' was clearly realistic enough.

The last decade has been one of further debate brought about by new evidence and of very limited theoretical advance, especially in so far as new integrated views were concerned. There have been signs of disintegration and disenchantment with the theoretical field *in toto*. The modernisation approach was simply restated by a few of the ex-colonial civil servants or politicians and defended with new vigour and argument by some neo-orthodox Marxists who looked again at the 'growth' and doubted the 'gap'.[22] Some interesting things have been said from different perspectives about the 'packages' of modernising characteristics about cognitions, about ecology and about the socially destructive propensities of technological revolution so far as the Third World is concerned.[23] A number of attempts were made to use the concept of 'mode of production' as an alternative to the models of dependency.[24] Frank presented rectifications of his views as did a number of major 'dependency' theorists, especially in the important reanalysis of F. H. Cardoso and others in Latin America.[25] On the 'same side' in terms of the broad divisions of views, the works of Samir Amin gained considerable support with many of the 'Third World' economists, of the 'left' as well as of the 'right'.[26] In 1974 E. Wallerstein commenced publication of a major study offering a global view of the origins of capitalist economy.[27] While following the views of 'dependency theorists' in many major matters (inclusive of a strong 'holist' tendency,[28] and the equating of the spread of capitalism with that of the global market), Wallerstein gave new historical depth to the analysis offered. He put in focus of his historiography the forms of world-wide division and internationalised control of labour and the resulting diverse modes of its use. Relevantly to our case, he extended accordingly the earlier conceptual schemes suggesting a societal category 'in between' the capitalist 'core' and the 'peripheries' (and typified by the prevalence of share-cropping in agriculture and mining commencing 'the long sixteenth century'). It would include the old empires in decline, caught in the process of capitalist peripheralisation. Tsarist Russia would be a prime example of this societal category, entering the global system somewhat later. More was done in terms of building up foundations by the social historians who traced the diverse roads of different states/social transformation (e.g. the comparison of Russian and Polish history by P. Anderson).[29]

All in all the debate of the 1970s and 1980s did not result in major conceptual breakthroughs. The fundamental approaches of the 1960s underwent further elaboration and revision under each other's impact and in the light of the new evidence. A major division still lies between the views by which 'developing societies' are an essentially similar but backward version of 'classical' capitalism and those who see it as a different social form, venue and set of possibilities, in need of discrete theoretical structures. Unsatisfactory as this state of theoretical affairs is for lovers of ideological final solutions, the conceptual 'fact' of different approaches in evidence cannot be disposed of by a clever logical trick, an executive decision or by an empiricist computation. One must make a choice, follow it up through concrete cases and then consider the results. Our study accepts in this spirit the view that the 'developing' or 'peripheral' societies should be treated as a diverse form of social organisation and looks at Russia in that light.

* * *

The adopted theoretical alternative is to advance further along the line of Baran's initial insight, while attempting to meet and rectify its limitations. The more recent term and self-description of such a view (with such rectifications) as the theory of 'dependent development' will be used. It builds on major conceptual elements of the past debate like Sweezy's comment about the plausibility of different capitalisms and Hobsbawm's refusal (quoted above) to accept as self-evident the universality of the feudalism-to-capitalism road of transition.[30] It rejects holist analysis of 'systems' of the kind that assumes a single dynamic and logic of the 'centre' governing it and/or economic determinism of some type. It rejects as well the evolutionist solutions, by which societal forms are essentially different steps along the necessary capitalist road (into socialism, for those who are socialists). The 'uneven' and combined development of different societies would mean to that approach not only different speeds and 'clocks' but also different 'roads', each with its own consistencies, potentials and logic. Also, a major message of the last generation was that of the growing disconnection between imperialism and colonialism.[31] The Arab proverb that people resemble their times more than their fathers seems to hold true in this case. One can restate it: people resemble cousins of the not-quite-common parentage but similar life-context, more than their own 'fathers'. Colonial history, of some and not of others, does not falsify the generalisations offered when we talk of 'dependent development'. Its decisive social characteristics are not defined by the colonial past but by the international and intra-national present. (The fact that 'developing societies' are so often equated with 'post-colonial' countries is an analytically interesting and under-analysed distortion of vision if, say, Turkey is the example.)

The conceptual sense of the societal category discussed is based on the assumption of a specific type of social structure, social reproductions and patterns of social transformation. It goes without saying that this composite picture should be treated not as a shopping-list of unrelated items or a blueprint of an engine's exclusive components. It is 'a system' of different and often contradictory tendencies and dynamics, related by a variety of 'degrees of freedom' and possible substitutions, to follow the somewhat mechanical metaphor.

The concept of 'dependent development' as recently used indicates a specific placement of the societies in question in the context of an international capitalist system.[32] Within the global hierarchies of institutionalised power, capital and science, the 'developing societies' are at the weaker pole, a weakness that if left to the forces of the 'free market' tends indeed to cumulate. Also, this 'placement' opens those societies to domination and exploitation by powerful 'partners'. At the same time the metaphor of 'developing societies' being the 'global proletariat', while not totally devoid of illumination, is badly biased, because 'developing societies' do not produce the bulk of goods consumed by the 'metropolitan' nations. Nor are they a homogeneous 'camp', homogeneously rural or homogeneously poor.

The internal economic context of the countries of dependent development is characterised by extensive 'disarticulations'. Strategic elements of it operate within the international networks controlled mostly by the multinational companies. Enclaves of foreign-produced and controlled modern technology coincide with archaic techniques of production, and mass under-employment. A fundamental frontier of economic 'disarticulation' usually lies between the massively peasant smallholder agriculture plus the peasant-in-town groups plus extensive 'informal economies' and the 'modern' industries and finance. At the core of the political as well as economic power-structures stands a state machinery that has been variously described as 'over-grown', 'strong' and/or 'state capitalist'. Those expressions try to present and to explain a bureaucratic system that monopolises not only administrative control and the powers of repression but also the direct assignment of social privileges, the powers of the largest employer, the direct control of major parts of production, and/or foreign trade, of the mass media, etc. Extraordinarily high rates of exploitation correspond in the 'developing societies' with the spread of repressive regimes, breakdown of consensus, often military dictatorships involving semi-official 'torture squads' as a day-to-day system of governing.

The effective control of the industry and finance of the 'developing societies' lies in the hands of a 'triple alliance' of international capital, state 'technocrats' and the local bourgeoisie (linked at times with large landlords). Up to a point the state apparatus acts as a 'gate keeper' for foreign capitalism, serving it but also attempting to control it. The working compromise of those forces, with the first two supreme and the third correspondingly servile (but far from powerless), define the day-to-day running of a dependent economy. It means constant shifts and confrontations by capital in search of quick profits whereby often the state enterprises act as the only effective instrument of long-term investments and capital accumulation. It means also that systematic exclusion of the plebeian masses from any economic gains of 'dependent development', forms part of the process of 'economic growth', with increasing social polarisation and tensions to follow. (A consequent transfer by the multinationals of a labour-intensive production process to countries of a cheap and repressed labour force was a major determinant of the recent wave of industrialisation within some of the 'developing societies'.) Specific class structure, ethnic divisions, political characteristics and ideological currents are generated by such a setting. The plebeian mass of manual labourers and of the often destitute 'lumpen bourgeoisie' of go-betweens together with the major parts of the local bourgeoisie are mostly devoid of impact upon the actual political life of the country, despite the parliamentary procedures usually being kept as a legitimating device. To that extent, the rhetoric term 'popular masses' is realistic as the antonym of the governing elite and may explain the nature of revolutionary eruptions and the ideologies of protest that cross-cut class boundaries of any description.

'Dependent development' is a process of social reproduction of extensive and extending inequality on both as international and local scale. The consistency of the international 'gap' is the expression of its fundamental 'laws of motion' while many more localised 'gaps' and disarticulations follow similar patterns. So do the patterns of repression, the typical cognitions of social reality and the ideologies of its change.

B. THE EDGE OF EUROPE

Historical analysis of an event or a period does not terminate with its contemporaries, mainly because hindsight throws new light and offers new illuminations. Since 1917, Russia has been first and foremost treated as the country in which the socialist experiment commenced, for good or evil. This particular hindsight is very much with us, explicit and implicit, reinforced by the drama and the grotesque in every news dispatch. It has facilitated some teleological explanations of Russian history (by which all which happened had to happen), and at the other pole, claims that all is accident, perplexity or bad luck. Looking back did offer also some useful analytical insights into Russia's revolutionary transformation and the socialist attempts elsewhere and since. What remained less clear is the extent to which the recent debate about the nature of the so-called 'developing societies' throws light on the history of Russia/USSR. Societies and economic conditions never exactly repeat themselves, but identity is not, of course, a condition for comparative analysis. During the period we are talking about, Russia was a country with a massive peasant population, a per capita annual income of less than 100 dollars, a major presence of foreign capital and a government pursuing industrialisation policies in a world increasingly dominated by 'the West', that is, the main capitalist industrial societies. Does not all this sound familiar to every student of the contemporary world?

At the turn of the century, Russia was a 'developing society', arguably the first of its kind. This generalisation denies neither the development of the 'classical' capitalism in it nor the uniqueness of its history. These notwithstanding, the major characteristics of what a few generations later came to be called 'dependent development', were increasingly evident in Russia. The international context and the grip of foreign capital were already referred to and were recognised in the extra attention given then in Russia to the problems of the types of 'development', the 'gap', and economic 'growth', as well as of capital accumulation, sovereignty and foreign finance. Evans's concept of the 'triple alliance' of capitals ruling industry – the foreign, the state and the local – was pertinent there, as was the parallel tendency of state planners to equate industry with modernity and Westernisation. Severe strains of economic and social disarticulations and steep class divisions were evident. Major enterprises, especially mining, have often linked into international economic circuits with little relation to the economy within which the bulk of the Russians lived. Heavy under-employment on a national scale went hand in hand with a shortage of skilled and 'reliable' labour. The largest factories of Europe, manned extensively by part-peasants, coincided with and were linked to pre-mechanical crafts and thousand-year-old farming methods. The advance of industry, urban-isation and literacy were paralleled by a widening gulf between the social 'top' and the rural and city poor. The level of exploitation of the producers was high, manifest and brutal, and so was the overall extent of state control and the repressions evoked by any 'disobedience' or even unauthorised initiative from the philanthropists. Political dissent was building up, expressed in the bottled-up resentment of the plebeian classes as much as in the ideologically and ethically expressed challenges of the intelligentsia.

Russia's immediate opportunities for rapid economic development and transformation, activated in the spells of industrial growth during 1892–9 and 1909–13, were on the whole better than those in the mainstream 'developing societies' of today. The powerful and highly centralised Russian state was able to mobilise considerable resources and, to an extent, check foreign political and economic pressures. The rise in world prices of foodstuffs and, in particular, of grain, had ensured a consistently positive balance of payments and helped towards the national 'capital formation'. The sheer size of the country has often been cited as a major advantage for rapid economic advance. The size of the population as a potential consumers' market, the extensive territory of Russia and its mineral riches would by that view facilitate 'economic growth'. Russia's Asiatic sector could play the role of an amalgam of British India and the American Wild West, that is, of an exploited minerals and cotton producing colony and of an 'open frontier'.

Yet the chances for these favourable i.e. 'growth'-facilitating economic conditions in Russia to persist were anything but good. To return to Timasheff's 'mental experiment' but to make it somewhat more specific, 67 per cent of the value of exports was agricultural primary produce as late as 1913 and nearly all of the rest were the products of mining.[1] It was the increase in foodstuff prices in the early twentieth century that secured the overall export figures. Once the First World War was over, the terms of trade were to become increasingly unfavourable to primary products and specifically to foodstuffs.[2] Moreover, as Atallah's major study of the period puts it, 'except under specific conditions, the long term movement of the terms of trade between industrial and agricultural products will be against agricultural products'.[3] The basic determinant of Russia's positive balance of payments and a 'booster' of its internal market was on the point of an extended downward turn.

The second source of the 'positive balance of payments', of the capital investment and economic development, was external (i.e. conditioned by the policy of encouraging foreign investment and sharply increasing the foreign debts of the government).[4] It was assumed by many that without the influx of foreign capital, the spectacular development of Russian industry would be altogether impossible. Estimated foreign investments during the period 1898–1913 were 4225 million roubles, of which about 2000 million roubles were comprised of state loans. The hold of foreign capital was growing. In particular, while during the 1881 to 1913 period about 3000 million roubles were taken out of Russia in foreign profits much was reinvested. By 1914, the holding of foreign capital in Russia was 8000 million roubles. This included foreign ownership of up to two-thirds of Russia's private banking and extensive foreign ownership of mines and of large private manufacturing enterprises.[5] A generation later Mirsky summed up the actual or the emerging results of that development in stating that, 'by 1914, Russia had gone a good part of the way toward becoming a semi-colonial possession of European capital'.[6] Already by 1916 the cost of the war had more than doubled foreign debts, clearly but a beginning of what was in store. It had also increased further Russia's technological dependency on its Western allies. If 'undisturbed', to use Timasheff's term for proceeding along the same line of development, Russia would have faced in the post-First World War period a massive and increasing crisis of foreign payments and of further loans just to pay off the old ones, together with the dividends and the payments for foreign expertise and imports. We know such scenarios well from our contemporary Latin America, Africa and Asia, be it Brazil, Nigeria or Indonesia.

Even the magnitude of Russia could not be viewed solely as a blessing. The empire had been created by conquest and lived by suppression of the national identity of the majority of population in which ethnic Russians accounted for less than half. Repression could keep the country together. But to see the tsardom perpetuating 'undisturbed' into the future, despite its ethnic heterogeneity and inequalities, was unrealistic. Even the hope that the land mass of Russia would solve the problem of its 'surplus population' was false. Despite high mortality rates, the percentage of annual population growth in Russia had doubled during the 1880–1910 period.[7] The absorption capacity of Asiatic Russia was limited. The actual land per capita rates in European Russia were rapidly decreasing. A 'population explosion' was beginning to build up, with consequences once again familiar from the 'developing societies' of today. The cities absorbed only about one-quarter or one-third of the rural natural growth. Without it changing or without what Gershenkron referred to as the 'Malthusian corrective' (i.e. war, famine and plague) or else without a labour-absorbing agricultural breakthrough (in an unpromising economic context of the prices downturn and lack of massive investment) the rural 'surplus population' could not but proceed to grow.

By the turn of the century, the awareness of these crises in the making was growing among 'the educated' of Russia. The resulting debate was not unlike that of the 1950s and 1960s in UN research units such as

Prebish's ECLA or between Baran's friends, the Marxist economists centred around the *Monthly Review* of New York. There was a major difference of the date under consideration, however. It supported for tsarist Russia neither an iron law of deterioration nor a self-evident extrapolation of the economic boom of 1909–13, that is, in the language of our own generation, neither a version of Dependency Theory nor a modernisation scenario. To say that the socio-economic development of Russia was then a race against time, with the result still in the balance, is neither a rhetorical turn of phrase nor an eclectic refusal to 'stick one's neck out' by offering a firm answer. It was for once supported by statistical evidence. Figures show that during the period in question, Russia was neither catching up, nor was it clearly falling behind its Western competitors. Between 1861 and 1913, the estimated growth rates of Russia's national income per capita were close to those of the European averages, but half the figure for Germany. Russia was doing better than the cross-national averages of the countries outside Europe, but the growth of its national income was considerably lower than in the USA and Japan.[8] A further worsening of Russia's chances in that race was anticipated which made the time factor crucial. In such contexts what counts particularly is not only the matrix of causes, trends and objective *determinants* but conscious conflicts and state policies, that is, the active seeking of alternatives by those in power, the forces they could command, the challenges presented to them and the way they were understood and met. The Russians increasingly came to view the future in terms of the ability of the tsardom and its policies to outweigh the effects of cumulative backwardness and global inequality, or else, in terms of a revolution that would radically change the character of Russia, removing the tsardam altogether as the main obstacle to the country's advance.

To those in the government in whose view 'modernisation' was necessary while a revolution was out of the question, the future has mostly presented itself as an alternative of a German-style rapid economic advance to join the dominant industrial societies or else a cumulative political and economic decline to the status of 'another China', that is, a society of poverty and increasing internal contradictions, an easy prey to powerful foreign imperialists. *Ex post factum* and with the experience of the last generation before our eyes, such a designation of the choices is inadequate, but far from spurious. It offers a division in the terms within which major aspects of Russian history may be considered.

Significantly for such comparisons, Russia entered the new century at a time when models of what has come to be referred to as 'classical' capitalism, (i.e. the generalised model of England of 1780–1870) were becoming less and less relevant to the actual capitalist societies of the day. A few intellectual forerunners excepted, the theory was clearly lagging behind, for it took a century for the social analysts to catch up in earnest with the fact of the non-repetition of the social characteristics of the British 'industrial revolution'.[9] It took much less time than that for the practitioners of politics and economics to grasp this point.

The first inkling of a new pragmatic understanding of these matters appeared within the governing elites of Germany, Japan and Russia. By that time, between the lucky first-comers (i.e. those societies that benefited from the early development of a mercantile, industrial and colonial capitalism) and between the 'other' (often colonised) people, a third intermediate group could be distinguished. It consisted of those countries that reached the thresholds of massive industrialisation somewhat later than the first-comers, but without having their economies distorted by recent foreign conquest and/or colonialism.

The USA headed this list, but was manifestly exceptional owing to particularly favourable conditions. Outside its southern regions of slave-and-cotton economy, it lacked entrenched pre-capitalist classes, structures and traditions. It was far enough away to eschew Europe's political tensions, and yet close enough to benefit from its markets, labour and experience. Its 'growth' was well served by the farming of the independent smallholders in the 'empty territories' (i.e. lands sparsely populated by peoples who could be defeated, locked up in 'reservations' or exterminated). The same held for the weakening of the British, French and German global grip when they duelled for world rule in 1914–18.

The core of the 'third group' consisted of the triad of Germany, Japan and Russia, the last usually at the bottom of the list in terms of its socio-economic and political indexes and achievement. In spite of the many differences with regard to their conditions and history, all of these countries showed marked similarities of government policies and guiding ideologies. At their centre was an attempt to escape what would be called today 'dependency' and 'cumulation of disadvantages', by a powerful intervention of the state, aimed to assure rapid industrialis-ation. In the words of Witte, the 'man in charge' of the Russian economy, 'the experience of all people shows that only those economi-cally independent are able fully to exercise their political might . . . China, India, Turkey, Persia and Latin America are politi-cally feeble in direct proportion to their economic dependence on foreign industry'. Consequent on that experience, 'in our times the political might of the great states called upon to play a role in history is based not only on the spirit of its people but in their economic system. . . . The international rivalry would not wait.' This view assumes a powerful, autocratic and aggressive government effectively opposing external pressures while suppressing any 'internal political obstacles', be it socialist agitation, demands of ethnic 'minorities' or even reactionary impulses within the landed 'ruling class'. The aim was to advance 'by hook or by crook', modernising the army, promoting capital accumulation, facilitating industrialisation, relegating agriculture to a secondary place within the national economy.[10]

For three decades the Russian government doggedly followed 'the German path'. Bunge, Vishnegradskii, Witte, Kokovtsev – a succession of finance ministers – professed policies of directed economic development and energetic government intervention, within which the all-out support for home industry was central. Government policies facilitated high profit margins for the industrialists, low wages, and the squeezing of peasant economy for the sake of urban capital formation. Yet, whatever the effort, the model or the pretence, Russia's advance was still no match for that of Germany. It was on the battle-field and in the confrontations of international politics and finance that the fact of the matter was first manifested. From a first-class world power in the first half of the nineteenth century, the Russian state has deteriorated, by the turn of the century, into a second-class force. The Crimean War of 1854–5 was followed by the diplomatic defeat by the 'European powers' at the Berlin conference in 1878, the military defeat by Japan in 1904 and retreat before Austrian pressure in 1908. All these rebuffs signalled and contributed to this growing international weakness. Simultaneously, the severity of the economic crisis at the turn of the century has shown how shaky the economic growth of Russia was. Social and ethnic contradictions and revolutionary pressures added to the internal weakness. Given the build-up of political and economic crises and the increasingly doubtful ability on the part of the Russian tsardom to dominate the international and local scene and to mobilise resources, Witte's political design and the later prediction-by-extrapolation by Timasheff of a development able to make Russia into another Germany were anything but prudent.

This is the point where the significance of the other horn of the dilemma of 'either Germany or China' comes into its own. The China of the day was to the contemporaries a synonym of declining ancient glory, but mostly a chief example of a victim of foreign political and economic predators which, despite its formal independence, was increasingly dominated and exploited. 'Vicious circles' of popular impoverishment, the population outrunning resources and a growing 'compradore' stratum of the economic agents of Western companies were reported from there. The carving up of China was becoming a favourite pastime of imperial generals and international conferences. The less the Russian similarity to Germany, the more realistic the comparisons to China as seen by the educated Russians of those times (i.e. to a social category of what would be called today a 'developing society'). Russia was the first country in which the syndrome of such conditions and problems appeared within the context of political independence of long standing, of a successful competition in the past with the more 'modern' Western neighbours and a country possessing a numerous intellectual elite, trained in advanced European scholarship and deeply involved in social analysis and in radical political action. That is why Russia was also to become the first 'developing society' to begin and recognise itself as such.

As often happens, a new drama was enacted in old terminological garb. Also, the new understanding manifested itself in political strategies and decisions rather than in academic treatises. Despite this, the actual message and its originality were clear. While theory stumbled behind, the actual leaders of Russia recognised that the theory drawn from 'classical' capitalism, even when superficially adjusted, was insufficient for the type of society Russia was and/or was becoming.

The self-understanding and the corresponding state strategies of 'classical capitalism' were first substantially amended in a 'Bismarckian way', theorised by Friedrich List and accepted by the whole of the 'middle group' of capitalist developers. List challenged the fundamental assumption of the British political economy concerning mutual advantages of free trade. He believed that a transitional period of 'protectionism' must secure the 'maturing' of the German industry before it would be able to compete 'freely' with Great Britain. He defended therefore state intervention in markets and finance, that is, the policies that came to be expressed eventually in the German Custom Union (the *Zollverein*), a major step towards the country's unification under the leadership of Prussia. Russia's practising economist increasingly adopted the perspective offered by List. Witte went so far as to have List's book personally translated and to order his officials and aids to study it. Yet, transferred to Russia, the Listian policies failed to produce German-like results. The consequent crisis, rebellion and the dismay that culminated during the 1905–7 revolution, was reflected in a new parcel of strategies of social transformation. These are crucial to the understanding of the 'developing societies' of today and, in turn, understandable only in the light of their experience.

It was in Russia that a 'second amendment' of the initial theories of 'classical' capitalism took shape, offering a theoretical expression and a testing ground for a new type of 'revolution from above' – the 'Stolypin Reforms' of 1906–14. Russia's revolutionary epoch was linked into, overlaid with and productive of major conceptual revolution. Its first message of originality was that the spontaneity that underlaid the British case of industrialisation indeed could not, as List had argued, work similarly for the newcomers. But the solution he designed, i.e. that of a market-directed (and enclosing) state intervention, was in their case insufficient. Only the fundamental restructuring of the whole social fabric could lay foundations for the List-like policies and the Western-style industrialisation to follow in a Russia-like society. A 'revolution from above' had to remove obstacles before capitalism could succeed. That was not the end of the experimentation that the history of Russia was to offer. Stolypin's 'revolution from above' was rapidly followed by its fundamental alternative – the first 'revolution from below' typical of 'developing societies' and effectively executed and theorised following the lessons of revolutionary experience of 1905–7 enhanced in 1917–21.

That is why it is not accidental that while numerous 'Western' intellectual fashions come and go, the analytical tenets of Russian experience and scholarship of those times are remarkably fresh when issues of 'economic growth' and of the underprivileged component of mankind in the 'developing societies' are addressed, be it peasants, the 'state apparatus' or the intelligentsia, classes, elites or revolutionary cadres, agrarian reform, capital accumulation or 'hidden unemployment'. That is also why Witte and Lenin, as well as Stolypin and Stalin, so often sound as if they were directly addressing politicians and militants of our day on different sides of the ideological barriers in 'developing societies' the world over. To a considerable degree they have exhausted the range of alternative strategies available up to now, conceptually and actually (or should Mao be added?).

To recapitulate, specific characteristics of Russia as a 'developing society' made it differ significantly in social structure from other catching-up members of the industrialising societies (i.e. the USA, Germany and Japan) and to parallel a different category of societal development. That is not what major Western historians of Russia usually assume. To quote the most authoritative American economic historian of Russia, to Gerschenkron, 'quantitatively, the differences were formidable . . . 'but' . . . the basic elements of a backward economy were on the whole the same in Russia of the [eighteen] nineties as in Germany of the [eighteen] thirties'.[11] (Gerschenkron proceeded then in the same study to follow a contrary road, i.e. to name major qualitative differences such as the nature of financing, and pointed to the face that being a latecomer may change the very nature of the country's development, especially when 'industrial progress' is defeated by a 'Malthusian counter-revolution' or 'social tension' which assumes 'sinister proportions'.) The writings of Von Laue carried the unilinear assumption still further, disposing of Gerschenkron's fruitful ambivalence by a view externalising fully the sources of change. To him a 'cultural slope' continued inside Russia the 'gradient issuing from Western Europe'. What was taking place in Russia was a 'vast revolution from without', that is, an 'expansion of Europe' in which 'there is no blending of old and new [i.e. 'Western'] . . . the old was being ruthlessly subverted'.[12]

Despite the dissimilarity of the sources quoted, the authorities and the terminology used, Soviet scholars have been facing similar dilemmas and conducting a similar debate. The arguments about foreign capital and its impact, about the actual extent of Russian economic advance before the revolution, about the 'feudal remnants' in it, etc., were used as a vehicle for it. A major field in which the issue was explicated was that of agrarian history, which explains its significance for the general debate and in academic confrontations of past, present and, doubtlessly, future. Nobody has as yet used directly a 'developing societies' model for an alternative explanation challenging the unilinear view there, but the accentuation of specificity of the social transformation in the Russian countryside, of 'semi-feudalism' and of the peculiarities of 'the imperialist epoch' have often carried a similar message. Lenin's favourite abuse of *aziatchina* (Asianness), when talking of Russia, was never properly explored for insight, but used time and time again in the Soviet debate to stress the specificity of Russian capitalism, its 'semi', that is, not-quite-capitalist and not-quite-Western Europe, nature. Fundamental differences and arguments were often hidden behind quantitative designation, that is, capitalism was very strongly 'semi' to some, less 'semi' to others and not 'semi' at all to those whom already Marx called 'the Russian admirers of the capitalist system' (i.e. Russia's consistent evolutionists).[13]

The shadow of the fundamental debate between Soviet historians entered also via the consideration of what the 'imperialist epoch of capitalism' meant where Russia was concerned. The 1968 multi-volume of USSR history[14] and an important expression of the attempts to explore new frontiers, offered a middle position. It began by proclaiming as the new general insight of scholarship at the turn of the century 'deviations in the development of capitalism . . . from the *usual* norms of the capitalism of free competition'.[15] That insight was said to be crystallised and advanced by Lenin's new theory of imperialism 'as the last stage of capitalism'. The textbook proceeded to discuss in these terms Russian specificity in the 1900–17 period. The general characteristic it singled out was the 'contradictory correspondence' of monopolist capitalism (which, to the authors' view, did not principally differ from West European imperialism, and which commenced at the same period as its West European version) with 'military feudal imperialism', represented by the tsarist state.[16] This social formation was said to be ruled by a corresponding class coalition – the political alliance between the squires and the top layer of imperialist bourgeoisie which was constructed in the weak post-1906 parliament – the *Duma*. A tendency of financial capital to conserve rather than destroy the 'early capitalist modes of production' in Russia, and the repressive nature of the tsarist policies at the Russian ethnic peripheries, were also pointed out thus recovering valuable past insights.[17] The nature of the 1905–7 revolution was defined as a treble conflict and dynamic: proletarian, peasant and ethnic.[18] The analytical gains of that view were considerable if somewhat uneven. The model caught well the complexity of the Russian social and political confrontations. It failed to account for some major characteristics representing a new road, a typical/specific pattern of societal transformation. It also bypassed some political forces of major significance. Since the late 1870s the Soviet textbooks seem to have moved back in accentuating once more the 'classically' capitalist image of pre-revolutionary Russia.

The difficulties of the general problems reviewed are clearly not of the type that can be resolved by simply piling up data, archival documents or figures. The significance and necessity of close scrutiny of evidence is not in question, but it is rather the conceptualisation of it that has made it opaque. When scholars stumble over words or hide behind them, the way forward, however tiresome, is to proceed with dissecting terms for their analytical meaning. This cannot end with the critique of somebody else's analytical efforts and 'loose ends'. Our book proposes 'dependent development' as Russia's major social characteristic. What does it mean in (the) terms of social analysis?

C. THE RUSSIAN 'PERIPHERY': THE GENERAL, THE TYPICAL AND THE SPECIFIC

The question 'Was the Russian case one of "capitalism" or of "feudalism", an "oriental despotism", a "developing society", a "*de facto* colonialism" or something else?' is badly put in one fundamental sense. As an approximation or intellectual shorthand it may suffice, but it is epistemologically naïve to mix two levels and languages of discourse: that of social reality and its theoretical models.[1] It goes without saying that these relate and it is within the process of relating them (which W. Baldamus has well called one of 'double fitting'[2]), that a systematic knowledge of society is born. There is, however, no logical way to reduce those languages one into another. Theoretical models do not reflect reality directly, simply, or fully, but are meaningfully selective representations of some of its properties, in the light of a general theory assumed. Models focus on some aspects of reality, thereby necessarily caricaturing it. It is for this reason that 'the price of employment of models is eternal vigilance'.[3]

That is also why the query: 'Is this society capitalist or feudal, etc.?' must be ever followed by two mental sub-clauses: 'If so, in what sense?' and 'What precisely do we learn and/or subtract from our perception by the use of this concept?' Social reality does not conform fully into any logical mould. Models of social structure do not exhaust it and therefore do not exclude *all* other models. The validity of alternative models may coincide and their illuminations may cumulate.

The characterisation of Russia as a 'developing society' should be supplemented first by the answer to the questions of its additional characteristics of parallel significance. A way to begin is to categorise the characteristics of our case, that is, a society, a period and an international context, into *the general, the typical* and *the unique*. Put succinctly and limited to the most significant features only, those would be: for the general – capitalism, for the typical – a 'developing' (or 'peripheral') society, for the unique (or 'specific') – the Russian state history, ethno-history and some of the characteristics of rural (i.e. the mass of the population) Russia.

The Russia of that day cannot be understood outside the context of capitalism and its 'laws of motion' operating both internationally and intranationally. The most dynamic, richest in investment and most productive branches of Russian economy as well as of the international political economy into which Russia linked as a junior partner, were capitalist in the sense attached to that term by the classical economists and by Marx. The major dynamics and axis of advancing social division of labour were bound to mechanisation and to 'economic' mechanisms of exploitation of wage labour. Within it the maximisation of profits and accumulation of capital operated as a structurally overriding determination. The concept of 'extended reproduction' by a capitalist 'mode of production' caught such processes well, as long as one remembers the concept's limitations and that not only economic but also social meanings are involved. While reproducing itself, the capitalist system invaded and transformed not only social structures of production but also those of class generation, ethnic consolidation, urbanisation, changes in collective consciousness, etc. It operated not as an itinerary of those 'factors' but as a powerful system, linked by the logic of institutional interdependence and aggressive capacity to spread.

There are two reminders that must be attached to this 'drawing with a thick brush' of capitalist determinants in Russia. The impact of the state in societies where industrial capitalism had been advancing with particular speed since the middle of the nineteenth century was more noticeable than at the point of its inception. Simultaneously, the international characteristics of political economy advanced and deepened, to be recognised as a necessary aspect of capitalism. In consequence, the notion of capitalism came to differ substantially from its early formulations. Second, an admission of the speed and drive of capitalist advance does not equal the acceptence of a totally integrated model and functionalist interpretations of it, that is, of 'its' ability to transform everything after its own image, or to adjust it totally to its 'needs'. The direction of social change cannot simply be deduced or extrapolated from it, nor is the logic of capitalism the only one available or operating. A 'finger of Midas' principle by which everything capitalism touches turns 'capitalist', in actuality as well as in theory is unrealistic and misleading. So is the image of capitalism simply devouring 'past forms' at its pleasure.

The unique/specific that most profoundly characterised the Russian social scene at the turn of the century and made its mark as its past within its present was represented particularly by the Russian state, ethnos and peasantry. The 'past' can be understood here only in its linkage and response to the more contemporary social forms, the ability to readjust and to hold on. That being granted, 'past' is indeed 'tenacious . . . never fully lost'.[4]

The power of the Russian state apparatus, its share of resources, its control over the population and its legal claims exceeded those elsewhere where capitalism was on the march. To categorise it as 'an intermediate form between European Absolutism and Asian Despotism'[5] offered an image of some descriptive strength, but little else. The term an 'over-developed state' used by Alavi fits the case better but in a way that differs significantly from the original usage.[6] The Russian state was not initially the creation of eighteenth- or nineteenth-century colonisers; the significance of it becomes clear if we remember some of the shared characteristics of the two most significant revolutions of the twentieth century, the Russian and the Chinese. Those characteristics were an extensive size, massive peasantry and 'Western penetration' but also a long history of a sovereign 'state apparatus' now facing multiple imperialisms. Such coincidences are not usually accidental. The tsardom's historical roots, international context and its military–political and economic organisation made for its consistency and effectiveness. The European absolutism was reflected in it, as were the 'Oriental' vestiges and forms (especially if we do not discard the Golden Horde and consider Byzantium 'Oriental'). But Russian tsardom was, to a degree that is usually understated, a sovereign Russian invention, building from the available institutional 'bricks' new structures of control responding to specific conditions.[7] It was the socially constituted decline in these inventive and regenerative capacities that formed a major aspect of Russia's political crisis.

Closely linked to the inception of the Muscovite State was the ethnogenesis of the Russians. Massive processes of consolidation and 'extended reproduction' of cultural patterns, language usage, fundamental symbols of identification and self-identification, as well as of related political loyalties, wielded together massive populations of Slav, Finnic and Turki origins. The Orthodox church played a major role in the construction and the delimitation of the Russian ethnos. This homogeneity, once established, achieved a momentum of its own, to become of major significance for the history of mankind. It was central to the Russian state's ability to rule not only by force but also through the mute consensus of the majority of the population and to tap and use its loyalties in times of crisis. The leading role of recent Soviet scholarship in attempting to unravel ethnic history as a particular dimension of social reality is not accidental: the relevance of this 'problematique' is deeply rooted in history as well as in the daily political experience of Russia/USSR.[8]

Finally, during two centuries only, the Russian peasants moved all the way from the payment of tribute (legitimated by the need to fight off or to keep peace with the southern nomads and softened by high territorial mobility and strong communal organisations) to unheard-of levels of exploitation and cattle-like enslavement of more than nine-tenths of the Russians. Within another century came the emancipation from serfdom which made peasantry not only 'free' but landowning. The state played a decisive and explicit role in this and made the transformation rapid. As against all these fundamental changes, the centuries-old Russian communal structures were transfigured but survived. It was explained by the fact that the commune kept its major functions, inclusive of what both Mourer and Marx referred to as the 'only shield of popular liberty of the past'.[9] Other characteristics of peasanthood held also, especially the operation of the family production units and the numerical pre-eminence of peasants in Russia. A massive majority of Russians lived within the peasant communes which differed significantly from the rural communities typical of Russia's neighbours, as well as its own Polish, Baltic, Caucasian and Central Asian internal peripheries.

*   *   *

It is only while stipulating the general and the unique tenets of the structure of Russian society that its categorisation as a 'developing society' and/or a political economy definable as a case of 'dependent development', can be considered for the discrete insights it offers. The fundamental significance of classifying the Russia of the period in that way lies in the type of social tension, crises, subsequent dynamism and prospects such an approach indicates and the analytical categories it offers. Central to it are the typical contradictions of such countries' political economy, the distinctive collective conflicts and the particular ideological/moral crisis linked to revolutionary agencies of change. It helps to map out and specify the context and the nub of the main forces and impacts that challenged the tsardom 'from inside' in 1900–7 and were to play out the final power-game of the tsardom's destruction in 1917.

The 'Witte System' named and vividly described by Von Laue,[10] was intimately linked with a Witte-type crisis, which directly represented the characteristics of 'dependent development' and closely paralleled much of what we encounter today in Latin America, South Asia and Africa. The growing international debt and linked financial and technological dependence endangered long-term 'growth' and made the whole 'national economy' vulnerable and volatile, especially when facing international economic 'downturns' or a war effort. State-supported industrialisation facilitated severe crises of agriculture and of rural society, increasingly treated as a milking cow and a dumping place of 'modernisation' and 'growth' focused elsewhere. Agriculture represented a large majority of the Russian labour force using archaic means of production, and locked within an economy where much of the potential investment fund was being removed by the squires, merchants and state. The need for broader internal markets to 'steady' the local manufacturing clashed head-on with the short-term 'needs' of taxation and the profit maximisation by the most powerful capitalist interests. Frequent substitution of 'private entrepreneurs' by state capitalism and by foreign banks led to the severe impediments discussed above. Between 1863 and 1914 the population doubled and so did the rates of 'natural growth', putting increasing pressure on the available resources. The super-exploitation of the mass of the producers linked 'economic growth' to the polarisation of the population, the poorer part of which showed an absolute or relative decline of economic well-being. Urbanisation, treated by the majority of Russian leaders and scholars as the long-term resolution of the problem of rural 'over-population', was inadequate for that as long as the growth of extra-agricultural employment was outrun by population growth. Spontaneous 'vicious circles' and 'bottle necks' within the Russian economy combined with the impacts of the state-and-foreign-capital strategies adopted and forcefully promoted by the government to produce a permanent economic and social crisis.

General crisis of economy and society does not translate directly into an actual social confrontation but those correspond closely and causally. At the highest levels of income there was in Russia what Thomas More has described in another time and age as 'a certain conspiracy of rich men', determined to become richer. Where the poor were concerned, Russian political economy was productive of over-crowded city slums where life was cheap, day-to-day survival harsh, and frustrations extreme. It was also productive of the growing hopelessness of villagers in the most populous part of rural Russia. These were reservoirs of poverty and class hatred ever arrayed against the manor houses and the 'nice quarters' of well-being and respectability, behind the protective walls of the 'forces of order'. 'Economic growth' meant different things to Russia's different sectors. In class terms, the old well-established wealth and the newly made fortunes were matched by the persistent poverty of the workers' compounds, peasant villages and artisan teams. Some of the regions, especially the spoils of eighteenth- and nineteenth-century conquest, operated as internal colonies of the realm. The 'gaps' were increasingly evident; a Russian would use for them the term *kolol glaza* – 'it stabbed the eye'. This increasingly bred revolt also in the 'nice quarters'.

The 'dependent development' found its expression therefore not only at the general level of the economic flows malfunctions and transformations but also at the distinct dimension of class generation and conflict. The grand approximation of class analysis has been for a century the main method for the mapping out of fundamental social conflicts, mostly to make sense of the political life of the parliamentary democracies of Western Europe. The theory of political elites, be it Mosca or Pareto, run a clear second to them.[11] A social class was defined as the major sub-group of the formally equal contemporary society. Common and discrete positions and basic interests within the system of political economy delimited it and made for distinctive consciousness, identity and self-identification shaped further by the conflicting relations with other classes. Social classes represented therefore 'objective' as well as 'intersubjective' phenomena, not only a set of determinants rooted in political economy (and resulting in typical tendencies of behaviour by individuals) but also as actual collectivities recognising themselves as such and with different degrees of 'classness'.[12]

The class map of the societies caught within 'dependent development' differs from that of mid-nineteenth-century Western and Central Europe, where class analysis was born. That is why, when transplanted directly from one to another, it often tends not only to approximate (which, as argued above, any concept does) but to mislead. As for Russia in the 1890s to 1917, the 'disarticulated' system of political economy meant different processes of class structuring operating side by side. There were the main pre-capitalist social classes which, while changing in a number of ways, retained cohesion, many specific characteristics, and substantial numbers: the squires and the peasants. There were the capitalist classes with particular extra colouring: the entrepreneurs with a strong mercantile rather than industrialist flavour, and the industrial wage labourers, with strong peasant connections. There were important inter-category groups, for example, peasants who were part-time construction workers or some large landlords carrying pre-capitalist titles in service of capitalist enterprises. There were finally the classes specific to the societies discussed, or, at least, firstly recognised within them.

Some of the historians of Russia have resolved this complexity by a neat model of four social classes representing the semi-feudal/semi-capitalist nature of society, that is, the squires and the peasants surviving from feudalism and rubbing shoulders with the capitalists and wage workers of the brave new world.[13] This extended the two-class societal models in a way which was relevant but insufficient. To improve on it one must consider in which way such classes differ within the 'dependent development' context, to extend further their list and to review the parallel and different social conflicts of major significance. It was Sweezy who pointed out the typical historical curve of working-class militancy: from the relative conservatism of the days of the manufacture, via a peak in the early stage of industrialisation and towards decline as industrialisation diversifies it and the 'service industries' grow.[14] Somewhat later Wolf discussed the 'second wave' of peasant militancy stimulated by early confrontation with capitalism.[15] The point is that these two radical potentials tend often to meet for a time within the context of 'dependent development'. On the other hand, a new hierarchy is established within the 'plebeian camp', limiting its ability to act collectively. Workers of the large-scale industries are usually capable of self-organisation but they do not represent the 'lowest of the low'. As against the peasants and the unskilled half-employed and 'marginal' workers, the skilled and semi-skilled industrial working class is a relatively privileged minority. Below them stand men without a steady job and income. Beneath these are the racial minorities, women and youngsters. Outside the industrial centres are the villages from which a steady stream of unskilled labour proceeds to come into towns to join the unskilled labour and the slums or poor quarters.

We have discussed already in the text above some basic characteristics of 'the great 4' classes of Russian society. Something more should be added concerning the state apparatus and the intelligentsia. The exceptional power of the state, the extensive nature of its economic grip as owner, producer, employer and controller of resources, combined with the peculiarities of modern (i.e. Western-style educational and bureaucratic) structures to produce two more types of class-like entities whose interdependence and *modus operandum* lie not in political economy as 'classically' defined (or, at least, not only in it). That is particularly important if we keep in focus not only the general consideration of social conflict and class relations but also the 'social actors', practical knowledge of society and conscious intentionality of action. The social structuring of the top ranks of the state hierarchy was determined by interests and logic of operation defined differently then that of profit-maximisation and production, but establishing all the same consistent group interests, structural conflicts of interest with major social classes, typical patterns of cognition and specific ideologies expressed as the 'sectional interests' of the state funtionaries but, more often, through the concept of 'national interest'.

The link between the Russian bureaucrats with the squires was significant but decreasing. For the Russia of the period, the university diploma or its equivalents were becoming the necessary passport into the middle and top ranks of the state bureaucracy and into the army officer corps. In this way the personnel of the 'state apparatus' overlapped increasingly with that of the 'educated stratum', a social characteristic it has shared, paradoxically, with Russia's most ferocious critics of its social order – the 'intelligentsia'. However, origins cannot substitute for the main determinants of any class analysis worth its name, that is, for the study of prevailing economic group-interest, typical ways of personal enhancement, and the consequent political and ideological expression. In all these, clear particularities were displayed by the officialdom of Russia. We discussed it in Chapter 1.

In its 'classical' form, class analysis had adopted the view that while other types of social conflicts exist they are inferior to and/or utilised by class conflict in determining social relations, in the construction of the collective consciousness and in the establishing of political camps or alliances. This was often enough but not always so. In particular, the ethnic divisions have often proven in Russia as significant as class conflict, or more so, in the defining of political camps. On the other hand, when ethnic patterns have corresponded with occupational divisions, this has resulted in ethno-classes of particularly mobilising and defining force (e.g. the Polish nobles, the Russian bureaucrats, the Beloruss peasants and the Jewish craftsmen in the north-west of European Russia).

*   *   *

Parallel to the general crisis of the Russian political economy and the growing and increasingly explicit conflict between major social groups was an ideological/moral crisis expressed in perceptions, concepts and values. At least to begin with, it found its main carrier and form of expression in the assault on the tsarist state by the Russian 'intel-legentsia' which judged it inadequate by the standards of progress, justice and national interest.

The creation of a Western-educated elite was the result of diffusion of what was defined as science, knowledge and modern education. One cannot treat it simply as an educational phenomenon, for it related knowledge and assumptions drawn from industrial societies to the peculiarities of the social structure of a 'developing society'. The cultural heritage and the intellectual training made the Western-educated elite into a group of outsiders in their own country, divided both from the plebeian mass of the population and the traditional power holders in it.

Inter-Russia processes added to this group particularisation. Commitment to 'rationality' and 'modernity' defined in the light of the experience of Western Europe (of which they were acutely if often inaccurately aware) put educated Russians at odds with their direct environment. On the personal level there were several possible ways for resolving the consequent conflict. The 'acceptance of reality', that is, a job in the administration or else in the 'free professions', was one. Emigration was another. The withdrawal to one's 'Cherry Orchard' estate was a time-honoured way for an alienated squire. All these solutions were both objectively and subjectively limited in the context of Russia. In the middle of nineteenth century a growing number of Western-educated Russians had found themselves within a particular marginal position. Theirs was the world of writings, read and produced, a territory-less purer part of Russia, a 'republic of letters'. They were emerging as a social grouping, self-recognised and recognisable as such. Their ranks were increasingly swelled by sons of social classes/estates different to that of nobility, that is, children of clergy, urbanites from a mixed background, the carrier-seeking members of ethnic minorities (often restricted in the choice of the official occupation, e.g. Jews, Poles and later the Baltic Germans), even a few peasants – a mixed group that came to be referred to as *raznochintsy*, i.e. 'men of different ranks'.

Characteristically the word 'intelligentsia' was introduced via Russian into other languages.[16] Formal definitions have related it mostly to 'mental labour' and university training. Its nature and functions can be understood only while related to the broader social context, that is, in our case that of 'dependent development' and of the highly repressive state. Conscious self-identification and positioning *vis à vis* different social forces were particularly significant here. Despite their university training and characteristically 'mental' labour, the managers of the Russian state and much of its economy were excluded, and excluded themselves, from Russian intelligentsia. The same was true for most of the army officers and the mass of the Russian clergy (which received its education in the religious seminaries and academies). On the other hand, most of the Russian 'liberal professions' and many of its best engineers or agronomists would see themselves definitely as part of it. So did the majority of Russian revolutionaries in the nineteenth century. At the core of this group and most influential within it were the Russian men of letters, its writers, poets, dramatists and 'publicists' (i.e. the more thoughtful journalists). The nature and the prevailing mood of the intelligentsia was dramatically yet accurately described by I. Berlin:

it did not mean simply educated persons. It certainly did not mean intellectuals as such . . . the Russian intelligentsia, because it was small and consumed by a sense of responsibility for their brothers who lived in darkness, grew to be a dedicated order, bound by a sense of solidarity and kinship. Isolated and divided by the tangled forest of a society impenetrable to rational organisation, they called out to each other, in order to preserve contact. They were citizens of a state within a state, soldiers in an army dedicated to progress, surrounded on all sides by reaction. . . . In the land in which the intelligentsia was born, it was founded, broadly speaking, on the idea of permanent rational opposition to the *status quo*, which was regarded as in constant danger of becoming ossified, a block to human thought and human progress.[17]

Two more short citations from the tsardom's top dignitary and Russia's foremost writer can supplement that picture. From the memoirs of Witte: 'The tsar [*gosudar'*] has once remarked at the dinner table . . . that one should order the Academy of Sciences to remove this word [*intelligentsia*] from the Russian dictionary'. From Bulgakov's *The White Guard*: 'You are a socialist, are you not? Like all intelligent people'.[18]

The particular 'marching army' of this group were the university students, inclusive of the 'permanent' ones (i.e. those who were unable to finish their education but held on to the university environment and formed a community around it). The universities and the colleges for advanced training (i.e. Forestry, Engineering, etc.) provided a natural base for organisation. In a condition involving the illegality of any opposition and with every social club or organisation supervised by the authorities, a base where young intelligentsia could organise itself and 'talk things out' was increasingly important and their conflict with both state and university authorities endemic. They were linked closely with young intellectuals engaged in the occupations of 'service to the people', especially teachers, medics, *zemstvo* agronomists, etc.

The Russian intelligentsia confronted directly the state apparatus. Its top bureaucrats have seen themselves as acting to enhance Russia's international standing, promote its economy and secure the eternal promise of the Russian autocracy. That had to be done by controlling and containing the two explicit challenges of capitalism and of intelligentsia with a third threat, one of popular revolt, looming in the background. The growth of capitalism disrupted the familiar ways of ruling and administrating. The initial policy of simple incorporation of new technologies, stripped of their disagreeable social and political characteristics (i.e. 'Western' weapons but no 'Western' constitutional rule), was increasingly difficult to execute. Not only education but the co-operation of the educated was needed. Yet a major sector of the Russian 'educated' stratum was locked in growing conflict with the tsardom and its officials. This was well expressed in the very transformation of the term 'intelligentsia' from 'a value-neutral' description of individual capacity or intellectual attainment, into the synonym of bitter social criticism and moral condemnation of the state and its dignitaries. Any outward sign of comfort given or co-operation with the state bureaucracy was treated as treason or corruption. The counter-culture of the intelligentsia took particular pride in refusing to serve the state or capitalist entrepreneurs in any capacity and especially in major issues of social hegemony and ideological control. (As for the bourgeoisie, N. Mikhailovskii had declared in the 1880s to universal acclaim that 'the Russian intelligentsia would and should be ashamed of marching in step with it'.)[19] Apart from a few exceptional periods (when these attitudes shifted under the impact of a nationalist wave triggered off by war or by the Polish 'mutinies'),[20] the Russian intelligentsia faced all brands of the Russian 'establishment' as a hostile force. What made this stand out even more sharply, was that the intelligentsia was opposed directly by senior and middle-range bureaucrats who often came from similar social backgrounds and educational establishments. But most of the state dignitaries were increasingly at a loss as to how to deal with the new times: with 'subjects' who expressed 'opinions', merchants who were not humble, peasants who wandered around, cities that 'exploded', Jews who resided in Petersburg, Finns who claimed autonomy, but especially so with the highbrows who spent their time denouncing the rightful authorities and even the Most Sacred Person of His Imperial Majesty. In the latter part of the nineteenth century the 'state' was increasingly challenged by disruptive forces and at their core the spontaneous processes associated with capitalism and the conscious revolt of the intelligentsia.

As a silent background and a potential arbiter to the unequal duel in which intellectual fireworks and personal sacrifice of Russia's brightest young men and women, faced the crass obstinacy and the seemingly overwhelming strength of those who ruled Russia, stood the Russian plebeian masses. It was the struggle for their 'hearts and minds' that formed the crux of the political history of the Russian tsardom and was to define its abrupt end in 1917.

D. STATE AND REVOLUTION

In 1862 a sequence of five *Unaddressed Letters* was written in Russia. Their dramatic significance lies as much in their symbolism and setting as in their content. Despite the title, and indeed accentuated by it, was the fact that the addressee was manifestly known. It was the Emperor and the Autocrat of all Russias, Alexander II, 'the Emancipator', at the Winter Palace. The sender's address was nearly as famous and as symbolic. It was the Peter and Paul fortress-prison of Petersburg that held Russia's most dangerous political criminals. The author was Nikolai Chernyshevskii, Russia's 'man of conscience' and foremost writer on politics, economics and aesthetics. A self-taught, dour and stubborn man of extensive knowledge, little *savoir-vivre* and unbending moral convictions, he well represented the *raznochintsy*, the first generation of Western-educated Russians not to come from the nobility. (Typical of many of them, Chernyshevskii was a cleric's son from a provincial town, i.e. Saratov, of past and future revolutionary fame.) He was careful not to break any laws and did not belong to any political organisation. He used his pen to oppose with the full strength of his convictions the way Russian society and state functioned and, despite the harsh hand of the censor, attacked it time and time again, clearly if indirectly, in the journal he edited – the *Contemporary* (*Sovremennik*). Despite 'remaining within the law', Chernyshevskii was arrested and spent two years of preliminary confinement in the fortress. While his judges struggled with the regrettable lack of proof of actual law-breaking, he wrote his *Unaddressed Letters* and a didactic novel entitled *What is to be Done?* about new men and women, on which generations of Russian intelligentsia were to be educated. He was eventually convicted of high treason and sentenced to life imprisonment with hard labour in Siberia, never to regain his freedom. With fine understanding of the symbolism of the occasion, his judges sentenced him also to a 'civil execution': on a grey morning he was taken out of prison to have a sword broken over his head by a hangman, signifying loss of all rights and privileges, and then transported directly to Siberia. The *Unaddressed Letters* were banned by the censor as were (following his sentence) most of his writings, but they circulated hand-to-hand inside and outside Russia. In 1873 another rebel, writer and social theorist, unknown to Chernyshevskii, read the *Unaddressed Letters* in his English exile and was sufficiently impressed to have the first of them personally translated and to promote their publication. The translator's name was Karl Marx, and with as keen a recognition of the man's worth as that of the judges in

Petersburg he was to refer to Chernyshevskii admiringly in the second edition of *Capital* in 1872 as 'that great Russian scholar and critic'.[1]

The significance of the *Unaddressed Letters* is, however, not only that of the charged symbolism of their political setting. Their theoretical content has stood remarkably well the test of time. There were two major components. The bulk of the argument was a systematic denunciation of the way 1861 emancipation reform was carried out, making clear how little it actually resolved the peasant's plight, how much it was hedged and twisted by the bureaucracy and why it would eventually lead to a plebeian revolt against all the Russian upper classes stood for, good and bad alike. Second, the opening Letter addressed the general social context of the debate and of the political conflict in contemporary Russia. It recognised a fundamental socio-political division of the Russians into three groupings very different in size. A remarkably apt anticipation of political divisions of Russia half a century later, Chernyshevskii's insights were also deeply relevant for other countries and for generations to follow. He had this to say to the tsar:

You are displeased with us: Let that be as you choose: no one can command their feelings, and we are not seeking your approval. Our aim is a different one, which you probably have as well: to be of service to the Russian common people (*narod*). Consequently, you must not expect real gratitude from us, nor must we from you, for our respective labours. A judge of them does exist, outside your numerically restricted circle, and outside even our circle which, though far more numerous than yours, still represents only a negligible fraction of the tens of millions of people whose welfare we and you would like to promote. If this judge knew all the facts of the case and could deliver an assessment of your labour and ours, any explanations between you and us would be superfluous.

Regrettably, this is not the case. You, he knows by name; yet being completely alien to your mental universe and your milieu, he certainly does not know your thoughts or the motives which guide your actions. Us, he does not know even by name.

. . . You tell the people: you must proceed like this. We tell it: you must proceed like that. But in the people's midst, almost everyone is slumbering.

. . . The truth is equally bitter for you and for us. The people does not consider that anything really useful to it has resulted from anyone's concern about it. We all, separating ourselves from the people under some name or other – under the name of the authorities, or under the name of this or that privileged stratum; we all, assuming we have some particular interests distinct from the objects of popular aspiration – whether interests of diplomatic and military power, or interests of controlling internal affairs, or interests of our personal wealth, or interests of enlightenment; we all feel vaguely what kind of outcome flows from this complexion of the people's view. When people come to think: 'I cannot expect any help in my affairs from anyone else at all', they will certainly and speedily draw the conclusions that they must get down to running their affairs themselves. All individuals and social strata separate from the people tremble, at this anticipated outcome.

The five Letters of terse prose analysing and condemning the inadequacies of the 1861 emancipation of Russia's serfs were concluded as follows: 'I am aware, dear sir, that I have broken the rules of propriety in thrusting myself with my explanations upon a man who had in no way asked me for them; so it will be no surprise to you if I do not adhere to those rules at the conclusion of my correspondence either, and do not sign in the customary way "always at your service" or "your most humble servant" but sign simply – N. Chernyshevskii'.[2] Within a year he was serving his sentence of hard labour for life in Siberia.

Chernyshevskii's text as well as his life story represented a new political map and a new type of dissent. His text described and analysed a social world twice divided. First, it was split into the politically mute plebeian world (the 'common people' – *narod*) as against the extremely thin layer of polite society, the educated, the potential rank-holders, those better off who could also write to each other and dance with each other at social occasions, those who counted. They were well separated from the plebeian mass by a protective wall of the army, the police lower ranks, the lower clerks, clerics and bailiffs, the NCOs of Russian society. Second, those better off and educated in the Western sense were divided in turn by their own images and standards as much as by their formal status, into, on the one hand, the official Russia of top rank-holders (*sanovniki*) and of the upper-class 'world' (*svet*) (i.e. the tsar's closest social environment). On the other hand, (but partly overlapping) stood those whom the Russians called 'society' (*obshchestvo*), that is, those with claim or pretence to spiritual depth, to the understanding of social relations, and appreciation of science, of arts and of progress – the 'public opinion' of the day, critical of 'official Russia'. The *raznochintsy* played an increasingly important role in that milieu but frequently they were children of 'the empire's first estate' of the nobility. These people, or at least the politically more conscious of them, came to be referred to increasingly as *intelligentsiya*. They were particularly sensitive to the leading men of ideas (*poveliteli dum*) of every generation: its poets, its writers, its theorists, its secular moralists and its dreamers. It was the moral leadership of this group that in the 1850s and 1860s sat heavily on the shoulders of Chernyshevskii as well as of Hertzen, Belinskii and a few more, making them consequently hated and adored. It was for that honour that Chernyshevskii paid by his life sentence in Siberia. The gendarmes and bureaucrats who had Chernyshevskii sentenced were right in sensing a new and powerful threat.

*   *   *

Russia has had its share of 'old dissent', which in essence belonged to the days of Muscovy and the commencement of the empire. There were centuries of plebeian struggle in defence of the 'old rights', that is, the partly imagined and partly true memories of times when a commoner was free of servitude and bondage. The encroachment of officers and nobles, clerks and clerics, the whole Draconian and crushing power of the state, had been resisted generation after generation in a long sequence of battles and some major peasant and Cossack wars, which were all eventually lost. Since the death by torture of Pugachev and his main followers in 1774, the 'official Russia', that is, the state and the church, the bureaucrats and the nobles, had for a period of 125 years ruled the ocean of under-dogs with relatively few ripples. The imperial wars and conquests had derailed some of the class conflicts, channelling into nationalist moulds the energy of protest, but also added new groups of those who were not Russian to the camp of resistance. Their struggles for ethnic rights spanned the 'old' and the 'new' dissent and were at times allied to both. They also failed or, at least, so it seemed by the end of the nineteenth century.

Europe knew another type of 'old dissent', for a time much more productive of actual political results and social transformation than the plebeian struggle and the peasant wars. The dominant class of warriors and/or squires confronted kings and dignitaries in a constant 'tug of war' over power and privileges. They have often lost when royal mercenaries (usually with the help of the burghers), reduced the nobles to submission. At times, it was the nobles who reduced kings to the status of figurative heads of state, the 'first among equals' of the nobility social estate. Deputies of nobility elected kings and imposed treaties in Poland and Hungary. Since the early Romanovs such ideas constituted treason and were effectively curbed in the tsardom of all Russias. Its *Zemskii sobor*, an assembly of deputies of 'estates', had disappeared from the scene by the seventeenth century. The 'municipal freedoms' expressed in *veche* had been reduced even earlier. The boyars and the *dvoryane* of the Moscovite grand dukes were from inception courtiers and servitors rather than princelings or a 'nation' of an organised and autonomous social estate, claiming its rights and liberties. Their 'class organisations' established by Catherine II's Charter of Nobility were disjointed and limited in scope.

The new type of dissent was initiated by men of knowledge, of ideas and of moral values, that is, those who, as a Russian contemporary would put it, 'had a soul'. To 'have a soul' was to seek justice and to accept values higher than obedience to the state authorities. The 'knowledge' and ideas in question were new in texture by being secular, general rather than pragmatic, dealing with humans rather than with 'things'. Those men were without exception stimulated (at times negatively) by the writings, views and moods of 'Europe' (i.e. the Europe that was not Russia). Not quite children of the Renaissance, because the Reformation and the scientific revolution of the seventeenth century were not realised in Russia, they were, figuratively speaking, their 'nephews', that is, the once-removed kinsmen related via the European social philosophy of Enlightenment as expressed in particular in the nineteenth-century writings of Schelling, Hegel, Fourier and Feuerbach.

The voice of the new dissent was first heard under the long rule of Catherine II, which saw also the Charter of Nobility and the execution of Pugachev. Its first lonely harbinger was, arguably, Alexander Radishchev. As in the case of Chernyshevskii, his biography aptly represented the general political context of the Russian tsardom of his day. An enlightened nobleman who had studied at the University of Leipzig and travelled extensively abroad, and a state official afterwards, he published in 1790 a volume entitled *Journey from St Petersburg to Moscow* which followed in form a contemporary European fashion. The book offered a bitterly eloquent critique of serfdom and of the management of the country on all levels. It was passed by the censor but enraged the Empress who, according to her secretary's memoirs, 'has most graciously commented that he [Radishchev] is a rebel, worse than Pugachev'.[3] Radishchev was tried and sentenced to execution, which was eventually commuted to life exile in Siberia. Permitted to return after Catherine's death, he was appointed to one of many committees considering administrative reforms but rapidly ran foul of its chairman. Threatened by renewed imprisonment if he did not 'learn how to behave', he committed suicide in 1802.

During the nineteenth century the new dissent recorded several more 'firsts'. In the 1820s came Russia's first attempt to active 'modernising' reforms by a military *coup d'état*. The 1812 march to Paris in the wake of the Napoleonic Wars had left a powerful impression on the young officers – in those days, Russia'a foremost group of educated nobility. The high hopes for major reforms under Alexander I were disappointed. As a result, a variety of secret societies sprang up. Most of their members were army men. Their creed, size and cohesion differed, but uniformly they craved for constitutional government and the abolition of serf-dom.[4] Klyuchevskii has caught well a particular 'intelligentsia' aspect of their mental outlook: 'whereas . . . fathers have been Russians educ-ated to become Frenchmen, the father's sons were French-educated men longing to become Russian'.[5] The constitutionalist struggle of Colonel Riego in Spain was treated by all of them as a model and an inspiration. Many of these conspirators were sons of Russia's most prestigious hereditary and landowning nobility. Russia's foremost poet, Pushkin, publicly expressed sympathy for their views, without actually belonging to one of the societies. The rebellion broke out prematurely, triggered off by arrests and a crisis of succession that followed Alexander I's death. In December 1825 (hence the nickname 'Decembrists' given to its or-ganisers) troops that were never quite told what the upheaval was all about, were led into the streets of the capital by their officers – members of the secret societies. The rebellion in Petersburg and in the South was quickly defeated by loyalist troops. Five of its leaders were executed and many more exiled to Siberia. The execution of Ryleev, a promising poet and a civilian, provoked Poland's foremost poet Mickewicz's stinging description of Russia as 'a land which murders its prophets'.[6]

The next 'first' was the essentially secular and 'sociological' debate about the nature of Russia in its relation to the West: the debate between the 'Westerners' (*Zapadniki*) and Slavophiles. It began in the 1830s, triggered off by the *Philosophical Letters* of P. Chadayev, a personal friend of many Decembrists, who in the wake of their defeat and under the heavy hand of Nikolai I declared that Russia belonged neither to the Western nor the Eastern civilisations, nor did not it represent a civilisation of its own; it was 'an intellectual lacuna'.[7] In the furore that followed, the tsar personally ordered Chadayev to be considered mad and had him repeatedly subjected to medical inspection. Abuse flew freely also from less official sources, but a debate was launched, its participants dividing into two major camps. Those who considered Russia backward and called for modernisation, understood as Europeanisation, came to be referred to as 'Westerners'. Peter the Great was their hero, commencing a process that now required to be completed. As against them, the Slavophiles believed in the uniqueness of Russia's social and spiritual nature and destiny, different from and superior to what Europe had to offer. They subsequently idolised pre-Petrine Russia and considered the German-infested bureaucracy, set up by Peter, to be the main obstacle to the natural harmony between the autocrat and the people that would have prevailed otherwise, with Orthodox Christianity offering its norms. They were deeply counter-revolutionary, and, while advocating freedom of speech and the revival of *Zemskii Sobor*, objected to constitutionalism and Western parliamentary rule. V. Belinskii was probably the most outspoken and influential of the Westerners while the Slavophiles were well represented by A. Khomyakov and by K. Aksakov.[8] Both groups were critical of Russia's actuality. Despite the conservatism, religiosity and monarchism of the Slavophiles, their writings and journals were subsequently frowned upon and often repressed by the censorship.

Finally, the most important 'first' of the new dissent was the creation of revolutionary populism – Russia's first indigenous socialist ideology and movement. Its main theorists were Hertzen, Chernyshevskii and Lavrov and its most powerful political expression was the People's Will party (*Narodnaya volya*). The movement was also influenced by the views of Bakunin and Tkachev, but never fully identified with them.[9]

It was Hertzen who commenced the particular theoretical position associated with Russian populism.[10] His views evolved from initial Westerner assumptions, through a critical analysis of Western Europe and of the 1848 revolution. From the outset he refused the Slavophile mystical and religious belief in intrinsic Russian peculiarities, but eventually was not prepared either to treat Russia simply as a more backward equivalent of Western Europe. To Hertzen, Russia was not unique or 'spiritual', but its social structure and potentials differed from Western Europe in a manner to be taken into consideration in the shaping of its socialist future. The fact that Russia could draw on the West European experience was new. The legal equality and constitutional rights the Russian liberals were beginning to demand had already proven insufficient. Hertzen was akin to the West European socialists and considered one of them in demanding social equality and the full emancipation of the exploited classes which would become the masters of a better world. In the Russian context, that meant the destruction of serfdom and the rise of the peasantry. Chernyshevskii, and later the *Land and Liberty* movement, were to adopt all those positions but to represent them inside Russia (Hertzen emigrated and set up Russia's first 'free press' in exile). These 'populists of the interior' were to develop Hertzen's initial analysis further and to add the blaze of martyrdom, of direct action and, eventually, of revolutionary struggle.

There was considerable originality in the way populist theorists and their movement approached the future of Russia. They assumed the possibility and desirability for Russia to bypass the capitalist stage and to proceed directly to a socially just society. This view and preference was rooted in the concept of 'uneven development' – a radical departure from the prevalent evolutionism of the day, first suggested by Chadayev. Not Russian uniqueness or supremacy but rather the 'global' context of Russian history would lead to an alternative path of development. The advance of industrial capitalism in Western Europe was central to it. On the other hand, the fact that the peasant commune, by now dormant in Europe, was still operative in Russia, could and should be put to use in the building of the new just world. To Hertzen, while Western Europe must progress from the political liberties achieved and from the rampant individualism of the capitalist society towards growing communality of the social structure, peasant Russia should keep its communalist structure while advancing towards liberty, to meet at socialism's junction. Put in the Hegelian idiom of the day by Chernyshevskii, the 'synthesis' of the future world would therefore resemble the initial 'thesis' of pre-capitalist and pre-class communities rather than its capitalist 'anti-thesis'. Tsardom's obstinate conservatism defined the revolutionary nature of the social transformation due to occur.

Without being fully accepted by the Russian populists, the writings of Bakunin had stimulated in their ranks a belief in mass spontaneity, an insurrectionist 'mood' and a particular hostility towards state centralisation. Later, the writings of Tkachev came to exercise an opposite influence in so far as revolutionary action was concerned, stressing the significance of 'Jacobin' centralism and of resolute minorities in revolutionary confrontation was well as the significance of the time factor: to delay a revolution might mean losing the chance to bypass capitalism in Russia.

The theorists of revolutionary populism considered the tsardom Russia's main capitalist force, representing not only a 'Mongol-like oppression', but generating, linked with and maintaining capitalism and capitalists. The state and state apparatus were central to the populist social analysis and designation of enemies. As against its power and capitalism-inducing strategies, the populists put their trust in the 'labouring class', which to Chernyshevskii included 'peasants, daily labourers and permanent wage workers' (it was to become peasants, workers and intelligentsia in later populist writings), united by the common enemies. It was the class war (with classes differently defined than in Marx or in Ricardo) that was eventually to transform Russia. Populist demanded not only parliamentary democracy but social equality. Since the nature of the main enemy entailed a repressive political regime and a social regime of inequality, both embedded in the state, it meant a necessarily combined revolutionary struggle for liberty and social justice. The goal was to establish a socialist Russia.[11]

A point to remember in view of the 'brainwash' of the latter generations, the Russian populists of the 1860s and 1880s were socialists in their own eyes as well as those of Western Europe. When resident in Western Europe, they joined as a matter of course the local socialist parties, edited their newspapers, were active in the 1st International. Its Russian section (located in Switzerland and led by Utin) consisted fully of populist *émigrés*, followers of Chernyshevskii. It elected Marx as its representative on the General Council of the International which he accepted with manifest pleasure. The leaders of the People's Will kept contact with French, German Polish and British socialist parties and were in direct relations with Marx in London. Friendship and appreciation between Marx and the People's Will were often mutually expressed the differences of approach were acknowledged and treated by both sides as deriving mostly from the Russian particularities.[12] It was Lavrov who 'on behalf of the Russian socialists' offered the eulogy read-out on Marx's grave. As a member of the 1st International, a founding member of the 2nd one, and a participant in the Parisian Commune, he well represented the living link between Marx, the West European socialist movement and the Russian revolutionary populism.

Finally, the Russian populists offered a set of images and views that linked what would be today treated as 'social sciences' with a different type of discourse and was described (and badly misnamed) as 'subjective sociology'.[13] It was a combination of social, psychological and ethical considerations about the place and duties of the intelligentsia in an oppressive and changing world. The issue of the two meanings of truth (*pravda*): truth as realism (*istina*) and truth as justice (*spravedlivost'*), was part of this debate. So was the place of ascetism as radicalising simplicity and of revolutionary activism as a way of life. The later terminology of 'professional revolutionaries' and 'cadres' within Leninism stemmed directly from these views. So did the belief in the educating and purifying force of revolutionary experience in the creation of new men and women. Conceptually, those views related the populist creed to an analysis of the role of ideas in history, enhancing their weight and offering a rationalist and libertarian theory of social advance. Most importantly it was a call for action.

By 1873 the views of the theorists and discussion within clandestine 'circles' were transformed into a political movement of growing coherence and numbers. The appeal of the theorists were reacted to by hundreds of young men and women who, in the summer of 1874, left the comfort of their well-endowed families to 'go to the people', that is, to go to the villages to propagate the populist cause among the peasantry. They were met with bewilderment by the peasants, denounced, and rapidly rounded up by the police. That was not the end of the matter, however. The radicals drew conclusions from their failure and reformed accordingly. By 1877 a new wave of populist propagandists went into villages. This time, most of them had trained beforehead in skills useful to the peasants: carpentry, metalwork, etc. They came now to settle permanently and in larger groups – 'colonies' – and were more ready for a long and slow haul. They established also an effective national organisation, the Land and Liberty, with a network of clandestine branches and printing presses all through European Russia.

By the end of the 1870s the populist movement reached its next stage. The results of the work in the villages were still barely to be seen. The authorities were fairly effective in precluding the attempted political re-education of the peasantry. In the populist ranks arrest followed arrest. The majority within the Land and Liberty leadership concluded that the state's oppressive power must be broken first, before the spiritual emancipation and social transformation of plebeian Russia could be proceeded with. In their own words, 'Social reform in Russia is revolution. Under our political regime of absolute despotism and denial of the right and of the will of the people, reform can be only achieved by a revolution'.[14] This new insurrectionist strategy was objected to by a minority that wanted to proceed with the movement's earlier village-centred approach (the *'dereven'shchiki'*). In 1879 the two wings parted company. The majority established the People's Will Party, the minority formed the Black Repartition organisation, each of them with its own clandestine journal that took its name from the organisation it represented.

The People's Will rapidly outpaced its rivals and for a few years came to dominate the Russian political scene. They shifted their 'cadres' into major towns, moving rapidly and effectively to organise army officers, workers and students for an insurrection. Immense energy was shown in establishing clandestine networks of new organisations, printing presses, etc. Wage workers rather than peasants were now considered central in the immediate battle but not because of the intrinsic socialist qualities of the proletariat but for tactical reasons, that is, their concentration at the urban centres where the political power lay. In accordance, a particular 'workers programme' was prepared, 'workers cricles' set up and the first Russian newspapers specifically aimed at the urban wage workers were printed. An adopted 'tactic of terror' against the top dignitaries of the state led to some of the People's Will's most spectacular exploits. It aimed to 'shake' the tsardom and its leaders, to break their confidence and the totality of their grip. The People's Will hoped that, pursued with sufficient energy, such attacks would make the government forces retreat or waver, and wake the mass of the people from their political slumbers, destroying the belief in the irresistaibility of the state. The Executive Committee of the People's Will, both a national leadership and a top organisation for terrorist action, adopted as its direct aim the killing of Alexander II.

In the confrontation that followed, the People's Will was eventually defeated. The initial impact of the organisation had led to a considerable panic at the top (the establishment of 'dictatorship' of General Loris-Melikov, etc.).[15] In 1881 the People's Will succeeded in killing Alexander II, but no popular insurrection followed and most of the Executive Committee members were imprisoned and/or executed within a year. The party re-formed, establishing new leadership, which in turn was arrested. Then, the powerful Military Organisation of army officers who joined the People's Will, preparing for the possibility of a military uprising, was destroyed by betrayal and arrests. New executions, imprisonments and exile followed. In 1884 came one more major attempt to re-establish the People's Will's national structure by G. Lopatin, a member of the General Council of the 1st International, and Marx's personal friend. It was crushed by a new wave of arrests. For all practical purposes that was the end of the party of People's Will. The last localised attempt to renew and proceed with its action took place in 1887, when a group of students, who adopted the name of *Revolutionary Fraction of the People's Will*, attempted to kill Tsar Alexander III. It ended, once again, in arrests and the execution of its participants, who included Alexander Ulyanov, Lenin's elder brother.[16]

The continuity between the 'generations' of the Russian new dissent was considerable, at times implicit yet ever powerful, enhanced by personal contacts and intimately related to Russian literature. Many of the social theorists of Russia were poets, novelists or literary critics;

indeed, the very division between types of writing was never clear. Pugachev, who led his Cossack and peasant rebels when Radishchev was a young man, was first described in realistically human terms by Pushkin, who befriended the Decembrists and exchanged with their prisoners in Siberia poetic messages, all of the educated Russians knew by heart. His closest personal friend was Chadayev, the author of the 'Philosophical Letters'. It was also Pushkin who initiated the journal *Contemporary*, which was eventually edited by Chernyshevskii and suppressed with his arrest. The young Hertzen had admired the Decembrists while the young Chernyshevskii has said that he 'admired Hertzen more than he admired any other Russian'[17] and explicitly set out to follow his tracks. (They clashed eventually, but that came long after Chernyshevskii's 'formative period'.) The name of the Marxist newspaper *Iskra* (the 'spark') was taken directly from the Decembrists' poetic answer to Pushkin, while Lenin took the name for his book devoted to party organisation from Chernyshevskii's novel *What Is to Be Done*, which he admired. A memorial column to the founding fathers of Russian socialism was erected in the first flush of the Bolshevik victory and still stands in the Alexander Park next to the Kremlin. The names, allegedly Dostoevsky (to be judged by the impact of his prose rather than by his political views), selected by Lenin, run from Marx to Fourier and end with Chernyshevskii, Lavrov, Mikhailovskii and Plekhanov. In truth one should have added here literary figures such as Tolstoy, Nekrasov, Chekhov and, of course, Pushkin, whose memorial, nearby in Moscow, reads:

And long my people will remember me
For my gift has served the right affections
In this cruel age I glorified liberty
And called for loyalty to the defeated.[18]

The third line was initially: 'Following Radishchev I glorified liberty', but was sacrificed to the gods of censorship. The Russian intelligentsia well knew its history and, through it, knew themselves.

It was the defeat of the People's Will that set the internal political scene of Russia in the two decades beginning from the middle of the 1880s, that is, the period that preceded the 1905–7 revolution. The drama of rejection of the first wave of young populist idealists by the peasants, the gallows, prisons and exile that followed and decimated a whole generation of activists, the immense sacrifice that ended in total defeat and a conservative backlash of the 'counter-reforms', were never forgotten by the Russian political opposition. Yet, on the other hand, the knowledge of it caused many latter-day observers to underestimate the long-term achievements of the revolutionary populism of the 1870s and 1880s. They established a model of political action, the crux of which lay in a small and tightly knit organisation of revolutionary intelligentsia whose main enemy was the state power and whose long-term strategy was the penetration and channelling of the spontaneous protest of the mass of Russia's under-dogs, workers and peasants, aiming to turn them into a political force. The problem of 'Why did it not succeed?' was hotly discussed, but the fundamental social map and the revolutionaries' task was set out already in Chernyshevskii's image of the double division of the people of Russia and of the coming plebeian war. The problem of 'cadres' v. masses and the class analysis of the revolutionary action, as the necessary initial phase of state destruction, were acknowledged and analysed as central and due to dominate any future considerations. The strength of this approach lay in its coming from and addressing the specific political and social conditions of tsarist Russia and countries with parallel characteristics. That is why it survived in the theory and organisational structures of all of the Russian revolutionary movements that followed.

On the other hand, there was the immediate and powerful experience of the defeat of the People's Will, both conceptual and political. The people of Russia did not rebel at the sign of the tsar's killing. The membership of People's Will was dead, incarcerated or on the run. This destruction left the field of dissent to those who considered the revolutionary action premature or altogether misconceived. They consisted of three major strands. First, after failing to make much impact as a separate branch of populism, the core of the *Black Repartition* leadership emigrated and rapidly converted to Marxism. They reformed in Switzerland and established there the Emancipation of Labour organisation, led by Plekhanov and Axelrod. They came now to accept the necessity of a capitalist stage in Russia's development and of a proletarian revolution as the one possible road to socialism. The failure of People's Will was explained accordingly, that is, as the result of an attack that was premature in class terms and therefore utopian and doomed. The eyes of the Emancipation of Labour group were on Germany, its rapid social and economic transformation during the 1880s and 1890s, as much as the repeated electoral victories of the German Social Democratic Workers Party. By the 1890s Plekhanov came to treat Russian peasantry *in toto* as a bottle-neck of stagnation, to be disposed of as a necessary condition for the advance of capitalism and democracy, to be followed in due time by the proletarian victory in its struggle for socialism. The movement they initiated was increasingly referred to as the Social Democrats.

Next, groups and individuals who proceeded to adhere to the broad populist tradition but refused its revolutionary implications, and therefore survived, came increasingly to speak on behalf of populism. As the hope for insurrection receded and its proponents were physically out of the scene, a 'politics of small deeds' was increasingly being stressed: education, agrarian advance, the welfare needs of the peasants and workers, etc. These views of a non-revolutionary ('legal') populism was finding a social carrier in the professional *zemstvos* employees. Within the *zemstvos* such populist members of the intelligentsia often allied with Marxists of similar inclinations and with liberal nobles, with whom they shared the wish to follow the 'small deeds', that is to serve the educational, economic and legal advance of the plebeian masses. A third strand of dissent, Russia's liberalism, developed within the enlightened landed nobility active in the *zemstvos* but also in the urban 'free professions': lawyers, medical doctors, university professors, etc. They were 'Westerners' to a man in their wish to have Russia progress towards the West European patterns of political organisation, that is, parliamentary rule and constitutional government. To them, political liberty and a democratised (i.e. curtailled in its powers) state administration was the way to secure advance in other fields, that is, activate the Russian economy, stimulate education, enhance personal initiative, etc. They were hostile to, or at least wary of, the revolutionary and anti-monarchist *élan* of the People's Will, but ready to co-operate with the Left in the pursuit of welfare and educational schemes as well as in some demonstrations of political opposition. With Marxists – especially the 'legal' Marxists – they have much in common, including 'Westernism', belief in evolution and in the supreme significance of economic progress, and the drive for parliamentary democracy. Their hostility was turning increasingly against the 'official Russia', which harassed the elected regional authorities and repressed expressions of the literate public opinion, its journals and associations.

On the government side, the experience of People's Will reflected in the designation of potential enemies and 'unreliable elements' as well as in the methods by which those were to be defeated or controlled. The main enemy was the 'terrorist', and as this disappeared the situation seemed essentially safe. Special attention was given to potential 'military rebels' among the officers. The main unreliable elements were seen as the 'rootless' people, that is, the intelligentsia and the wage workers, who were to be carefully watched and controlled, with particular attention given to any contacts between the 'educated' and the 'uneducated'. The long-winded theoretical tracts of Marxists or of other scholastic radicals were treated as a marginal nuisance. On the other hand, the mildly constitutionalist reformers and professionals in the local authorities were systematically cautioned, dismissed or exiled.

During the 1890s the gloom of the defeat and executions of members of the People's Will and of the counter-reforms of Alexander III was lifting within the Russian political dissent. The opposition became increasingly active. Contacts were being restored, some of the revolutionary exiles were coming back, new activists were joining the fray. The 1891 famine had proved once more the tsarist state's outrageous crassness and incompetence, as against the relative efficiency of the humanitarian initiative of Russian 'society', that is, the *zemstvo* authorities and the 'free professions'. By the mid-1890s clandestine groups were growing faster than was their eradication by the police. Attempts began to establish political parties or equivalent nation-wide organisations in Russia proper. (In the Polish, Finnish and Latvian provinces clandestine parties were already active.) The framework that shaped these attempts was that of three major ideological streams: Marxist, liberal, and populist, but ethnic divisions and considerations of political strategy added to the complexity of the emerging political structures.[19] The picture at its most general was one of rapid transformation of Russia's political scene – a rising wave of political dissent and of a parallel self-critical trend between the tsars' nobles and bureaucrats.

In his first book concerned with party organisation in those days, Lenin had hotly advocated the need for 'demarcation' before any unification into a political party could take place. The issue was certainly rife within each of the ideological, ethnic and strategy-oriented streams and sub-streams of Russian political dissent. It was through a process of constant attempts at unification, of arguments, demarcations and re-marcations, punctuated by arrests and escapes that the map of twentieth-century Russian political parties was being established. At the turn of the century the essential shape of the main political organisations challenging the tsardom could already be seen but programmes, organisational prescriptions and membership were still very fluid when the revolution of 1905–7 put the nascent political parties of Russian dissent to their supreme test. It was then that the unexpected characteristics of a political revolution that failed and the high drama of its experience resulted in a conceptual revolution due to play a major role in the transformation of Russia and the world at large. Its essence was the acceptance, often implicit, of Russia's specificity as a 'developing society' and the fact that this moment of truth was put to political use by monarchists radicalised by a revolution, and by revolutionaries, taught new realism by its surprises and its eventual defeat.

Notes and References

The references to each section within chapters form a separate unit, that is, op. cit. refers to items already listed in the section.

Abbreviations used:

ES	*Entsiklopedicheskii slovar'*, Brokhauz and Efron (St. Petersburg, 1891–1906).
KA	*Krasnyi arkhiv* (published in Moscow, 1922–41 by the Central Archive Department of RSFSR, later of USSR).
NES	*Novyi entsiklopedicheskii slovar'*, Brokhauz and Efron (St Petersburg/Petrograd, commenced 1910 (unfinished)).
OSPN	*Obshchii svod pervoi vseobshchei po imperii resul'tatov razrabotki dannykh perepisi naseleniya* (St Petersburg, 1905).
PSS	V. Lenin, *Polnoe sobranie sochinenii* (Moscow, 1967–9 (5th edn)).
SD	Social Democrat (group or party, i.e. the *RSDRP*).
KD	The Constitutional Democrats, i.e. the Party of Popular Freedom.
SR	Social Revolutionary (group or party, i.e. the *PSR*).

INTRODUCTION

1. T. Shanin, *Late Marx and the Russian Road* (London, 1983) p. 17.

1 THE RUSSIAN TSARDOM: PAST AND PRESENT

The making of Russia

1. K. Marx and F. Engels, *Selected Writings* (Moscow, 1973) vol. I, p. 398.
2. M. Bloch, *The Historian's Craft* (Manchester, 1954) p. 93; A. Nasonov, *Russkaya Zemlya* (Moscow, 1951).
3. G. Vernadsky, *A History of Russia* (New Haven, 1948, 1953) vols II, III; B. Grekov, *Kievskaya rus'* (Moscow, 1953); V. Pashuto and L. Cherepnin, *Drevnerusskoe gosudarstvo* (Moscow, 1965); D. Obolensky, *The Byzantine Commonwealth* (London, 1971).
4. The legitimate rule in 'feudal' Europe was, on the whole, as Bloch put it, the 'hereditary vocation not of an individual but of a dynasty', the actual 'heritability in the direct line' to be validated by the consent of the upper stratum of the nobles. M. Bloch, *Feudal Society* (London, 1961) vol. II, chs 28 and 31. (For the quotation, see pp. 383–5.) See also R. W. Southern, *The Making of Middle Ages* (London, 1978) pt II; and G. Jones, *The History of the Vikings* (Oxford, 1984).

Some of the Russian historians denied the period of Scandinavian domination at the origins of the Kievan state with the same vehemence with which the claims were made by others of 'no impact whatever' of the nomads and of the Steppe on Russian history. Such exercises are not unlike other nationalist claims of tribal purity concerning ethnic history, that is, at their best a one-sided bias; at their worst, racialist bigotry.

5. For the legal structure of the princely rule in Kiev and its socio-legal groupings, see in particular M. Vladimirskii-Budanov, *Obzor istorii russkogo prava* (St Petersburg, 1909). Also, references in note 3 above.

6. A major way to read back into history later prejudices and miscomprehensions has been a tendency to present pastoral economies as 'a stage' on a unilinear developmental ladder, placed between the primitive origins of mankind and the stage of peasant farming which proceeds to rise still farther towards the industrial society as the climax of human advance. For example, see J. Bronowski, *The Ascent of Man* (London, 1973). As against such deductive constructs, see the more specific and realistic studies, like L. Gumilev, *Drevnie Tyurki* (Moscow, 1967) who speaks of the pastoral economy as the 'most developed form of production, nearly incapable of further improvement' (ibid, p. 4). See also L. Kreder, *The Social Organisation of the Mongol-Turkic Pastoral Nomads* (Bloomington, 1963); and A. Khazanov, *Nomads and the Outside World* (Cambridge, 1984).

7. Kreder, op. cit.; Khazanov, op. cit.; also E. D. Phillips, *The Royal Hordes* (London, 1965); L. Gumilev, *Poiski vymyshlennogo tsarstva* (Moscow, 1963).

8. Gumilev, *Drevnie*, op. cit.; J. Saunders, *The History of the Mongol Conquest* (London, 1971), ch. 1; *The Times Atlas of World History* (London, 1981) p. 127.

Many authoritative dictionaries of the English language and most native English speakers do not differentiate between the inhabitants of Turkey and those who belonged to a category much broader ethnically, linguistically, geographically and historically. We shall follow the Russian more specific usage in dividing between Turks, that is, natives of Turkey, and *Turki*, that is, members of the Turkic sociolinguistic group of Asian pastoral origins that would include also Kazakhs, Turkmenians, Azerbaydzhanis, Uzbeks, and in the past Cumans, Khazars etc. (in Russian, *Turki* or against *Tyurki*).

9. Ibn Khaldun, *The Muqaddimah* (New York, 1958).

10. See Vladimirskii-Budanov, op. cit., p. 25. Gumilev, op. cit., p. 310. Also O. Suleimanov, *Az i ya* (Alma Ata, 1975). This study of relations between the Russians and the Turki nomads, especially the Cumans, by a Kazakh intellectual who identified ethnically with the latter, has run into a hostile reception clearly fuelled by Russian nationalism.

11. *Yazychnik* (Russian for pagan) from Yazyk Niki (Turki) – a man of Steppe; *Koshchei* (the bogey-man of Russian legend) from Koshchshshchi (Turki) – a nomad; *Polovets* (Russian for Cuman) from Pol (Slav) – a man of Steppe (based on Suleimanov, op. cit., pp. 150–9). The author, a poet himself, has given particular attention to the linguistic expressions of the Russian/Turki relations. He has summed up his findings as follows: 'The attitude of the monks to the men of the Steppe was trasferred to the contemporary

historians. Rome has named all of the non-Romans (even the Greeks) barbarians. The Chinese chronicle did not consider human either Indians or Iranians. Arabs who have given the world Algebra and Astronomy appeared in the European chronicles only as Saracen, i.e. pagans, and nothing else' (ibid, p. 164).

12. Gumilev, op. cit.; Saunders, op. cit.; Vernadsky, op. cit., vol. III; also B. Spuler, *History of Mongols* (London, 1972); M. Prawdin, *The Mongol Empire: Its Rise and Legacy* (London, 1967).

13. Khan Tochtamysh of the Golden Horde was addressed in the correspondence with the French kings as 'Emperor of the Russians' while the Russian princes have often referred to the Khan as 'the tsar'. B. Ischboldin, *Essays on Tatar History* (New Delhi, 1963) pp. 33ff.

14. We shall return below to the impact of the Orthodox church on Russian history.

15. Vladimirskii-Budanov, op. cit., p. 149; Obolensky, op. cit., ch. 8.

16. F. Braudel, *The Mediterranean and the Mediterranean World in the Age of Phillip II* (New York, 1966). The study is limited to a region of the author's choice but shows significant similarities to developments in some other areas as for example, England, Persia and, as discussed below, Russia.

17. Vernadsky op. cit., vols II, III and IV (1959); V. Bernadskii, *Novgorod i novgorodskie zemli v XV veke* (Moscow, 1961); D. Likhachev, *Novgorod velikii* (Moscow, 1959); A. Nikitskii, *Istoriya ekonomicheskogo byta velikogo novgoroda* (The Hague, 1967); V. Yanin, *Novgorodskie posadnike* (Moscow, 1962).

18. Vladimirskii-Budanov, op. cit., p. 93.

19. M. K. Liubavskii, *Ocherk istorii Litovsko-russkogo gosudarstva* (Moscow, 1915); N. Vakar, *Belorussia* (Cambridge, 1956); Vernadsky, op. cit., vol. IV; S. Kutrzeba, *Historia ustroju polski w zarysie* (Krakow, 1949); H. Lowmianski, *Studia nad poczatkami spoleczenstwa i panstwa litewskiego* (Wilno, 1931–2); J. Phitznen, *Vitold von Litauen* (Prague, 1930). See also note 22.

20. Ibid. Also *The Times Atlas*, op. cit., pp. 140–1.

21. Vernadsky, op. cit., vol. IV, p. 237.

22. J. Dowiat, *Polska-panstwem sredniowiecznym europy* (Warsaw, 1968); B. Wlodarski, *Polska a rus* (Warsaw, 1966); O. Halecki, *Dzieje unii jagielonskiej* (Krakow, 1919); A. Kamin'ski, 'The Szlachta of the Polish–Lithuanian Commonwealth and Their Government', in I. Banac et al., *The Nobility in Russia and Eastern Europe* (New Haven, 1983); K. Chodynicki, *Kosciol pravoslavny a rzeczpospolita polska 1370–1632* (Warsaw, 1934); J. Fedorowicz, *A Republic of Nobles* (Cambridge, 1983). Also note 20 above.

23. N. Rozhkov, *Russkaya istoriya* (Moscow, 1919–26). The view was upheld also in the works of many of the latter Western (and 'non-Marxist') historians, for example, J. Blum, *Lord and Peasant in Russia* (Princeton, 1964) p. 151.

24. The conceptual re-tooling called for would need also a more attentive look at the ethno-processes, a general task that exceeds our brief. Something more will be said below about the ethnic crystallisation of the Russian nation, the impact of the Orthodox Church and the state on it, etc.

The state: formation of an empire

1. M. Vladimirskii-Budanov, *Obzor istorii russkogo prava* (St Petersburg, 1909) p. 79 (the text quoted was written in 1477). Changes of similar type but lesser in extent formed part of the establishment of absolutism elsewhere. For example, since the time of Henry VIII of England, 'the King would be addressed, not as "Your Grace", but as "Your Majesty", a unique being exalted above all others in both Church and State' as testified by A. R. Meyers, *Pelican History of England* (Harmondsworth, 1966) p. 212.

2. Quoted after *Polnoe sobranie zakonov russkoi imperii* (St Petersburg, 1911). For major discussions of the processes within which the centralist nature of Muscovy was established, see L. V. Cherepnin, *Obrazovanie russkogo tsentralizirovannogo gosudarstva* (Moscow, 1960); P. Anderson, *Lineages of the Absolutist State* (London, 1974); R. Pipes, *Russia under the Old Regime* (London, 1974); S. Veselovskii, *Feudal'noe zemlevladenie v severo – vostocrhnoi rusi* (Moscow, 1947).

3. V. Klyuchevskii, *Boyarskaya duma drevnei Rusi* (Moscow, 1888); Also G. Vernadsky, A History of Russia (New Haven, 1953), vol. III, pp. 359–63; A. Leont'ev, *Obrazovanie prikaznoi sistemy upravleniya* (Moscow, 1961).

4. See Vladimirskii-Buganov, op. cit., pp. 115–49; also, V. Klyuchevskii, *Istoriya soslovii v Rossii* (Moscow, 1913).

5. R. Hellie, *Enserfment and Military Change in Muscovy* (Chicago, 1971) pp. 267–73.

6. ibid, pts I and III, which date the decisive stage of 'gunpowder revolution' in Muscovy to the seventeenth century.

   The *Gulyai gorod*, a mobile fortress of wooden walls mounted on wheels, was a sixteenth-century Russian invention used in the struggle against the Tatar and Lithuanian cavalry.

7. Klyuchevskii, *Istoriya*, op. cit., p. 188 (italics added). For basic evidence, see *Razryadnye knigi 1475–1598* (Moscow, 1966).

8. ES vol. 47, pp. 46–7. By the nineteenth century the name of the category was changed to that of *podatnoe sostoyanie*.

9. See below, pp. 78–81. The picture becomes clearer in evidence from the seventeenth century. For a authoritative study, see R. E. F. Smith, *Peasant Farming in Muscovy* (Cambridge, 1977).

10. ibid, p. 226.

11. Klyuchevskii, *Istoriya*, op. cit., p. 192.

12. Vernadsky, op. cit., vol. IV, pp. 104–7.

13. V. Klyuchevskii, 'Kurs lektsii', *Sochineniya* (Moscow, 1957) vol. III; Also A. Zimin, *Oprichniki Ivana Groznogo* (Moscow, 1964); A. Zimin, *Reformy Ivana Groznogo* (Moscow, 1960).

14. For example, S. F. Platonov, *Boris Godunov* (Petrograd, 1921); R. Skrynnikov, *Boris Gudunov* (Moscow, 1978).

15. For a recent study and discussion of sources, see A. Man'kov, *Ulozhenie 1649 goda* (Leningrad, 1980).

16. A. Yanov, *The Origins of Autocracy* (Berkeley, 1982).

17. E. Golubinskii, *Istoriya russkoi tserkvi* (The Hague, 1969); N. Nikol'skii, *Tserkov'i istoriya rossii* (Moscow, 1967); Yu. Solov'ev, *Holy Russia* (Paris, 1959). Also R. W. Southern, *The Making of the Middle Ages* (London, 1978) pts 3 and 4; Vernadsky, op. cit., vol. IV.

18. Smith, op. cit., pp. 232–6.
19. ibid, p. 221.
20. J. Blum, *Lord and Peasant in Russia* (New York, 1961) pp. 117–276; also, Hellie, op. cit., pt I, Smith, op. cit., chs 6–10; B. D. Grekov, *Krest'yane na Rusi* (Moscow, 1952).
21. V. Klyuchevskii, *Kurs russkoi istorii* (Moscow, 1937) vol. III, p. 11.
22. Vernadsky, op. cit., vol. IV, pp. 249–68; K. Abaza, *Kozaki* (St. Petersburg, 1890); P. Longworth, *The Cossacks* (London, 1969).
23. ibid; I. Smirnov *et al.*, *Krest'yanskie voiny v Rossii XVII–XVIIIvv.* (Moscow, 1966); Hellie, op. cit., Robinson, op. cit., ch. 1; N. Firsov, *Pugachevshchina* (St Petersburg, 1907); *Pugachevshchina* (Moscow, 1926–31); Y. Shvetsova, *Krest'yankaya voina pod predvoditel'stvom stepana razina* (Moscow, 1954–62).
24. V. Klyuchevskii, *Petr velikii sredi svoikh sotrudnikov* (St Petersburg, 1902); M. Raeff, *Peter the Great, Reformer or Revolutionary* (Boston, 1963); M. Bogoslovskii, *Petr I, materially dlya biografii* (Moscow, 1940–8).
25. See below, pp. 27, 34.
26. Klyuchevskii, *Istoriya*, op. cit., p. 203.
27. Vladimirskii-Buganov, op. cit., p. 240.
28. See in particular the work of M. Raeff concerning the *Polizeistaat* in Central and Eastern Europe, for example, his 'The Well-ordered Police State and the Development of Modernity', *The American Historical Review*, vol. 80, no. 5, 1975; see also G. Barraclough, *The Origins of Modern Germany* (Oxford, 1947) ch. 12.
29. V. Nazarevskii, *Tsarstvovanie imperatritsy ekateriny II* (Moscow, 1913); I. Grey, *Catherine the Great* (London, 1961); A. Brikner, *Istoriya ekateriny vtoroi* (St Petersburg, 1885); Y. Limonov, *Pugachev i ego spodvizhniki* (Moscow, 1915); Klyuchevskii, *Kurs*, op. cit., vol. 5; V. Klyuchevskii, 'Evgenii Onegin i ego predki', *Rossiya i pushkin* (Kharbin, 1937).
30. For an illuminating discussion of the issue, see M. I. Finley, *Ancient Slavery and Modern Ideology* (Harmondsworth, 1983) especially ch. 3.
31. For the discussion of the nadir of serfdom in Russia, see G. T. Robinson, *Rural Russian Under the Old Regime* (New York, 1949); ch. 11; Klyuchevskii, *Kurs*, op. cit.; Blum, op. cit.; see also section below, p. 000.
32. For example, P. Alston, *Education and State in Tsarist Russia* (Stanford, 1969); and S. Starr, *Decentralisation and Self-Government in Russia 1830–1870* (Princeton, 1972).
33. As portrayed in heterogeneous sources, for example, *Istoriya sssr* (Moscow, 1968) vols IV, V and VI; P. Kabanov, *Kurs lektsii po istorii sssr 1860–1917* (Moscow, 1963); M. Florinsky, *Russia* (New York, 1953) vol. II; H. Seton-Watson, *The Russian Empire 1801–1917* (Oxford, 1967).
34. The most dramatic of the cases was that of M. Speranskii who rose from humble origins to become the closest adviser to Alexander I, prepared at his request a project of fundamental reforms of Russian state machinery and ended up in exile, with the core of his suggestions abandoned.
35. For a discussion of the emancipation of serfs, see Robinson, op. cit.; Blum, op. cit.
36. We shall return to the issue in Chapter 3 and again in the companion volume, *Revolution as a Moment of Truth* (forthcoming).
37. See below Chapter 5, section D.

The State apparatus

1. The official 'small title' of the emperors of Russia, which appeared in most of the major state documents.
2. See M. Raeff, 'A Well-ordered Police State and the Development of Modernity', *The American Historical Review*, vol. 80, no. 5, 1975. He described the Russian state executive as characterised by 'separation of public and private, regularity and objectivity, arrogance and self-righteousness' and by the 'brutal didactism of the emperors'.
3. ES, vol. 47, p. 47; Significantly for the new self-images related to the period beginning with Peter I, it speaks of 'benefiting the state' rather than of serving the tsar.
4. For example, there was no legal maximum of length of the working day within the state service and no payment for 'extra hours'. The work schedule was defined by the will of one's superiors.
5. That proscription was left fairly vague at the top of the ranking order.
6. For an excellent review of the duties and privileges of the state service, see NES, vol. 14, item '*Gosudarstvennaya sluzhba*'.
7. For relevant passages of Max Weber, and O. Hintze, see R. Benedicts, *State and Society* (London, 1968) pp. 296–303 and 154–69.
8. The contemporary Prussian officials, even when dismissed from the state service, would keep a major part of their pension. Lack of clearly defined rights of tenure has made M. Raeff go as far as to conclude that 'there was no true bureaucracy' in Russia because of the strength of its autocracy' – an overstatement that makes a very useful point (Raeff, op. cit.; see also his 'The Russian Autocracy and Its Officials', in H. McLean *et al.*, *Russian Thought and Politics* (Grauenhage, 1967) p. 90).
9. Privileged access to some position, especially within the army for the sons of nobility also appeared, of course, in other countries – for example, in contemporary Germany and France.
10. The majority of Russia's top state administrators were university graduates by the end of nineteenth century. Half of them graduated in law.
11. See, for example, *Pazheskii ego imperatorskogo velichestva korpus: za sto let 1802–1902* (St Petersburg, 1902) vols 1 and 2. See also for discussion, Yu. Solov'ev, *Samoderzhavie i dvoryanstvo v kontse 19ogo veka* (Moscow, 1973) and C. Black, *The Transformation of Russian Society* (Cambridge, 1960) especially pts 2 and 3. (P. Zaionchkovskii in his *Pravitel'stvennyi apparat samoderzhavnoi rossii v XIX v.* (Moscow, 1979) p. 21, has expressed doubts as to the actual significance of the 'Pazheskii korpus' in the training of the bureaucratic elite.)
12. About one-third of the top ranks (one to four) were reported in 1902 to be held by owners of landed estates, mostly 'hereditary nobles'. In 1853 it was more than half (Zaionchkovskii, op. cit., pp. 90–8. The quotation comes from V. Leikina-Svirskaya, *Inteligentsiya v rossii vo vtoroi polovine XIX veka* Moscow, 1971) p. 74.
13. K. Marx, the Civil War in France', in K. Marx and F. Engels, *Selected Works* (Moscow, 1973) vol. 2, p. 217.
14. For further discussion, see T. Shanin, 'State, Class and Revolution: Substitutes and Realities', in H. Alavi and T. Shanin, *Introduction to the Sociology of Developing Societies* (London, 1982).

15. Table xx (the division of the population by occupation) on which the figures presented in the section are based, in OSPN, vol. 2, pp. 256–71 and 296–7.

16. *Statemen Handbook for Russia* (St Petersburg, 1896) vol. 1, section: 'Armed Forces'.

17. See Chapter 2.

18. A. Lopukhin, *Nastoyashchee i budushchee russkoi politsii* (Moscow, 1907); P. Zavarzin *Rabota tainoi politsii*, Paris, 1924; C. E. Black, *The Transformation of Russian Society* (Harvard, 1980) pp. 164–90; E. Smith and R. Lednitskii, *The Okhrana: the Russian Department of Police* (Stanford, 1967).

19. The figures of teachers varied in different reports. In particular, the figures of Ministry of Education were consistently higher than those presented by the population census. (The official figures of the ministry for 1903 were 213 000 in *Ezhegodnik rossii*, 1905 (St Petersburg, 1906) p. 507.) This discrepancy is too large to be simply explained as the result of the rapid development of Russian education in 1897–1905 and must reflect differences of accounting – for example, the way the part-timers were treated, etc.

20. For example, of the 17 000 medical doctors and superintendents registered, 3200 were employed by the army and the navy and not less than half of the rest received their salaries from 'public employers', that is, mostly the state and the *zemstvos* (ES, vol. 13, pp. 894–5).

21. Orthodox clergy within the districts of a mostly non-Orthodox population received a salary on par with the state officials.

22. The census showed about 30 000 priests of 'other churches' i.e. not of the established 'Orthodox' church. Their ambivalent political status in representing loyalties which were not quite Russian and preserving elements of 'other' ethnic cultures, have opened them frequently to persecutions by the state officials and virulent propaganda by the 'orthodox' priesthood. It also made them, at times, into major organisers of ethnic defiance.

23. Zaionchkovskii, op. cit., p. 71.

24. An extensive literature of memoirs about life at the tsar's court, offers information that is relevant here, for example, the very informative A. A. Mosolov, *At the Court of the Last Tsar* (London, 1935). For a considerable amount of information and gossip, often malicious, see S. Yu. Witte, *Vospominaniya* (Leningrad, 1924) vols I, II and III. For the ways the tsar was connected to and briefed by the 'state organs', see also Zaionchkovskii, op. cit. Solov'ev, op. cit. Also *Tsarskii listok* (Paris, 1909) for examples of the reports submitted.

25. Once again there is a vast literature of memoirs relevant to the field. For example, see A. Ignatiev, *Pyat'desyat let v stroyu* (Moscow, 1950).

26. See *Ministerstvo vnutrennykh del 1802–1902: istoricheskii ocherk* (St Petersburg, 1902) for the history of the ministry and an interesting insight into its structure and development.

27. D. K. Rowney, 'Higher Civil Servants in the Russian Ministry of Interior Affairs', *Slavic Review*, vol. 31, 1972, pp. 101–10 as well as Zaionchkovskii, op. cit., ch. 4.

28. Taken from the files of the Russian State Archives, now at Leningrad – the TGIA(L). (File 1276, 0.19, Ed. 22.)

29. For figures of national income, see S. Prokopovich, *Opyt ischisleniya narodnogo dokhoda* (Moscow, 1918) pp. 66–9. It would have been also more than 100 times the wages of a male worker in agriculture (N. Rubakin, *Rossiya v tsifrakh* (St Petersburg, 1912) p. 160, (to which an estimated increase of 50 per cent during 1900–13 was added). One rouble amounted roughly to half a US dollar of those days.
30. *Spisok chinov departamenta politsii* (St Peterburg, 1913).
31. N. Rubakin, 'Mnogo v rossii chinovnikov', *Vestnik Evropy*, 1910, p. 133.
32. ibid, p. 132. See also N. Rubakin, *Rossiya v tsifrakh* (St Petersburg, 1912) pp. 60–70, for further discussion of the officialdom's income.
33. *Spisok*, op. cit., Zaionchkovskii, op. cit., pp. 177–8.
34. For a comparable discussion of the problem of corruption within the 'official bureaucracy' of 'developing societies', see for example W. F. Wertheim, 'Sociological Aspects of Corruption in South East Asia', in R. Benedicts, *State and Society* (London, 1968) pp. 561–80; also, G. Myrdal, *Asian Drama* (New York, 1971).
35. The government refused to establish *zemstvo* authorities in the ethnically unreliable 'peripheries', for example, the Polish provinces of the 'Visla Region' and the north-west of European Russia.
36. *Statemen Handbook for Russia*, op. cit., section: 'Local Authorities'.
37. A spectacular example of such governmental actions was the 'purge' of the *zemstvo* of Tver' in 1904, when for 'insubordination' its *zemstvo* authorities were suspended and six of their elected officers exiled from the province by an administrative order of its governor.

State v. society

1. See above, pp. 4, 8–9.
2. D. Obolensky, 'Russia's Byzantine Heritage', *Oxford Slavonic Papers*, vol. I, 1950, p. 37 (italics added). The author limited his acceptance of outside impacts in medieval Russia mostly to those of the 'parent culture' of Byzantium, refusing similar treatment to the Golden Horde. See also G. Ostrogorsky, *History of Byzantian State* (Oxford, 1968).
3. Obolensky, loc. cit.; also, N. Baynes, *The Thought-World of East Rome* (London, 1947).
4. Obolensky, loc. cit., pp. 45–51; V. Savva, *Moskovskie tsari i vizantiiskie vasilevsy* (The Hague, 1969); S. W. Eisenstadt, *The Decline of Empires* (Englewood Cliffs, 1967) esp. sections 4 and 14.
5. G. Vernadsky, *A History of Russia* (New Haven, 1953) vol. III, pp. 205–20. The comparison with Doomsday Book introduced in England after its conquest is self-evident and suggestive. See for further discussion and documentation, B. Spuler, *History of Mongols* (London, 1972) chs I, II and V, especially pp. 78–86. It is also interesting to compare the Muscovite and Turkish models of statehood which incorporated a number of similar 'ingredients' in their administrative traditions – a point developed in G. Vernadsky, *Opyt istorii evrazii* (Berlin, 1934) pp. 104–8.
6. Vernadsky, op. cit., pp. 108, 128 and 337–85.
7. A. de Tocqueville, *The Ancient Regime and the French Revolution* (London, 1955); P. Anderson, *Lineages of the Absolutist State* (London, 1974);

I. Wallerstein, *The Modern World System* (New York, 1974) especially ch. 3; R. Pipes, *Russia Under The Old Regime* (London, 1974) especially ch. II.
8. A. Gramsci, *Selection from Prison Notebooks* (London, 1978) pt 2.
9. See, for example, K. Pobedonostsev, *Reflections of a Russian Statesman* (London, 1898).
10. P. Baran, 'On the Political Economy of Backwardness', in R. Rhodes, *Imperialism and Underdevelopment* (New York, 1970) p. 300.
11. For example, the 'official displeasure' and repressions aimed at the Slavophiles (see p. 213).
12. Quoted after Pipes, op. cit., p. 243.
13. Yu. Solov'ev, *Samoderzhavie i dvorianstvo v kontse XIXgo veka* (Moscow, 1973) p. 75.
14. See T. Shanin, *Russia 1905–07: Revolution as a Moment of Truth*, chs 1 and 2.

Addendum 1 A society: a snapshot of Russia

1. *Obshchii svod po imperii rezul'tatov razrabotki dannykh pervoi perepisi naselenia* (St Petersburg, 1905) vols 1 and 2 (referred to further as OSPN).
2. The Russian subjects who resided in Finland or in the protectorates of Bukhara and Khiva, as well as the Russian sailors at sea, were incorporated in the census.
3. For further discussion, see Chapter 5.
4. OSPN, vol. 2, pp. i–iv. Also NES, vol. 9, pp. 914–35. For the new estimates mentioned, see V. Kozlov, *Natsional'nosti SSSR* (Moscow, 1982) p. 38.
5. OSPN, vol. 1, pp. xvi–xx and tables XIII–XVI; the Russian sectarians, mostly the Old-Believers (*Starovery*) formed 2.6 per cent of the population (OSPN, vol. 2, p. xxxiii).
6. OSPN, vol. 1, pp. xvi–xx and table IX.
7. See *Ezhegodnik Rossii 1905* (St Petersburg, 1906) pp. 507–8 and 526.
8. ibid.
9. OSPN, vol. 1, pp. xiii–xiv, tables VI and VIII–X.
10. ES, vol. 4/d, p. xix.
11. OSPN, p. xiii.
12. ibid, vol. 2, tables XX–XXIII.
13. ibid, pp. 256–63. The numbers of top administrators and senior army officers, etc. were actually specified in the census. For clergy, merchants and the 'free professions', one-tenth was assumed to belong to the top and/or managing group. Of the 'hereditary nobility', 10 per cent was added to represent the large landowners who did not appear within the other categories mentioned, a figure that is close to the one reported for landowners with income above 1000 roubles per annum for 1906 (see Chapter 3).
14. A. Rashin, *Naselenie rossii za 100 let* (Moscow, 1956) pp. 96–9. Also, *Ezhegodnik Rossii 1906* (St Petersburg, 1907) pp. lvi–lxxv; a later study has estimated the members of 'rural' estates (i.e. of peasantry with fairly small admixtures of Cossacks and 'aliens') to provide 20 per cent of Russia's urban population in 1858 and 43 per cent in 1897 (Ya. Vodarskii, *Naselenie rossii za 400 let* (Moscow, 1973) p. 114).

15. OSPN, op. cit., pp. xx–xxi; also ES, op. cit., p. v.
16. OSPN, vol. 1, pp. iii–iv, tables III–V.
17. ES, op. cit., vol. 4/d, p. xi.
18. Rashin, op. cit., pp. 44–7.
19. OSPN, p. xiii. As non-peasants by their legal status who would qualify as peasants in social sense, the editors of the census named the Cossacks, a major part of aliens (*inorodtsy*), and about half of the urbanites by 'social estate' (*meshchane*). On the other hand, peasants 'by estate', who permanently resided in towns, were subtracted from this estimate.

2   RUSSIAN PEASANTS: HOUSEHOLD, COMMUNITY AND SOCIETY
The peasant household

1. For discussion of the generic and the specific in the features of peasantry, see E. Wolf, *Peasants* (New York, 1966); B. Galeski, *Basic Concepts of Rural Sociology* (Manchester, 1972); T. Shanin, *Peasants and Peasant Societies* (Harmondsworth, 1971); T. Shanin, 'Defining Peasants: Conceptualisations and Deconceptualisations', *Sociological Review*, vol. 30, no. 3, 1983. For a historical context, see E. Le Roy Ladurie, 'Peasants', in *The New Cambridge Modern History* (Cambridge, 1979) vol. XIII.
2. V. Mukhin, *Obychnyi poryadok nasledovaniya krest'yan* (St. Petersburg, 1888) p. 151.
3. NES, vol. 17, p. 519.
4. As expressed in the widespread peasant saying, 'a crab isn't a fish and a woman isn't a person' (*rak ne ryba, baba ne chelovek*). A study of typical peasant time-budgets in the 1920s has shown that a peasant woman spent nearly as much time on 'productive work' as the male peasant (1905 v. 1935 hours per annum) but simultaneously spent much more time on 'housework' (2229 v. 622). This meant as much as one-third more of 'work time' spent by a woman than by a man. See A. Bol'shakov, *Sovremennaya derevnya v tsifrakh* (Leningrad, 1925) p. 100.
5. G. T. Robinson, *Rural Russia Under the Old Regime* (London, 1932) p. 66. Until 1906 the head of the household could have a member of his household arrested, sent back to his village under escort, or flogged by simple application to the peasant court.
6. N. Makarov, *Krest'yanskoe khozyaistvo i ego interesy* (Moscow, 1917) p. 71; within the Russian rural studies that position was first clearly stated in A. Vasil'chakov's early classic, *Zemlevladenie i zemledel'e v Rossii* (St Petersburg, 1879) p. xxv, to say: 'A family here means not so much kinship, parents' control or inheritance but an economic unit.'
7. V. Aleksandrov, *Russkie* (Moscow, 1967) pp. 17–99. See also J. Blum, *Lord and Peasant in Russia* (New York, 1964) ch. 20, and A. Anfimov, *Krest 'yanskoe khozyaistvo evropeiskoi Rossii* (Moscow, 1980).
8. V. Den, *Kurs ekonomischeskoi geografii* (Leningrad, 1925) pp. 188 and 211.
9. Robinson, op. cit., p. 104. The meaning of 'subsistence' was, of course, far from absolute and varied between areas, households and periods.
10. For an analysis of the peasant's occupation, see Galeski, op. cit., ch. 3. As late as in the census of 1926, 95.3 per cent of the working rural population of Russia named 'farming' as their only or main occupation (*Statisticheskii*

spravochnik za 1928 g. (Moscow, 1929) p. 44). For a good discussion of *promysly* see A. Anfimov, *Ekonomicheskoe polozlence i klassoraya* (Moscow, 1984) Ch. 1, who estimated that by the turn of the century 14 million peasants engaged in them at least to some extent. He claimed for some reason the term to be an invention of officialdom and populists.

11. An expression taken from a classic study of another peasant society: W. Thomas and F. Znaniecki, *The Polish Peasant in Europe and America* (New York, 1958) vol. I, p. 107. In empirical terms it has been expressed within the Russian peasantry in 'virtually universal marriage for both men and women' (P. Chap, 'Marriage and Peasant Joint Family in Russia' (MS), p. 13). That applied both in the times of serfdom (when the squires have often ordered it directly) and afterwards.

12. *Zemel'nyi kodeks RSFSR* (Moscow, 1924). The peasant land being treated as 'family patrimony rather than belonging to the person who inherited it' had ancient roots. See J. Blum, *Lord and Peasant in Russia* (Princeton, 1961) p. 81.

13. For a systematic discussion of property and inheritance under the Russian peasant customary law, see T. Shanin, *The Awkward Class* (Oxford, 1972) appendix B; for a good compilation and a discussion of the Russian peasant legal customs concerning property, see Mukhin, op. cit.; also, O. Khauke, *Krest'yankoe zemel'noe pravo* (Moscow, 1914); A. Leont'ev, *Krest'yanskoe pravo* (St. Petersburg, 1909).

14. V. Aleksandrov, *Sel'skaya obshchina v Rossii* (Moscow, 1976) especially ch. VI. Also the work of Chap, op. cit., who pointed out the 'non-European' marriage pattern of the Russian peasants – the differences of ages between spouses was small in rural Russia and extensive partitioning was taking place (which was true also in the last century of serfdom, 1782–1858).

15. See A. Chayanov, *Byudzhetnye issledovaniya* (Moscow, 1929). For a short discussion, see Shanin, op. cit., ch. 4 and 'Measuring Peasant Capitalism', in E. Hobsbawm *et al.*, *Peasants in History* (Calcutta, 1980). For the classical work that set these studies in motion throughout Russia, see F. Shcherbina, *Svodnyi sbornik po 12 uezdam* (Voronezh, 1897). For substantive discussion of the evidence see Anfimov, op. cit.

16. For a fundamental taxonomy of peasant production, see N. Malita, 'Agriculture in the Year 2000', *Sociologia Ruralis*, 1971. See also T. Shanin, 'The Nature and Logic of Peasant Economy', *The Journal of Peasant Studies*, vol. I, nos. 1 and 2, 1973.

17. See Chapter 3. pp. 117–18.

18. For a compilation of studies concerning the reasons of 'labour emigration' (*otkhod*), see P. Maslov, *Agrarnyi vopros v rossii* (St Petersburg, 1908) vol. I, ch. XVI (especially the table on page 417). The most prominent reasons indicated in 1899 in Samara by the migrants themselves were land shortage, a 'bad year' of failure of crops and the shortage of opportunities of wage labour in one's own locality, in that order.

The peasant commune

1. B. Galeski, *Basic Concepts of Rural Sociology* (Manchester, 1972) ch. 2. The word *mir* used by the Russian peasants to describe both the peasant commune and its communal assembly means also 'world' and

'peace' in Russian. The expression is significant of the major characteristic of a peasant ideal of community living.

2. For a good comparative discussion, see L. Danilova and V. Danilov, 'Problemy teorii i istorii obshchiny', in *Obshchina v Afrike* (Moscow, 1978).

3. G. Pitt-Rivers, 'The Closed Community and its Friends', *Kroeber Anthropological Society Papers*, no. 16, p. 957, 1957.

4. See p. 82.

5. R. Redfield, *Tepoztlan: A Mexican Village* (Chicago, 1946; first published in 1930); O. Lewis, *Life in a Mexican Village: Tepoztlan Re-Studied* (Urbane, 1951); G. M. Foster, 'Interpersonal Relations in Peasant Society', *Human Organization*, vol. XIX, no. 4, 1960–1.

6. V. Aleksandrov, *Sel'skaya obshchina v rossii* (Moscow, 1976) p. 5, tells us that while there was one publication only concerning peasant communes in the 1850–5 period, it increased to ninety-nine in 1856–60 and proceeded to increase to reach a grand total of 2000 for the 1876–1904 era. The decades to follow, and especially the 1920s, have seen further considerable increases in those figures.

7. See, for a formal summary of peasant social and legal organisation, A. Rittikh, *Krest'yanskii pravoporyadok* (St Petersburg, 1904).

8. In some cases, a kind of super-commune evolved with several communes holding some lands in collective possession and dividing it firstly by communes and then by households. These super-communes have been particularly in evidence in the areas of comparatively recent colonisation, that is, south-east European Russia and Siberia.

9. See *Statistika zemlevladeniya 1905 g.* (St Petersburg, 1907) p. 129; *Svod statisticheskikh svedenii po sel'skomu khozyaistvu Rossii* (St Petersburg, 1902–6) pt III, pp. 2–3.

10. Rittikh, op. cit.; also T. Tsytovich, *Sel'skoe obshchestvo* (Kiev, 1911) pp. 48–60.

11. For example, A. Leont'ev, *Krest'yanskoe pravo* (St Petersburg, 1909) pp. 8ff. Also, there are many vivid descriptions by the Russian writers, especially those of rural origin or with rural experience, for example, G. Uspenskii, N. Virta, etc.

12. Stepniak, *The Russian Peasantry* (London, 1888) p. 36; Tsytovich, op. cit., pp. 48–56.

13. Leont'ev, op. cit., pp. 94–5; Tsytovich, op. cit., p. 17.

14. NES, vol. 23, pp. 326–8; G. T. Robinson, *Rural Russian Under the Old Regime* (New York, 1949) p. 119; see also pp. 32 and 48 above. In 1889 the authority of peasant magistrates was extended further as part of the conservative counter-reforms.

15. See O. Khauke, *Krest'yanskoe zemel'noe pravo* (Moscow, 1914) pp. 83–7; I. Izgoev, *Obshchinnoe pravo* (St Petersburg, 1906) pp. 38–40.

16. By the beginning of the century some agricultural innovations were at times reported, that is, more complex crop cycles, industrial crops, etc. However, until the end of the period discussed the three-field system with an obligatory fallow remained prevalent in all the major regions of Russia. See V. Aleksandrov, *Russkie* (Moscow, 1967) p. 20.

17. *Statistika*, op. cit., p. 11.

18. See, for example, the comparative discussion in H. H. Stahl, *Traditional*

Romanian Village Communities (Cambridge, 1980).
19. A. Haxthousen, *Studien uber die inner-Zustande, das Volksleben und insbesondere die landlichen einrichtungen Ruslands* (Hannover, 1847–52) vols. 1–3.
20. The debate was initially expressed in the clash between I. Belyaev and B. Chicherin, the second representing the so-called 'State School', that is, those who have seen the commune as a fairly recent state creation for fiscal purposes mostly. For a summary of the debate, see L. Vdovina, 'Vopros o proiskhozhdenii krest'yanskoi obshchiny v russkoi dorevolyutsionnoi istoriografii', *estnikmoskovskogo universiteta*, no. 4, 1973 and V. Danilov, 'K voprosu o kharaktere i izuachenii Krestiyanskoi pozemel' noi obshchiny v rassii', in *Problemy sotsiano-ekonomicheskoi istorii rossii*, Moscow, 1971.
21. To be discussed in Chapter 5, section C. Also see T. Shanin, *Late Marx and the Russian Road* (London, 1983).
22. I. Chernyshev, *Agrarno-krest'yanskaya politika Rossii* (Petrograd, 1918).
23. A. Kaufman, *Russkaya obshchina v protsese ee zarozhdeniya i rosta* (Moscow, 1908). See also his *Sbornik statei* (Moscow, 1915).
24. For example, Le Roy Ladurie in *The New Cambridge History* (Cambridge, 1970) vol. XIII, about the French rural communes and Danilov and Danilova, op. cit., about Africa today. For an important collection of specific studies concerning the Russian peasant communes, see *Ezhegodnik po agrarnoi istorii* (Vologda, 1976) vol. VI. For a contemporary Soviet version of the State School views see Yu. Alekeev in *V. I. Lenin i problemy istorii*, Leningrad, 1970 (argued against by Danilov, K voprosu, op. cit.).
25. Aleksandrov, *Sel'skaya*, op. cit., pp. 314–15.
26. ibid, p. 177.
27. That is, serfs who did not belong to a squire but directly to the state.
28. Quote after Vdovina, op. cit., p. 38.
29. For discussion of the commune in post-revolutionary Russia of 1917–27, see T. Shanin, *The Awkward Class* (Oxford, 1972) pt III; D. Male, *Russian Peasant Organisation Before Collectivisation* (Cambridge, 1971); for a more recent excellent study of those matters by a Soviet scholar, see V. Danilov, *Sovetskaya dokolkhoznaya derevnya* (Moscow, 1977, 1979) (2 vols published and one more promised). For the period of Stolypin reform, see also Robinson, op. cit., chs XI–XII.

Peasantry: models and history

1. R. Redfield, *Peasant Society and Culture* (Chicago, 1956) p. 169.
2. Fei Hsiao Tung, 'Peasantry and Gentry', *American Journal of Sociology*, vol. LII, no. 1, 1946.
3. E. Wolf, *Is the Peasant a Class Category Separate from Bourgeois and Proletarian?* (Notes for a Talk) (Binghampton, 1977).
4. For further discussion of peasant taxonomies, see T. Shanin, 'Defining Peasants: Conceptualisations and De-conceptualisations', *Sociological Review*, vol. 30, no. 3, 1982, which links with the writings of Wolf, B. Galeski, V. Danilov, etc.
5. For discussion of the definitions of peasant economy, see in particular Chapter 4.

6. For further discussion the companion volume, *Russia 1905–07: Revolution as a Moment of Truth*, ch. 3.

7. The term 'cultural pattern' is used in the sense expressed by C. Wright Mills, in *Power, Politics and People* (New York, 1962) p. 406: 'The lenses of mankind through which men see: the medium by which they interpret and report what they see', etc.

8. Expressed in the tendency of the peasant court to pass judgement either 'according to the man' (*po cheloveku*) or 'according to conscience' (*po sovesti*), that is, when the personality of those involved and the social implications of the judgement carried explicitly more weight than objective circumstances or legal precedent. This approach has also accounted for the typical tendency of the peasant magistrates, 'to divide the sin by half' (*delit' grekh popolam*), that is, to resolve a property-conflict by the division of the property rather than to pass a judgement totally in favour of one side, however 'right'. See V. Mukhin, *Obychnyi poryadok nasledovaniya u krest'yan* (St Petersburg, 1888) p. 311.

9. A. Herzen, *Izbrannye folozofskie proizvedeniya* (Moscow, 1946) vol. ii, p. 253.

10. For discussion of the evidence concerning the Printers' Union of Moscow, see p. 118 below. For some further evidence of a parallel type, see P. Maslov, *Agrarnyi vopros Rossii* (St Petersburg, 1905) vol. I, p. 368.

11. T. Shanin, *The Awkward Class* (Oxford, 1972) pt II.

12. A. Kroeber, *Anthropology* (London, 1924) p. 284; Redfield, op. cit., p. 31.

13. J. H. Boeke, *Economics and Economic Policy of Dual Societies* (New York, 1953).

14. ibid, pp. 4, 12, 40–1 and 101–6.

15. For critical discussion, see T. G. McGee, *The South East Asian City* (London, 1971); C. Geertz, *Pedlars and Princes* (Chicago, 1963); B. Roberts, *Cities of Peasants* (London, 1978) pp. 110—15.

16. For example, T. Parsons, *The Evolution of Societies* (Englewood Cliffs, 1977); L. Althusser and E. Balibar, *Reading Capital* (London, 1970) especially pt 3.

17. K. Marx and F. Engels, *Selected Writings* (Moscow, 1950) vol. I, p. 303.

18. See the important insights of Barington Moore, *Social Origins of Dictatorship and Democracy* (Harmondworth, 1967) pt III.

19. The first article of the Russian General Statute of Emancipation 1861.

20. See G. T. Robinson, *Rural Russia under the Old Regime* (New York, 1949) p. 96.

21. For discussion, see Robinson, op. cit., ch. V; also NES, vol. 23. For the documentation of the process in which the decisions concerning emancipation took shape via the work of the committees that prepared legislation, see *Zhurnaly sekretnogo i glavnogo komitetov po krest'yanskomyu delu* (St Petersburg, 1915) vols 1–3. For the estimate of the size of the 'cut-off' land, see Robinson, op. cit., p. 87.

22. Robinson, op. cit. p. 66.

23. For discussion, see Shanin, op. cit., pt 3. A recent study of a Soviet rural sociologist went even further along the time scale. After having described the way of living of pre-revolutionary rural Russia, it stated: 'On the whole this characteristic way of life, determined by the forces of production,

remained nearly unchanged until the post-war times [i.e. post 1945] (V. Staroverov, *Sovetskaya derevnya na etape razvitogo sotisializma* (Moscow, 1976) p. 12).

24. See p. 80.

Addendum 2   Peasants: averages, diversities, socio-economic differentiation

1. OSPN, vol. I, p. 1.
2. *Svod statisticheskikh svedenii po sel'skomu khozyaistvu Rossii* (St Petersburg, 1902) pp. 1–19; see also D. Male, *Russian Peasant Organisation Before Collectivisation* (Cambridge, 1971) and Y. Taniuchi, 'A Note on the Territorial Relations Between Rural Societies, Settlements and Communes', *Discussion Papers, University of Birmingham* (CREES, series Rc/D, no. 3, 1966).
3. In the north-west of European Russia, on the lands that used to belong to the Lithuanian state, the impact of the so-called *voloki* reform of Crown lands in 1557 enhanced single holdings, weakening the peasant communities. (For discussion, see G. Vernadsky and M. Karpovich, *A History of Russia* (New Haven, 1959) vol. IV, pp. 225–6.) The same applied to the impact of the German landownership patterns in the areas of Latvian and Estonian peasantry.
4. Particularly interesting and influential were the regionalisations by trade and industry (V. Semenov Tyan'-Shanskii, D. Mendeleev, and V. Varzar), by natural diversity (V. Viner and A. Skvortsov), by the type of farming (A. Vasil'chakov) and by the marketability of rural produce (V. Lenin). The most advanced pre-revolutionary regionalisation centred on types of rural production was carried out by A. Chelintsev, *Selskoe khozyaistvo i lesovodstvo* (St Petersburg, 1910). For a more recent review, see E. Karnaukhova, *Razmeshchnie sel'skogo khozyaistva Rossi v period kapitalisma* (Moscow, 1951) ch. 3; W. H. Parker, *An Historical Geography of Russia* Chicago, 1968) chs 11–17.

   For specific characteristics of peasant economy and society in the ten Polish *guberniyas* (the 'Visla region'), relevant also to some of the non-Polish villages in the Western parts of European Russia in the late nineteenth century, see J. Chalasinski, *Mlode pokolenie chlopow* (Warsaw, 1936).
5. Reviewed in T. Shanin, *The Awkward Class* (Oxford, 1972)
6. ibid, pt II.
7. The value of another potential source of relevant data, the military censuses of horse ownership, was considerably limited by the non-simultaneous collection of evidence and the fact that only horses of potential military use were recorded. For a summary of the 1900–6 studies, see *Ezhegodnik Rossii 1907* (St Petersburg, 1908) pp. lxxviii–lxxxiv.
8. For the demographic figures, see OSPN, vol. I. The authors of the land census were clearly not sure of their ground, for they have offered (in a footnote) an alternative computation assuming a family size of 5.3 with the resulting figure of 'occupied outside agriculture' down to 12.5 million; see also A. Rashin, *Naselenie rossii za sto let* (Moscow, 1956).
9. Shanin, op. cit., ch. 4.

10. Published initially in *Mir bozhii*, no. 8, 1905. Quoted after A. Bol'shakov and N. Rozhkov, *Istoriya khozyaistva rossii* (Leningrad, 1925) vol. 2, pp. 267–71. For the source of the evidence, see OSPN, vol. II.

11. A. Anfimov, *Krupnoe pomeshchich'e khozyaistvo evropeiskoi rossii* (Moscow, 1969) p. 375.

12. Lenin, PSS, vol. 16, p. 203.

13. *Statisticheskoe opisanie kaluzhskoi gubernii* (Kaluga, 1897–8) vols 1 and 2.

14. M. Sulkovskii, *Klassovye gruppy i proizvodstvennye tipy krest'yanskikh khozyaistv* (Moscow, 1930) pp. 61–3. Another authoritative study back in the pre-revolutionary times has estimated the average plot sufficient for the upkeep of a peasant family to be 8 des. of land. Once again it contradicts Lenin's categories quoted but indicates that about half of the Russian peasants suffered from insufficiency of land (malozemel'e) (S. Prokopovich, *Agrarnyi krizis i meropriyatiya pravitel'stva* (Moscow, 1912) p. 9).

15. Lenin has added the figure of the small private land holdings to that of the holders of common lands, disregarding those who held both an allotment and private land. Our own estimates used the communal lands as base, amending it by the notional average of 1 des. of private land per household as an approximation of private land owned by the 'middle peasants' stratum. It is substantiated by Prokopovich's estimate of an average 1.12 des. of private land per peasant household in a somewhat latter period (S. Prokopovich, *Agrarnyi krizis i meropriyatiya pravitel'stva* (Moscow, 1912) p. 9–13).

16. For discussion, see Shanin, op. cit., chs 6 and 7.

17. OSPN, vol. I, pp. v–viii and 16–17.

18. See B. Kodomtsev, *Profesional'nyi i sotsial'nyi sostav naseleniya evropeiskoi rossii* (St Petersburg, 1909) pp. 47 and 60. S. Strumilin has approached it in a different manner by estimating the whole amount of full-time and part-time rural wage labour and then presenting it in 'full-time worker units'. His result was about 9.5 per cent of mature rural labour appearing as 'wage labour' (i.e. 4.5 million units). (See his *Naemnyi trud v sel'skom khozyaistve* (Moscow, 1926) p. 8.) It indicated once more that most of this labour came from members of family farms.

19. I. Pisarev, *Narodonaselenie SSSR* (Moscow, 1962) pp. 66 and 71.

20. For example, Lenin, PSS, vol. 27, pp. 135–225; and among his ideological foes and later, N. Sukhanov in *Puti sel'skogo khozyaistva*, nos. 6–7, 1927, etc. For discussion, see Shanin, op. cit., ch. 6.

21. Using categories of land holding that were somewhat lower than in the Kaluga study published fifteen years earlier, he concluded that the peasants of Penza gub. divided as follows:

    Better off (12 des. plus)　　15%
    Middle (4.5–12 des.)　　　　51%
    Poor (1–4.5 des.)　　　　　　30%
    Landless (up to 1 des.)　　　4%

    Itogi otsenochno-statisticheskogo izsledovaniya penzenskoi gubernii (Penza, 1913) p. vi.

22. *Statistika*, op. cit., p. 129; the next category of households with 1–2 des. of land was still only 4.7 per cent of the total number.

23. OSPN, vol. II, pp. 296–7; also vol. I, p. 161.

3 THE DEVELOPMENT OF CAPITALISM IN RUSSIA

The New America's star

1. OSPN, vol. I, pp. 256–67, 296, iii and xii. The 2 500 000 inhabitants of Finland were accounted for separately. (Discussed above in Addendum I.)

2. V. Den, *Kurs ekonomicheskoi geografii* (Moscow, 1925). See also ES, vol. IV/DX.

3. S. Prokopovich, *Opyt ischisleniya narodnogo dokhoda 50 gub. evropeiskoi rossii* (Moscow;, 1918) pp. 65–6. (The figures are for European Russia, which held three-quarters of the population of the empire.)

4. For production per capita figures, see P. Lyashchenko, *Istoriya narodnogo khozyaistva SSSR* (Moscow, 1952) vol. II, pp. 414–15; also A. Finn-Enotaevskii, *Kapitalism v rossii (1890–1917 gg)* (Moscow, 1925) vol. I, p. 189, and *Sbornik statistiko-ekonomicheskikh svedenii po sel'skomu khozyaistvu rossii* (St Petersburg, 1914) p. 2; the 1900 report of the Minister of Finance to the Tsar: S. Witte, 'O polozhenii nashei promyshlennosti', *Isotrik marksist*, nos. 2–3, 1935, p. 132.

5. *Sbornik statistiko-ekonomicheskikh svedenii,* r, op. cit., pp. 597–9 (excepting the populations of Scandinavia and Montenegro).

6. Prokopovich, op. cit., p. 26.

7. Witte, op. cit., p. 131.

8. *Krest'yanskaya sel'sko-khozyaistvennaya entsiklopedia* (Moscow, 1925) vol. II, p. 18. For further discussion, see Chapter 4.

9. A. Rashin, *Naselenie rossii za sto let* (Moscow, 1956) p. 98; Prokopovich, op. cit., p. 67.

10. L. Lubny-Gertskykh (ed.), *Trudy kolonizatsionnogo nauchnoissledovatel's-kogo instituta* (Moscow, 1926) vol. II, p. 7; N. Turchaninov and A. Domrachev, *Itogi pereselencheskogo dvizheniya po 1914 gg. vklyuchitel'no* (Petrograd, 1916) pp. 44–5 and 66–8.

11. OSPN, vol. I, pp. xvi–xx.

12. See the companion volume *Russia 1905–7: Revolution as a Moment of Truth.*

13. See below, Chapter 5, pp. 215–17.

14. Aleksander Blok, 'Novaya Amerika', in *Sochineniya* (Moscow, 1955) p. 396.

15. For relevant discussions of capitalism as a system of political economy and its broader social and historical implications, see P. Sweezy, *The Theory of Capitalist Development* (New York, 1954); J. Schumpeter, *The Theory of Economic Development* (Cambridge, 1936); S. Kuznets, *Modern Economic Growth* (New Haven, 1966); M. Barratt Brown, 'Marx's Economics as a Newtonian Model', in T. Shanin, *The Rules of the Game* (London, 1972); J. Robinson, *Economic Philosophy* (Oxford, 1962); R. Hilton, *The Transition from Feudalism to Capitalism* (London, 1976).

16. For discussion of different approaches to progress, see S. Pollard, *The Idea of Progress* (Harmondsworth, 1971); F. Engels, *The Origins of the Family, Private Property and the State* (London, 1968) ch. 9; W. Warren, *Imperialism: Pioneer of Capitalism* (London, 1980); T. Shanin, *Late Marx and the Russian Road* (London, 1983).

Industry, capital and 'uneven development'

1. See P. Lyashchenko, *Istoriya narodnogo khozyaistva SSSR* (Moscow, 1952) vol. II, pp. 414–15; also A. Finn-Enotaevskii, *Kapitalizm v Rossii (1890–1917 gg.)* (Moscow, 1925) vol. I, p. 169, and *Sbornik statistiko-ekonomicheskikh svedenii po sel'skomu khozyaistvu Rosii* (St Petersburg, 1914) p. 2; M. Wolf and G. Mebus, *Statisticheskii spravochnik po ekonomicheskoi geografii* (Moscow, 1926) chs. II–VII. Also, the excellently written W. H. Parker, *An Historical Geography of Russia* (Chicago, 1969).
2. P. Khromov, *Ekonomicheskoe razvitie Rossii* (Moscow, 1967) pp. 405–7.
3. ibid. For a good discussion see also M. Tugan-Baranovskii, 'Sostoyanie nashei promyshlennosti za poslednee desyatiletie', *Sovremenneyi mir*, no. 2, 1910, pp. 27–53.
4. ibid; also Lyashchenko, op. cit., pp. 123–7.
5. M. Dobb, *Soviet Economic Development since 1917* (London, 1960) p. 38; also Khromov, op. cit., pp. 96, 138 and 146–8; L. Eventov, *Inostrannye kapitaly v russkoi promyshlennosti* (Moscow, 1931) especially the figures on p. 17.
6. M. Tugan-Baranovskii, *Russkaia fabrika* (Moscow, 1938) chs 4 and 5.
7. ES, vol. 4/D, pp. 1–lxvii. The expression 'registered' (*tsenzovaya*) indicates the more substantive units of production that were taken account of by the census of industries.
8. ibid; also Lyashchenko, op. cit., p. 149; M. Wolf and G. Mebus, *Statisticheskii spravochnik po ekonomicheskoi geografii* (Moscow, 1926) p. 249.
9. R. Portal in an important discussion of the Russian economic and social history in *The Cambridge Economic History of Europe* (Cambridge, 1965) vol. VI (the figures of craftsmen pp. 841–2); Wolf and Mebus, op. cit., pp. 248–9, quote an estimate of 3.7 million labourers (often part time) and an annual produce of 1528 million roubles for the handicrafts and cottage industries of Russia in 1912–13. A. Rashin, 'O chislennosti rabochikh rossii', *Istoricheskie zapiski*, vol. 46, 1950, p. 150, suggested 3.5 million for 1913. Other and probably overstated figures quoted were 5.5 million labourers, mostly part-timers employed in the crafts of European Russia (S. Prokopovich, *Opyt ischisleniya narodnogo dokhoda 50 gub. evropeiskoi rossii* (Moscow, 1918) pp. 19–20 and 58) while for all of the empire 7.5 million was cited or even as many as 12 million (A. A. Rybnikov, *Kustarnaya promyshlennost' i sbyt kustarnykh izdelii* (Moscow, 1913) pp. 15–17). All sources agree that about four-fifths of those were peasants' supplementary engagement in non-farming work.
10. Prokopovich, op. cit., pp. 65–6. The figures are limited to European Russia (which held three-quarters of the population of the empire).
11. See, in particular, M. Falkus, 'Russian National Income, 1913: A Revaluation', *Economica*, vol. XXXV, nos. 133–40, 1968, and A. Vainshtein, *Narodnyi dokhod Rossii* (Moscow, 1969).
12. Prokopovich, op. cit., p. 26.
13. For discussion, see p. 143.
14. R. Goldsmith, 'The Economic Growth of Tsarist Russia 1860–1913', *Economic Development and Cultural Change*, vol. 9, 1961.

15. ibid, p. 463 (using 1900 base). A German study quoted by Khromov, op. cit., p. 284, has assumed an even steeper advance of the main Russian industries in the 1890s, that is, more than doubling within the decade and for a time outstepping in speed the advance of Germany (and showing similar averages of growth in 1900–13). Also, see Lyashchenko, op. cit., p. 213.
16. Lyashchenko, op. cit., 99. 146–7.
17. L. Eventov, *Inostrannye kapitaly v russkoi promyshlennosti* (Moscow, 1931) especially p. 17. Eventov's work was based mainly on that by P. 01' *Inostrannye kapitaly v Rossii* (Moscow, 1925). See also I. Gindin, *Banki i promyshlennost'v Rossii* (Moscow, 1927). For somewhat different figures, see Lyashchenko, op. cit., p. 156.
18. Eventov, op. cit., pp. 20–1.
19. Gindin, op. cit.; also his *Gosudarstvennyi bank i ekonomicheskaya politika tsarskogo pravitel'stva* (Moscow, 1960).
20. See extended discussion edited by V. Bobykin, I. Gindin and K. Tarnovskii in *Istariya sssr* 1959, no. 3.
21. Leshchenko, op. cit., pp. 407–8 and 414–15; Wolf and Mebus, op. cit., pp. 319–25 ff. A. Bol'shakov and N. Rozhkov, *Istoriya khozyaistva rossii* (Moscow, 1926) vol. 2, p. 293, vol. 3, pp. 13–20.
22. S. Strumilin, *Ocherki sovetskoi ekonomiki* and (Moscow, 1930) p. 29.
23. Tugan-Baranovskii, op. cit., pp. 308, 342 and 375.
24. *Chislennost' i sostav rabochikh v Rossii* (St Petersburg, 1906); also A. Pogozhaev, *Uchet chislennosti i sostava rabochikh Rossii* (St Petersburg, 1906).
25. Pogozhaev, op. cit.
26. *Chislennost'*, op. cit., pp. vii–x and xiii–xiv.
27. E. M. Dementev, *Fabrika, chto ona daet naseleniyu i chto u nego beret* (St. Petersburg, 1893) followed by B. Kademtsev, *Professional'nyi i sotsialnyi sostav naseleniya evropeiskoi rossii* (St Petersburg, 1909) and many others.
28. Pogozhaev, op. cit., p. 25.
29. A. Svavitskii and V. Sher, *Polozhenie rabochikh pechatnogo dela v Moskve* (St. Petersburg, 1909) pp. 8–28.
30. Bol'shakov, op. cit., vol. 2, p. 271. Our estimate of the total labour is 90 per cent of the 15 to 60 age groups within the population, less 10 per cent for those unavailable for physical or social reasons. Should a higher estimate of 15 per cent for the 'non-working' component be used, the consequent figures would be: wage labour 15.8 per cent, industrial wage labour 5.5 per cent. For discussion of availability of female labour, see Addendum 2.
31. See, for example, C. M. Cippola, *The Fontana Economic History of Europe: The Middle Ages* (London, 1977) pt 2.
32. Lyashchenko, op. cit., ch. XV; V. Laverychev, *Krupnaya buzhuaziya v poreformennoi rossii 1861–1900* (Moscow, 1974); V. Dyakin, *Samoderzhavie, burzhuaziya i dvoryanstvo 1907–1911* (Leningrad, 1978); A. Nifontov, 'Formirovanie klassov burzhuaznogo obshchestva v russkom gorode, *Istoricheskie zapiski*, no. 54, 1955.
33. Laverychev, op. cit., p. 70.
34. Dyakin, op. cit., cit., p. 7.
35. ibid, p. 9.
36. Laverychev, op cit., p. 71, as against OSPN, vol. II, pp. 263 and 296.
37. In particular, the novels of the many so-called *bytoviki* who described

critically the day-to-day life of Russia's different social strata, like A. Serafimovich and the politically radical writers like M. Gorki.

38. Pogozhaev, op. cit., pp. xix–xxiii.
39. A. Rashin, *Naselenie rossii za 100 lt* (Moscow, 1956) pp. 96–9; I. Pisarev, *Narodonaselenie SSSR*, (Moscow 1962) *Narodon.*
40. For a highly illuminating study (despite its 'progressist' bias) of the historical background of Russian urbanisation, see N. Rozhkov, *Gorod i derevnya v russkoi istorii* (St Petersburg, 1902). See also NES, vol. 14, pp. 299–309; Parker, op. cit.
41. ES, op. cit., pp. v–vi.
42. Sostoyanie gorodskikh poselenii imperii i usloviya zhizni v nikh, *Ezhegodnik Rossii, 1906* (St Petersburg, 1907) pp. lix–lxix.
43. *Report of the Minister of Finance to HM the Emperor on the Budget of the Empire for 1899* (St Petersburg, 1898) p. 20.
44. For the relevant tables of the British censuses of late nineteenth century, see E. Black, *Victorian Culture and Society* (New York, 1974) pp. 62–9. The parallel percentages of employment in the other key occupations were much closer. In Great Britain those employed in the armed forces, state administration and in 'liberal professions' were 1.1 per cent, 1.0 per cent and 0.7 per cent respectively while the Russian figures for 1897 were 0.75 per cent, 0.99 per cent and 0.61 per cent.
45. Interestingly, the development of this concept as a major amendment or challenge to the prevalevant evolutionism of nineteenth-century Europe finds its beginning in Russia (i.e. the writing of P. Chadaev developed and put to further use by the revolutionary populists of the 1850s–1880s). For discussion, see T. Shanin, *Late Marx and the Russian Road* (London, 1983). (See Chapter 5).
46. Goldsmith, op. cit., pp. 442 and 451; for further discussion, see section D.
47. Lyashchenko, op. cit., p. 408; A. Gerschenkron, in C. Black, *The Transformation of Russian Society* (Cambridge, 1960) pp. 50–1.

The state as an economy

1. The 'last' of the stages (i.e. that of our own times) is usually missing from such textbooks for the reason well explained by one of Marc Bloch's high-school teachers who taught him that 'since 1830 there has been no more history. It is all politics' (M. Bloch, *The Historian's Craft* (Manchester, 1954) p. 37).
2. I. Pososhkov, *Kniga o skudnosti i bogatstve* (Moscow, 1951); NES, vol. 14, pp. 328–30.
3. Or put in the language of the Anglo-Saxon academic *politesse*, he was 'a man who may not always have known the dividing line between personal and public interest' (T. H. Von Laue, *Sergei Witte and the Industrialization of Russia* (London, 1963) p. 24). The book offers a good introduction to the 'Witte system (i.e. of tsardom's basic economic strategy in the 1890s).
4. P. Lyashchenko, *Istoriya narodhnogo khozyaistva SSSR* (Moscow, 1952) vol. II, p. 185; also *Statistika zemlevladeniya 1905* (St Petersburg, 1907) p. 11.

5. Lyashchenko, op. cit., pp. 184–7, 593 and 594.
6. Bogolepov's estimates in L. Martov, P. Maslov and A. Potresov, *Obshchestvennoe dvizhenie v Rossii v nachale XXgo veka* (St Petersburg, 1909) vol. I, p. 172.
7. A. Bol'shakov and N. Rozhkov, *Istoriya khozyaistva Rossii* (Leningrad, 1925–6), op. cit., vol. II, p. 232. Lyashchenko, op. cit., p. 192.
8. I. Gindin, *Gosudarstvennyi bank i ekonomicheskaya politika tsarskogo pravitel'stva* (Moscow, 1960); NES, op. cit., vol. 14, pp. 456–66. Gerschenkron has spoken of private speculative banking and state financing as the two main ways of industrialisation to date. A Gerschenkron, 'Economic Backwardness in Historical Perspective', in B. Hoselitz, *The Progress of Underdeveloped Areas* (Chicago, 1953) pp. 9–19.
9. NES, vol. 18, pp. 447–62.
10. ibid, p. 451.
11. A. Bol'shakov and N. Rozhkov, *Istoriya khozyaistva rossii* (Leningrad, 1925) vol. 2, p. 232..
12. Lyashchenko, op. cit., pp. 386–8 and 391–2.
13. The percentages were arrived at by relating a sum total of state income from its properties plus regalia (post office, etc.) to the sum total of state income less the peasant redemption payments. See also Lyashchenko, op. cit., p. 582 (figures for 1900).
14. Lyashchenko, op. cit., p. 390.
15. ibid, p. 391.
16. ibid, pp. 414–17.
17. NES, vol. 18, p. 831.
18. Bogolepov in Martov etc op. cit., p. 43; A. M. Anfimov, *Krupnoe pomeshchich'e khozyaistvo evropeiskoi Rossii* (Moscow, 1969) pp. 255–7; Von Laue, op. cit., p. 103; V. Den, *Kurs ekonomicheskoi geografii* (Moscow, 1925) pp. 288 and 309.
19. In the report of S. Witte as published in *Istorik marksist*, no. 2, 1935, p. 133.
20. For interesting insight, see F. Stern, *Gold and Iron* (London, 1977) ch. 16. For figures, see L. Eventov, *Inostrannye kapitaly v russkoi promyshlennosti* (Moscow, 1931) pp. 24–7.
21. In 1905 a further step in a similar direction was taken when the payment of the war debts as the expenses of suppressing the 1905–7 revolution had to be financed.
22. Witte, op. cit., p. 136.
23. See ES, vol. 4/D, pp. lxx and xxi; Lyashchenko, op. cit., pp. 282 and 715; also Prokopovich, op. cit., p. 79.

Rural economy: labour and land

1. V. Den, *Kurs ekonomicheskoi geografii* (Leningrad, 1925) pp. 186–90; also A. Bol'shakov and N. Rozhkov, *Istoriya khozyaistva Rossii*, Leningrad, 1926, vol. II; ES, vol. 49, p. 182.
2. See Den, op. cit., chs IV and V. For figures of the 1910 census of agricultural equipment, see N. Oganovskii (ed.), *Sel'skoe khozyaistvo Rossii v XX veke* (Moscow, 1923) pp. 122–3.

3. See R. Goldsmith, 'The Economic Growth of Tsarist Russia 1860–1913', *Economic Development and Cultural Change*, vol. 9, 1961, p. 447, as against P. Khromov, *Ekonomicheskoe razvitie rossii* (Moscow, 1967) p. 513, which seems clearly to understate his figures. See also ES, op. cit., pp. xliii–xlix, which support Goldsmith's assumptions.

4. See E. Karnaukhova, *Razmeshchenie sel'skogo khozyaistva Rossii v period kapitalizma* (Moscow, 1951) chs 5–6.

5. A. Vainshtein, *Oblozheniya i platezhi krest'yanstva* (Moscow, 1924) p. 32; N. Rubakin, *Rossiya v tsifrakh* (St Petersburg, 1912) p. 158, suggested the figure of 32 per cent. Anfimov pointed out how much Russian wage labour was restricted by job availability. He estimated that, varying in degree, 14 million peasants were involved in crafts and trades, one-third of them outside their localities. See A. Anfimov, *Ekonomicheskoe polozhenie i klassoraya* (Moscow, 1984) p. 224. Contemporaries assumed less figures.

6. For their actual value, see Vainshtein, op. cit., pp. 41 and 43. We shall return to the issue in the text below.

7. S. Strumilin, *Ocherki ekonomicheskoi istorii Rossii i SSSR* (Moscow, 1966) pp. 205–14; see also A. Anfimov, *Krest'yanskoe khozyaistvo evropeiskoi Rossii* (Moscow, 1980) pp. 171–2.

8. OSPN, vol. 1, pp. v–vi and 254–7; ES, vol. 4/D, p. xxi; A. Anfimov, *Krupnoe pomeshchich'e khozyaistvo evropeiskoi Rossii* (Moscow, 1969) ch. 5.

9. *Statistika zemlevladeniya 1905* (St Petersburg, 1907) p. 137.

10. ibid, pp. 136–7 and 188–9.

11. ibid, p. 141; the figure represents in fact the surplus of land sold over land bought by the nobles. The land market was buoyant and there were nobles who proceeded to purchase land (V. Kosinskii, *Osnovnye tendentsii v mobilizatsii zemelnoi sobstvennosti* (Prague, 1925) ch. 1).

12. Vainshtein, op. cit., pp. 39–42; A. Anfimov, 'K voprosu of kharaktere agrarnogo stroya evropeiskoi rossii XX v.', in *Istoricheskie zapiski* (Moscow, 1959) vol. 65, pp. 127 and 134. For different (and lower) figures see S. Dubrovskii, *Sel'skoe khozyaistvo rossii v period imperializma* (Moscow, 1975) pp. 144–54; the debate was inconclusive.

13. Anfimov, *Krupnoe*, op. cit., pp. 71–3 and 79; A. Chelintsev, 'Pomeshchich'e khozyaistvo v Rossii pered revolyutsiei', in *Zapiski Instituta izucheniya Rossii* (Prague, 1925) vol. I.

14. Lenin has referred to it as a system that was not an European or capitalist 'way of economy' but 'a Turkish and feudal one' (Lenin, PSS, vol. 23, p. 275).

15. *Svod statisticheskikh svedenii po sel'skomu khozyaistvu Rossii* (St Petersburg, 1906) pt III, pp. 4–5.

16. The actual estimates of the size of this discrepancy varied widely. Figures for 1900 based in part on the military census of horses suggested the following percentages:

	Land owned	Horses owned	Land sown, inclusive of the rented lands
Peasants and Cossacks	67.4	92.7	90.5
Private owners, less those above	32.6	7.3	9.5

(NES, vol. 18, pp. 513–14.)

On the other hand, the Ministry of Agriculture estimates (not fully comparable in terms of area) in *Svod statisticheskikh svedenii po sel'skomy khozyaistvu Rossii*, op. cit., vol. II, tables I–IV, has claimed for the nobles of European Russia in 1900 as much as 15.3 per cent of total horses. For the evidence of the rapid drop of the share of agricultural implements held by the non-peasant owners, see Anfimov, 'K voprosu', op. cit.

17. For figures see Dubrovskii, *Sel'skoe*, op. cit., pp. 115–25 and Anfimov *Krupnoe*, op. cit., chs 3–4 and 7–8. Dubrovskii remarked that the only thing such nobles did accumulate was their debts.

18. A. Vainshtein, *Narodnyi dokhod Rossii i SSSR* (Moscow, 1969) pp. 58–9. For comparison with the large landowners in Europe, see A. J. Mayer, *The Persistence of the Old Regime* (New York, 1983). It shows that while in Great Britain or Germany their most significant income often also came from outside agriculture, it was related to coal, transport and city properties rather than to 'state service'.

19. For supporting evidence, see Anfimov, *Krupnoe*, op. cit., pp. 271–4.

20. ibid, pp. 289–90 and 294–9. Russian novels of the nineteenth century have well expressed that phenomenon (e.g. in the figure of Oblomov and Zatertyi in the widely read novel *Oblomov* by I. Goncharov).

21. A. Nifontov, *Zernovoe proizvodstvo rossii vo vtoroi polovine XIX veka* (Moscow, 1974) p. 280.

22. L. Lubny-Gertsykh, *Dvizhenie naseleniya na teritorii SSSR* (Moscow, 1926) pp. 6–7; A. Chuprov, *Vliyanie urozhaev i khlebnykh tsen na nekotorye storony ruskogo narodnogo khozyaistva* (St Petersburg, 1897). There was an estimated one 'surplus' labourer' per peasant household. The 1914 government figures admitted to half of Russia's districts producing less than half the minimal consumption requirements of its rural population. See *Sel'sko-khozyaistvennyi promysel v Rossii* (Petrograd, 1914) section *story khlebov'* and pp. 114–24.

23. V. Den, *Kurs ekonomicheskoi geografii* (Moscow, 1925) p. 193.

24. G. T. Robinson, *Rural Russia under the Old Regime* (New York, 1932) p. 115.

25. ibid, p. 219; A. Rashin, Naselenie Rossii za sto let (Moscow, 1956) p. 98.

26. ES, vol. 4/D, p. xxxv; A. Kaufman, *Agrarnyi vopros v Rossii* (St Petersburg, 1918) p. 44. These somewhat higher figures are due probably to variations in the areas considered.

27. Karnaukhova, op. cit., ch. 4. A government committee was set up to study 'the problem of impoverishment of the Rural areas of Central Russia'. It spoke first of 9 *gubernyas* relevant and latter of 18. For discussion see M. Simonova 'Prolema "oskudneniya" tsentra' in *Problemy sotsial'no-ekonomicheskoi istorii rossii*; Moscow, 1971.

28. F. Lorimer, *The Population of Soviet Union* (Geneva, 1946) pp. 14–15.

29. P. Lyashchenko, *Zernovoe khozyaistvo i khlebotorgovye otnosheniya Rossii i Germanii* (Petrograd, 1915) pp. 3–4, 11 and 51. For 1898 the average for 1896–1900 was taken.

30. Nifontov, op. cit., pp. 266–7, 275 and 284.

31. ES, vol. 4/D, p. xlv.

32. Anfimov, *Krupnoe*, op. cit., p. 474. Also, *Sbornik statistikoekonomicheskikh svedenii po sel'skomu khoziaistvu* (Petersburg, 1914) pp. 113–14.

33. Nifontov, op. cit., p. 315.
34. ibid, pp. 242–6 and 272–4; Karnaukhova, op. cit., ch. 6.
35. Prokopovich, *Opyt izucheniya narodnogo dokhoda 50 gub. evropeiskoi rossii* (Moscow, 1918), pp. 33 and 44.
36. ES, volume 1/D, p. xlviii, li; Anfimov, *Krest'yanskoe khozyaistvo evropeiskoi rossii* (Moscow, 1980) pp. 150–7; Den, op. cit., pp. 200–2.
37. P. Lyashchenko, *Russkoe zernovoe khozyaistvo* (Moscow, 1927) pp. 11 and 51. The averages increased from 16.8 per cent in 1891–5 to 19.5 per cent in 1906–10.
38. ibid.
39. For example, the changes introduced by the District Agronomist Zubrilin in the Volokolamsk *uezd* of Moscow gub.
40. For estimates, see T. Shanin, *The Awkward Class* (Oxford, 1972) ch. 4.
41. Lyashchenko, *Russkoe*, op. cit., pp. 311–12. Also, Den, op. cit., pp. 184–6. For the estimated one-quarter shortage of grain produced in Russia so far as the consumption needs of its rural population are concerned, see ES, vol. 4/D, p. xlix v. For the different view of Nifontov, op. cit., pp. 285–98 (especially p. 285 where he speaks of grain production 'increasingly in excess of the consumption needs of the rural population').
42. The evidence concerning peasants crafts and trades is not very adequate but its general patterns were never contested. See, for example, *Krest'yanskaya sel'skokhozyaistvennaya entsiklopediya* (Moscow, 1925) vol. II, pt III, section 3; L. Mintz, *Otklod krest'yanskogo naseleniya na zarabotki v sssr* (Moscow, 1925) ch. 1; Rubakin, op. cit., ch. 32, etc.
43. For evidence of the 'negative profit' of peasant households, see, for example, Anfimov, 'K voprosu', op. cit., pp. 133 and 141; A. Peshekhonov *Krest'yane i rabochie* (St. Petersburg, 1806) pp. 61–5; Anfimov, *Ekonomicheskoe*, op. cit., chs 1, 3.
44. Khromov, op. cit., p. 355; Anfimov, op. cit., vol. 2, pp. 186–8. Also Anfimov, 'K voprosu', op. cit., p. 132, quotes estimates by S. Strumilin to say that the rent component of the inputs in grain production increased between 1887–8 and 1912–14 much faster than the inputs total value.
45. R. Manning, *The Crisis of Old Order* (Princeton, 1982).
46. During the first twenty years following the emancipation, the peasant communes were legally free to sell allotment lands and not only to buy them. The figure of land actually sold is indicative of the actual conditions and processes. It was 0.2 per cent of the total (M. Florinsky, *Russia* (New York, 1955) p. 1103). For the process of land purchase by peasants, see Anfimov, *Rossiiskaya*, op. cit., ch. 3. A recent article estimated that peasant redemption and land purchases payments amounted to 4400 million Roubles in 1863–1910 (*Istoriya SSSR*, no. 5, 1983, p. 75).
47. *Report of the Minister of Finance to HM the Emperor on the Budget of the Empire* (St Petersburg, 1899) pp. 19–21.
48. Vainshtein, op. cit., pt I, also pp. 114–30. For re-evaluation of the figures see Anfimov, *Ekonomicheskoe*, op. cit., ch. 3.
49. Estimates of Bogolepov in Martov op. cit., vol. I, pp. 169–77. For evidence see *Materialy uchrezhdennoi 16 noyabrya 1901g. kommissii* (St Petersburg, 1905) vol. I, p. 79.

50. Anfimov, *Krupnoe*, op. cit., p. 82.
51. For example, A. Engel'gardt, *Chernozemnaya Rossiya* (Saratov, 1902).
52. In 1900 the average price of a des. of land was, in European Russia, 67.4 roubles. The average annual rural wages in the Black earth region were 60 roubles (V. Svetlovskii, *K voprosu o sud'bakh zemlevladeniya v Rossii* (St Petersburg, 1907) pp. 58 and 67; V. Koval'chenko, *Rossiya v kontse XIX veka* (St Petersburg, 1900) p. 548).
53. The archives of the 2nd *Duma*, TsGIA(L), The second *Duma* Fond, file 784, p. 19.

4 THE PEASANT ECONOMY: SEMI-FEUDALIST, SEMI-CAPITALIST OR WHAT'S-ITS-NAME?

Capitalism, rural proletarians, kulaks

1. See in particular the debate in major professional journals, both 'Western' and 'local' concerning the rural component of the 'developing societies' of today (i.e. *Sociologia Ruralis, Peasant Studies, Journal of Peasant Studies, Economic and Political Weekly* (Bombay), *Journal of Contemporary Asia*, etc.).
2. It goes without saying that the equality of peasantry with autarky by some writers make it disappear. Such conceptual tricks help little when social reality is concerned. For discussion see the next section.
3. S. Prokopovich, *Opyt ischisleniya narodnogo dokhoda* (Moscow, 1918) p. 78.
4. C. Geertz, *Agricultural Involution* (Berkeley, 1963).
5. A. Anfimov, *Krest'yanskoe khozyaistvo evropeiskoi Rossii* (Moscow, 1980) p. 193.
6. A. Chayanov, *Theory of Peasant Economy* (Homewood, Ill., 1966) ch. 2; K. Kautsky, *Die Agrarfrage* (Hanover, 1966), chs 2c and 6b; Lenin, PSS, vol. 19, p. 343.
7. Especially N. Danielson (under the pseudonym Nikolai-on) and V. Vorontsev (the V.V.) as against P. Struve, 'Critical Notes on the Question of Economic Development of Russia', and V. Lenin, 'The Problem of Markets', PSS, vol. 1.
8. V. Lenin, *The Development of Capitalism in Russia* (Moscow, 1974) p. 176.
9. ibid., p. 198. Annenskii presented his figures concerning 1887 in the book edited by A. Chuprov, *Vliyanie urozhaev i khlebnykh tsen na nekotorye storony russkogo narodnogo khozyaistva* (St Petersburg, 1897).
10. Lenin, PSS, vol. 12, pp. 249–50.
11. A. Anfimov, *Krupnoe pomeshchich'e khozyaistvo evropeiskoi Rossii* (Moscow, 1969) p. 380.
12. A. Anfimov, 'K voprosu ob opredelenii ekonomicheskikh tipov zemledel'cheskogo khozyaistva', *Voprosy istorii sel'skogo khozyaistva* (Moscow, 961).
13. Lenin, PSS, vol. 19, p. 325.
14. In an unsubstantiated passage of his last book, *Krest'yanskoe*, op. cit., p. 7 (published in 1980), Anfimov retreated from his analysis of 1959. Scholars will be judged by the highest points of their originality and achievment and not by recantation, be it as it may.

15. I. Chernyshev, *Agrarnyi vopros v rossii* (Kursk, 1927) p. 87. The author has described these figures as 'extremely small'.
16. T. Shanin, *The Awkward Class* (London, 1972) pt 2.
17. ibid, ch. 3.
18. M. Simonova, *Stolypinskaya agrarnaya reforma v tsentral'no chernozemnom raione* (Moscow, 1953) p. 462. A. Dubrovskii made a similar point when speaking of peasant pauperisation in the central gub. of Russia, stressing that it 'was not compensated by the development of the capitalist economy . . . and led to the impoverishment of the agriculture as a whole' (*Stolypinskaya zemel'naya reforma* (Moscow, 1963) p. 29).
19. Kautsky, op. cit., chs 4, 5 and 6.
20. Lenin, PSS, vol. 27, pp. 185–205.
21. M. Mikhelson, *Russkaya mysl' i rech'* (St Petersburg, 1903) vol. I. Also, and along similar lines, B. Dal', *Tolkovyi slovar' zhivogo russkogo yazyka* (St Petersburg, 1907) vol. 2, p. 551, who adds to his list of characteristics also 'those who live by cheating'.
22. D. H. Ushakov, *Tolkovyi slovar'russkogo yazyka* (Moscow, 1934).
23. R. Gvozdev, *Kulachestvo-rostovshchestvo* (St Petersburg, 1899) p. 1.
24. ibid.
25. K. Tarnovskii, 'Problemy agrarno-kapitalisticheskoi evolyutsii', *Istoriya Rossii*, no. 1, 1970, p. 77. For one of the relatively few collections of actual quantitative evidence concerning rural usury in the period, see V. Blagoveshchenskii, *Melkii kredit v derevne* (Moscow, 1906). His study of Ufa gub. has reported an average of 36 per cent of interest paid (as against the legal 12 per cent) and the fact that loans were taken mostly 'as the result of poverty' and not 'for the sake of investment in production' (ibid, pp. 9 and 22).
26. K. Marx, *Capital* (Harmondsworth, 1976) vol. I, p. 645; P. Baran, *The Political Economy of Growth* (New York, 1962) pp. 194–6ff.
27. Lenin, *Development of Capitalism*, op. cit., p. 188, which speaks on the other hand of 'the important proposition that independent development of merchants' and usurers' capital in our countryside retard the differentiation of peasantry (ibid) and returns elsewhere to the distinction between 'peasant bourgeoisie *and* the rural usurers'.
28. See, for discussion, M. Levin, 'Who was the Soviet Kulak?', *Soviet Studies*, no. 2, 1966. Also, Shanin, *The Awkward Class*, op. cit., pt III. In the period of collectivisation a word *podkulachnik*, i.e. 'under-Kulak' – was designed for similar purpose.

Capitalism, agrarian markets, productivity

1. K. Tarnovskii, 'Problemy agrarnoi istorii Rossii perioda imperializma v sovetskoi istoriografii', *Istoricheskie zapiski*, nos. 78 and 83, 1968–9.
2. ibid, vol. 78, pp. 31–2.
3. 'While correctly defining the direction of development we have mistakenly defined the point it reached' (i.e. an 'over-estimation of the extent of capitalist development within the Russian agriculture') (Lenin, PSS, vol. 16, pp. 268–9).

4. ibid, vol. 31, pp. 417–18.
5. A. Anfimov, 'K voprosu of kharaktere agrarnogo stroya evropeiskoi rossii v nachale XX v.', *Istoricheskie zapiski*, no. 65, 1959, p. 121.
6. For example, the study of M. Gefter, 'Stranitsa iz istorii marksizma XX veka', *Istoricheskaya nauka i nekotorye problemy sovremennosti* (Moscow, 1969). The volume and its editor (then head of the Sector of Historical method of the Institute of History in Moscow) were harshly attacked by ideological authorities, see J. Gleisner, 'Old Bolsheviks Discuss Socialism' Leeds, 1983. For discussion, see also K. Tarnovskii, 'Problemy agrarno-ekonomicheskoi evolyutsii Rossii', *Istoriya SSSR*, May–June 1970, pp. 65–78.
7. A. Shestakov, *Kapitalizatsiya sel'skogo khozyaistva Rossii*, Moscow, 1924 and V. Kosinskii *Osnovnye tendentsii v mobilizatsii zemel'noi sobstvennosti*, Praha, 1924 (who declared it to be a law of private property, expressing necessary progress, ibid., p. XI). For the clearest exposition of the view see N. Rozhkov, "Teoreticheskie predposylki resheniya agrarnogo voprosa" *Voprosy dnya*, Moscow, 1906.
8. For discussion, see T. Shanin, *Russia 1905–7: Revolution as a Moment of Truth* (forthcoming).
9. I. Koval'chenko and L. Milov, *Vserossiiskii agrarnyi rynok* (Moscow, 1974); S. Trapeznikov, *Leninizm i agrarno-krest'yanskii vopros* (Moscow 1967) vol. I.

   For the most significant earlier studies of the trade in grain, see A. Chelintsev, *Russkoe sel'skoe khozyaistvo pered revolyutsiei* (Moscow, 1928) and P. Lyashchenko, *Khlebnaya torgovlya na vnutrennikh rynkakh rossii* (St Petersburg, 1912). Both seem to indicate conclusions different from those of Koval'chenko and Milov, but the figures cannot be related directly.
10. The view that rural Russia was totally capitalist in the 1880s was voiced in the 1920s as well as in our own generation both inside and outside the USSR (e.g. M. Balabanov, *Ocherki po istorii rabochego klassa v rossii* (Moscow, 1925) pt II; S. Hinada, 'The Russian Peasant Movement in the Era of Imperialism', *Hokudai Economic Papers*, vol. 3, 1972–3). Koval'chenko and Milov did not state it but consistent in their mode of analysis they declared that the labour performed in exchange for land rented (*otrabotki*) (i.e. Lenin's major index of 'pre-capitalist survivals') was also 'capitalist in its objective sense' (p. 369). Once that is accepted, Annenskii' figures must result in a fully capitalist image of rural Russia in 1887.
11. Koval'chenko and Milov, op. cit., pp. 365–6. For a new study along similar lines of the peasant Budget Studies at the turn of the nineteenth century, see I. Koval'chenko, 'O burzhuaznom kharaktere krest'yankogo khozyaistva evropeiskoi rossii', *Istoriya SSSR*, 1983, no. 3, especially pp 73–81. Its particulars will be considered in a forthcoming volume, Shanin, op. cit., chapter 4.
12. For an important discussion of the non-capitalist characteristics of communal lands see K. Shabunya, *Agrarnyi vopros i krest'yansxoa dv izhenie v belorussii* (Minsk, 1962).
13. ibid, pp. 367, 374.
14. A. Nikofontov, *Zernovoe proizvodstvo Rossii vo vtoroi polovine XIX veka* (Moscow, 1974). This particular piece of deductionism treated as common

sense (and thereby free from the need for any substantiation) is widespread in the works of the Soviet economic historians (e.g. P. Khromov, *Ekonomicheskoe razvitie rossii* (Moscow, 1967) p. 512).

15. See, for example, J. Harriss, *Rural Development* (London, 1982). Also, the interesting analysis of the frontier between the peasant and the capitalist family farming by V. Danilov discussed below, in p. 169.

16. A. G. Frank, *Capitalism and Underdevelopment in Latin America* (New York, 1967); accepted also by I. Wallerstein, *The Modern World System* (New York, 1974).

17. See, for example, I. Oxaal, T. Barnett and D. Booth, *Beyond the Sociology of Development* (London, 1975). Also, H. Alavi and T. Shanin, *Introduction to the Sociology of 'Developing Societies'* (London, 1982).

18. For discussion, see E. Laclau, 'Feudalism and Capitalism in Latin America', *New Left Review*, no. 67, 1971.

19. H. Friedmann, 'World Market, State and Family Farm', *Comparative Studies in Society and History*, vol. 20, no. 4, 1978, p. 549. Its findings correspond to those of J. Harriss, *Rural Development* (London, 1982) which centred on Europe.

20. I. Stalin, 'Na khlebnom fronte', *Voprosy leninizma* (Moscow, 1947) p. 186 (first published in 1928); the corresponding percentages of production were declared to be 12, 38 and 50.

21. Nemchinov proclaimed it in 1964 at the celebrations to mark his award of Doctorate Honoris Causa at Birmingham in Great Britain. For a discussion of the specific characteristics of the late-colonised south-east of European Russia, see E. Druzhinin, 'Genezis kapitalizma na yuge i yugo-vostoke evropeiskoi rossii', in *Materialy po istorii sel'skogo khozyaistva i krest'yanstva SSSR* (Moscow, 1980). See also Addendum 2 above.

22. I. Koval'chenko in *Problemy sotsial'no-ekonomicheskoi istorii Rossii* (Moscow, 1971) pp. 188–91. For a contrary view, see V. Danilov, *Sovetskaya dokolkhoznaya derevnya: sotsial'naya struktura, sotrial'nye otnosheniya* (Moscow, 1979) pp. 169–70 and 184.

23. A. Chayanov, *Theory of Peasant Economy* (Homewood, Ill., 1966) chs 3 and 4.

24. A Chayanov, *Byudzhety krest'yan starobel'skogo uezda* (Kharkov, 1915).

25. For further discussion, see T. Shanin, 'Defining Peasants: Conceptualisations and De-conceptualisation', *Sociological Review*, vol. 30, no. 3, 1982.

Peasant economy: modes, production and history

1. See for discussion, B. Galeski in T. Shanin, *Peasant and Peasant Societies* (Harmondsworth, 1976) item 10.

2. For example, the arguably mistaken interpretation of the Chayanov school of thought as relating to Sombart's consumptionist definition in K. Tarnovskii in *Istoricheskie zapiski*, no. 72, 1962, pp. 32–41.

3. See T. Shanin, 'The Nature and Logic of Peasant Economy', *Journal of Peasant Studies*, vol. I, nos. 1 and 2, 1973–4.

4. J. Harriss, *Rural Development* (London, 1982) and the relevant debate conducted by *Political and Economic Weekly* (Bombay) in the 1970s; see also H. Wolpe, *The Articulation of Modes of Production* (London, 1980); T. Shanin, 'Defining Peasants: Conceptualisations and De-conceptual-

isations', *Sociological Review*, vol. 30, no. 3, 1982.

5. Unless, of course, one equates feudalism with 'petty mode of production' as in M. Dobb's contribution in R. Hilton, *The Transition from Feudalism to Capitalism* (London, 1976)p. 165.

6. H. Bernstein in Harriss, op. cit., p. 160. The somewhat peculiar grammar that treats peasantry as plural is reproduced as in the original text for the issue may be not only semantic. H. Alavi has recently commented that 'Peasants are able to survive a little longer because of the logic of their own economic situation . . . not because capital "wills" it so' (H. Alavi and T. Shanin, *Introduction to the Sociology of the 'Developing Societies'* (London, 1982) p. 190).

7. For example, the work of K. Baratov on the 'Agrarian Question in Turkey', reviewed in *Journal of Social Studies*, no. 19, 1983.

8. For discussion, see Shanin, 'Defining Peasants', loc. cit. For the discrepancies between the standard Marxist interpretations and Marx's own view on that matter, see T. Shanin, *Late Marx and the Russian Road* (London, 1983) pt II.

9. See Galeski, op. cit.

10. ibid. Also, N. Malita, 'Agriculture in year 2000', *Sociologia Ruralis*, vol. XI, 1971; for general characterisation of peasant family farms, see p. 000 above.

11. Bernstein in Harriss, op. cit., p. 160.

12. Discussed further in Shanin, 'Defining Peasants', loc. cit. The contemporary relevance of family farming for differential rural histories is much wider than acknowledged. See, for example, W. Goldschmidt, 'Large Scale Farming and the Rural Social Structure', *Rural Sociology*, no. 43 (3), 1978, for California, USA and the work of H. Friedmann cited on p. 163.

13. Following an argument offered by P. Corrigan, 'Feudal Relics or Capitalist Moments', *Sociology*, vol. II, 1977, but logically 'inverted' on its author's advice.

14. V. P. Danilov, L. V. V. Danilova and V. G. Rastyanikov in *Osnovnye etapy razvitiya krestyanskikh khozyaninstv* (Moscow, 1977).

15. G. Djurfeld, 'What Happened to the Agrarian Bourgeoisie and Rural Proletariat under Monopoly Capitalism', *Acta Sociologica*, no. 3, 1981.

16. R. Brener, 'The Agrarian Roots of European Capitalism', *Past and Present*, no. 97, 1982 (which follows an earlier piece in *Past and Present*, no. 70, 1976, considering the impact of peasant resistance on enserfment).

17. In Hilton, op. cit., p. 160.

18. G. Djurfeld in Harriss, op. cit., pp. 147 and 143.

19. M. Dobb, *Soviet Economic Development Since 1917* (London, 1960) p. 39.

20. R. Goldsmith, 'Economic Growth of Tsarist Russia 1860–1913', *Economic Development and Cultural Change*, vol. IX, 1961, p. 447.

21. M. Bloch, *The Historian's Craft* (Manchester, 1954) p. 155.

5 RUSSIA'S MORPHOLOGY OF BACKWARDNESS: PRESENT AND FUTURE

A type of 'development': the 'growth' and the 'gap'

1. N. Timasheff, *The Great Retreat* (New York, 1946) pp. 34 and 394–5.

2. N. Timasheff, 'The Russian Revolution', *The Review of Politics*, no. 4, 1943, p. 440.

3. See, for example, V. Treml, *The Development of the Soviet Economy: Plan and Performance* (New York, 1968) (in particular G. Warren Nutter's contribution). It goes without saying that this example represents but one of many.

4. That is, usually the variations or extensions of W. W. Rostow, *The Stages of Economic Growth, a Non-Communist Manifesto* (Cambridge, 1960).

5. A. G. Frank, 'The Post-War Boom: Boom for the West, Bust for the South', *Journal of International Studies*, vol. 7, no. 2, 1978, p. 153.

6. See *World Development Report* (New York, 1980) chs 4 and 5. The report states that 'The gap in income per person (between 'developing' and 'industrual' countries) has widened . . . the gaps in education and in health narrowed' (ibid, p. 35). See also A. Hoogvelt, *The Third World in Global Development* (London, 1982) ch. 1 (tables).

7. S. P. Trapeznikov, *Agrarnyi vopros i leninskie agrarnye programmy v trekh russkikh revolyutsiyakh* (Moscow, 1967) vol. I, pp. 13–14.

8. For discussion, see H. Alavi and T. Shanin, *Introduction to the Sociology of 'Developing Societies'* (London, 1982).

9. ibid. See also S. Pollard, *The Idea of Progress* (New York, 1968).

10. Put in a nutshell by N. Smelser, *Social Change in Industrial Revolution* London, 1972) introduction. See D. Lerner, *The Passing of Traditional Society* (Cambridge, 1963); S. Eisenstadt. *Modernisation: Protest and Change* (Englewood Cliffs, 1966); T. Parsons, *The Evolution of Societies* Englewood Cliffs, 1977).

11. For discussion of alternative views on the left, see T. Shanin, *Marx and the Russian Road* (London, 1983); A. Walicki, *The Controversy Over Capitalism* (Oxford, 1969).

12. G. Plekhanov, *Nashi raznoglasiya* (Geneva 1885); I. Stalin, *Voprosy leninizma* (Moscow, 1947) (especially the section devoted to dialectical and historical materialism, written in 1938); W. Warren, *Imperialism: Pioneer of Capitalism* (London, 1980).

13. *The Oxford English Dictionary* (Oxford, 1972) p. 786.

14. J. A. Hobson, *Imperialism: A Study* (London, 1908); R. Hilferding, *Finanz Kapital* (Vienna, 1910); R. Luxemburg, *The Accummulation of Capital* (first published 1913); N. Bukharin, *Imperialism* (first published in 1915); V. I. Lenin, 'Imperializm kak vysshaya forma kapitalisma' (1917) PSS vol. 27; for historical debate, see G. Palma, 'Depedency', *World Development*, vol. 6, 1978; H. Magdoff, *Imperialism: From Colonial Age to the Present* (New York, 1978); G. Arrighi, *The Geometry of Imperialism* (London, 1978).

15. For discussion of the new stage of debate that commenced in 1927, see Magdoff, op. cit., T. Kemp, *Theories of Imperialism* (London, 1967): C. G. Lee, 'An Assimilating Imperialism', *Journal of Contemporary Asia*, vol. 2, no. 4, 1972. See also H. Alavi and T. Shanin, *Introduction to the Sociology of Developing Societies* (London, 1982) pts I and II.

16. G. Myrdal, *The Economic Theory and Underdeveloped Regions* (London, 1967).

17. For example, R. Prebish, 'The System and the Social Structure in Latin America', in I. Horovits *et al.*, *Latin Americal Radicalism* (New York, 1967) but mainly his views as expressed by the reports of UN bodies, e.g. *Toward a New Trade Policy of Development* (New York, 1964). For the impact of

Prebish on other leading economists of Latin America and further development of those views see, for example, C. Furtado, *Development and Underdevelopment* (Berkeley, 1967).

18. P. Baran, *The Political Economy of Growth* (New York, 1962) (first published in 1957).

19. In particular, P. Baran, 'On Political Economy of Backwardness', in R. Rhodes, *Imperialism and Underdevelopment* (New York, 1970). The book presents an excellent selection substantiating that view.

20. A. G. Frank, *Capitalism and Underdevelopment in Latin America* (New York, 1967); H. Bernstein, *Underdevelopment and Development* (Harmondsworth, 1973); I. Oxaal, T. Barnett and D. Booth, *Beyond the Sociology of Development* (London, 1975); I. Roxborough, *Theories of Underdevelopment* (London, 1979); Alavi and Shanin, op. cit.; also, an enormous number of articles in relevant journals.

21. In, particular, the argument of E. Laclau, 'Feudalism and Capitalism in Latin America, *New Left Review*, no. 67, 1971.

22. For example, see J. E. Golthorpe, *The Sociology of the Third World* (Cambridge, 1975) as against G. Kay, *Development and Underdevelopment: A Marxist Analysis* (London, 1975); C. Leys, 'Underdevelopment and Dependency', *Journal of Contemporary Asia*, vol. 7, no. 1, 1977; W. Warren, *Imperialism: Pioneer of Capitalism* (London, 1980).

23. P. Berger, *Pyramids of Sacrifice* (Harmondsworth, 1979); M. Coldwell, *The Wealth of Some Nations* (London, 1979); I. Ilich, *Tools of Conviviality* (London, 1973).

24. For example, H. Alavi in Alavi and Shanin, op. cit. (especially the table on p. 188) stressed as a major dimension of analysis the inability of the colonial economy to reproduce itself autonomously and the matrix of determinations established thereby.

25. For major criticism that came from the very ranks of the theorists of 'dependency', see F. H. Cardoso, 'Dependency and Development', in Alavi and Shanin, op. cit. See also his *Dependency Revisited* (Austin, 1973).

26. Beginning with S. Amin, *Accummulation on a World Scale* (New York, 1974).

27. I. Wallerstein, *The Modern World System* (New York, 1974) (and the volumes to follow).

28. For example, it is not the case that two forms of social organisation existed side by side, or could ever so exist. The world economy has one form or the other. One it is capitalist, relationships . . . are necessarily redefined in terms of the governing principles of a capitalist system' (ibid, p. 92).

29. P. Anderson, *The Origins of an Absolutist State* (London, 1978).

30. P. Sweezy, *Four Lectures on Marxism* (New York, 1982); E. Hobsbawm, 'From Feudalism to Capitalism', in R. Hilton, *The Transition from Feudalism to Capitalism* (London, 1976) especially the passage quoted above on p. 171.

31. See A. Emanuel and H. Alavi, in Alavi and Shanin, op. cit., pt I.

32. For an illuminating discussion of the issue in relation to the evidence of a major developing society' of large size within the contemporary world, see P. Evans, *Dependent Development: The Allience of Multi-National, State and Local Capitals in Brazil* (Princeton, 1979).

The edge of Europe

1. A. Bol'shakov and N. Rozhkov, *Istoriya khozyaistva Rossii* (Moscow, 1926) vol III, pp. 13–16.
2. M. Atallah, *The Long-Term Movement of the Terms of Trade between Agricultural and Industrial Products* (Rotterdam, 1958) pp. 3–3 and 72–9; Lamartine Yates, *Forty Years of Foreign Trade* (London, 1959) pp. 38–45, 62–72.
3. Atallah, op. cit., p. 79.
4. See p. 132 above.
5. P. A. Khromov, *Ocherki ekonomicheskogo razvitie Rossii* (Moscow, 1967) pp. 134 and 144–8; P. I. Lyashchenko, *Istoriya narodnogo khozyaistva Rossii* (Moscow, 1952) vol. II, p. 644. See also Event'ev, by whose estimates foreign capital formed by 1914 43 per cent of the shareholding capital in Russian industrial, banking and trading private enterprises (L. Eventov, *Inostrannye kapitaly v russkoi promyshlennosti* (Moscow, 1931) pp. 17 and 37–41).
6. D. Mirsky, *Russia, A Social History* (London, 1952) p. 269.
7. A. Rashin,*Naselenie Rossii za sto let* (Moscow, 1956) p. 98.
8. R. W. Goldsmith, 'The Economic Growth of Tsarist Russia 1860–1913', *Economic Development and Cultural Change*, vol. 9, 1961, pp. 474–5; also P. Khromov, *Ekonomicheskoe razvitie rossii* (Moscow, 1967) p. 398; S. Prokopovich, *Opyt ischisleniya narodnogo doklada* (Moscow, 1918).
9. A century has passed between Friedrich List and the generation of Gunnar Myrdal and Paul Baran, still very much lonely voices crying in the wilderness of Stockholm and Stanford, USA, respectively in the mid-1950s. See F. List, *The National System of Political Economy* (London, 1909) initially published 1841. For discussion, see F. F. Clairmonte, *Economic Liberalism and Underdevelopment* (London, 1960) especially ch. 10.
10. The quotation comes from S. Witte, 'O polozhenii nashei promyshlennosti', *Istorik Marxist*, nos. 2–3, 1935, p. 133. Already in his early 1893 Annual Report about the State Budget, Witte declared that in Russia 'as a result of the special historical conditions' and of 'the weak development of the habits of self help among the population' [! T.S.] 'the whole burden of the struggle with public misfortune falls inevitably upon the government'. Cited in C. E. Black, *The Transformation of Russian Society* (Cambridge, 1960) p. 215.
11. A. Gerschenkron, 'Economic Backwardness in Historical Perspective', in B. Heselitz, *The Progress of Underdeveloped Area* (Chicago, 1953) pp. 18 and 27.
12. T. Von Laue, 'Imperial Russia at the Turn of Century', in R. Bendix, *State and Society* (Berkeley, 1973) pp. 438 and 422. Interestingly, in the same source the brightest political adviser of the US establishment, S. Huntingdon, moves sharply in the opposite direction when the 'Second World' of today is concerned, declaring that for 'the modernising countries of this century . . . it is in Moscow and Peking not in Washington that this lesson is to be learned', 'this' standing for 'accumulation and concentration of power' as a 'primary need' (ibid, p. 199). Once again the grasp of immediate politics seemed to have outdistanced the more abstract brands of

social analysis and the understanding of historical continuities relevant to the case.

13. Marx drafts of the letter to Zasulich, in T. Shanin, *Late Marx and the Russian Road* (London, 1983) p. 100.
14. *Istoriya SSSR* (Moscow, 1968) vol. VI, devoted to the 1900–17 period and prepared by a team of historians headed by A. L. Sidorov and K. N. Tarnovskii.
15. ibid, p. 8.
16. ibid, pp. 9–10.
17. ibid, p. 11.
18. ibid, pp. 12–13 and 24–7.

The Russian 'periphery': the general, the typical and the specific

1. For further discussion, see T. Shanin, *The Rules of the Game: Cross Disciplinary Essays on Models in Scholarly Thought* (London, 1972).
2. W. Baldamus, 'The Role of Discovery in Social Sciences', in ibid, pp. 294–5.
3. R. B. Brentwaite, *Scientific Explanation* (Cambridge, 1953) p. 93.
4. M. Raeff, 'The Well Ordered Police State'. *The American Historical Review*, vol. 80, no. 5, 1975, p. 1221. For relevant discussion, see P. Corrigan, Feudal Relics or Capitalist Monuments', *Sociology*, vol. II, 1977.
5. The view expressed originated with Plekhanov and was typical of most of the younger Marxist theoreticians of Russia in the period reviewed. The quotation comes from L. Trotsky, *1905* (Harmondsworth, 1971) p. 8 (first published in 1906).
6. H. Alavi, 'State in Post Colonial Society', *New Left Review*, no. 74, 1972.
7. The significance of the multiple imperialism and of administrative invention was impressed on me by the comments of Philip Corrigan of University of Toronto, and Israel Shahak of Hebrew University, Jerusalem, respectively.
8. Works of the senior members of the Institute of Ethnography and Ethnology in Moscow and Leningrad (e.g. V. Kozlov, Yu. Bromley, D. Olderogge, U. Arutunian and the significant alternative position established by L. Gumilev).
9. T. Shanin, *Late Marx and the Russian Road* (London, 1983) p. 108; Marx related the particularities of the Russian peasant commune, its relative stability and future potentials, to its advanced form (i.e. being based on neighbourhood rather than on kinship).
10. T. H. Von Laue, *Sergei Witte and the Industrialisation of Russia* (London, 1963).
11. G. Mosca, *The Ruling Class*(New York, 1939); V. Pareto, *The Mind and Society* (London, 1935); also in a very different context, C. Wright Mills, *The Power Elite* (New York, 1956); T. B. Bottomore, *Elites and Society* (London, 1964).
12. S. Ossowski, *Class Structure in Social Consciousness* (London, 1963); R. Bendix and S. M. Lipset, *Class Status and Power* (London, 1968) pts I, III and IV; also see T. Shanin, 'Class, State and Revolution: Substitutes and Realities', in H. Alavi and T. Shanin, *Introduction to the Sociology of the 'Developing Societies'* (London, 1982).

13. For example, A. Pankratova in *Pervaya russkaya revolyutsiya* (Moscow, 1951).
14. P. Sweezy, 'The Proletariat of Today's World', *Tricontinental*, vol. 9, 1968; E. Wolf, *Peasant Wars in the Twentieth Century*(New York, 1969).

    Another way to approach the issues of the extent of 'classness' is to accept with Wallerstein a one-class system as widely spread for reasons, and in the terminological context, suggested in I. Wallerstein, *The Modern World System* (New York, 1974) pp. 354–7. Also, Corrigan, loc. cit., for discussion of the complexity of the class-generating social context at the 'peripheires of capitalism'.
15. See, for example, V. Belinskii, 'Letter to Gogol', written in 1847 (for the version in English see B. Dmytryshyn, *Imperial Russia: A Source Book 1700–1917* (Hinsdale, 1974) pp. 221–8). The quotation from N. Mikhailovskii, *Otechestvennye zapiski*, no. 12, 1881, pp. 201–5. See also Leikina-Svirskaya, op. cit., chs 1, 9 and 10.
16. The discussion of the concept of 'intelligentsia' is too extensive to be reviewed here. For major relevant items, see J. Kautsky, *Political Change in Underdeveloped Countries* (New York, 1967); A. Gramsci,*Selection from Prison Notebooks* (London, 1973); J. H. Billington, *Fire in the Minds of Man* (London, 1980) and an interesting sequence of relevant studies in *Dedalus*, 1972 (especially the paper by S. N. Eisenstadt). In the USSR a most useful study was published by V. Leikina-Svirskaya, *Inteligentsiya v Rossii vo vtoroi polovine XIX veka* (Moscow, 1971); and a companion volume about 1900–19 in 1981 also clandestinely published, M. Bolkhovskii, *Sud'ba Revolyutsionno—sotsialisticheskoi inteligentsii Rossii. Materiyaly samizdata*, 1980, No 13/80.
17. I. Berlin in *The Listener*, 2 May 1968.
18. M. Bulgakov, 'Belaya gvardiya', *Povesti* (Moscow, 1978) p. 189; S. Witte, *Vospominaniya* (Moscow, 1960) vol. 2, p. 328.
19. N. Mikhailovsskii in *Otechestvennye Zapiski*, 1881, No. 12, p. 205.
20. For example, the patriotic frenzy (led by people like the ex-liberal M. Katkov) that swept the Russian society during the Polish uprising of 1863 and led to the collapse of the influence of Hertzen's journal-from-abroad which refused to submit to it.

State and revolution

1. See F. Venturi, *Roots of Revolution* (London, 1960) ch. 5. For discussion of Marx's attitude, see T. Shanin, *Late Marx and the Russian Road* (London, 1983). (Especially the contribution by H. Wada.)
2. For the text and comment see Shanin, op. cit., pts 3 and 1 respectively.
3. *Bol'shaya sovetskaya entsiklopedia* (Moscow, 1941) vol. 48, p. 78.
4. The social reforms envisaged by members of the 'secret societies' varied from the radical and centralist (often referred to as 'Jacobine') programme of P. Pestel', who led the movement in the south, to the milder suggestions of N. Muraviev, the leader of the secret societies in Petersburg.
5. Quoted after V. Klyuchevskii, *A History of Russia* (New York, 1960) vol. 5, p. 172.

6. Adam Mickewicz, 'Do Przyiacieli Moskali'.
7. P. Chadayev, *Sochineniya i pis'ma* (Moscow, 1913–14).
8. A. Hertzen, *Byloe i dumy, Sochineniya*, Moscow, 1956, vol 5, chaps XXIX, XXX; See A. Khomyakov, *Izbrannye sochineniya* (New York, 1955); K. Aksakov, *Polnoe sobranie sochinenii* (Moskow, 1861–80); V. Belinskii, *Polnoe sobranie sochinenii* (St Petersburg, 1900–17). For an illuminating discussion, see I. Berlin, *Russian Thinkers* (Harmondsworth, 1978). Elements linking the 'Westerners' and the populist credo appeared in the views of the so-called Petrashevtsy group which operated within Russia in the 1848 period (V. Leikina Svirskaya, *Petrashevtsy* (Moscow, 1966)).
9. See Venturi, op. cit.; Shanin, *Late Marx*, op. cit.; Berlin, op. cit. Also V. Khoros, *Ideinye techeniya narodnicheskogo tipa* (Moscow, 1980) and A. Walicki, *The Controversy over Capitalism* (Oxford, 1969).
10. ibid. For a basic source see *Kolokol* (Moscow, 1964) vols I and II.
11. Shanin, *Late* Marx, op. cit., especially pp. 43–8, 69–71 and 206–7. The programme of the People's Will Party began as follows: 'In our fundamental convictions we are socialists and populists. We are convinced that only upon a socialist basis can humanity embody freedom, equality and fraternity . . . . We are convinced that only the will of the people can sanction social forms' (ibid, p. 207). See also Walicki, op. cit.
12. Ibid. For a long list of Russian populists active within the 1st International, especially within its pro-Marx and anti-Bakunin wing, see B. Henberg, *Pervyi internatsional i revolyutsionnaya rossiya* Moscow, 1962).
13. Especially the *Historical Letters* by P. Lavrov. For discussion, see Berlin, op. cit., and Khoros, op. cit.
14. From an editorial statement of *Narodnaya volya*, no. 3 (dated 1 January 1880).
15. P. Zaionchkovskii, 'Verkhovnaya rasporyaditel'naya kommisiya', in *Voprosy istorii sel'skogo khozyaistva, krest'yanstva i revolyutsii* (Moscow, 1961) pp. 254–71.
16. Venturi, op. cit., Shanin, op. cit. See also for a study of the People's Will party by a senior police officer drawing extensively on police sources, A. Spiridovich, *Revolyutsionnoe dvizhenie v rossii* (Petrograd, 1916) vol. II.
17. Venturi, op. cit., p. 140.
18. Alexander Pushkin, 'Ya pamiatnik sebe vozdvig'.
19. For a highly illuminating political review of the clandestine organisations of the period, see the report to the tsar of the Provisional Office of the Ministry of Justice, concerning 'cases of crime against the state for 1897 and a short review of anti-governmental movements within the empire during 1894–97' in *Revolyutsionnoe dvizhenie v Rossii* (St Petersburg, 1907).

Index of Names

Index of Subjects